NATIONAL
GEOGRAPHIC

GUIDE TO THE
National Parks
of Canada

NATIONAL GEOGRAPHIC

GUIDE TO THE

National Parks
of Canada

NATIONAL GEOGRAPHIC
Washington, D.C.

CONTENTS

Pages 2–3: Bat Star (*Asterina miniata*) group, Gwaii Haanas National Marine Conservation Area Reserve, British Columbia. Opposite: Winter sunrise on Waskesiu Lake, Prince Albert National Park, Saskatchewan.

Plains bison, Riding Mountain National Park, Manitoba

THE HEART OF CANADA

More than 130 years ago, the leaders of the young nation of Canada showed great vision and foresight. In 1885, they embraced a relatively new concept and decided to create Canada's first national park—just the third such park in the world.

Twenty-six square kilometres of land around a bubbling hot spring was set aside as "a public park and pleasure ground for the benefit, advantage and enjoyment of the people of Canada." This area has grown to be known as Banff National Park and is part of a family of protected areas that span some 350,000 square kilometres—equivalent to the size of Germany.

Today, Banff is among the 46 national parks, four national marine conservation areas, and one national urban park considered to be one of the finest and most extensive systems of protected natural heritage areas in the world. Within this system are six UNESCO World Heritage sites inscribed for their Outstanding Universal Value to Humanity.

Parks Canada is committed to protecting the special environment of these places for all time and providing Canadians and visitors from around the world with opportunities to experience and enjoy them. These national parks and national marine conservation areas represent the very best that Canada has to offer. They are the heart of Canada and tell the

variety of our landscape from coast to coast to coast.

They include world-renowned names such as Gwaii Haanas, Nahanni, and Jasper, as well as more recently established ones such as Qausuittuq National Park, Nááts'ihch'oh National Park Reserve, and Rouge National Urban Park.

They may be a site for a cherished annual family vacation or a once-in-a-lifetime dream destination in some of the wildest and most remote places on Earth.

No matter their names or where you find them, the breathtaking scenery, incredible wildlife, and inspiring surroundings of Canada's national parks and national marine conservation areas provide us with remarkable gateways to nature, adventure, and discovery.

Here, visitors can camp in the shadow of towering mountains, paddle down rivers flowing through canyons carved over thousands of years, observe birds along traditional migration routes, and walk through ancient forests. The unforgettable experiences are made all the more memorable by the learning opportunities Parks Canada offers through interpretive walks, indigenous programming, and innovative activities.

If you have already discovered some of the incredible wonders of Canada's vast network of protected wilderness, this guide will encourage you to explore further. If you are thinking about visiting us for the first time, I can promise you incredible memories that will last a lifetime.

Parks Canada's extraordinary team looks forward to offering you a warm welcome. We invite you to enjoy some of the greatest places on Earth.

— DANIEL WATSON *Chief Executive Officer*
Parks Canada

stories of who we are, including the history, cultures, and contributions of indigenous peoples. Parks Canada is proud to work with more than 300 indigenous communities across the country in conserving, restoring, and presenting Canada's natural and cultural heritage. We are committed to a system of national heritage places that recognize the role of the indigenous people of Canada and the traditional use of these special places.

Canada's national parks and national marine conservation areas are a source of pride for all Canadians and an integral part of our identity. From British Columbia's temperate rain forest and the plains of the Prairies to the deep blue waters of the Atlantic Provinces and vast Arctic tundra, they are found as far north and south as Canada goes. These incredible places celebrate the beauty and infinite

Dawn, Ingonish Beach, Cape Breton Highlands National Park, Nova Scotia

USING THE GUIDE

Each of Canada's 46 national parks, four national marine conservation areas, and one national urban park offers fun, adventure, and splendour. Exploration can be done on your own, with a guide if you choose, or perhaps only with a mandatory guide or outfitter, depending on the accessibility, and safety of the environment.

Coverage of each park begins with a portrait of its natural wonders; ecological setting; history; and, sometimes, its struggles on behalf of endangered species and its means of protecting it from human intrusion. These parks were established not only for people to enjoy but also for the preservation of ecosystems. Of Canada's 10 UNESCO World Heritage sites inscribed for their outstanding natural heritage, six of them include one or more national parks.

Before starting off on your own, use this guide to preview the parks. You'll notice that each park introduction is followed by the following three how-and-when sections:

How to Get There

Many of the national parks are not in close proximity to one another, so you may need to plan several trips to make the most of what they have to offer. Allow enough time in your travel schedule to get from place to place, as roads may be rugged or crowded, and base your itineraries on time rather than on mileage. When visiting the more remote destinations, contact the park staff for guidance on how and when to go.

When to Go

All parks have a lot to offer at different times of the year. To avoid crowds, visit a popular park during the off-peak months (April, May, or late August), and time your arrival for early on a weekday. In many parks, fall is glorious, and autumn vistas coincide with a relative scarcity of visitors. Summer brings wildflowers, and with winter comes snow-swept beauty that beckons backpackers, campers, cross-country skiers, and snowshoers. Most parks are open year-round, but off-season visitor facilities may be limited or nonexistent. Consult the Information & Activities section for each park.

How to Visit

Give yourself time to savour your surroundings. No matter how long you decide to stay, the How to Visit section recommends itineraries and suggests the amount of time to allot. In the parks of the Far North, the visitor must allow extra time for contingencies related to travel schedules and weather. Don't be afraid to explore on your own or, if necessary, with a guide. And don't neglect the Excursions at the end of many park entries. They generally include national historic sites within 100 km (60 mi) of the parks.

OTHER FEATURES OF THE GUIDE:

Maps

The park maps were prepared as an aid in planning your trip. For more detail on trails and other facilities inside a park, call the park, or visit the Parks Canada website at *www .parkscanada.gc.ca.*

Always use park maps or detailed topographic maps when travelling within park borders. Park maps indicate specially designated wilderness areas that are managed to retain their primeval beauty. They also include hiking trails, which are marked for safety or protection of environmental species, and which you should not stray from.

For a list of map symbols, see p. 394.

Information & Activities

This section, which follows each park entry, offers detailed visitor information. Call, write, or visit the park's website *(www.parkscanada.gc.ca)* for further details.

Regional brochures for the parks can be downloaded online at *www .parkscanada.gc.ca/eng/voyage-travel/ index/pdf.aspx.*
Entrance Fees. The prices listed in Canadian dollars throughout the book are average prices. The daily entrance fees at the time of printing range from $5.80 to $9.80 for adults; $4.90 to $8.30 for seniors (65 and older); $2.90 to $4.90 for youth (ages 6–16); and $14.70 to $19.60 for a family or group (up to seven people in a single vehicle). You can purchase daily entry passes at the park. Check the Parks Canada website *(www.parkscanada.gc.ca)* for all current prices.

Visitors can purchase online an annual Parks Canada Discovery Pass for entry into national parks, national marine conservation areas, and national historic sites. The pass provides unlimited access to 100 park properties. The current cost for the annual Discovery Pass is $67.70 for an adult, $57.90 for seniors, $33.30 for youth, and $136.40 for a family/ group. The passes are available at *www.parkscanada.gc.ca/pass* or by phone at (888) 773-8888, and at information or visitor centres within individual parks.

Pets. Although you might want to bring your pet along, pets can attract and antagonize wildlife. If they are permitted on hiking trails, they must be leashed. Refer to specific park information or inquire ahead for restrictions.

Accessible Services. This section of the guide lists places within the parks, including visitor centres and trails, that are accessible to visitors with disabilities.

Special Advisories
• Take care when visiting parks; accidents do occur. Most of them are caused by recklessness or failure to heed warnings.
• Stay away from wild animals no matter how harmless they may appear. Do not feed them or touch

them—not even the smallest animals.

• Try not to surprise a bear. Wear bear bells, whose jingle will alert them to your presence. If one approaches, scare it off by yelling, clapping your hands, or banging pots. Store food in bear-proof containers; keep food out of sight in your vehicle, with windows closed and doors locked, or suspend it at least 4.5 m (15 ft) above ground and 3 m (10 ft) out from a post or tree trunk.

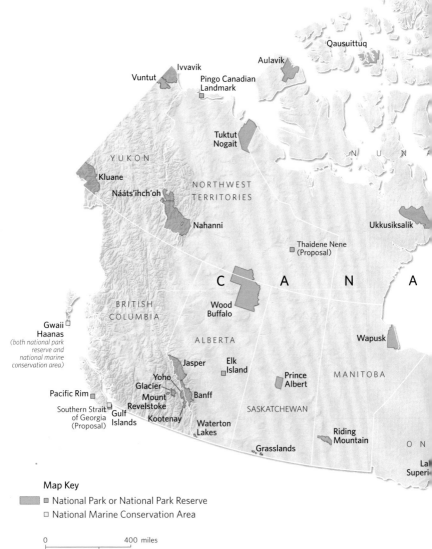

Quttinirpaa

Qausuittuq

Aulavik

Ivvavik

Vuntut

Pingo Canadian Landmark

Tuktut Nogait

YUKON

Kluane

Nááts'ihch'oh

NORTHWEST TERRITORIES

Nahanni

N   U   N   A

Ukkusiksalik

Thaidene Nene (Proposal)

C   A   N   A

BRITISH COLUMBIA

Gwaii Haanas
(both national park reserve and national marine conservation area)

Wood Buffalo

ALBERTA

Wapusk

Jasper

Elk Island

Prince Albert

MANITOBA

Pacific Rim

Yoho
Glacier
Mount Revelstoke

Banff

Southern Strait of Georgia (Proposal)

Gulf Islands

Kootenay

Waterton Lakes

SASKATCHEWAN

Riding Mountain

O   N

Grasslands

Lal Superi

Map Key

■ National Park or National Park Reserve
□ National Marine Conservation Area

0   400 miles
0   400 kilometers

- Know your limitations. If you are not fit, don't overexert yourself.
- Boil or chemically treat water that doesn't come from a park's drinking-water tap.
- Heed all park warnings—they are posted for your protection.
- Plan for delays: passes closed by snow; scheduled pickups delayed because of weather conditions; road blockages resulting from construction, fallen rocks, landslides, or smoke.

Check road regulations as you enter a park. Along some roads you will not be able to manoeuvre large campers or RVs.

Campgrounds. The Campground Reservation Service (877-737-3783, *www.reservation.pc.gc.ca*) handles reservations for 23 parks: Banff, Bruce Peninsula, Cape Breton Highlands, Elk Island, Forillon, Fundy, Georgian Bay Islands, Grasslands, Gros Morne, Gulf Islands, Jasper, Kejimkujik, Kootenay, Kouchibouguac, La Mauricie, Mingan Archipelago, Pacific Rim, Prince Albert, Prince Edward Island, Riding Mountain, Terra Nova, Thousand Islands, and Waterton Lakes. Check early for availability.

Hotels, Motels, & Inns. This guide lists a sampling of accommodations as a service to readers. The lists are by no means comprehensive, and listing does not imply endorsement by the National Geographic Society or Parks Canada. The information can change without notice. Many parks keep lists of the lodgings in their areas, which they will provide on request. You should also contact local visitor centres and provincial tourism offices for suggestions.

ATLANTIC
PROVINCES

Page 12: top, Autumn foliage, Cape Breton Highlands; middle, Atlantic puffin; bottom, Canoeing in Kejimkujik. Page 13: Grazing sheep in Gros Morne. Above: Mill Falls on the Mersey River, Kejimkujik.

ATLANTIC PROVINCES

Sprinkled from Labrador to Nova Scotia, these eight national parks and two national park reserves show off the beauty of mountain building, erosion, and glaciation and a shoreline nearly 9,656 km (6,000 mi) long. At Terra Nova, visitors can hike and bike in a boreal forest. Gros Morne amazes visitors with expansive views of mountains, valleys, and a freshwater fjord. At Torngat Mountains, local Inuit guides share their knowledge of flora and fauna. Cape Breton

Highlands includes part of the scenic Cabot Trail. Kejimkujik boasts old-growth forests, hills called drumlins, and one of the world's largest collections of petroglyphs. Prince Edward Island looks just like the rolling landscape described in *Anne of Green Gables,* the beloved novel by island resident L. M. Montgomery. Kouchibouguac is considered one of the best biking destinations among these parks, while Fundy ties for the highest tidal range in the world.

A double rainbow arches over Terra Nova.

▶ TERRA NOVA

NEWFOUNDLAND & LABRADOR
ESTABLISHED 1957
399 sq km/99,000 acres

On the northeast coast of Canada's most easterly province, a boreal forest dares embrace the forbidding North Atlantic. Terra Nova National Park, whose name derives from the Latin for Newfoundland, is about a two-hour drive from Bonavista, where early European explorer Giovanni Caboto (John Cabot) "discovered" North America. Fittingly, the park's rocky extremities continue to stretch into the sea—an ageless geological invitation to explorers far and wide.

Terra Nova, the oldest national park in Newfoundland and Labrador, protects an interesting collection of diverse habitats: woodlands, ponds, marshes, and bogs, as well as the occasional granite promontory and a significant stretch of coastline.

This Eastern Island boreal forest represents what is historically a traditional Newfoundland landscape. History, however, is changing. The area's once vibrant evergreen and deciduous forest is fading as moose—browsing on balsam fir, birch, maple, and other species—have been literally eating away at the forest understorey.

Moose are the second largest land animal in North America (bison are the largest). An adult male will grow up to 2 m (7 ft) in height at the shoulder, weigh anywhere from 380 to 720 kg (840–1,600 lbs), and consume almost 10,000 calories per day. Not native to Newfoundland, they were introduced to the island in 1904, at a time when the Newfoundland wolf still existed. Today the Newfoundland wolf is extinct, and moose have no natural enemies aside from black bears and human hunters. Unchecked, they will decimate portions of Terra Nova's forest.

It's an important forest to maintain: Terra Nova is one of the few remaining homes of the threatened Newfoundland marten, a subspecies unique to the island and one of only 14 mammals native to it. There are thought to be only 300 of these animals left in existence. Other animals evident throughout the park include black bears, ospreys, lynx, Atlantic salmon, and bald eagles.

How to Get There

Because Terra Nova is located on the island of Newfoundland, travel there must include some element of air or sea transportation.

The closest airport is Gander International, which will put you approximately 90 km (56 mi) west of the park. The next closest airport, albeit larger and with a more frequent flight schedule (which often translates to cheaper rates), is 259 km (161 mi) to the east in the province's capital city, St. John's. Deer Lake, home to the smallest of the three airports, is 380 km (242 mi) west of Terra Nova. If you fly to Newfoundland, you'll have to rent a vehicle upon arrival.

It is possible for you to drive to Newfoundland provided you're prepared to travel by ferry from North Sydney, Nova Scotia, to either Argentia (126 km/78 mi east of the park) or Port aux Basques (655 km/407 mi west). The 14-hour

Argentia crossing operates seasonally from mid-June to September, while the 4.5- to 8-hour Port aux Basques run operates year-round.

The park is also accessible via personal watercraft (GPS co-ordinates 48 34 45.35 N; 53 56 51.31 W). Docking and launch facilities can be found at Salton's Brook.

Once you're on the island, finding the park is simple. Trans-Canada 1 runs through the park for 40 km (25 mi). Along the way, you'll find clearly marked signage indicating campgrounds, swimming areas, hiking trails, and other park attractions.

When to Go

As Newfoundland rarely experiences the extreme highs and lows of other locales with comparable latitude, Terra Nova is open for year-round enjoyment. On average, the coldest temperatures during the winter are around minus 15°C (5°F), while the warmest summer temperatures are around 22°C (72°F). Note, however, that electrically serviced campsites are only available during the summer season.

Endangered Newfoundland marten

Pitcher plant

How to Visit

With few exceptions, the park's broad offering of activities and habitats is readily accessible. Of Terra Nova's 11 hiking trails, ranging in length from 1 to 32 km (0.6–20 mi), you'll find nature walks that are appropriate for young children as well as people who enjoy a slower pace (some trails are even negotiable by wheelchair). Also on tap are hikes that test the most fit and resilient individuals.

There's freshwater swimming, mountain biking, kayaking, and canoeing in the warmer months, as well as cross-country skiing and snowshoeing during the winter.

Reservations are highly recommended, particularly for campsites with electrical service as opposed to primitive areas (i.e., wilderness camping sites without services or facilities). On-site information kiosks about various campgrounds are open seasonally.

Of particular note are the on-site shower and laundry facilities (yes, there is hot water). Although you may want to bring provisions with you, there is a convenience store in Newman Sound Campground that carries all the essentials and a small selection of prepared food items.

Deciding what you'd like to do depends on the type of adventure

you're looking for. Regardless of the specific activity, however, always remember to follow the golden rule: Other than footprints, leave behind no evidence of your presence.

SANDY POND & MARINE EXHIBIT AT THE VISITOR CENTRE
a full day

Though Terra Nova's camping facilities are superb, even a day visit is

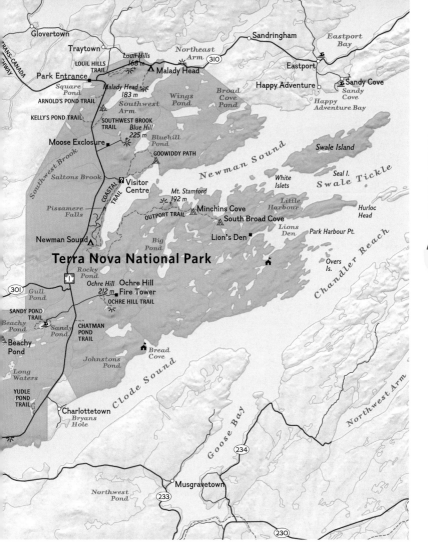

time well spent. Plan to arrive early in the morning and head directly to **Sandy Pond.** While waiting for the sun to warm the day, ease into the park with a leisurely 3-km (2 mi) stroll around the pond.

Along the route, be on the alert for beavers, ducks, and assorted local flora such as the provincial flower, the pitcher plant. Most often found in marshy areas, the pitcher plant is easily recognizable due to its inverted red-wine flower and hollow cone-like leaves. These

"cones" capture water, which in turn traps insects—a fact you will come to appreciate once you've been properly introduced to Terra Nova's prodigious population of blackflies and mosquitoes.

Walk complete, stake your claim to a portion of Sandy Pond's sand beach, notable because most beaches in this province are comprised of less hospitable gravel and rock. The water here is always warmer than most Newfoundland ponds, due to the shallow water depths.

Sandy Pond

When you've tired of swimming, have lunch at one of the many picnic tables conveniently spaced nearby. If you didn't bring lunch with you, purchase a snack at the concession stand. While there, rent a canoe for an enjoyable paddle and a new perspective of Sandy Pond.

Time does have a way of slipping away from you at Terra Nova, but if you aren't too tired and want to experience the oceanic side of the park, head to the **Marine Exhibit** at the visitor centre at Salton's Brook. Here, you'll find interactive displays about the North Atlantic marine life around the park. Children of all ages will especially enjoy the touch tanks and the opportunity to hold a live crab or sea star in their hands.

If you weren't hungry at Sandy Pond but are feeling peckish now, step into the on-site Seaside Cafe for soup and a sandwich. Finish what's been a very full day by exploring the seaweed- and shell-strewn shore around the visitor centre.

OTHER HIKES & ACTIVITIES

If the setting sun finds you at the ocean's edge with the wind tickling your hair and the scent of salt water tingling in your nose, pause for a moment to slowly inhale. Should that breath of North Atlantic air leave you wistful for more, remember that life is too short for regrets. Plan your next trip to include at least a week in the park, and create an itinerary that encompasses the guided boat tour (departing Salton's Brook twice daily, mid-May–early Oct.), introducing your children to Terra Nova's junior naturalist programs, or taking part in the weekly campfire singalong.

You might even tread the paths of the Beothuk. Sadly, Newfoundland's original native inhabitants became extinct in 1829, their demise blamed on confrontations with Europeans, disease, and increased competition for food. Though they lived throughout the island, they were particularly populous along the northeast coast. Hiking along the **Ochre Hill Trail** (named for the red dye with which the Beothuk coloured themselves on ceremonial occasions), it isn't difficult to imagine you're sharing the path with quiet moccasin-clad feet. It's a gentle reminder that, though the park itself is a youthful 59 years, the land it protects is ageless.

TERRA NOVA NATIONAL PARK
(Parc national Terra-Nova)

INFORMATION & ACTIVITIES

VISITOR & INFORMATION CENTRE
Visitor Centre located at Salton's Brook. Phone (709) 533-2942. Open from May to October.

SEASONS & ACCESSIBILITY
Park open year-round; no winter services.

HEADQUARTERS
Glovertown, NL A0G 2L0. Phone (709) 533-2801. www.parkscanada.gc.ca/terranova.

FRIENDS OF TERRA NOVA
Heritage Foundation for Terra Nova National Park Glovertown, NL A0G 2L0. hftnnp@gmail.com.

ENTRANCE FEES
$6 per person ($5.00 senior, $3.00 youth); $15 per group per day. Check www.pc.gc.ca/terranova for a full list of entry and service fees.

PETS
Dogs must be on a leash. Pets permitted at the beaches but must be kept off the beach and boardwalk at Sandy Pond.

ACCESSIBLE SERVICES
The Visitor Centre, Heritage Trail, and boardwalk at Sandy Pond are all accessible to wheelchairs.

THINGS TO DO
Swimming at Sandy Pond (freshwater) and at Eastport and Sandy Cove beaches (saltwater). Fishing for trout and salmon in season; ice fishing at Dunphy's Pond in February and March (permit $10 per day, $34 per season). Call (709) 533-2801 for the status of closed waters and for catch-and-possession limits.

Hiking and bicycling are also available, as well as beach volleyball at Eastport Beach. Canoes and paddleboats are available for rent at Sandy Pond.

SPECIAL ADVISORIES
• Watch for wildlife when driving with poor visibility.
• Keep campsites clean and tidy to avoid attracting wildlife.
• Report fires or suspicious smoke to park staff or call (709) 533-2801.
• No open fires or charcoal barbecues permitted in Newman Sound Campground.

OVERNIGHT BACKPACKING
Primitive campgrounds on Outport Trail and Dunphy's Pond Trail. Canoe route through Sandy Pond, Beachy Pond, and Dunphy's Pond. Call (709) 533-2801.

CAMPGROUNDS
Electrical sites $29 per night, nonelectrical sites $26 ($24 and $19 respectively with Early Bird Pass). **Newman Sound,** 278 sites (150 with electricity), open year-round with The Nature House Activity Centre, grocery store, laundromat, day-use area, and outdoor theatre. **Malady Head,** available June to September. Unserviced campsites with washrooms, kitchen shelters, playground, fire pits, a filling and dumping station, and a day-use area. $22 per night; $17 with Early Bird Pass. Call (877) 737-3783 or visit www.pccamping.ca.

HOTELS, MOTELS, & INNS
(unless otherwise noted, rates are for a 2-person double, high season, in Canadian dollars)

Inside the park:
Charlottetown, NL A0C 1L0
Clode Sound Motel and Restaurant 8 Main St., (709) 664-3146. guestservices@clodesound.com; www.clodesound.com. $120-$220.

Outside the park:
Port Blanford, NL A0C 2G0:
By d'Bay Cabins (709) 543-2637. info@bydbay.com; www.bydbay.com. $110-$117 for two nights.
Terra Nova Resort & Golf Community (709) 543-2525. info@terranovagolf.com; www.terranovagolf.com. $109-$350.

View from the Long Range Mountains down to Western Brook Pond

▶ GROS MORNE

NEWFOUNDLAND & LABRADOR
ESTABLISHED 1973
1,805 sq km/446,000 acres

Surrounded by silent granite guardians whose tips stretch into endless sky to regularly converse with clouds, you might feel the natural and unavoidable impulse to look up. Succumb to the temptation. But don't forget—an equally impressive and revealing story lies patiently beneath your feet.

That the literal French translation of *gros* is "big" seems a criminal understatement when applied to Gros Morne National Park. Even words like "immense" and "majestic" fail to do it justice.

This, the third largest of Atlantic Canada's national parks, is host to a gargantuan panorama of natural wonder: Newfoundland's second highest peak (standing 806 m/2,622 ft), ocean viewscapes, a freshwater fjord sheltered by towering cliffs, the highest waterfall in eastern North America, sandy beaches, sea stacks, and sea caves.

All of this natural beauty helps account for the park's listing as a UNESCO World Heritage site. The scenery, however, is a by-product of Gros Morne's greatest gift: a highly visible example of plate tectonics. Here, on the isolated and uninhabited mountaintops of western Newfoundland, you will find one of the world's best examples of continental drift and the physical remnants of collisions and separation that took place hundreds of millions of years ago. Here, deep ocean crust and rocks from the Earth's mantle lie exposed for all to see. Glaciation has added a coastal lowland, alpine plateau, fjords, glacial valleys, waterfalls, and lakes to this breathtaking landscape.

How to Get There

Of the four commercial airports in Newfoundland, Deer Lake Regional is the closest—a mere 32 km (20 mi) from the park entrance. It offers direct flights from Toronto, Montreal, and Halifax.

If you're driving or cycling to Gros Morne, you'll have to catch the ferry from North Sydney in Nova Scotia (www.marine-atlantic.ca). A six-hour ferry ride will land you in Port aux Basques, 300 km (186 mi) from the park entrance. If you take the 14-hour North Sydney–Argentia crossing (mid-June–Sept.), it's a 570-km (354 m) trip to the park. For both ferries reservations are a must, but be prepared for delays due to weather.

When you've landed in Newfoundland, take Trans-Canada 1 to Deer Lake. Then leave the highway and head 32 km (20 mi) north along Rte. 430 (also known as the Viking Trail) to the park entrance in Wiltondale. From here you will have the option to head south on Rte. 431 toward Glenburnie, Woody Point, or Trout River, or continue north on Rte. 430 toward Rocky Harbour, Norris Point, St. Paul's, or Cow Head.

When to Go

Precipitation is a given in Gros Morne, with some form of it falling every two days on average. Summer can bring rain and fog, which sometimes creates an otherworldly atmosphere for summit seekers. For winter visitors, the rain, drizzle, and fog give way to thick falls of the white stuff that ski, snowshoe, and snowmobile enthusiasts adore.

Given the extreme differences in elevation throughout the park, temperatures and wind speeds can quickly fluctuate. As long as visitors are of the non-complaining sort and come prepared with multiple layers and water-resistant clothing, Gros Morne is a park to be adored year-round. Check with park officials prior to setting out. The Gros Morne Mountain trail is closed in spring to minimize soil erosion and human interference with animal habitats and breeding. It is also closed for hiker safety as late-melting snow beds often conceal the trail. The Long Range Traverse is a multiday recognized by National Geographic as one of the world's 15 best hikes. For local weather updates, visit www.weatheroffice.gc.ca.

How to Visit

Truly appreciating the natural wonder of Gros Morne requires several days and extended excursions along challenging uphill trails. However, the park also is prepared to play host to many different age levels, with shorter, easy walks on level ground, lots of coastal access, and great sandy and cobbled beaches. Accessible via a walk along a 3-km (2 mi) boardwalk, the boat tour of the landlocked Western Brook Pond fjord is richly rewarding.

There are five frontcountry camping locations in Gros Morne, most of which have playground facilities. Combined, they have a total of 217 unserviced campsites; 25 have electrical and water hookups and 10 have alternate accommodations (oTENTiks and rustic cabins). Green Point's 31 beachside sites were upgraded in 2016 to include showers and

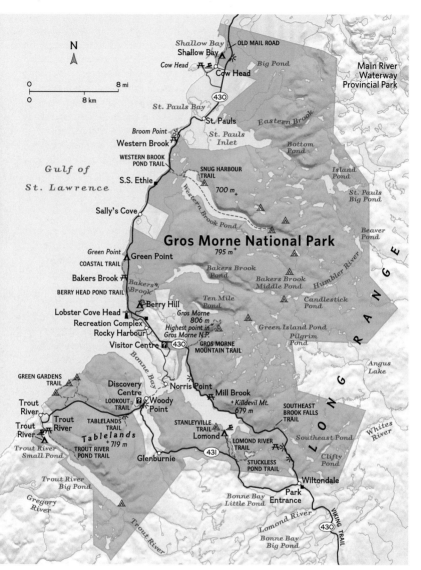

flush toilets. Each campground has something different to offer, from wide-open grassy areas to water views to glorious mountain vistas.

TABLELANDS
a full day

Start your morning at the Discovery Centre at the south end of the park (there's no mistaking its vibrant yellow hue and impressive circular facade). Spend some time enjoying its modern comforts and informative displays about the area. You can catch an art exhibit or sometimes a presentation from the artist-in-residence if you're there at the right time.

The **Tablelands Trail** parking lot is 4 km (2.5 mi) west of the Discovery

Camping, Lomond Campground

Centre. Make sure you're carrying a couple of bottles of water and are dressed for the weather. Wear hiking boots. The climbs are challenging, but the views from the top are well worth it. Enjoy an avalanche of sensory information. Note the seeming isolation atop this ancient slab of the Earth's mantle, the wind whispering in your ears, the feeling of the sun's rays as they warm you and this ageless rock into a golden mood, the sight of a verdant mountain with cottony clouds as its crowning glory. With the jaw-dropping descent comes the realization that you really did climb that high. In addition to the surreal views from every angle—whether hiking the Tablelands on high or down below—this is a rare opportunity to get up close and personal with peridotite, a type of rock usually found in the Earth's mantle. Rarely ever seen on the surface, it forms below the Earth's crust, deeper than 10 km (6.6 mi) or more below ground. It was launched to the surface by continental collision about 470 million years ago. Rich in iron, chromium, and nickel but lacking nitrogen, potassium, and phosphorus, peridotite discourages plant growth. Don't be deceived by the low-growing plants here. They are tough, some are extremely rare, and they may be decades, even centuries, old.

Centre along Rte. 431. You'll find yourself immediately stepping out on the rust-tinted Mars-like landscape of this impressive geological feature. If time is limited, you can hike just a segment of the Tablelands. The Tablelands Trail is an easy hike along an old gravel road bed. You'll pass pitcher plants (with a thirst for insects) and tough, rare flora able to grow on toxic rock. There is a guided hike at 10 a.m. from June through September—it's free with your park pass. To learn at your own pace there is an Explora app.

For real off-trail adventures there are two options. Blast up to the top of the **Bowl,** a glacial cirque, and back down again in about three hours. For a long, otherworldly adventure, plan an 8-to-10-hour hike up the back of Winterhouse Canyon, and along its upper edge to get back to the Bowl, then head down to the parking lot. A park guide leads folks up to the top of the Bowl twice weekly during peak season.

Before setting out you will want to pick up a map at the Discovery

OTHER ATTRACTIONS

There are freshwater ponds to swim in and fjords to explore, wildlife to see and kayaks to paddle, communities to visit and trails to hike—not the least of which is the strenuously rewarding 16-km (10 mi) round-trip expedition to the top of **Gros Morne Mountain** itself.

GROS MORNE NATIONAL PARK
(Parc national du Gros-Morne)

INFORMATION & ACTIVITIES

VISITOR & INFORMATION CENTRES
Gros Morne Visitor Centre Hwy. 430, 3 km (2 mi) east of Rocky Harbour. Open May to October. **Discovery Centre** Hwy. 431 at Woody Point. Open late May to early October.

SEASONS & ACCESSIBILITY
Park open year-round.

HEADQUARTERS
Rocky Harbour, NL A0K 4N0. Phone (709) 458-2417. grosmorne.info@pc.gc.ca; www.parkscanada.gc.ca/grosmorne.

FRIENDS OF GROS MORNE
Gros Morne Co-operating Association Rocky Harbour, NL A0K 4N0. Phone (709) 458-3610. info@grosmornetravel.com; www.visitgrosmorne.com.

ENTRANCE FEES
$10 per person, $20 per group per day (winter, $8 per person, $16 per group per day); $49 per person, $100 per group per year.

PETS
Pets permitted but must be leashed at all times. Dogs not permitted on boat tours.

ACCESSIBLE SERVICES
The visitor centres, Lobster Cove Lighthouse, campground service buildings, and boardwalk section of the Berry Head Pond Trail are wheelchair accessible. An all-terrain wheelchair is available at the visitor centre; call in advance for booking.

THINGS TO DO
Backcountry hiking **Long Range Traverse** (3–4 days) and **Northern Traverse** (3 days), both unmarked routes. Reservations required ($25 reservation fee). There is a limited number of groups per day. Backcountry permit required ($85 and $70 per person).

Fishing permits free, but provincial licence and tags required for salmon fishing (for a fee). Kayaking in **Trout River Pond** and **Bonne Bay.** Boat ramps at Trout River Pond, Mill Brook, and Lomond day-use areas. Powerboats permitted on Trout River Pond and Bonne Bay.

Boat tours on **Western Brook Pond** (July–Sept.); call (709) 458-2016 or (888) 458-2016 for reservations. Cruises available on Bonne Bay.

Indoor swimming at Recreation Complex (late June–early Sept.); unsupervised outdoor swimming at **Shallow Bay, Lomond** (saltwater), and **Trout River Pond** (freshwater). Cross-country skiing,

EXCURSIONS

L'ANSE AUX MEADOWS NATIONAL HISTORIC SITE
ST. ANTHONY, NL

This living history site at the northernmost tip of the Great Northern Peninsula is so far the only authenticated Viking site in North America. Here you'll discover the excavated remains of the base camp used by Leif Eriksson around A.D. 1000. Open June to early October. Located north of St. Anthony, but to get there, you must turn off Hwy. 430 onto Hwy. 436, about 10 km (6.2 mi) south of St. Anthony. (709) 623-2608 (in season only); (709) 458-2417 (rest of the year).

snowmobiling, self-guided tour of **Lobster Cove Lighthouse** (late May–early Oct.) and **Broom Point**; (early June–mid-Sept).

SPECIAL ADVISORIES

- Onshore winds common mid-morning to mid-afternoon. Boaters should check the forecast before setting out.
- The beach at the mouth of Western Brook is dangerous for swimming due to currents. Elsewhere, use caution in choosing where to swim.
- If hiking in the backcountry call (709) 458-2417 for information.
- If travelling in avalanche zones, you should be trained in avalanche safety and carry safety and rescue gear.

OVERNIGHT BACKPACKING

Primitive/backcountry campsites along **Green Gardens, Stanleyville, Gros Morne,** and **Snug Harbour** trails. Sites are equipped with picnic tables, pit toilets, and tent pads (where necessary). Open fires not permitted, so bring camp stove. Permit required; first-come, first-served basis. Visit www.pccamping.ca or call (877) 737-3783. Fees: $10 overnight, $70 per season.

CAMPGROUNDS

Gros Morne National Park offers 227 drive-in and eight oTENTik (a cross between a tent and a cabin) campsites at five Parks Canada campgrounds. All campgrounds are semi-serviced. Rates range from approximately $16 primitive to $120 for an oTENTik. **Trout River Pond,** 44 sites, boat launch. **Lomond,** 29 sites, ideal for fishing and boating, first-come, first-served. **Berry Hill,** 69 sites and 2 group sites. **Green Point,** 31 sites, near fishing area, self-registration. **Shallow Bay,** 52 drive-in sites, near sand beach and outdoor theatre. Group camping is $6 per person, per night. All-season camping at Green Point only. For Berry Hill, Shallow Bay, and Trout River Pond, reservations are available at www.reservations.parks canada.gc.ca. (877) 737-3783 or TTY (866) 787-6221.

HOTELS, MOTELS, & INNS

(unless otherwise noted, rates are for a 2-person double, high season, in Canadian dollars)

Outside the park:

Fisherman's Landing Inn P.O. Box 124, Rocky Harbour, NL A0K 4N0. (709) 458-2711. www.fishermanslandinginn.com. $159.

Sugar Hill Inn Norris Point, NL A0K 3V0. (888) 299-2147. www.sugarhillinn.nf.ca. $170–$235.

For more accommodations visit www.newfoundlandandlabrador.com.

PORT AU CHOIX NATIONAL HISTORIC SITE
PORT AU CHOIX, NL

The limestone bedrock throughout the Port au Choix area has preserved evidence of 5,500 years of indigenous history, including a 4,000-year-old slate bayonet and the antler harpoon used by a Groswater Paleo-Eskimo. Open mid-June to mid-September. Drive 110 km (68 mi) north of Gros Morne. Turn off the Viking Trail at Port Saunders and drive through to Port au Choix. Take Point Riche Road to the visitor centre. (709) 861-3522 (in season only); (709) 458-2417 (rest of the year).

Small glacier near Mount Caubvick/Mont D'Iberville

▶TORNGAT MOUNTAINS

NEWFOUNDLAND & LABRADOR
ESTABLISHED 2005
9,700 sq km/2,400,000 acres

The region of Torngait was named after Torngak, the most powerful spirit in Inuit mythology. Torngat Mountains National Park remains a spiritual place where visitors from around the world have the unique opportunity to experience the power of Torngait with warm and welcoming Inuit who call this place home.

Coming to a sharp point at the northeasternmost edge of continental Canada, Torngat Mountains National Park covers a wedge of land between northern Quebec and the Labrador Sea. Rising from a rugged and barren coastline, this mountain range at the tip of Labrador is home to the highest peaks on mainland Canada east of the Rockies (the highest being Mount Caubvick at 1,652 m/5,420 ft). Massive glacier-carved fjords cut into the land along a coastline flanked by saw-toothed mountains, some more than 1 km (0.6 mi) high. Exposed cliffs put their ancient underlying geologic formations on display.

As you travel through this land the most striking elements against the green velvet landscape are the surreal, luminescent blue icebergs that stud the dark waters along the coast and the nanuk—the polar bears that wander the shores. Wildlife in the park includes wolves, arctic foxes, peregrine falcons, and the world's only tundra-dwelling black bears. On the migratory path of the George River caribou herd, once the world's largest, this region is also home to the Torngat Mountains caribou herd.

Established in 2005 after a collaborative negotiation between the Canadian government and the Inuit of Nunatsiavut and Nunavik, Torngat Mountains is the first national park in Labrador. The park is operated and managed through a cooperative management regime that recognizes Inuit as equal partners and values the importance of mutual respect and trust. When you visit the park, you experience this practice of working together as you explore the landscape and learn about the place from both local Inuit and Parks Canada staff perspectives.

How to Get There

There are no roads to the Torngat Mountains. Access is through charter air flight, cruise ship, or snowmobile. Most visitors access the park through the Inuit-owned and -operated base camp and research station, with all-inclusive trips arranged from Goose Bay, Labrador. Contact the Nunatsiavut Group of Companies (www.torngatbasecamp.com).

Private charter flights to Saglek Bay airstrip, located just south of the park boundary and the base camp, may be arranged from Goose Bay through Air Labrador (www.airlabrador.com), Innu Mikun (www.provincialairlines.ca), or Kuujjuaq in Nunavik (northern Quebec) through Air Inuit (www.airinuit.com). The journey from the Saglek airstrip to the base camp requires a boat or a helicopter ride.

Expedition Cruise ships travel to the park and into some of the fjords.

For an updated list of cruise companies, check the Cruise Newfoundland and Labrador website (www.cruisetheedge.com). Those who seek to arrange their own travel into the park should contact Parks Canada to secure permits and arrange orientation sessions (888-922-1290).

When to Go

The summer season is short and the mildest weather occurs from mid-July to mid-August. For spring conditions, March and April can be good times to travel to the park by snowmobile.

The temperature in the park is typically 20°C (68°F) in the summer, but can also reach 30°C (86°F) or drop below freezing. Mean temperature in the winter is –16.5°C (2°F).

Climatic conditions, influenced heavily by latitude, altitude, and coastal currents, can change rapidly. Heavy wind, fog, and strong rain can sweep in, grounding planes and boats.

How to Visit

Last year about 450 visitors came to the Torngats, more than one-third of whom visited on cruise ships, zipping ashore on zodiacs for day excursions. The 150 or so visitors—including scientific researchers—who came for a more immersive visit stayed at the base camp.

Like most remote locations, the Torngats can be time-consuming and expensive to reach. To have a meaningful experience of the area, a trip of at least one week is recommended.

TORNGAT EXPERIENCE

In the summer, organized expeditions and Parks Canada operations are run from the Torngat Mountains Base Camp and Research Station in kANGIDLUASUk (St. John's

A food cache at North Arm attests to Inuit history.

Harbour) in Sallik (Saglek) Bay, in
the southern reaches of Torngat
Mountains National Park. Here,
visitors have access to a variety of
accommodations and a dining hall.
Freshwater, flushing toilets, and hot
showers bring the amenities of home
to this remote camp. Other notable
features include a power generator
and 10,000-volt electric fence that
keeps out curious (and hungry!)
bears. There is plenty of opportunity
for interaction with Inuit staff and
visiting researchers over meals in
the dining hall and during evening
activities.

Polar bear safety is of paramount
concern in the park. Parks Canada
recommends that visitors hiking in
the park, especially those on overnight
trips, engage the services of trained
and experienced Inuit bear guards
who are hired by the base camp to
accompany hikers outside the safety
of the electric fence.

It's common practice for Inuit to
periodically turn around and survey
the land behind them to make sure
they're not being stalked. Visitors
need to be very diligent about prevent-
ing wildlife encounters and be appropriately prepared to deter wildlife.

Artifact from a Thule sod house, Nachvak Fjord

Parks Canada's mandatory visitor
orientation includes a bear safety talk,
followed by a video that presents polar
bear knowledge from Inuit elders.
Along with the awe-inspiring scale of
the landscape of the Torngats, living
in close proximity to wild predators is
part of the experience that makes this
park special.

INUIT GIFT

Torngat Mountains isn't just about
grand landscapes. The national park
is considered by many as a gift from
the Inuit to Canada, and interaction
with the Inuit staff and guides—most
of whom have lived on this land for
generations—can easily be the richest
part of your visit here.

Southwest Arm, Saglek Fjord

Arctic hare

This isn't just their homeland in the conceptual sense. As you glide along the banks of a fjord, your Inuit guide might point to the spot where his mother was born. Or he may spot wildlife off in the distance, a polar bear or caribou, that would otherwise have gone unnoticed. He might even kneel down to show you a Ramah chert shard tool nestled in the tundra or the faint remains of a tent ring—evidence of the ancient past of Inuit, Dorset, or Thule habitation.

Until fairly recently, most Inuit were seminomadic subsistence hunters, inextricably tied to the land, with an intimate knowledge of the habits of wildlife. Experiencing traditional Inuit harvesting practices can be as hands-on as rolling up sleeves to help skin a seal or just simply observing. Others may prefer to fish for arctic char, wander in the tidal zone picking mussels, or gather berries. It's also possible to join the guides on their hunt for ducks and seal.

Excursions from base camp are usually made by boat. A typical day trip might take you to Sallikuluk (Rose Island), where thousands of archaeological features dating back 5,000 years are located. Here, you can see sod-house excavations, tent rings, food caches, and hunting blinds. Among the hundreds of traditional stone burial sites found all over the island, one mass burial site houses repatriated ancestral remains.

Another popular outing takes you to the north arm of **Sallik (Saglek) Fjord,** about three hours by boat from base camp. Along the way, crumbling cliffs of gneiss—shot through with striations—tower along the shore. Some of the rock in this area is 3.9 billion years old, putting it among the oldest on the planet. At the end of the inlet, you can go ashore for a meal of freshly caught arctic char and traditional *panitsiaks* (bannock) baked on the hot rocks of a beach fire.

NORTHERN LIGHTS

Wherever you stay in the park, you will have the opportunity to view *atsanik*—the northern lights. On a good night, swaths of green light may arc across the night sky before seeming to turn to liquid that appears to drip down from the heavens in molten tendrils. If you haven't already felt the spirits inhabiting the park, the magnificence of the northern lights alone may inspire you to reconsider.

TORNGAT MOUNTAINS NATIONAL PARK
(Parc national des Monts-Torngat)

INFORMATION & ACTIVITIES

VISITOR & INFORMATION CENTRE
Parks Canada has a visitor reception and orientation tent at the **Torngat Mountains Base Camp and Research Station** in St. John's Harbour in Saglek Bay that generally welcomes visitors from late July to the end of August. For information call Parks Canada's administrative offices in Nain, Labrador, (709) 922-1290 or (888) 922-1290.

SEASONS & ACCESSIBILITY
Park open year-round; visits recommended in March and April and from early July to September. No road access or facilities. Aircraft landing requires permit from parks, issued on a case-by-case basis only. Access to Inuit lands on the coast at Iron Strand Beach requires permission from the Nunatsiavut Government; call (709) 922-2942.

PARKS CANADA OFFICES
Box 471, Nain, NL A0P 1L0. Phone (709) 922-1290 or (888) 922-1290. torngats.info@pc.gc.ca; www.parkscanada.gc.ca/torngat. Torngat Mountains Base Camp and Research Station organizes all-inclusive trips to the Torngats and manages the base camp. P.O. Box 1000, Stn. B., Happy Valley-Goose Bay, NL, A0P 1E0. (855) TORNGAT (867-6428); basecamp@ngc-ng.ca

FRIENDS OF TORNGAT MOUNTAINS
Torngat Arts and Crafts, P.O. Box 269, Nain, NL A0P 1L0. Phone (709) 922-1659. torngatartscrafts@gmail.com.

ENTRANCE FEE
No entry fee.

PETS
Pets must be under control at all times.

ACCESSIBLE SERVICES
None.

THINGS TO DO
Hiking, mountain climbing, backcountry skiing, sailing or motorboat tours along the coast.

SPECIAL ADVISORIES
- All visitors must register before entering and leaving Torngat Mountains National Park either by phone, fax, or in person at the Parks Canada offices in Nain or George River.
- Travel with experienced Inuit polar bear guards is strongly recommended.
- The weather is highly variable. In summer, temperatures can drop from mild during the day to below freezing at night. Dress appropriately.
- Do not plan on using wood for cooking. Build only small fires in emergencies, and ensure they are extinguished when you are done.
- Do not remove artifacts or disturb features at archaeological sites.
- Only Inuit are permitted to carry firearms in the park.

CAMPGROUNDS
No designated campsites or facilities. Backcountry camping protocols are discussed with Parks Canada staff during registration.

HOTELS, MOTELS, & INNS
(unless otherwise noted, rates are for a 2-person double, high season, in Canadian dollars)

Outside the park:
Atsanik Lodge Sand Banks Rd., Nain, NL A0P 1L0. (709) 922-2910. $150–$165.
Auberge Kuujjuaq Inn Kuujjuaq, QC J0M 1C0. (819) 964-2903. reservations kuujjuaqinn@tamaani.ca. $225.

For more accommodations options contact the Fédération des coopératives du Nouveau-Québec (FCNQ), (514) 457-3249 or (866) 336-2667, www.fcnq.ca.

Swallow Harbour

▶ AKAMI-UAPISHK^u-KAKKASUAK-MEALY MOUNTAINS

NEWFOUNDLAND AND LABRADOR
ESTABLISHED 2015
10,700 sq km/2,644,028 acres

In Mealy Mountains National Park Reserve, deep interior valleys carve through ancient sugarloaf granite. Bounded by flashing salmon rivers, the cold Labrador Sea, and the brackish waters of 160 km-long (100 mi) Lake Melville, this largest federal park in eastern Canada is the primarily undisturbed haunt of wolves and caribou. No roads run through the park. Few visitors access its subarctic beauties, except for a handful of snowmobilers in spring, some summer boaters along its watery fringes, and anglers travelling in light aircraft. The local people have a long and deep connection to the Mealy Mountains, where they continue to trap, fish, and hunt.

The Innu call it Akami-Uapishk^u (pronounced kami-wa-pushku), meaning White Mountains Across, while Inuit refer to it as KakKasuak, an Inuttitut word for "mountains." The origin of the term "Mealy" is not certain, although one theory links it to an old term meaning "spotted," because of the snow patches that persist well into summer. The park's loftiest summits lie in the English Mountains, a remote range deep in the park's interior. Here, an unnamed peak rises incrementally above its neighbours to 1,180 m (3,871 ft), the highest point in the Mealys. Walking is good at this altitude, over bare rock, tundra, and ground-hugging alpine cover, but large swathes of *krummholz*—called tuckamore in eastern Canada—create a daunting barrier on some lower slopes. This wiry stunted spruce is so old and tough from years of slow growth—one specimen is 340 years old—that it is impossible to push through and must be skirted or scrambled over awkwardly.

While the mountains farther west are lower and less precipitous than the English range, they still commonly reach 600 to 900 m (2,000 to 3,000 ft). Their bare, rounded tops are a favourite with caribou, which brought Inuit

and Innu hunters to the Mealy Mountains each winter. Caribou numbers have declined sharply throughout Labrador, possibly due to natural population cycles. The entire park area is identified as critical habitat for the threatened Mealy Mountains caribou herd. The most accessible portions of the park are its coastlines—the northern border along Lake Melville and the long strip of sand beach known as the Wunderstrands ("the strand") along its eastern boundary. Archaeologists believe that this beach may be the Wunderstrands mentioned in the Viking sagas of Eric the Red: "They also gave name to the strands, calling them Furðustrandir, because it took so long to sail by them."

The beach begins just 13 km (8 mi) by boat from the town of Cartwright, which is accessible by ferry or by a gravel spur road off the Trans Labrador Highway.

The 54-km (34 mi) sweep of the strand is broken in only one spot, by the rocky finger of Cape Porcupine. The strand begins at Sandy Point,

Cape Porcupine

A hiker pauses in the Mealy Mountains highlands.

near the mouth of the salmon-rich North River, and ends at the abandoned fishing village of West Bay to the north. West Bay is also one of the few spots sheltered from the Atlantic rollers that always wash the beach and that prompted an early park advocate to tout this coastline as a potential surfing mecca.

The strand may be far from the mountains after which the park is named, but its comparative accessibility and some relief from biting insects, its historical importance, together with its pleasant hiking, its wilderness views, and its wildlife, will make it one of the icons of Canada's 46th national park. Fresh wolf and bear tracks are common along the sand beach. Black streaks of titanium lace the sands.

At high tide, the beach turns too narrow in spots for hiking, but visitors can continue along a low sandy berm fringed with sea grass. Inuit women from the nearby town of Rigolet, the southernmost Inuit community on the Labrador coast, still gather this grass to sew into traditional waterproof baskets.

Archaeologists have studied the Wunderstrands for evidence of past habitation, including the broken keel mentioned in Viking sagas, but the acidic soil has yielded few artifacts.

These days, all of Canada's northern parks involve local First Nations and Inuit communities in planning and management, but Mealy Mountains is unique in the coming together of several groups to co-operatively manage the park with Parks Canada. These include the Innu—a First Nations group related to the Cree and historically known as the Naskapi and Montagnais—as well as the Inuit-run Nunatsiavut government of northern Labrador and the NunatuKavut, formerly the Labrador Metis Association.

How to Get There

While Mealy Mountains National Park Reserve is not as geographically remote as some other northern parks, just getting to Labrador can be

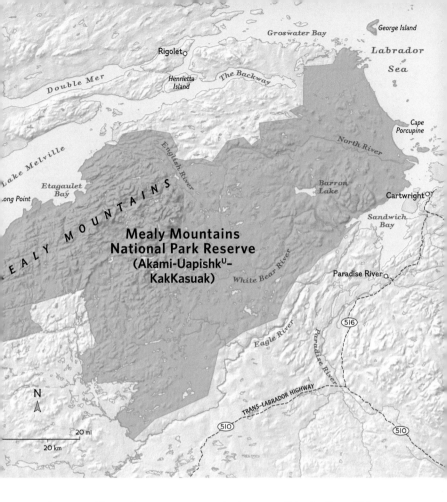

an adventure. The main gateways to the park, Goose Bay and Cartwright, are accessible from southern Canada by a partially gravel road called the Trans Labrador Highway. Goose Bay is typically a hard two-day drive from southern Quebec. Rigolet is another gateway, accessible by air or ferry from Goose Bay and by ferry from Cartwright. Cell phones work in most Labrador communties, but not all.

Eastern visitors may shorten the gravel section of their journey by taking the ferry from St. Barbe, on the island of Newfoundland, to Blanc Sablon, Quebec, and driving north from there. Happy Valley-Goose Bay

is also accessible via direct flights from Deer Lake, St. John's, Halifax, and Montreal.

The strand is a short boat ride or kayak trip from Cartwright, but the only practical way into the mountainous portion of the park is by floatplane or helicopter from Goose Bay. Helicopters typically carry four to six passengers, depending on the amount of baggage brought along. Most bush planes are Twin Otters and have room for up to eight people and their gear.

Ambitious hikers may be tantalized by views of the Mealys from Lake Melville, near Goose Bay, but in most places, a wide apron of impas-

The Wunderstrands

sible bog and dense forest separates the lakeshore from the mountains.

When to Go

In June, the long Labrador winter gives way abruptly to summer. But summer is also the time when the region's infamous mosquitoes and blackflies dominate the park's interior. While mosquito numbers are reasonable in the mountainous areas of the park, blackflies are legion, and therefore few locals venture inland at that time of year. Experienced visitors prefer to wait until late August or September, when the biting hordes have diminished.

Summer backpacking is possible for those willing to experience the park in headnets and bug jackets, or for those who base themselves near the park's windswept summits. Along the coastal portions of the park, cool ocean breezes keep the insect population manageable; this area of the park may be hiked all summer long.

In the park's interior, early October can be cool but lovely, with brilliant red and yellow vegetation carpeting the slopes, but winter can set in at any time.

For hardy snowshoers and backcountry skiers, March–April offers longer days and milder daytime temperatures. But this is still serious, remote winter travel in potentially hostile weather.

How to Visit

In the summer months, two or three cruise ships ply the Labrador coast, and they sometimes stop at the strand. An outfitter in Cartwright offers kayaking as well as boating tours to the beach, from which you can hike and even camp out—as long as future pickup is arranged.

Each spring, residents from Happy Valley-Goose Bay and neighbouring towns will continue to access the Mealy Mountains by snowmobile to visit personal cabins as part of the local agreement that underpins the formation of the park.

The white-water streams that spill from all sides of the Mealy Mountains down to sea level are largely rocky and unnavigable, even for kayaks. An alternative option for amphibious travel here is a modern lightweight packraft. It weighs little, packs to the size of a sleeping bag, and can be inflated in a few minutes for short crossings of ponds and small lakes.

A backpacking trek, based in the high windswept ranges above the

AKAMI-UAPISHKᵁ-KAKKASUAK-MEALY MOUNTAINS
(Réserve de parc national Akami-Uapishkᵁ–KakKasuak–Monts Mealy)

INFORMATION & ACTIVITIES

SEASONS & ACCESSIBILITY
Open year-round, but best times for interior travel are March–April (skiing, snowshoeing) and late August–September. The coastal areas may be visited all summer long.

VISITOR & INFORMATION CENTRES
At press time, there are no visitor centres. For general information, 709-458-2417. mealymountains.gmp@pc.gc.ca.
www.parkscanada.gc.ca/mealymountains

ENTRANCE FEE
To be determined.

PETS
Yes, on a leash.

THINGS TO DO
Hiking, snowshoeing, backcountry skiing, fishing.

SPECIAL ADVISORIES
• The Mealy Mountains are a remote backcountry environment, and visitors should be equipped for heat, snow, insects, wind, and rain—sometimes all in the same day.
• There are black bears and polar bears in the park. Precautions must be taken to ensure safety.

CAMPGROUNDS
No designated campsites or facilities. Visitors may camp anywhere in the park except at archaeological and ecologically sensitive sites. Contact Parks Canada for more information.

TOUR OPERATORS
Adventure Canada 14 Front St. South, Mississauga, ON, L5H 2C4 1-800-363-7566 info@adventurecanada.com; www.adventurecanada.com.
Experience Labrador 20 Lethbridge Lane, Cartwright, Labrador, NL A0K 1V0 709-938-7444 experiencelabrador@gmail.com; www.experiencelabrador.com.
Park Lake Lodge Goose Bay Airport, Dakota Dr., Hanger 13, P.O. Box 1527, Station B, Happy Valley-Goose Bay, NL AOP 1EO. www.parklakelodge.com.

AIR CHARTER COMPANIES
Canadian Helicopters (709) 896-5259.
Universal Helicopters (709) 896-2444.
Air Labrador (709) 896-6730.
Provincial Airlines (877) 576-3140.

FERRY
Rigolet and Cartwright are accessible from Happy Valley-Goose Bay on the *Northern Ranger*, a supply boat that doubles as a passenger ferry. www.tw.gov.nl.ca/ferryservices/schedules/h_goosebay_nain.html.

HOTELS, MOTELS, & INNS
Internet sites, including destinationlabrador.com and tourismnunatsiavut.com, offer accommodations options.

krummholz and most of the blackflies, is the best way to get intimate with the heart of the mountains, while avoiding the main obstacles to enjoyment. Floatplanes can land on some of the larger lakes, but then conveying gear higher through difficult terrain is required. For a small party, a helicopter shuttle from Happy Valley-Goose Bay is the best way to go. Note that the Mealy Mountains offer a backcountry experience, in which parties must be self-sustained and prepared for pickup delays that can sometimes last days because of weather.

Franey Trail lookout on the Cabot Trail, Cape Breton Highlands

Sweeping vistas where land meets sea

▶ CAPE BRETON HIGHLANDS

NOVA SCOTIA
ESTABLISHED 1936
948 sq km/235,000 acres

Cape Breton Highlands National Park was the first national park designated in Atlantic Canada. The Cabot Trail, a world-famous scenic highway, runs along parts of the coastal borders on both sides of the park and crosses the highlands. Renowned for its hiking trails, the park is home to a diverse mix of boreal and temperate species not found elsewhere in Canada.

The human history of northern Cape Breton reaches back 8,000 years. Paleo-Indians have lived here about 4,000 years. Portuguese, French, Scottish, Irish, and Dutch immigrants settled here from the 1600s onward, and there continues to be a rich cultural history in the region that is active and engaging.

The park is often referred to as the place "where the mountains meet the sea." The dominant feature of this region is the elevated plateau, surrounded by the Atlantic Ocean and divided by steep-walled river canyons; northern species and habitats on the plateaus coexist with the more temperate habitats and species of the lowlands. Consequently, there is much diversity.

Approximately 88 percent of the park is forested. The plateau or upper reaches is dominated by both boreal and taiga vegetation and is part of the worn-down Appalachian mountain chain that stretches from Georgia to Newfoundland. The boreal land region of this plateau features large swaths of coniferous trees, sprinkled with barrens and wetlands. Most of the population of Nova Scotia's endangered Canada lynx live here, as well as moose, hare, grouse, and marten. The taiga land region of the plateau features a tundra-like landscape characterized by scrub forest, barrens, and bogs.

In the lowlands, the Acadian forest includes a mix of northern and temperate plants and animals. Most noteworthy are the old-growth stands—more than 350 years old—as well as some pure sugar-maple stands found only in the northern part of this species' range.

The park has been shaped by the Gulf of St. Lawrence, which flanks it on the westward side, and the Atlantic Ocean to the east. The shorelines range from rocky shores and dramatic headlands to cobbled and sandy beaches. A healthy marine food chain includes krill, lobster, and salmon. Minke whales, pilot whales, fin whales, and harbour seals are seen along the coast. Around 230 species of birds frequent various sections of the park, the most noticeable being bald eagles.

The park has seven campgrounds, 26 hiking trails, numerous beaches, and a world-class golf course. Bordering communities have seasonal amenities, recreational programs, and cultural activities.

How to Get There

Airports are located in Sydney, in Cape Breton, and Halifax, in mainland Nova Scotia. From Sydney, take Rte. 125 to Hwy. 105, then take the exit to the English town ferry or continue on to the Cabot Trail at the St. Ann's exit. Driving time is two hours.

If driving from Halifax, take Hwy. 102 to Truro, then Hwy. 104 to the Canso Causeway that links mainland Nova Scotia to Cape Breton Island. Allow three hours to reach Cape Breton. At this point you need to decide which park entrance/visitor centre you want to check into: Ingonish Beach or Chéticamp.

For the Ingonish Beach entrance, take Hwy. 105 to exit 11 at Southaven. Follow the Cabot Trail north to the visitor centre. Driving time is two hours. Approaching the park from the west side, once you've crossed the Canso Causeway, follow Rte. 19 (the Ceilidh Trail) along the coast to Margaree Forks, then follow the Cabot Trail to Chéticamp. Allow two hours. The park entrance is 10 minutes from Chéticamp.

When to Go

The park is accessible year-round. The best time to go depends on your interests. Bird-watchers may prefer spring and early summer, as there is less foliage and chances are better for spotting birds, although peak breeding activity is June through July.

Hiking is great from May to November, when the ground is usually snow free. Some people prefer to hike in the fall as there are no flies and fall foliage is spectacular. It's also when the Celtic Colours International Festival and the Hike the Highland Festival take place, which is a bonus.

The best time for cycling is summer and fall. Ocean temperatures warm up by July and start to cool off in October. Although there is limited infrastructure during the winter, snowshoeing and skiing in the park can be a once-in-a-lifetime experience; valleys and plateaus become veritable winter wonderlands.

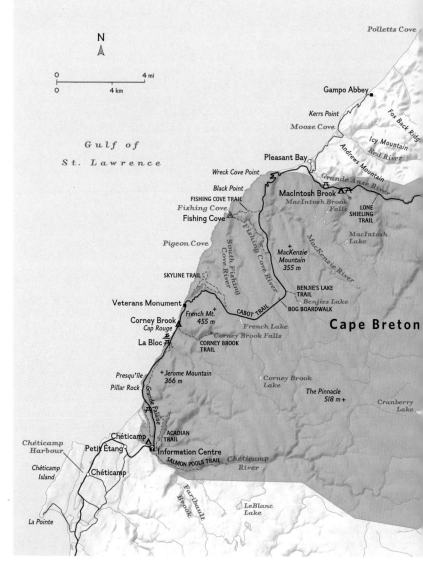

N

Gulf of
St. Lawrence

Polletts Cove

Gampo Abbey

Kerrs Point
Moose Cove

Fox Back Ridge
Icy Mountain
Red River

Pleasant Bay

Andrews Mountain

Grande Anse River

Wreck Cove Point

Black Point

FISHING COVE TRAIL
Fishing Cove
Fishing Cove

MacIntosh Brook

MacIntosh Brook
Falls

LONE
SHIELING
TRAIL

MacIntosh
Lake

Pigeon Cove

South Fishing Cove River

Fishing Cove River

MacKenzie River

MacKenzie
Mountain
355 m

SKYLINE TRAIL

BENJIE'S LAKE
TRAIL
Benjies Lake
BOG BOARDWALK

Veterans Monument

Corney Brook
Cap Rouge

La Bloc

French Mt.
455 m

CABOT TRAIL

French Lake

Corney Brook Falls

CORNEY BROOK
TRAIL

Cape Breton

Presqu'île
Pillar Rock

Jerome Mountain
366 m

Corney Brook
Lake

The Pinnacle
518 m

Cranberry
Lake

Grande Falaise

Chéticamp
Harbour

Chéticamp

Petit Étang

Chéticamp
Island

Chéticamp

ACADIAN
TRAIL

Information Centre

SALMON POOLS TRAIL

Chéticamp
River

La Pointe

Faribault
Brook

LeBlanc
Lake

How to Visit

The possibilities are endless. You can be as busy or as laid-back as you please. The best place to start is at one of the visitor information centres located at either end of the park. The views and vistas are spectacular no matter where you enter the park.

INGONISH BEACH TO SOUTH HARBOUR

a full day

Pack a lunch. Begin at **Ingonish Beach** and head for the stunning view at a rocky, 375-million-year-old granite headland. Here you can see northern gannets, cormorants, seals, and the

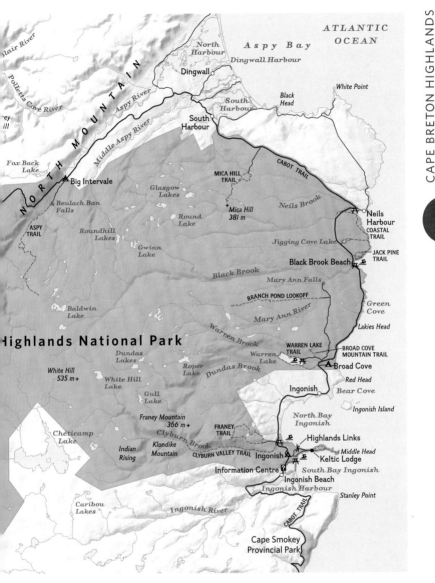

occasional whale. Next head to **Black Brook Beach,** nestled in a cove. Go for a swim while you enjoy views of the waterfall, or hike the **Jack Pine Trail,** which leads to views of the rugged Atlantic coast. Drive on north through **Neils Harbour,** where you can get ice cream in a lighthouse, and continue on the alternate route

to **White Point** for a picnic and fabulous views of the northern highlands falling abruptly into the Atlantic. Carry on another 10 minutes to **South Harbour.** Not listed on most maps, the stunning yet rather secluded beach here draws few visitors.

If it's not too late, on the way back consider a three-to-four-hour hike to

Mica Hill, along a breathtaking trail that winds through Acadian mixed forest and stunted taiga as it climbs to the windswept highlands plateau. Otherwise, check out interpretive activities and night hikes to finish off your day. Starlit evenings at **Warren Lake** are magical, with loon and owl calls echoing through the forest.

CHÉTICAMP TO NORTH MOUNTAIN & BACK

a full day

From Chéticamp head toward Pleasant Bay, where the Cabot Trail turns inland. Your first stop is **Benjie's Lake.** The trail leads through boreal forest to a viewing platform from which songbirds, moose, and raptors are often spotted. Next is **Lone Shieling,** where you'll see a reproduced Scottish crofter's hut.

Ascending **North Mountain,** you'll see the oldest rocks in Nova Scotia—more than one-billion-year-old Grenville gneiss and anorthocite. At the top, look down on **Aspy River,** whose slopes are especially resplendent in the fall.

As you descend on the return trip toward **Pleasant Bay,** look for the sparkling waters of the Gulf of St. Lawrence in the V of the mountains. If it is time for lunch, drive to the picnic area at **MacIntosh Brook,** where a 20-minute hike leads through an old-growth forest to a lovely waterfall. After lunch, ask one of the locals for directions to **Gampo Abbey,** a Buddhist monastery perched on the coastline, or the **Whale Interpretation Centre.** Tours are available in summer.

On your way back to Chéticamp, stop at the lookout where the road narrows to a ridge called the **Boar's Back.** About 305 m (1,000 ft) below is **Fishing Cove,** once a tiny Scottish settlement reached only by footpath or boat, and now a wilderness campsite.

Your next stop is **the Bog,** a 15-minute walk on a boardwalk with several interpretive panels. The treasures here include frog eggs, orchids, and carnivorous plants.

If you want to see a moose, head for the **Skyline Trail.** You'll need two to three hours; it's worth keeping to the right and walking the entire loop. Part of the trail leads to a dramatic headland overlooking the **Gulf of St. Lawrence,** where you're likely to catch sight of bald eagles and pilot whales.

As you travel back toward Chéticamp, enjoy the views from the Cabot Trail. Pull over at Veterans Monument where you may see gannets plummeting 20 to 30 m (66–98 ft) in a nearly vertical dive for food. Next, pull over at **La Bloc,** a picnic area with a great beach. End your day with a visit to **Pillar Rock** at Presqu'ile. If there's been a wind, the waves hitting the rock will be mesmerizing.

KAYAKING

The shore along the western side of the park just above **Chéticamp** up to Corney Brook is accessible in several places. If you paddle north along the coast, you'll pass by **Jumping Brook** and find yourself beneath some towering cliffs. A little farther on you'll find a large sea cave with a high, vaulted ceiling. If the tide is up, you'll be able to paddle all the way in.

Farther up the coast is Cape Breton Highlands' backcountry campsite, Fishing Cove. Paddle in on the beach, and enjoy spectacular sunsets.

Experienced kayakers can launch at Pleasant Bay and paddle to **Pollets Cove.** Pack a few apples for the horses that may greet you. If the winds rise and the seas become agitated, you will want to wait for calmer waters to paddle out. Bring extra food.

On the Atlantic Coast, the best

A tranquil view of a Cape Breton sunset

launching and takeout points are the beaches at Neils Harbour, Black Brook, Broad Cove, and Ingonish. On both coasts there are outfitters where you can rent gear or hire guides for paddling excursions.

HIKING, BIKING, & MORE

Up for a challenge? Hike to **Franey,** a two- to three-hour loop from the Ingonish Visitor Centre. At the top, follow the narrow gravel trail near the lookout for a breathtaking view of the **Clyburn Brook canyon** and the Atlantic.

For a more relaxed pace, spend the afternoon playing golf at the world-famous **Highlands Links,** considered the best public course in Canada. Or head to **Ingonish Beach,** named one of the top 25 Canadian beaches by *Canadian Geographic Traveller.*

Or challenge yourself: Find the red chairs placed around the park to savour the views of Parks Canada's absolute favourite places. Or, complete 10 short hikes in one day! If you have two or more days, you could explore all the trails that lead to a waterfall, including **Mary Ann Falls, Beulach Ban Falls,** or **MacIntosh Brook Waterfalls,** and **Corney Brook trails.**

Or go geocaching; 14 caches are strategically placed throughout the park including an Eco-Cache, Cultural Cache, Earth Cache, and the Parka's Campground Kid Cache. Learn more at the visitor centres.

Cycling can be hugely rewarding along the **Cabot Trail.** A number of private companies offer personalized tours, and many provide shuttle service to get up the steep hills.

Lively interpretive programs are offered June–August. Offerings, often hands on, focus on everything from moose to local history and take you to some of the park's most cherished places. The Skyline Sunset hike, Seeing in the Dark, and How to Hook a Mackerel are just a few programs, along with a star party in August. Schedules are available at the visitor centres, campgrounds, and online.

Local communities host dozens of suppers, ceilidhs, cultural events, and festivals throughout the region. Check local papers and community bulletin boards or ask park staff for more information.

CAPE BRETON HIGHLANDS NATIONAL PARK
(Parc national des Hautes-Terres-du-Cap-Breton)

INFORMATION & ACTIVITIES

VISITOR & INFORMATION CENTRES
Chéticamp Visitor Centre Western en-trance near Chéticamp. Phone (902) 224-2306. Nature bookshop, exhibits, and family-friendly activities. **Ingonish Visitor Centre** Eastern entrance in Ingonish Beach. Phone (902) 224-2306.

SEASONS & ACCESSIBILITY
Park open year-round; full services from late May to late Oct.

HEADQUARTERS
Ingonish Beach, NS B0C 1L0. Phone (902) 224-2306. www.parkscanada.gc.ca/cape breton.

ENTRANCE FEES
$8 per person, $20 per group per day; $40 per person, $100 per group per year. (A group is up to seven people in one vehicle.)

PETS
Pets must be on a leash at all times. Owners must control noise levels.

ACCESSIBLE SERVICES
Many of the washrooms and lookouts are accessible, as are the Chéticamp Visitor Centre, the Ingonish Visitor Centre, some campsites, and the Bog and Freshwater Lake Trails.

THINGS TO DO
A variety of interpretive events for the whole family in June, July, and Aug. One-third of the **Cabot Trail,** celebrated for picturesque views, runs through the national park. For drivers and cyclists, this is one of the most visited regions in Canada. Cape Breton Highlands National Park is home to six superb beaches. Choose between salt water and freshwater. Fishing permits $10 per day, $35 per year.

The park offers 26 hiking trails, ranging from easy strolls to challenging climbs with panoramic views of canyons, highlands, and coasts. The trails provide a chance to explore the complex habitat of northern Cape Breton Island. Fishing permits $10 per day, $35 per year. **Golfing** at **Highlands Links** *(www.highlandslinksgolf.com).* For tee times, call (800) 441-1118.

Centuries-old traditions, fresh seafood, the Cape Breton fiddle, and dances are what the local communities are all about. Mi'kmaq, Scottish, and Acadian cultures are alive and well here. At the end of the day, be sure to indulge in some good old Cape Breton hospitality.

EXCURSIONS

ALEXANDER GRAHAM BELL NATIONAL HISTORIC SITE
BADDECK, NS

Teacher, inventor, and humanitarian, Alexander Graham Bell accomplished wonders. Located in Baddeck, this site celebrates the life of the man who was a pioneer in education, communication, and transportation. Original artifacts, airplane and hydrofoil replicas, audiovisual presentations, and interpretation tell the story. Programs and activities for all ages. (902) 295-2069. 95 km (60 mi) southeast of Cape Breton Highlands National Park on Hwy 105.

SPECIAL ADVISORIES

- Avoid wildlife encounters, especially with coyotes, black bears, or moose. To report incidents, call (877) 852-3100.
- Rogue waves and riptides can be a concern during and after storms.
- Blackflies and mosquitoes are common in the summer; bring insect repellent.

OVERNIGHT BACKPACKING

Permit required for backcountry trekking. Wilderness camping at **Fishing Cove** campground, accessible only on foot, with tent pads, food cache, and pit privy. Beach nearby. For information and reservations for backcountry camping, call (902) 224-2306.

CAMPGROUNDS

Open year-round; full services available from late May to early October. Unlimited length of stay; for information on camping for longer than 7 nights, visit park website. Maximum 4 people per site. For reservations call (877) 737-3783 or visit www.reservation.pc.gc.ca. Reserve one of 20 oTENTiks ($100) or 10 equipped campsites ($70).

Chéticamp, open year-round, has hot showers, kitchen shelters with wood stoves, group fireplaces, playgrounds, and an outdoor theatre. Full services available from mid-May to late Oct.; flush toilets and kitchen shelters available year-round.

Serviced campsites with electricity, water, and sewer $35 per night. Serviced campsites with electricity $29 per night; unserviced campsites with washroom building (toilets and showers) $26 per night. **Ingonish Beach,** unserviced campsites with washroom building (toilets and showers) $26 per night. Winter camping available. **Broad Cove,** open late June to early September. Serviced campsites with electricity, water, and sewer $35 per night; unserviced campsites with washroom building (toilets and showers) $26 per night. **MacIntosh Brook** and overflow unserviced campsites with washroom building (toilets only) $22 per night. **Corney Brook,** unserviced campsites with washroom building (toilets only) $24 per night. **Big Intervale,** primitive campground with pit privies $18 per night.

HOTELS, MOTELS, & INNS

(unless otherwise noted, rates are for a 2-person double, high season, in Canadian dollars)

Outside the park:
Surrounding communities offer an array of services, amenities, and experiences. For restaurants, lodging, events, and more, visit www.cbisland.com or www.novascotia.com.

FORTRESS OF LOUISBOURG NATIONAL HISTORIC SITE
LOUISBOURG, NS

Founded by the French in 1713, later fortified and twice besieged, Louisbourg was demolished in the 1760s. Today the Fortress of Louisbourg stands as the largest reconstruction project in North America. In the summer, interpreters in period clothing re-enact 18th-century life. Year-round, trails offer hiking with spectacular scenery. Each season offers special programs and activities. (902) 733-3552. 140 km (87 mi) from park on south side of Cape Breton Highlands National Park.

Sable Island horses

▶ SABLE ISLAND

NOVA SCOTIA
ESTABLISHED 2013
30 sq km

Sable Island has long loomed large in the imaginations of sailors, adventurers, and maritime Canadians. A crooked smile of a sandbar, its exact length expands and contracts—with the wind and the waves—all the time. It is a place where wild horses outnumber hardy residents by a very wide margin. Sable Island National Park Reserve is both beautiful and strange, a skinny stretch of land where sand dunes walk the width of the island and shipwrecks—some 350 of them—haunt its perilous shoals.

The island once known as the "Graveyard of the Atlantic" for the many shipwrecks along its shores was also home to a penal colony in the 16th century. Sable Island is one of Canada's newest national parks, and due to its isolated nature, as is the case with the country's remote northern parks, is not highly visited.

Despite that, Sable Island continues to fire a sense of adventure and capture hearts across the country and the world.

How to Get There

Set 175 km (109 mi) off the Nova Scotia mainland, Sable Island occupies a very remote position. Accessed mainly by boat, the park reserve—home to a resident population of just a half dozen people, mostly Parks Canada and Environment Canada staff—welcomed only 120 visitors in 2015. Small charter aircraft also service the island. Because there is no landing strip, planes must land on a flat spot on the beach. Perhaps the easiest way to visit Sable is with an expedition cruise company. As of 2016, Adventure Canada and One Ocean Expeditions both offer yearly itineraries that include one-day visits to the island that are escorted by Parks Canada staff and an onboard expedition team.

When to Go

Visitors are limited to single-day experiences between June and October. The best weather can be experienced in August, when the sun (often) shines and the frequent fog of the spring and early summer months is less likely. The island shelters the world's largest breeding colony of grey seals, which pup in December and January but molt in May and June, at which time a large number haul themselves up out of the water and onto Sable's beaches. The park reserve is also home to a small resident colony of harbour seals, which pup from the middle of May to the middle of June.

Sable is part of a key migratory flyway. More than 350 bird species have been recorded here, including vagrants unknown on the Nova Scotia mainland. Sixteen species breed during the spring and summer. The endangered Ipswich sparrow is the most famous. This subspecies of the Savannah sparrow breeds only here. Fish and eels populate the freshwater ponds, and six species of invertebrates are endemic to the island.

How to Visit

Arrivals on Sable are closely controlled and monitored, and the park reserve operates a registration system to ensure the protection of the island's resources and the safety of visitors. All guests must register prior to arrival. Parks Canada employees lead mandatory orientation and safety briefings for all visitors, at Main Station.

Camping isn't permitted, and overnight stays are rare, although organized groups of visiting researchers are occasionally housed at Main Station. During a typical one-day visit from an expedition cruise, organized walking tours take visitors to the top of Bald Dune and past some of the island's largest freshwater ponds, places where wild horses gather.

There are no formal walking trails on the island. Visitors are encouraged to stay on the horse paths when available and are welcome to walk Sable's impressive natural features. Two long, parallel beaches flank the island, and the tips—known as the Eastern and Western Spits—are long and flat and comprised entirely of sand. The centre of the island is dominated by rolling dunes, some of Canada's highest.

HOME TO HORSES

Sable Island counts more than 550 wild, feral horses, ancestors of those animals likely left on the island by Loyalist merchants who would have either purchased or acquired livestock after the Great Expulsion, when, in 1749, the Acadians were expelled by the British.

While the island is a sandbar, it boasts unique conditions that have sustained the life of these strangely majestic horses. The freshwater ponds are fed by rainwater alone, and an abundance of green grass grows on the dunes. In the 1960s, the resident horses came very close to removal, but were saved by an unlikely source: a national letter-writing campaign undertaken by Canada's schoolchildren that implored Prime Minister John Diefenbaker to reconsider. He did, protecting the animals under the Canada Shipping Act, and the horses have continued to flourish here. And they're not alone.

Rabbits, cattle, and goats also were released on the island, with little success, and Sable once hosted a population of walruses, which hunters drove to extinction. Sable's shifting sands occasionally still reveal one of their tusks, discarded long ago. The island also is home to some 50,000 seals.

SHIFTING SANDS

The actual length of the park— a crescent-shaped island usually around 45 km (28 mi) long, and never wider than 1.5 km (0.9 mi)—is always in flux. In 2015, for example, the island was 7 km (4 mi) shorter than it was in 2014, a result of the blowing winds and rolling waters that surround it. The geographic features are constantly changing, too— one of the island's highest points, **Bald Dune,** has been blown clear across the island over the course of 40 years.

GRAVEYARD OF THE ATLANTIC

Sable figured prominently in sailors' lore and has long enjoyed an almost supernatural mystique. Set along one of the primary shipping lanes to the New World, the island is often por-

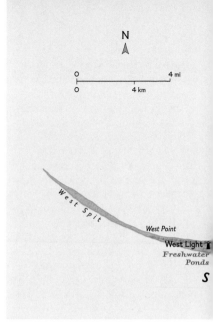

trayed in old maps as a much larger island, in some cases thousands of miles long, stretching far down the eastern side of North America. Seamen were aware—and wary—of the island. Indeed, Sable seems to have an almost preternatural ability to host the sinking of ships. There have been more than 350 shipwrecks since 1583, when the H.M.S. *Delight* gained the dubious distinction of being the first recorded shipwreck here. Sailing in support of the H.M.S. *Squirrel,* which was commanded by Sir Humphrey Gilbert, a British explorer, the *Delight* ran aground and sank, taking all of its valuable supplies— and most of its crew—with it.

Massive sandbars radiate from the island, which sits at the meeting point of the cold waters of the Labrador Current and the warm flow of the Gulf Stream. This position ensures an almost impenetrable curtain of fog that can descend at a moment's notice. There's also a particularly nasty long-shore current.

The waters were so dangerous that in 1801 Nova Scotia established

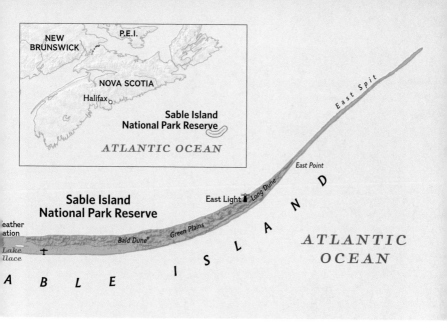

NEW BRUNSWICK

P.E.I.

NOVA SCOTIA

Halifax

Sable Island
National Park Reserve

ATLANTIC OCEAN

East Spit

East Point

Sable Island
National Park Reserve

East Light Long Dune

eather
ation

Lake
llace

Bald Dune

Green Plains

ATLANTIC
OCEAN

A   B   L   E   I   S   L   A   N   D

a series of lifesaving stations on the island—Canada's first such structures. At first, two lighthouses would attempt to signal peril to approaching ships. By 1895, a large main station along with an additional four satellite stations had been established. They were staffed by up to six men who lived on site with their families. Watchtowers and patrols on horseback added to the effort, but ships often foundered far from shore, meaning lifesavers were compelled to row hours out from Sable to rescue sailors in distress. In one famous incident, lifesavers rescued 170 people from the *Arcadia*, which struck a sandbar amid gale-force winds and fog. Very little of the original stations remain. The last staffed

Footprints along Sable Island's East Spit beach

Aerial view of Sable Island

lighthouse was automated in 1987. More recently, the island has served as a refueling station for Canadian Coast Guard helicopters, which continue the legacy of saving sailors in danger.

The island has served many purposes over the years, including a brief but terrible stint as a French penal colony. At the end of the 16th century, a marquis, with permission from King Henry IV, dropped some 70 imprisoned men—mostly beggars and tramps—on the island. Humble homes and a storehouse were built as part of their settlement.

The island was regularly resupplied, and islanders attempted to grow meagre gardens and catch fish. But then the marquis responsible for the colony fell on hard times, and those left on Sable were left to fend for themselves for an entire year. Starvation, cannibalism, and murder prevailed, and those dozen or inhabitants who managed to survive dug dens in the sand, built

fortifications out of shipwrecks, and wore uncured sealskins as clothing. When help finally came from France, legend has it that the prison's priest refused to leave, and that his ghost haunts this place still. Those who remained were transported back to France, and the king—impressed with their wild state and unmoved by their almost certain murderous guilt and hideous means of survival—rewarded them with silver coins.

On a more peaceful note, Sable is a place for plants. While the island's wild horses get much of the press, Sable's vegetation is also noteworthy. More than 190 plant species have been identified here, and 20 of those have a restricted distribution elsewhere. About one-third of the island is green, with most of it dominated by heathlike plants typical of dune environments. The island's extremities, however, host sand-tolerant plants, including sandwort and marram grass.

SABLE ISLAND NATIONAL PARK RESERVE
(Réserve de parc national de l'Île-de-Sable)

INFORMATION & ACTIVITIES

HEADQUARTERS
Parks Canada c/o Halifax Citadel National Historic Site, P.O. Box 9080, Station A, Halifax, NS B3K 5M7. (902) 426-1993 sable@pc.gc.ca; www.parks canada.gc.ca/sable.

SEASONS & ACCESSIBILITY
June to the end of October comprise the visitation season, with August–October being the optimum months. Sable Island is extremely isolated, and access to it is determined by constraints of weather and geography. Visitors either arrive by air charter or come ashore from private vessels, including small expedition cruise ships, that anchor offshore.

Visits to Sable Island National Park Reserve are carefully managed by Parks Canada through a registration system and provision of detailed trip planning and orientation information to ensure visitor safety and protection of the island's resources.

VISITOR & INFORMATION CENTRES
No visitor facilities.

ENTRANCE FEE
Fees based on services provided. See website for details.

PETS
Not permitted.

THINGS TO DO
Explore rolling windswept dunes and walk along beaches on both the north and south sides of the island. See wild horses, seals, birds, freshwater ponds, and remnants of the island's history. Experience the isolated nature of being on a remote island in the midst of the North Atlantic.

SPECIAL ADVISORIES
- Sturdy shoes for heavy walking on sand and layers of clothing, including a rain jacket, are essential.
- Be aware that walking on sand for prolonged periods can be more difficult than walking equivalent distances on hard surfaces or solid terrain.
- Vehicle use on Sable Island is restricted to activities in support of park administration and to facilitate research.
- Visitors are required to bring in all of the food and supplies that are required for their visit, including extra supplies to account for unexpected travel delays, and to pack out everything including garbage.
- Island wildlife, including horses and seals, are wild animals and must not be harassed, interfered with, or fed.
- In a national park, it is illegal to collect rocks, shells, animal specimens, plants, or cultural artifacts.

HOTELS, MOTELS, & INNS
As this book went to press, visits are limited to day trips. Visitors fly to and from Sable Island on the same day or spend the night in a vessel anchored offshore.

Twilight, Kejimkujik Seaside

▶KEJIMKUJIK

NOVA SCOTIA
ESTABLISHED 1967
404 sq km/100,000 acres

Referred to by staff and locals as "Keji," Kejimkujik National Park and National Historic Site teems with wildlife and boasts the greatest diversity of reptiles and amphibians in Atlantic Canada. The park is also home to ancient petroglyphs. Here, the Mi'kmaq cultural land-scape dates back centuries. Spanning waterways and forests, the park includes Kejimkujik Seaside, a 22-sq-km (8 sq mi) coastal area replete with a lagoon system and an abundance of beaches, bogs, wildflowers, and coastal wildlife.

In 1995, the inland portion of Kejimkujik was designated a national historic site because of its significant Mi'kmaq heritage. It is the only national park in Canada that has this dual designation. In 2001, UNESCO designated the five counties of southwest Nova Scotia as a biosphere reserve. Kejimkujik inland—which is situated next to the Tobeatic Reserve and the historic Shelburne River, a Canadian Heritage River—is part of this important biosphere.

The park has numerous lakes, many of them dotted with islands, and several with still waters. Features in the park also include fascinating barrens, old-growth forests, and elongated hills known as drumlins.

Many of the physical features of the park were sculpted during the last ice age.

Keji also has a large concentration of rare plant, insect, and animal species, many of them at risk of extinction. Great care and attention is paid to the preservation and propagation of these species, and the park has a number of educational programs in which visitors can take part.

How to Get There

Kejimkujik's inland portion is accessible from both major highways on either side of the province. From Hwy. 101 take exit 22 close to Annapolis Royal and head inland on Hwy. 8. Allow approximately 30 minutes from the exit. From Hwy. 103, take exit 13 at Bridgewater and follow the signs to Kejimkujik. Again, allow approximately 30 minutes from the exit.

To visit Kejimkujik Seaside, drive toward Liverpool. Continue west on Hwy. 103. Approximately 7 km (4 mi) past exit 22, turn left onto St. Catherine River Road; it's 6 km (3.5 mi) to the park entrance.

When to Go

Keji is open year-round. Spring and fall temperatures range from 10° to 15°C (50°–59°F), and summer temperatures reach upward of 24°C (75°F); in winter they can drop to -2– -10°C (14°–28°F). Winter camping is not permitted.

How to Visit

With more than 80 percent of the park accessible only by foot or canoe, Kejimkujik National Park offers backcountry experiences to suit every taste, from relaxing on a secluded island to traversing the park's ancient canoe routes. In fact, one of the best

ways to experience the park is by canoe—the vehicle of choice here for thousands of years.

It's easy to see why Albert Bigelow Payne was so eager to recount his journey here by penning *The Tent Dwellers* more than a hundred years ago. The famous author took a historic fishing trip with his friend Eddie Breck and two guides, Charles "the strong" Charleston and Del "the stout" Thomas. The book is hilarious, poignant, insightful—and for sale in the visitor centre.

Boats and bicycles can be rented by the hour or for up to a full week; fishing permits can also be purchased. Consider renting a canoe or kayak at Jake's Landing and paddling around Lake Kejimkujik, or make the drive to Merrymakedge for a picnic and swim.

Camping is hugely popular in Kejimkujik, with 254 unserviced and 118 serviced sites, which include electrified sites along with places for group tenting and backcountry wilderness camping along hiking trails and canoe routes. There also are 15 oTENTiks (a cross between a tent and a cabin), a yurt, and three rustic cabins,

Each camping site is equipped with two tent pads, a fire box, a picnic table, a privy, firewood, and a pulley device to hoist and safely store your food supply.

PETROGLYPH TOUR

a full day

For a one-day visit, sign up at the visitor centre for the **Petroglyph Tour** with a Keji interpreter. There are more than 500 petroglyphs in the park—the largest collection in North America. These images give a glimpse into the lives of the

Mi'kmaq and how they changed when the Europeans arrived. You'll hear stories of how these images came to be and why they are protected.

HIKES

A hiker's haven, Keji features 15 trails, ranging from the 0.2-km (0.1 mi) **Mersey Meadow** boardwalk loop to the challenging 19.5-km (12 mi) **Fire Tower Road** hike. **Mill Falls** (2 km/1 mi return) is an easy hike with a surprise ending, while the **Hemlocks and Hardwoods** 5-km (3 mi) loop will take your breath away when you see 400-year-old hemlocks. Six trails are also suitable for biking.

BIRD-WATCHING

Bird-watchers will have plenty to do at both the inland and seaside locations of the park. You can take part in a variety of monitoring programs, like the **Piping Plover Guardian Program,** or become a **LoonWatcher,** tracking pairs of loons in June or their chicks in August on one of 16 lakes in the park.

Keji lies within the Acadian forest zone, a transition between southern deciduous trees (hardwoods) and northern evergreen trees (softwoods). Pockets of original, ancient forests still stand tall in the park. Most impressive are the towering groves of old-growth eastern hemlocks: nature's cathedrals.

If you look up, you may see the northern goshawk, a swift and powerful hunting hawk that likes to nest in the hemlock stands.

KEJI AT NIGHT

Kejimkujik has been designated a Dark Sky Preserve by the Royal Astronomical Society of Canada

(see pp. 72–73). This means that Keji is an area in which active measures are taken to educate and promote the reduction of light pollution so that night skies reveal their glories.

Join park staff for a nighttime astronomy program. Bring a blanket and get ready to experience something very memorable, as Keji is one of the best places for night sky observation on the eastern seaboard. Kejimkujik dark sky programming

is unique as staff combine scientific data with Mi'kmaq legends in a spellbinding presentation.

OTHER ACTIVITIES

When visiting the park with children, check in with the visitor centre and pick up the Parks Canada Xplorer booklet. It offers great ways for kids ages 6–11 and their parents to discover and explore what makes Keji so special and unique.

Complete the activities and receive a certificate and special collectible souvenir.

The park also offers plenty of volunteer opportunities. You can join a core of scientists and trained volunteers and take part in a variety of projects ranging from searching for eastern ribbon snakes and examining their movement patterns to working on loon surveys or protecting Blanding's turtle eggs and tracking their hatchlings.

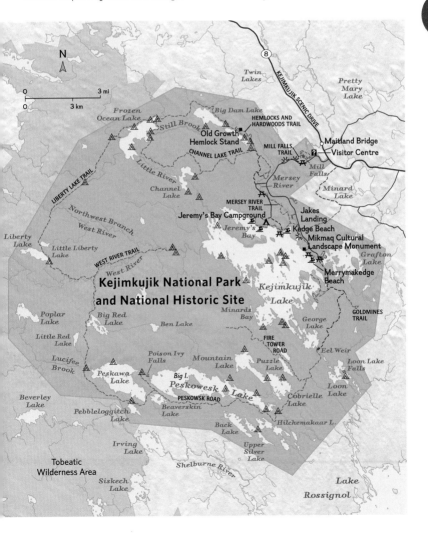

KEJIMKUJIK NATIONAL PARK
(Parc national Kejimkujik)

INFORMATION & ACTIVITIES

VISITOR CENTRE
Kejimkujik and National Historic Site Visitor Centre 3005 Main Parkway, Rte. 8, Maitland Bridge, NS B0T 1B0. Phone (902) 682-2772. Open mid-May to Thanksgiving.

SEASONS & ACCESSIBILITY
Visitor services available mid-May to Thanksgiving.

HEADQUARTERS
Kejimkujik National Park and National Historic Site Visitor Centre. Phone (902) 682-2772. www.parkscanada.gc.ca/kejimkujik.

FRIENDS OF KEJIMKUJIK
Friends of Keji Cooperating Association 50 Pinetree Crescent, Hammonds Plains, NS B3Z 1K4. info@friendsofkeji.ns.ca; www.friendsofkeji.ns.ca.

ENTRANCE FEES
$6 per person, $15 per group per day; $30 per person, $75 per group per season.

PETS
Owners must leash pets, pick up waste.

ACCESSIBLE SERVICES
The following are wheelchair accessible: visitor centre; boardwalk and viewing platform at **Mersey Meadow Trail;** picnic shelter, deck, and washrooms on **Mill Falls Trail;** six sites and one washroom at **Jeremy's Bay Campground;** washrooms and picnic sites at **Jake's Landing;** playground and picnic area at **Merrymakedge Beach.**

THINGS TO DO
Guided canoe outings, hiking, cycling, swimming, and fishing (April–Aug.; permit $10 per day, $34 per year). Rent canoes and bicycles at Jake's Landing.

SPECIAL ADVISORIES
- Bring portable camp stoves for backcountry camping. Open fires may be banned in dry conditions.
- Do not leave food unattended. Pack coolers in vehicles.
- Check with staff before going into backcountry to learn about avoiding wildlife.

OVERNIGHT BACKPACKING
Backcountry camping registration mandatory. 47 backcountry campsites, each with two tent pads, a firebox, a picnic table, a pit privy, and firewood. Backcountry guide and map available for purchase at the visitor centre. For reservations, visit www.reservation.parkscanada.gc.ca, call (877) 737-3783, or stop by visitor centre.

CAMPGROUNDS
Campgrounds open mid-May to mid-October; 60 sites open for winter camping. **Jeremy's Bay,** 368 sites (154 with electricity), near Kejimkujik Lake. Hot showers, washrooms, outdoor sinks, playgrounds, picnic tables, fireplaces, tent pads, dumping station, and outdoor theatre. 15 oTENTiks (a cross between a tent and a cabin) and 3 rustic cabins near Kejimkujk Lake. For reservations call (877) 737-3783 or visit www.reservation.parkscanada.gc.ca. Serviced sites with electricity $26 per night; unserviced sites with washroom facilities (toilets and showers) $25 per night. Primitive sites $26. Group camping at **Jim Charles Point** for families or organized groups, $5 per person.

HOTELS, MOTELS, & INNS
(unless otherwise noted, rates are for a 2-person double, high season, in Canadian dollars)

<u>Outside the park:</u>
Milford House 5296 Hwy. 8, South Milford, RR#4 Annapolis Royal, NS B0S 1A0. (877) 532-5751. www.milfordhouse.ca. $155–$200.
White Point Beach Resort Queens County, NS B0T 1G0. (902) 354-2711. www.whitepoint.com. $145–$240.
The Whitman Inn 12389 Hwy. 8, Kempt, NS B0T 1B0. (902) 682-2226. www.whitmaninn.com. $69–$125.
Caledonia Country Hostel Caledonia, NS. (902) 682-3266. www.caledoniacountryhostel.com. $60.

EXCURSIONS

FORT ANNE NATIONAL HISTORIC SITE
ANNAPOLIS ROYAL, NS

Canada's oldest national historic site and most attacked fort is full of wonder and intrigue. Its story reaches back more than 3,000 years to the Mi'kmaq. In the 1600s and 1700s, the French and the British set up forts and vied for supremacy. Fort Anne houses an impressive 2.4-by-5.5-m (8 by 18 ft) heritage tapestry, crafted by more than a hundred volunteers using some three million stitches. (902) 532-2397 or (902) 532-2321. 50 km (30 mi) north of park via Hwy. 8.

KEJIMKUJIK NATIONAL HISTORIC SITE
KEJIMKUJIK, NS

The entire landscape of Kejimkujik is designated as a national historic site and commemorates Mi'kmaq culture dating back thousands of years. Visitors can join a tour led by a Mi'kmaq interpreter and visit ancient rock carvings known as petroglyphs. The park has a rich history of aboriginal campgrounds and traditional canoe routes. Discover more in the park's visitor centre. (902) 682-2772.

MELANSON SETTLEMENT NATIONAL HISTORIC SITE
LOWER GRANVILLE, NS

Starting in the 1660s and for almost a century, the Melanson Settlement was home to Charles Melanson, Marie Dugas, and their descendants. This site was discovered during a survey for Acadian sites in 1984. Archaeologists eventually located the ruins of several cellars, and the site is now well documented. A short interpretive trail tells the story of this historic Acadian homestead. (902) 532-2321. 75 km (47.5 mi) north of park via Hwy. 8.

Lighthouse at Dalvay in Cavendish, on the north side of Prince Edward Island

▶ PRINCE EDWARD ISLAND

PRINCE EDWARD ISLAND
ESTABLISHED 1937
27 sq km/6,672 acres

Prince Edward Island National Park spans a spectacular stretch of land encompassing sand dunes, salt marshes, remnants of an Acadian forest, coastal headlands, beaches, and sandstone cliffs. This is the land that inspired Lucy Maud Montgomery's *Anne of Green Gables* and prompted an oil tycoon to build an elegant Victorian home here. Both Green Gables and Dalvay-by-the Sea are national treasures and showcased within the park.

Approximately 285 million years ago, a mountain chain existed in this region. Over time, its rivers deposited gravel, silt, and sand into a low-lying basin forming sandstone bedrock. As the glaciers retreated, Prince Edward Island gradually took shape.

Situated on the central north shore of Prince Edward Island, the park faces the Gulf of St. Lawrence, where sunsets are storybook-perfect. Although one of the smallest parks in Canada, it's a popular destination, with famous beaches and outstanding coastal landscapes. The other attraction is the lure of Lucy Maud Montgomery through her beloved 1908 novel, *Anne of Green Gables*.

The park's ecosystems support a variety of animal species and 400 different species of plants. Although there are no deer or moose on the island, coyotes, red foxes, raccoons, beavers, mink, and weasels are common. With more than 300 species of birds, including the endangered piping plover, the park plays a significant role in shorebird migration in spring and fall.

In 1998, the park expanded to include 4 sq km (990 acres) on the Greenwich Peninsula where rare, U-shaped dunes known as parabolic dunes are located. This is also the region where archaeological digs revealed that Paleo-Indians lived here 10,000 years ago. Evidence indicates that Mi'kmaq, French, Acadian, Scottish, Irish, and English were also early settlers here.

The park is bordered by a number of traditional farming and fishing communities, which adds to the cultural fabric of the island and enhances the visitor's experience.

How to Get There

A number of airlines fly into Charlottetown, the island's capital. Direct service is available from Halifax, Montreal, Toronto, and Ottawa with seasonal direct service from Boston, Detroit, and New York. Connecting service is available every day from Halifax International Airport.

If you are driving, there are two ways to approach the island. One is to take the 12.9-km-long (8 mi) bridge—the longest bridge over ice-covered water in the world—from Cape Jourimain in New Brunswick to Borden-Carleton on Prince Edward Island. The other is to board Northumberland Ferries *(www .peiferry.com)* for a 75-minute sail from Caribou, Nova Scotia, over to Wood Islands.

When to Go

Beach lovers and families will want to visit during July and August, when daytime temperatures range from 18° to 24°C (64°–75°F) and nights are warm. Park activities run full tilt during the operational season (late June–Sept.).

If you prefer solitude, spring and fall are the best seasons for hiking, kayaking, cycling, and bird-watching. Average daytime temperatures in both spring and fall range from 9° to 18°C (48°–64°F) during the day and 5° to 10°C (41°–50°F) at night. The fall tends to be balmy and quite warm until mid-October.

Birders have lots to observe in the park year-round; highlights include migration and nesting seasons. Seasonal dates determined by the migratory habits of most birds are: mid-March to late May (northerly migration), early June to mid-August (nesting season), and mid-August to mid-December (southerly migration).

If you are interested in adding culinary travel to your park experience, the island hops with a special food festival called Fall Flavours during the month of September.

How to Visit

There are three distinct segments of the park: **Cavendish, Brackley-Dalvay,** and **Greenwich,** each with its own unique characteristics. You'll need a vehicle to get from one to another. Once you have arrived, however, the best way to enjoy the park is by foot or bike.

Visitors to the Cavendish and Brackley-Dalvay sectors of the park will find supervised beaches, campgrounds, and a number of trails of easy to moderate difficulty adapted to both hiking and cycling.

Both Cavendish and Stanhope have full-service campgrounds; organized groups can contact the park to arrange for group camping at a unique campsite and day-use area. There is no camping offered at Greenwich, but private accommodations are located close by and it's only a 30- to 40-minute drive to Stanhope or Brackley. Natural and cultural history really come alive at evening campfire activities held at **Cavendish** and **Stanhope Campgrounds,** where interpreters present the park's heritage through storytelling and skits with the aid of costumes and music.

Along with your camp gear, consider bringing a kite. With all the wide-open spaces and gentle breezes, kite flying is a snap. Field glasses are also a good thing to have along as there's always something that you'll want to see up close and personal.

In-park interpretive activities such as guided walks, geocaching programs, and evening campfire presentations are listed in the visitor guide and posted throughout the park during the summer peak season. All activities are pre-

sented in both French and English and are delivered by experienced and engaging interpreters. Programs and activities change on a daily basis.

The key is to talk with park personnel. Find one of the many uniformed staff persons and ask for suggestions of things to do and places to go. They always have great ideas. Don't be surprised if one of the staff invites you to come along and see a hidden treasure or shares with you a favourite place. Known to be friendly, islanders are also a good source of information.

There is a wealth of scenic trails in the park, each with its own unique features. Meander along field edges and hedgerows, across floating boardwalks, or through mixed woodlands.

Discover spectacular vistas and a variety of species of birds and other wildlife. The trails vary in length as well as in sights and sounds. For details on hiking trails visit *www .pc.gc.ca/eng/pn-np/pe/pei-ipe/activ /activ-menu/.* Guided walks along trails in Cavendish and Greenwich are

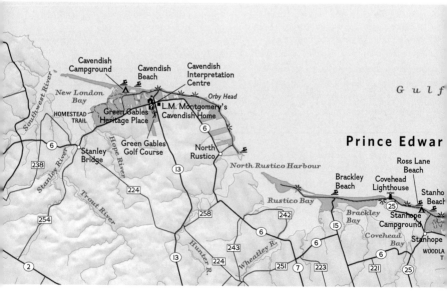

always a big hit. The focus is usually on wildlife, ecology, and other natural features of protected coastal areas, as well as the rich cultural history of Prince Edward Island's north shore.

Interpretive signage throughout the park enhances self-guided hikes and provides insights into the natural and cultural significance of each area.

CAVENDISH
a full day

If you are approaching from Confederation Bridge, head to Cavendish to experience **Green Gables Heritage Place** (separate fee applies). Kids enjoy the Xplorers Program and many onsite activities, including old-fashioned games and races. You'll also want to visit the home of Lucy Maud Montgomery (1874–1942). The bucolic setting has not changed since the author lived here.

Top up your day with a stroll or swim at the beach, famous worldwide for its sweeping shores and endless vistas. Golfers can enjoy a round at **Green Gables Golf Course,** designed in 1939 by Stanley Thompson, one of the world's most celebrated golf course architects. Or, if you like to run, walk, hike, or bike, select one of six unique trails to explore, such as the 8.8-km (5.5 mi) **Homestead Trail** and the wooded trail network at **Cavendish Grove.**

BRACKLEY TO DALVAY
a full day

Bird-watchers will want to start the day at **Brackley,** where **Covehead Wharf** offers the best place for shorebird-watching, especially at low tide, when exposed mudflats become popular feeding and resting grounds for dozens of species.

This is also one of the nesting grounds of the endangered pip-ing plover, which is monitored and protected by Parks Canada resource

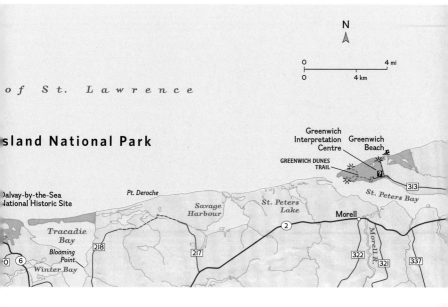

Greenwich Dunes Trail

conservation staff in closed-off sections. These sections offer excellent vantage points to observe the bird without posing a threat; if they are not present, many other species will equally delight. Checklists are available at visitor centres, campgrounds, and entrance kiosks.

Covehead Lighthouse and the surrounding shoreline make for an interesting stop between Stanhope and Dalvay-by-the-Sea. Look for the plaque on the lighthouse commemorating the infamous Yankee Gale storm of 1851, which wrecked close to one hundred ships and claimed the lives of more than 150 sailors.

On the **Bubbling Springs** and **Farmlands Trails,** look for the unmarked gravestones that mark the resting place of the sailors who perished in that storm.

In the afternoon, picnic or swim at **Ross Lane Beach.** Or drive over to **Dalvay-by-the-Sea** for high tea. Enjoy the famous sticky date pudding at this national historic site while admiring the building's exquisite late Victorian–style architecture.

Hikers will find eight trails in this part of the park, including **Gulf Shore Way,** which spans 10 km (6 mi) from Brackley to Dalvay-by-the-Sea and is also suitable for in-line skating. Walking or biking even part of this trail positions you for excellent views of the park's coastal ecosystems, and there are several stopping points and observation posts along the way. Bike rentals are available at Dalvay-by-the-Sea.

The **Reeds & Rushes Trail** is also hugely popular. Hike the trail early in the morning or around dusk and you may see some beavers. Just about any time of day you'll see hundreds of dragonflies, including sedge sprites, wandering gliders, and ruby meadowhawks.

GREENWICH
a full day

If you enter the island from Nova Scotia and have only one day to spend in the park, head for Greenwich. Although Greenwich is part of the park system, it is one of the island's best-kept secrets, and it can be far less crowded than Cavendish or Brackley-Dalvay. Nevertheless, it has a full range of services, including beach supervision, washrooms, change rooms, and showers as well as an indoor resting and picnic area.

Increasingly, outdoor-activity lovers are including the Greenwich portion of the park into their itinerary. Start your visit at the **Greenwich Interpretation Centre,** where you'll find a variety of interactive exhibits geared toward all ages—including a walk-over three-dimensional floor map and coastal environmental exhibit—that showcase the natural features and ecology of the park. Moreover, these exhibits highlight the rich cultural history of the Greenwich area, which has been inhabited by different cultural groups over the past 10,000 years.

Along with the exhibits there's an informative 12-minute multimedia presentation that will catapult you back in time. Kids can also sign up for the Parks Canada Xplorer Program.

Your visit to Greenwich won't be complete until you go for a hike on the **Greenwich Dunes Trail.** The longest and most popular of the three trails in this part of the park, the Greenwich Dunes Trail is a 4.5-km (3 mi) return trail of

moderate difficulty that features an interesting floating boardwalk. Along the trail you'll discover different ecosystems including field, forest, wetlands, and coastal systems while enjoying breathtaking views of Greenwich's parabolic dune system and associated counter ridges, or Gegenwälle—all rare dune formations.

The Greenwich Dunes Trail also leads to one of Prince Edward Island's most spectacular beaches. While unsupervised and not recommended for swimming, it boasts breathtaking views of the parabolic dune system. Upon your return, you will still have time for a stroll or swim on the supervised main beach at **Greenwich.**

The 1.25-km (0.8 mi) **Havre St. Pierre Trail** leads you to interpretive signage on an observation deck that explains the history of St. Peter's Bay and the rope-cultured mussel harvest that is part of the economic fabric of the island. The trail is wheelchair accessible.

The third trail, **Tlaqatik,** covers an easy 4.5 km (2.8 mi) through the

A summer sunset on the island's beach

Great blue herons, Tracadie Bay

sand dunes, with terrific views of the bay.

KAYAKING

One of the more interesting ways to take in the natural beauty of Prince Edward Island National Park is to kayak segments of the coastline. Consider paddling between **Tracadie Bay** and **Blooming Point. Covehead Bay** and **Brackley Bay** are also great spots, as is **New London Harbour.** Although not as well known, **St. Peter's Bay** and the rivers that flow into the bay, such as the **Morell, St. Mary's,** and **St. Peter's,** offer many kayaking pleasures.

Park staff can advise you about where to launch your boat and can also make suggestions on how to navigate the waters safely. Although you can't rent a kayak in the park, there are reputable outfitters in the nearby communities who have excellent gear for rent; some even offer day trips.

LONGER STAYS

3 days

For an extended visit, consider any combination of the above scenarios. For example, you may want to spend one full day in the Cavendish area, checking out Green Gables Heritage Place, relaxing on the beach, and hiking or cycling along the Homestead or Gulf Shore Way. Finish the day by taking part in an interpretive walk or enjoying an evening campfire.

A second day would give you a chance to explore the Brackley-Dalvay area and uncover its natural and cultural history, perhaps by taking in a popular bird-watching activity at Covehead Wharf or a guided pond walk in nearby Dalvay. Check the interpretive activity schedule, or visit these areas on your own if you've brought along binoculars and an appropriate bird or field guide.

Another full day can easily be spent exploring Greenwich, especially if the weather is fine.

VISITING IN WINTER

During the winter season, ice along the north shore gives the impression that the beach extends forever into the Gulf of St. Lawrence. Snowshoeing to the **Greenwich Dunes** is a breathtaking hike.

PRINCE EDWARD ISLAND NATIONAL PARK
(Parc national de l'Île-du-Prince-Édouard)

INFORMATION & ACTIVITIES

VISITOR & INFORMATION CENTRES
Cavendish Destination Centre Open May to September. **Greenwich Interpretation Centre** Open June to September.

SEASONS & ACCESSIBILITY
Park open year-round. Full services available in July and August.

HEADQUARTERS
2 Palmers Lane, Charlottetown, PE C1A 5V8. Phone (902) 672-6350. www.parks canada.gc.ca/pei.

ENTRANCE FEES
$8 per person, $20 per group per day; $39 per person, $98 per group per season.

PETS
Pets must be leashed and attended at all times. Dogs are not permitted on the beaches from April to mid-October.

ACCESSIBLE SERVICES
Brackley Beach and Stanhope Main Beach are wheelchair accessible, and a beach wheelchair is available free of charge.

THINGS TO DO
Interpretive activities are available throughout the park and **Green Gables Heritage Place** in the summer. Seven beaches for swimming; surfguards are on duty from late June to late August. Canoeing and kayaking are available on the ponds and in the Gulf of St. Lawrence; motorized watercraft are not permitted.

The private 18-hole Andersons Creek Golf Course is located within the park boundaries. Call (902) 886-2222 or visit www.andersonscreek.com.

SPECIAL ADVISORIES
- When swimming, watch for heavy surf, deep channels, currents, rocks, shallow sandbars, and rip currents.
- Do not get too close to the edges of the cliffs, as the rocks are eroding quickly.
- Arctic red jellyfish in the Gulf of St. Lawrence may sting. If you are stung, rub wet sand over the irritated area.
- Watch for poison ivy.
- Cycling helmets are mandatory.

CAMPGROUNDS
The park's two campgrounds are open June to September. Maximum number of persons per site is six. For reservations call (877) 737- 3783. **Stanhope,** 131 sites, oTENTiks (a cross between a tent and a cabin), fire pits, showers, playground, laundromat, and kitchen shelters. Interpretive programs in July and August. Organized group camping for up to 30 campers. **Cavendish,** 287 sites, oTENTiks, beach, fire pits, showers, playground, and laundromat. For both campsites: $28–$35 for serviced campsites with electricity, water, and sewer; $26–$32 for serviced campsites with electricity and water; $20–$26 for unserviced campsites with washroom building (toilets and showers); oTENTiks, $120.

HOTELS, MOTELS, & INNS
(unless otherwise noted, rates are for a 2-person double, high season, in Canadian dollars)

Outside the park:
Johnson Shore Inn 9984 Rte. 16, Hermanville, PE C0A 2B0. (902) 687-1340 or (877) 510-9669. www.jsipei .com. $180–$275.
Rodd Crowbush Golf & Beach Resort 632 Rte. 350, Morell, PE C0A 1S0. (902) 961-5600. www.roddhotels andresorts.com. $159–$319; 2-bedroom cottages $409–$619.
Shaw's Hotel 99 Apple Tree Rd., Brackley Beach, PE C1E 0Z4. (902) 672-2022. info@shawshotel.ca; http:// shawhotel.ca. $145–$320 for rooms, suites, and cottages.

For additional visitor information:
Prince Edward Island Tourism (902) 473-8570 or (800) 463-4734, www .tourismpei.com.

EXCURSIONS

ARDGOWAN NATIONAL HISTORIC SITE
CHARLOTTETOWN, PE

This site was the home of William Henry Pope, one of the Fathers of Confederation. It was also the scene of lavish entertaining during the historic Charlottetown Conference. Pope was an avid gardener and the property reflects his passion. Visitors are encouraged to stroll around the grounds and have a picnic. Parks Canada administrative offices are located inside. (902) 566-7050.

PORT-LA-JOYE–FORT AMHERST NATIONAL HISTORIC SITE
ROCKY POINT, PE

Established in 1720, the site served as a seat of government, port of entry, and colonial outpost during the Franco-British conflict period. It was also the location from which the tragic deportation of Island Acadians was administered in 1758. Enjoy the scenic views of the site from the grassy ruins of the historic earth-works and the interpretive panels along the Old Harbor Path. (902) 566-7626. 26 km (16 mi) south of Charlottetown via Capital Drive/ Hwy. 1.

DALVAY-BY-THE-SEA NATIONAL HISTORIC SITE
PRINCE EDWARD ISLAND NP, PE

Located on Rte. 6 in Prince Edward Island National Park, this Queen Anne Revival–style home was built in 1896 as a summer residence for Alexander McDonald, a Scottish-American oil tycoon. Dalvay-by-the-Sea now operates as a resort inn. Learn about the fascinating features of this home, how it was constructed, and the extravagant lifestyle of the original owner. (902) 672-2048. 35 km (21.9 mi) east of Cavendish via Hwy. 13.

L. M. MONTGOMERY'S CAVENDISH NATIONAL HISTORIC SITE
CAVENDISH, PE

This destination includes the site of Lucy Maud Montgomery's Cavendish Home and Green Gables Heritage Place, where the world-renowned author drew the inspiration to write *Anne of Green Gables*—the first of 23 novels. View a film and exhibits at the visitor centre, enjoy guided activities, and stroll to Montgomery's gravesite. Close by are the Haunted Wood Trail and Lovers Lane, featured in her books. (902) 963-7874. Palmer Land, Charlottetown.

PROVINCE HOUSE NATIONAL HISTORIC SITE
CHARLOTTETOWN, PE

Although July 1, 1867, marks the birth of Canada, delegates met for the first time in Province House in September 1864 to discuss the future of the British colonies in North America. No formal records of the Charlottetown Conference exist— only letters. While the building is closed for conservation work through 2017, visit the Confederation Centre of the Arts to see an impressive replica of the Confederation Chamber. (902) 566-7050. 2.5 km (1.5 m) south of park headquarters.

Preserving Starry Skies

Diamond dust. It looks as if the mighty hands of the gods spread a broad arc of diamond dust across the heavens. The sharp, cold glitter of thousands of distant stars encircles the sky with a ghostly embrace of ancient light. This is the Milky Way, our home galaxy. But only if you are lucky enough to be somewhere free of light pollution will you see its majestic splendour.

Comet Lulin as it passed near Saturn, in the early hours of February 24, 2009

When was the last time a view of the night sky sent shivers up your spine? Most North Americans live in urban areas where there is so much artificial light at night that the stars are only a faint memory. From cities and towns we see only a handful of the brightest stars. The rest are lost in an expanding glow of artificial light that is enveloping the world. Globally, more than 1.3 billion people—one fifth of the world's population—can no longer see the Milky Way with unaided eyes.

In the face of swelling populations and spreading urbanization, what can be done to save some of the night? The Royal Astronomical Society of Canada has initiated a Dark Sky Preserve (DSP) program (*www.rasc.ca/dark-sky-site-designations*). Working with partners like Parks Canada, the program has been remarkably successful in establishing areas where nature's night environment is protected and preserved for the benefit of all species, including humans.

"Parks Canada supports the DSP program," says Jonathan Sheppard, of Kejimkujik National Park and National Historic Site, "because it fits our mandate of protection, education, outreach, and visitor experience: protecting nocturnal ecology, implementing an energy-saving dark-sky-compliant lighting strategy for our facilities, teaching about astronomy and light control, working with astronomy partners, and creating new, engaging programs for visitors."

DSPs protect the night sky by controlling the number, placement, and design of lighting fixtures. No excess light spills over where it is not needed. Eliminating light pollution ensures visitors can appreciate the night while also providing plants and animals with the most natural habitat possible.

Every species on Earth is connected and interdependent. Can we afford to ignore half of the systems that sustain us? Life's systems have evolved, and continue to need, to experience the day-night cycle. It is necessary for our health and well-being.

Light pollution affects humans and wildlife, interfering with the growth, behaviour, and survival of nocturnal species everywhere. Many species need the day-night cycle to synchronize their biological rhythms. Some adapt behaviour in response to changing nighttime light levels from the lunar cycle. But light levels at night in urban and suburban areas are brighter than full moonlight.

Parks Canada is charged with protecting and presenting Canada's natural and cultural heritage, and fostering understanding, appreciation, and enjoyment of that heritage into the future. People come to Canada's national parks for recreation and to reconnect with nature. DSPs enable us to fully experience nature's diurnal cycle. We can see the stars and feel night's whispering magic. DSPs will become increasingly important as society becomes more urbanized with more people living in a 24-hour artificial day.

By lighting up the night we have divorced ourselves from our evolutionary history and cultural heritage. We have disconnected ourselves from Earth's life-sustaining natural systems. We are losing touch with our place in the universe.

We must dim the lights!

Parks Canada's Dark Sky Preserves are leading the way, becoming "dark beacons" of hope for the future of our natural environment. Come see the stars.

— MARY LOU WHITEHORNE, *past president and fellow,*
The Royal Astronomical Society of Canada

RASC Dark-Sky Preserves

The Royal Astronomical Society of Canada has certified 17 Dark-Sky Preserves in Canada to date. Nine* of these are part of the Parks Canada system. More are planned.
• Torrance Barrens Dark-Sky Preserve, ON—1999
• McDonald Park Dark-Sky Park, Fraser Valley, BC—2003 (from Fraser Valley Astronomer's Society)
• Cypress Hills Inter-Provincial Park Dark Sky Preserve, SK/AB—2004*
• Beaver Hills Dark-Sky Preserve, AB—2006 (from IDA)
• Point Pelee National Park, ON—2006*
• Mont-Mégantic International Dark-Sky Preserve, QC—2007
• Gordon's Park, Manitoulin Island, ON—2008
• Grasslands National Park, SK—2009*
• Kouchibouguac National Park, NB—2009*
• Bruce Peninsula National Park and Fathom Five National Marine Park, ON—2009*
• Mount Carleton Provincial Park, NB—2009
• Kejimkujik National Park, NS—2010*
• Fundy National Park, NB—2011*
• Jasper National Park Dark-Sky Preserve, AB—2011*
• Bluewater, Wiarton, ON—2012
• North Frontenac Township, ON—2013
• Wood Buffalo National Park, AB—2013*

View of Kellys Beach from the boardwalk

▶ KOUCHIBOUGUAC

NEW BRUNSWICK
ESTABLISHED 1969
239 sq km/59,000 acres

Kouchibouguac National Park covers an area of protected land on the eastern shore of New Brunswick. Representative of the maritime plain natural region and the Atlantic–Gulf of St. Lawrence marine region, it features a number of fascinating ecosystems, including the Acadian forest, bogs, salt marshes, tidal rivers, lagoons, open fields, and approximately 25 km (15 mi) of fragile white-sand dunes.

Pronounced koo-she-boo-gwack, Kouchibouguac is a Mi'kmaq word meaning "river of long tides." There are 26 known aboriginal archaeological sites in the park—a testimony to the park's rich cultural history. Acadian, Irish, and English settlers also lived and worked here, and their legacy lives on.

More than half of the park is occupied by forests, including significant stands of rare forest vegetation that are part of the Acadian forest. Peat bogs cover another 21 percent of the park. These bogs are about 5,000 years old and measure up to 6 m (20 ft) deep at their domed centres. Although salt marshes do not make up a large part of the park, 72 plant species have been identified here. In addition, several species of waterfowl breed in the park.

The Barrier Islands—a unique feature that includes a series of dune systems—span a small but significant portion of the park. Stretching 25 km (15 mi), these dune systems shelter estuaries, lagoons, and salt marshes in an intensely dynamic coastal environment.

Influenced by the presence of the Gulf of St. Lawrence, the dunes are ever changing as the result of the influence of tides, storms, and shifting sands.

The diverse wildlife and flora in the park includes salmon, eel, piping plovers, common terns, ospreys, mussels, crabs, and oysters along with widgeon grass and eelgrass. There are nine rare plants, including the rayless aster and southern twayblade. Recreational clam harvesting is encouraged and enjoyed.

How to Get There

The park is located in Kent County on New Brunswick's central eastern shore in an area known as the Acadian Coastal Drive. It is a one-hour drive north from Moncton, a four-hour drive from the Quebec border, or a four-hour drive northeast of Maine. Take Hwy. 15 to Shediac and then either Hwy. 11 heading north or the more scenic Rte. 134.

When to Go

The park is open year-round. Although the warmer months (May–Oct.) are the most popular, people are discovering the joy of winter activities. There are three trails specifically designated for winter walking, three for snowshoeing, a 22-km (14 mi) groomed trail system for cross-country skiing, and groomed trails for fat bikes.

Cozy warm-up huts with wood stoves are strategically placed along the trails, and winterized camping shelters are accessible by fat bike, ski, or snowshoe. Skis, snowshoes, fat bikes, and sleds for transporting young children or gear are available for rent.

How to Visit

Start at the visitor reception centre and plan to spend time at the interactive interpretive centre. Here you will get an overview of the natural and cultural aspects of the park, learn how it was created, and experience the four seasons through a lively audiovisual presentation. At the visitor centre you will also find detailed information about park activities.

If you have two or more days to spend, Kouchibouguac has a variety of camping options, with 311 campsites (both serviced and unserviced) as well as semi-primitive campsites for those who want to rough it—but not too much. Primitive campsites, accessible only by foot, bike, kayak, or canoe, are available for those who *really* want to rough it.

The park offers Step-on-Guide Services for motorcoach tours, organized groups, or families. Simply request that a park interpreter accompany you on a specific trail or for a particular activity and this will be arranged

Bicycling along a summer path

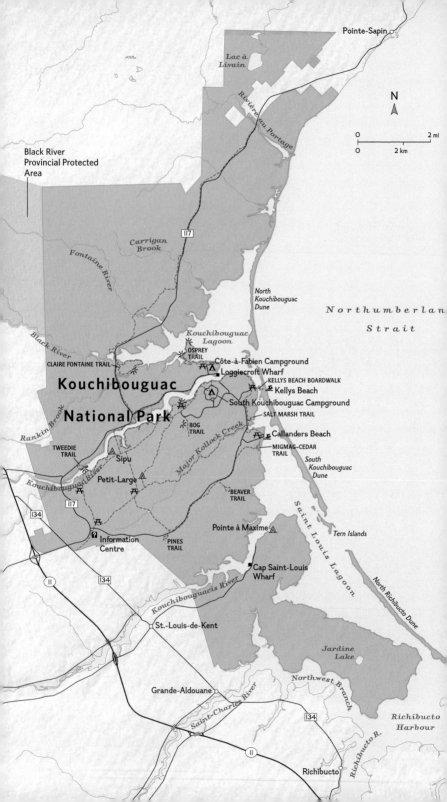

Pointe-Sapin

Lac à
Livain

Rivière au Portage

N

0   2 mi
0   2 km

Black River
Provincial Protected
Area

117

Carrigan
Brook

Fontaine River

North
Kouchibouguac
Dune

Northumberlan
Strait

Black River

Kouchibouguac
Lagoon

OSPREY
TRAIL

CLAIRE FONTAINE TRAIL

Côte-à-Fabien Campground
Loggiecroft Wharf

KELLYS BEACH BOARDWALK

Kellys Beach

Kouchibouguac

South Kouchibouguac Campground

SALT MARSH TRAIL

National Park

BOG
TRAIL

Major Kollock Creek

Callanders Beach

MIGMAG–CEDAR
TRAIL

Rankin Brook

TWEEDIE
TRAIL

South
Kouchibouguac
Dune

Sipu

Kouchibouguac River

Petit-Large

117

134

BEAVER
TRAIL

Saint Louis Lagoon

Tern Islands

Information
Centre

PINES
TRAIL

Pointe à Maxime

Cap Saint-Louis
Wharf

134

11

Kouchibouguacis River

North Richibucto Dune

St.-Louis-de-Kent

Jardine
Lake

Grande-Aldouane

Saint-Charles River

Northwest Branch

Richibucto
Harbour

134

11

Richibucto

Richibucto R.

(service available in spring, summer, and fall seasons only; advance notice is required).

HIKING & KAYAKING

With 60 km (37 mi) of bikeways, Kouchibouguac is recognized as one of the best biking destinations in Atlantic Canada. The trails are wide, relatively flat, and topped with fine gravel. If you plan to spend one day, rent a bike and choose one of the cycling loops. They range from 14 to 27 km (9–17 mi) and boast spectacular scenery. In winter there are groomed trails for fat bikes.

Rent a canoe or kayak and explore the lagoons or paddle along the **Kouchibouguac River** and see the **Great Leaning Red Pine Tree** growing out of a sandstone outcropping. The tree stretches horizontally over the river, and you can actually paddle underneath it. With eight Class I (flat-water) rivers flowing into the park, canoeing and kayaking are ideal and safe activities.

VOYAGEUR CANOE MARINE ADVENTURE
3 hours

For a unique adventure, book a three-hour excursion with a park interpreter and join a few others in the "grand canoe" for a trek to the **Barrier Islands,** where you'll see hundreds of grey seals. There are approximately 700 in the colony. Along the way you'll also likely see ospreys, bald eagles, and other bird species, including the second largest tern colony in North America. Paddling experience is not necessary; age limit is six years and up. Reservations are highly recommended as the canoe can only accommodate eight people at a time.

(506) 876-2443. Cost around $40 per person. 186 Rte 117, Kouchibouguac, NB E4X 2P1.

VISITING WITH KIDS

If you are visiting the park with children, consider making your way to **Kellys Beach,** where you can enjoy a swim, take part in an activity-filled festival (during camping season) or join a park interpreter for a hands-on activity to see what's lurking in a saltwater lagoon. Through the Lagoon Life Program, children learn all about crabs, sticklebacks, and moonsnails.

Another option is to buy a picnic lunch at Kellys Beach Canteen and then head to **Callanders Beach** (where there's a day-use area), a great place for young children as the water is warm and shallow. If you have time, check out the self-guided **Mi'kmaq Cedar Trail.** Chances are you'll be able to join a First Nations interpreter for a Mi'kmaq cultural experience.

Relaxing at a winter shelter

KOUCHIBOUGUAC NATIONAL PARK
(Parc national Kouchibouguac)

INFORMATION & ACTIVITIES

VISITOR CENTRE
Visitor Reception Centre Phone (506) 876-2443. Open mid-May to mid-October. Park attendants available from December to March.

SEASONS & ACCESSIBILITY
Park open year-round. Administration office open weekdays year-round.

HEADQUARTERS
186 Rte. 117, Kouchibouguac National Park, NB E4X 2P1. Phone (506) 876-2443. www.parkscanada.gc.ca/kouchibouguac.

FRIENDS OF KOUCHIBOUGUAC
Amica, Inc. Kouchibouguac National Park, 186 Rte. 117, Unit 1, Kouchibouguac National Park, NB E4X 2P1. Phone (506) 876-1234. amica@nbnet.nb.ca; www.friendsofkouchibouguac.ca.

ENTRANCE FEES
$8 per person, $20 per group per day; $39 per person, $98 per group per season. Reduced rates April to mid-June and September to end of November. Go to park website for current information.

PETS
Pets must be leashed and attended at all times. Pets are not permitted on the barrier islands or on the boardwalks leading to the barrier islands.

ACCESSIBLE SERVICES
The **Salt Marsh Trail, Mi'kmaq Cedar Trail,** and boardwalk at **Kellys Beach** are wheelchair accessible. All washroom facilities are also wheelchair accessible.

THINGS TO DO
Hiking; biking and fat biking (helmets mandatory); swimming (warm waters in Kouchibouguac inner bay, cooler waters in the Northumberland Strait); canoeing; and kayaking.

Bicycles and boating equipment available for rent at the Ryans Recreation Equipment Rental Centre (mid-May–mid-Sept.) near South Kouchibouguac Campground. Fishing permits $10 per day, $34 per year.

In winter, cross-country skiing, snowshoeing, fat biking, geocaching, and sledding. Cross-country skiing trail use $8 per person, $20 per group per day; $39 per person, $98 per group per season.

Kids aged six to 10 love the Club Parka and Xplorers programs. Children and adults can also take part in the Citizen Science Program with the added benefit of contributing to the park's ecological integrity. Join a group and participate in a mission to count aquatic species from the estuaries.

DARK SKY DELIGHTS

In 2009, the Royal Astronomical Society of Canada (RASC) designated Kouchibouguac National Park a Dark Sky Preserve (see pp. 72–73). This means the park minimizes lighting at night and encourages public awareness of the cultural heritage of the night sky. As a bonus there are several special activities and Star Fest events a year.

During one of these night-sky programs, you may witness the wonders of a meteor shower, glimpse planets, and hear stories, legends, and myths from Mi'kmaq folklore and as portrayed by the stars. Visitors are also introduced to the basics of astronomy and learn why the dark sky is important to the birds, bats, insects, and amphibians that live in Kouchibouguac. You can also observe Saturn's rings, craters on the moon, galaxies, and nebulae by using the park's special light-gathering telescopes.

SPECIAL ADVISORIES

- Wear minimum SPF 15 sunscreen at Kellys Beach; there is no natural shade.
- Contact the visitor centre to inquire about jellyfish conditions.

OVERNIGHT BACKPACKING

Fees for backcountry use and camping: $10 per person per night, $69 per person per year. Eight primitive campsites at **Petit-Large** open year-round and accessible by bicycle or on foot. Four canoe campsites at **Pointe-à-Maxime** accessible only by canoe and/or kayak. Four canoe campsites at **Sipu** accessible by canoe or on foot. Parking lot camping, $19 per vehicle per night, available mid-October to April.

CAMPGROUNDS

South Kouchibouguac, open mid-May to mid-October, has 311 campsites, which include more than 190 partially or fully serviced sites ($30–$40 per night), 15 oTENTiks (a cross between a tent and a cabin, $100 in peak season), and 3 equipped campsites with prospector tents ($70 per night). 103 sites are non-serviced.Campground has fireplaces, kitchen shelters, picnic tables, playgrounds, washrooms, and showers. Unserviced campsites with washroom building (toilets and showers) $27–$32 per night. $16 per night for primitive and backcountry camping. Rustic shelters available early December to late March; stove and firewood provided; accessible only by skiing and snowshoeing. **Côte-à-Fabien,** open mid-June to early September, 32 campsites with fireplaces, picnic tables, and pit toilets. Group camping $5 per person per night. For reservations call (506) 876-2443.

HOTELS, MOTELS, & INNS

(unless otherwise noted, rates are for a 2-person double, high season, in Canadian dollars)

Outside the park:
Kouchibouguac Resort 10983 Rte. 134, St. Louis, NB E4X 1W6. (506) 876-4317 or (888) 524-3200. www.kouch.com. $78–$165.
Maison Tait House 293 Main St., Shediac, NB E4P 2A8. (506) 532-4233 or (888) 532-4233. www.maisontait house.com. Rooms start at $159.

For additional accommodations options: www.tourismnewbrunswick.ca.

EXCURSION

BOISHÉBERT & BEAUBEARS NATIONAL HISTORIC SITE
BEAUBEARS ISLAND, NB

During the deportation of 1755, many Acadians followed French-Canadian officer Charles Deschamps de Boishébert, taking refuge on an island of the same name. Now Beaubears Island, it achieved fame for its shipbuilding in the early 19th century. The island contains part of an old-growth Acadian forest and can be reached via a short shuttle ferry (foot passengers only) from Nelson-Miramichi. (506) 876-2443. 52 km (32.1 mi) northwest of Kouchibouguac via Hwy. 134.

Sea kayaking on the Bay of Fundy

▶ FUNDY

NEW BRUNSWICK
ESTABLISHED 1948
206 sq km/50,900 acres

Time and tides wait for no man, the saying goes. And it's most true at Fundy National Park on New Brunswick's east coast, where, twice daily, the most dramatic tides in the world cover the ocean bed with up to 12 m (38 ft) of water—the equivalent of a four-storey building. Over the next six hours, the water then sluices back to reveal the sea bottom: mucky, covered with seaweed, and bursting with intertidal wildlife.

From expansive intertidal beaches to the mixed forest plateaus of the Caledonia Highlands, the special places protected within Fundy National Park are wholly influenced by the massive tidal range of the Bay of Fundy. Fundy National Park forms the heart of the UNESCO Fundy Biosphere Reserve, a designation that recognizes the uniqueness of the region's geological formations, terrestrial and marine ecosystems, and cultural heritage. Fundy is also designated as a Dark-Sky Preserve by the Royal Astronomical Society of Canada (see pp. 72–73), making it one of the best places to explore the night sky in Canada.

Travelling inland, you can walk, hike, or bike more than 100 km

(62 m) of trails that weave their way through coastal fog forests and rugged river valleys. Spring is marked by the return of shorebirds and a seaward migrating population of Atlantic salmon found only in the upper Bay of Fundy.

In the fall, the Acadian forest—a diverse assemblage of softwood and hardwood tree species—comes alive with brilliant red, orange, and yellow foliage dotted wirh the dark evergreen of 400-year-old red spruce and balsam fir.

How to Get There

Nearby airports include Moncton (an hour drive), St. John (1.5 hours), Fredericton (2.5 hours), and the larger airport at Halifax (4 hours). All airports have car rentals.

Bus terminals operate in Moncton and in the town of Sussex, just off Trans-Canada 2. Sussex is a 45-minute drive to the park and also has car rental services. Note that there is no public transportation to and from the park itself.

If you are driving to the park from Fredericton, head east on Trans-Canada 2 toward Moncton, turning south at exit 365 (Coles Island) and onto Provincial Hwy. 10 to Sussex. Then head northeast on Hwy. 1, turning east on Hwy. 114 (at exit 211) to the park. From St. John, drive northeast on Hwy. 1, then turn onto Hwy. 114 at exit 211. From Moncton, drive southwest, all the way on Hwy. 114.

When to Go

The park's visitor services, including campground and visitor centre, operate from May through Thanksgiving weekend. The summer months of July and August offer the best weather and a somewhat lower likelihood of stubborn fog, although morning fogs, common throughout the summer,

can be great for viewing.

For visitor centre hours go to *www.pc.gc.ca/eng/pn-np/nb/fundy/ visit/heures-hours.aspx*. Most campgrounds and campsites are seasonal, except for Headquarters Campground, which is open year-round. Ski and snowshoe trails are kept groomed, as is a tobogganing hill. The road to Point Wolfe closes with the first snow and reopens when it's clear in the spring.

How to Visit

If you are interested in seeing the tides, be prepared to spend a full day. Tidal timetables change, so check in advance and plan the timing of your visit around them. The federal Fisheries and Oceans timetable can be found online *(www.tides.gc.ca)*.

In addition to the tides, the park offers a nine-hole golf course designed by Stanley Thompson, a heated saltwater swimming pool just off Point Wolfe Road, hiking, shore exploration, camping, and night-sky viewing. The park is liberally peppered with iconic Canadian imagery for photographers lucky enough to catch sunlight instead of frequent morning fog (which usually burns off by mid-afternoon) in summer.

TIDAL EXCURSIONS

For most visitors to Fundy, the remarkable tides along the park's coastline are its major magnet. Tides—the regular rise and fall of the height of the sea—are caused by the gravitational pull of the sun and moon. There are two high and two low tides in a 24-hour period, with the time between a high and a low tide about 6 hours and 13 minutes. High tides move about an hour later every day because of the

FUNDY

motion of the moon's orbit relative to the Earth.

Spring tides, which happen twice monthly in conjunction with the new moon and the full moon, offer the most dramatic highs and lows. Neap (from the Old English word "nep," or nipped) tides, when the moon is in a quarter phase, are less dramatic.

Spring tides at the full or new moon phase sometimes coincide with the moon's perigee, the point when the moon is closest to the Earth. When this happens, tides in the 150-km-long (93 mi) **Bay of Fundy** can rise to 16 m (53 ft)—higher than anywhere else in the world.

Imagine the bay is a basin of water. Water in a basin will slosh from end to end (called a seiche) in response to a disturbance such as a tremor, big wind, or tidal push from the ocean. Because of the particular length of the Bay of Fundy, the timing or period of that sloshing in the bay coincidentally matches the timing of the tidal push from the Atlantic Ocean. These two separate water movements resonate with and amplify one another, resulting in the giant tides of the Bay of Fundy.

During spring, summer, and fall, park naturalists time daily group Beach Walks for low tide, the perfect time for a stroll along the seabed in rubber boots or aqua socks. Be prepared. Thick brown sea mud cakes the feet and legs of all who wander out onto the mudflats; you will get thoroughly mucky.

When the seafloor is exposed, it reveals what's called the intertidal zone, an array of tenacious organisms able to survive underwater for half the time and in the open air for the other half. Barnacles, periwinkles, little crabs, dog whelks, limpets and other crustaceans, and all sorts of seaweeds become visible. During

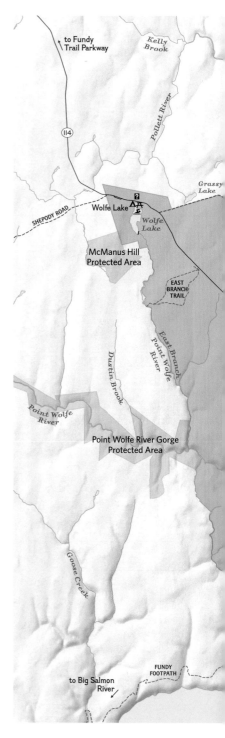

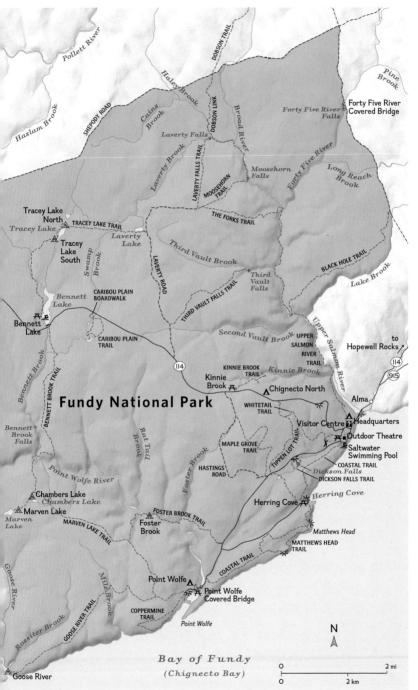

Pollett River

Haslam Brook

DOBSON TRAIL

Haley Brook

Pine Brook

SHEPODY ROAD

Cains Brook

DOBSON LINK

Broad River

Forty Five River Falls

Forty Five River Covered Bridge

Laverty Falls

LAVERTY FALLS TRAIL

MOOSEHORN TRAIL

Moosehorn Falls

Forty Five River

Long Reach Brook

Tracey Lake North

TRACEY LAKE TRAIL

Tracey Lake

Laverty Lake

Laverty Brook

THE FORKS TRAIL

Tracey Lake South

Swamp Brook

LAVERTY ROAD

Third Vault Brook

BLACK HOLE TRAIL

Lake Brook

Third Vault Falls

THIRD VAULT FALLS TRAIL

Bennett Lake

CARIBOU PLAIN BOARDWALK

Second Vault Brook

UPPER SALMON RIVER TRAIL

Upper Salmon River

to Hopewell Rocks

Bennett Lake

CARIBOU PLAIN TRAIL

114

Bennett Brook

BENNETT BROOK TRAIL

KINNIE BROOK TRAIL

Kinnie Brook

Kinnie Brook

115

Bennett Brook Falls

Kinnie Brook

Chignecto North

Alma

Fundy National Park

Rat Tail Brook

WHITETAIL TRAIL

Visitor Centre

Headquarters

Outdoor Theatre

Bennett Brook Falls

MAPLE GROVE TRAIL

Foster Brook

TIPPEN LOT TRAIL

Saltwater Swimming Pool

HASTINGS ROAD

COASTAL TRAIL

Dickson Falls

DICKSON FALLS TRAIL

Chambers Lake

Chambers Lake

Marven Lake

Point Wolfe River

MARVEN LAKE TRAIL

Foster Brook

FOSTER BROOK TRAIL

Herring Cove

Herring Cove

Marven Lake

Matthews Head

MATTHEWS HEAD TRAIL

Goose River

Mile Brook

GOOSE RIVER TRAIL

Point Wolfe

COASTAL TRAIL

Rossiter Brook

Point Wolfe

COPPERMINE TRAIL

Point Wolfe Covered Bridge

Point Wolfe

N

Goose River

Bay of Fundy
(Chignecto Bay)

0   2 mi
0   2 km

Hopewell Rocks

Covered bridge at Point Wolfe

bird migrations south or north, flocks of tiny shorebirds stop on the mudflats to load up on the tiny sea animals exposed at low tide.

The interpreters here are experts on their subject. They guide people on how the tides work and what happens to the area's ecosystem when tides are high and low.

HIKES & WATERFALLS

Trails for mountain biking and hiking, the park's top draw, cover more than 100 km (62 mi), with more on the way. Trails range from short jaunts, like the **Point Wolfe Beach Trail,** to the **Fundy Circuit,** which runs almost 50 km (31 mi) around the park. Requiring three to five days to complete, the

Fundy Circuit comprises seven trails linked together, with two wilderness campsites along the way (preregistration required), as well as a couple of campgrounds.

The 0.5-km (0.3 mi) **Caribou Plain Trail** boardwalk is accessible to wheelchairs and leads through a wetland bog with interpretive signs and an occasional moose wandering through the terrain. Beyond the wheelchair-accessible portion, another 2 km (1.2 mi) worth of wooded trail continues through to a wetland bog with plenty more wildlife.

The short **Shiphaven Trail** starts beside Point Wolfe Bridge at the gorge of the Point Wolfe River and leads about 1 km (0.6 mi) along a glacial ridge. Find interpretive panels marking an early logging dam and the remains of a sawmill that are slowly crumbling back into the river.

There are more than two dozen waterfalls in the park. The most popular, **Dickson Falls,** is relatively easy to reach on a 1.5-km (1 mi) trail loop, most of it boardwalk, with some stairs to climb and a number of interpretive signs along the way.

At the end of Laverty Road, the **Laverty Falls Trail,** another much loved trek, runs 5 km (3 mi) in total, out and back. A little all-natural wading pool at the foot of the 40-foot falls makes a handy midpoint cooling-off spot, but watch for slippery rocks. More ambitious hikers can make their way to Laverty Falls via **Moosehorn Trail** or the **Dobson Link,** which connects hikers to a larger, out-of-park network of trails leading all the way to Moncton.

FUNDY TRAIL PARKWAY

A 16-km (10 mi) paved parkway that edges the cliffs along the Bay from the village of St. Martins to Cranberry Brook Lookout, this scenic drive can be reached by taking Shepody Road west out of the park onto Hwy. 114 to St. Martins. The parkway entrance gate is about 10 km (6.2 mi) from the village. It's also less than an hour's drive from St. John, taking Trans-Canada 1 east to exit 137A, then following Hwy. 114.

The attractions here are legion: coastal scenery, hiking and cycling trails, the **Big Salmon River Interpretive Centre,** and a suspension footbridge. The **Fundy Footpath,** a world-class wilderness trek, stretches from the Big Salmon River all the way to the park (41 km/24 mi; about four days' worth of travel time for hardy hikers). The trail passes through the most remote stretch of coastal wilderness along the Eastern seaboard.

Once a hunting retreat for newspaper baron William Randolph Hearst and his friends, the wilderness **Hearst Lodge** is a handsome tribute to 20th-century great-outdoors architecture.

HOPEWELL ROCKS
a full day

Perhaps the most photographed site in New Brunswick, the **Hopewell**

Rocks—a half-hour drive north of the national park via Hwy. 114—are iconic conglomerate stone and red sandstone "flowerpot" rocks that tower up to 15 m (49 ft) or more in height at low tide. (One of the most famous formations collapsed in 2016.)

Once part of the sedimentary rock cliffs formed here millions of years ago, these formations are slowly eroding. In fact, in the centuries to come, the surging tides will completely wash the rocks away. New ones will form behind them, however, and geologists think there's enough conglomerate rock—that's the top layer of stone that wears away less rapidly than the underlying sandstone—to make more flowerpot rocks for about another hundred thousand years.

Begin the day exploring the ocean floor around the rocks at low tide, then poke around some of the caves gouged into the cliffs over the centuries. Take a lunch break at the park's restaurant while you wait for the tide to turn. Once the ocean begins moving toward high tide, meet up with one of the local kayaking outfitters and paddle around the tops of the very rocks whose bases you explored just hours earlier.

Independent kayakers can go it on their own, but you must stop at the visitor information desk first in order to sign a waiver and get permission to drive to the kayak launch area. The best timing is during the two hours prior to or following high tide, when beach access is easier. Outside that time window, water levels sink fast and you may have to drag your kayak across the sensitive mudflat ecosystem.

Though you can kayak in Fundy National Park at high tide as well, viewing the oddly comical formations of the Hopewell Rocks from two completely different dramatic angles

FUNDY

FUNDY NATIONAL PARK (*Parc national Fundy*)

INFORMATION & ACTIVITIES

VISITOR CENTRE
Phone (506) 887-6000.

SEASONS & ACCESSIBILITY
Fundy National Park's operational season runs from May long weekend until Thanksgiving long weekend. During winter, the Park is open for day-use activities such as snowshoeing and walking; however, visitor services such as the campgrounds and visitor centre are closed.

HEADQUARTERS
P.O. Box 1001, Alma, NB E4H 1B4. Phone (506) 887-6000. www.pc.gc.ca/fundy.

FRIENDS OF FUNDY
Fundy Guild Inc. 8642 Unit 2, Rte. 114, Fundy National Park, NB E4H 4V2. Phone (506) 887-6094. info@fundyguild.ca; www.fundyguild.ca.

ENTRANCE FEES
$8 per adult, $7 per senior, $4 per child, $20 per group per day; Seasonal: $39 per person, $98 per group.

PETS
Pets must be on a leash at all times.

ACCESSIBLE SERVICES
The visitor centre, **Caribou Plain boardwalk,** and **Point Wolfe Lookout** are all accessible to wheelchairs. Chignecto North and Headquarters Campground have wheelchair-accessible washroom facilities. Swimming pool and changing room facililties are wheelchair accessible.

THINGS TO DO
Hiking on more than 100 km (62 mi) of trails, mountain biking. Snowshoeing. Swimming in heated saltwater pool (late June–September; lifeguard on duty) and at Bennett Lake and Wolfe Lake beaches (unsupervised). Lake fishing (permits $10 per day, $34 per year).Tennis and lawn bowling (rent equipment mid-May–early Oct.). Golfing (mid-May–early October; $33 per day, $19 for 9 holes; for reservations call the Pro Shop (506) 887-2970). Canoe, rowboat, and kayak rentals at Bennett Lake. Sea-kayak rentals and tours available in the Village of Alma. Summer interpretive programs. Evening outdoor music and theatre events, stargazing, and campfire pro-

is a treat you can get nowhere else in the world.

VILLAGE OF ALMA

Located on the southeastern edge of the park, the fishing village of **Alma** makes a good base for enjoying local food and exploring everything that Fundy has to offer. At **Alma Beach,** low tides reveal more than 1 km (0.6 mi) of mudflats. Fishing boats can come and go from the harbour only at high tide. At low tide they are propped up by wobbly crates to keep them vertical.

There are two lobster fishing seasons in Alma, fall (mid-October–end of December) and spring (beginning of April–end of July). In between, the fleet gears up for scallop fishing. The fisheries are celebrated locally through the fall lobster fleet launch, an annual send-off for fishermen that tracks the opening of the season (sometimes in the middle of the night), and a chowder cook-off in the summer. Visit one of several lobster "pounds" to learn about fisheries and pick out your own lobster—sized as a canner (170–454 g/0.4–1 lb in weight), a market (454 g/1 lb and up), or a jumbo (more than 1,135 g/2.5 lbs).

Alma also has a Sunday market with local vegetables, baked goods, and crafts.

grams. Activity schedules posted online and throughout the park; call the visitor centre for details.

SPECIAL ADVISORIES
• The weather is variable. Wear layers and footwear with good traction and support.
• Watch for the rising tide; be aware of tide times posted on boards along trails. Call the visitor centre for information.

OVERNIGHT BACKPACKING
7 backcountry sites at **Goose River, Marven Lake,** Chambers Lake, **Tracey Lake,** and **Foster Brook.** Tent pads, fireboxes with wood, pit privies, and picnic tables. Backpacking stoves and drinking water recommended. Reserve online (www.reservations.pc.gc.ca).

CAMPGROUNDS
Campsites available on a first-come, first-served basis. For reservations call (877) 737-3783 or visit www.reservations.pc.gc.ca. **Wolfe Lake,** primitive campsite with pit privies $16 per night. **Point Wolfe Headquarters** and **Chignecto North** serviced with electricity, water, and sewer, $36; serviced with electricity and water only, $32; unserviced with washroom (toilets and showers), $26. **Chignecto South** group campground, $5 per person. Yurts and oTENTiks (a cross between a tent and a cabin, with electricity and hot showers), $90. **Headquarters** and Chignecto North open mid-May–mid-October; serviced campground with electricity. **Point Wolfe** mid-June–early October.

HOTELS, MOTELS, & INNS
(unless otherwise noted, rates are for a 2-person double, high season, in Canadian dollars)

Inside the park:
Fundy Highlands 8714 Rte. 114. (506) 887-2930. info@fundyhighland chalets.com; www.fundyhighland.com. $99–$125.

Outside the park:
Village of Alma, NB E4H 1N6
Parkland Village Inn 8601 Main St, (506) 887-2313, www.parklandvillage inn.com. $95–$155.

For a full directory of lodgings and other information go to www.villageofalma.com.

EXCURSION

MONUMENT LEFEBVRE NATIONAL HISTORIC SITE
MEMRAMCOOK, NB

Named for Father Camille Lefebvre, founder of the first French-language degree-granting college in Atlantic Canada, Monument Lefebvre has long been a centre of Acadian pride. In the mid-19th century, Lefebvre helped educate many leaders of the Acadian renaissance, a movement to reawaken and preserve Acadian culture. Today the building houses an exhibit chronicling the Acadians' history in Atlantic Canada. Guided tours are available. (506) 758-9808. 118 km (73 mi) northeast of park via Hwy. 114.

QUEBEC & ONTARIO

Page 88: top, Visitors at Lake Bouchard, La Mauricie; middle, Northern saw-whet owl; bottom, Dwarf lake iris.

QUEBEC & ONTARIO

From Mingan Archipelago in Quebec to Pukaskwa in Ontario, these parks represent Canada's wonderful inland waters. Mingan's islands are known for strange monoliths that trim the shore. Boaters paddle by, spotting seals, dolphins, and nesting seabirds. At the tip of the Gaspé Peninsula, Forillon marks one end of the Appalachians. Hikers at La Mauricie spot moose and black bear, while campers sleep, listening to loons singing on a lake. More than

Page 89: Sunset in Georgian Bay Islands National Park. Above: Brébeuf Island as viewed from Georgian Bay Islands National Park.

24 islands dot Thousand Islands, home to endangered plants like the American water willow. At Georgian Bay Islands, 63 islands pepper the shore, and visitors hike and camp in settings accessible only by boat. Visitors at Bruce Peninsula hike along the Bruce Trail, Canada's longest hiking trail, while Point Pelee draws serious bird-watchers. Hikers in Pukaskwa can follow a trail on the longest undeveloped shoreline on the Great Lakes.

ONTARIO

QUEBEC

Mingan Archipelago

Pukaskwa

Forillon

La Mauricie

Bruce Peninsula

Georgian Bay Islands

Thousand Islands

Lands Committed for Rouge

Point Pelee

Detail of granitic islets and reefs, Mingan Archipelago National Park

▶MINGAN ARCHIPELAGO

QUEBEC
ESTABLISHED 1984
151 sq km/37,313 acres

Famous for the largest concentration of erosion monoliths in Canada, the Mingan Archipelago National Park Reserve encompasses close to a thousand islands and islets sprinkled along 150 km (93 mi) from east to west. Although the park is restricted to the islands themselves, the sea shapes everything here—rocks, plants, wildlife, climate . . . even the visitor's experience itself.

The Mingan Archipelago tells a fascinating geological story. Difficult to imagine today, the sedimentary rock formations date back almost 500 million years to a time when a warm, shallow tropical sea covered today's St. Lawrence Lowlands region. Saturated with calcium carbonate and teeming with a diversity of marine organisms, the bottom of this ancient sea received a steady deposit of fine marine sediments and animal shells. Over tens of millions of years, they accumulated to form a blanket several kilometres thick that gradually turned to rock under its own weight.

With passing time, continents shifted, the sea receded, and this vast plateau of relatively soft and partly soluble rock found itself under the aggressive attack of erosion. Among other factors, rivers carved up the land, carrying away most of the material, but fortunately left behind several "hard to do" rocky mounds. After several other episodes of sea level fluctuation, these mounds became today's islands.

As if to decorate them still further, the sea continued to carve their shores, creating a mesmerizing array of monoliths, festooned cliffs, arches, and grottoes. At the same time, a surprising diversity of plant and animal species managed to establish itself on the islands. Due to the particular combination of geology and climate, many rare plants are found nowhere else in the region. In springtime, marine birds—such as puffins, razorbills, guillemots, terns, and kittiwakes—congregate on certain islands to form important nesting colonies, taking advantage of both island safety and a bountiful supply of food in surrounding waters. All of these and much more make the archipelago a unique part of our natural heritage.

How to Get There

Take Hwy. 138, driving about two hours east of Sept-Îles. The Mingan Archipelago stretches along the north shore of the Gulf of St. Lawrence between the towns of Longue-Pointe-de-Mingan and Aguanish. There are information and interpretation centres located in Longue-Pointe-de-Mingan and Havre-St.-Pierre, as well as information kiosks in Baie-Johan-Beetz and Aguanish.

When to Go

The best time to visit is from June to early September. The park is only accessible by boat, so unless you have your own kayak or boat, you will require the services of registered marine transportation companies, most of which operate only from mid-June to early September. It is recommended that you contact them

ahead of time to obtain information and make reservations.

How to Visit

The most popular way to visit the Mingan Archipelago is to take one or several of the boat tours offered by commercial marine transportation companies departing from Longue-Pointe-de-Mingan and Havre-St.-Pierre. Boat capacities vary from eight to 58 passengers. Tours usually last three to five hours and allow a visit to several different islands, often including one or two guided visits led by Parks Canada interpreters. Enjoy the cool ocean breeze and unbounded horizons. If you are lucky, you may see whales or seals along the way. Admire the spectacle of giant monoliths and festooned cliffs sculpted by the sea. Keep your eyes peeled for fossils embedded in the rock and dating back to a time so ancient that fish and other vertebrates had not yet evolved.

Once in the area, chances are you will want to spend a few more days exploring these unique islands at a more leisurely pace. Take a taxi boat and spend a couple of nights camping in the archipelago. Experience genuine island seclusion. Wake up to the rhythm of waves. Inhale the rich smells of the sea. Observe passing seabirds and whales. Relax and soak in the solitude. You will be smitten.

If camping is not your style, the taxi boats also offer numerous possibilities for day or half-day trips. There are relatively easy hiking trails on several different islands, varying in length from 300 m (0.2 mi) to about 10 km (6.2 mi), either in the interior or along the shoreline. Explore "your" island at your own pace. Relax and picnic along the way. Walk on a pebbled or sandy beach. Marvel at the unique and hardy

Longue-Pointe-
de-Mingan

Mingan

Île aux
Perroquets

Île Nue
de Mingan

La Grosse
Romaine

Île à Bouleaux
de Terre

Île à
Bouleaux
du Large

La Grande
Île

Chenal de
Mingan

Île
Quarry

Île du
Fantôme

Île
Niapiskau

Havre-
St-Pierre

Grosse île
au Marteau

Île du
Havre

Petite île au
Marteau

Île de la
Fausse Passe

Île St-
Charles

Baie
Nickerson

Baie Puffin

Île Ste-
Geneviève

Île à la Chasse

Refuge de Betchouane

Lac
à l'Ours

Ba
Joha
Be

Rivière Romaine

Rivière Mingan

N

0   12 mi
0   12 km

Mingan Archipelago National

Gulf of St. Lawrence

seashore flora. Venture onto the rocky flats at low tide. Discover the diversity of marine organisms that make their home in the tidal pools. Hike into the interior of an island and discover a diverse mosaic of unique ecosystems, each with its specific flora and fauna.

If you feel adventurous, try kayaking in the archipelago. Possibilities for day and multiday trips are endless, and kayak rentals and guided excursions are available. Whichever itinerary you choose, you are bound for an unforgettable experience of discovery and awe.

Whether you embark on a short three-hour boat tour or a 10-day

kayak journey, be sure to begin your stay by stopping at either of the two Parks Canada visitor information and interpretation centres located in Longue-Pointe-de-Mingan or Havre-St.-Pierre. Visit the exhibits on show. Talk to Parks Canada employees to discuss the different excursions that are offered. Obtain all necessary maps, information, and permits. And while you are there, take a tour of the Mingan Islands Cetacean Studies Centre adjacent to the Parks Canada information centre in Longue-Pointe-de-Mingan. It provides a fabulous opportunity for visitors to dive deep into the fascinating underwater world of whales.

Fog envelops Île aux Perroquets Lighthouse at dawn.

Mingan Archipelago National Park Reserve
includes all offshore islands between
Île aux Perroquets and Aguanish

ark Reserve

THE WESTERN ISLANDS

If you drive east from Sept-Îles along
Hwy. 138, stop in Longue-Pointe-de-
Mingan and take a boat tour or taxi
boat to visit Île aux Perroquets and
Île Nue de Mingan. Standing proud
and strong on **Île aux Perroquets,** at
the western end of the archipelago,
the old **lighthouse buildings** beckon the
visitor back to a time when there was
no road and the sea provided the
backbone of the local economy and
transportation system. For almost a
century, six different light keepers,
often accompanied by a helper and
some by their families, made their
home on this tiny isolated island during most of the year to ensure mariners steered clear of the forbidding
islands and shoals of the archipelago.
The light keepers are long gone, but
the island and surrounding islets are
still home to the many seabirds—
eiders, terns, guillemots, razorbills,
and puffins—that congregate here
during the nesting period.

Just east of Île aux Perroquets lies
Île Nue de Mingan, a treeless island
with fascinating Arctic and subarctic
vegetation, home to the southernmost patches of permafrost along
Canada's eastern coastline. This
peculiarity is likely due in part to a
microclimate caused by cold water

upwelling in the area, which at the
same time enriches the surrounding
waters, attracting several species of
seals and whales, a regular sight on
the water.

You can visit both islands during
the same three-hour tour, but if you
have the whole day, it is worthwhile
to make arrangements with the
tour operator and spend the rest of
the day hiking around Île Nue de
Mingan, a loop of about 8 km (5 mi)
along the shoreline. Note, however,
that this trail does not open until
mid-July in order to avoid disturbing
nesting seabirds.

Roseroot (*Sedum rosea*)

Another alternative for a full-
day activity is to take a longer tour
that also includes **Grande Île** and its
impressive monoliths. Camping is
also possible on either **Île Nue de
Mingan** or **Grande Île,** a unique experience as each campground is limited
to just two or four tents.

THE CENTRAL ISLANDS

The central part of the archipelago,
accessible from Havre-St.-Pierre, is
home to some of the largest islands
of the archipelago, as well as some of

the park's most stunning monoliths and rock formations. As a result of their size and relative proximity, these islands are less susceptible to the cooling effect of the sea and boast a diversity of ecosystems such as coniferous forests, bogs, barrens, small lakes, salt marshes, seashores, and cliff habitats.

To see the most imposing and famous monoliths, be sure to visit **Île Niapiskau** and **Île Quarry.** Short excursions with interpretive stops on each island are available. Day and multiday trips are also possible as both islands have campgrounds and hiking trails. Just across Île Niapiskau, you will find **Île du Fantôme** with its fascinating checkered reef flats and its trail across rocky barrens, home to a peculiar and hardy flora.

Less than a kilometre across from Havre-St.-Pierre, **Île du Havre** is a quickly accessible island offering seashore hiking possibilities as well as two campgrounds. Just east of it is easily accessible **Petite Île au Marteau,** which is sure to captivate

with its old **lighthouse buildings.** Go for a picnic, relax, and discover local culture and history. Still farther east, you will find **Île de la Fausse Passe** with its incredible festooned cliffs that you can admire directly from the water. And if seclusion is what you are looking for, spend a night or two camping on **Île à la Chasse,** a rarely visited island due to its remoteness.

THE FAR EAST

Besides protecting the sedimentary rock islands that make it famous, the national park reserve also encompasses a maze of a thousand small rose-coloured and often treeless Precambrian rock islands and islets sprinkled along some 70 km (43 mi) of coastline in the vicinity of Baie-Johan-Beetz and Aguanish. Home to the largest migratory bird sanctuary in Quebec, this area offers no tourist infrastructure for the time being. It can, however, be admired from two roadside viewpoints, at **Baie Pontbriand** and **Rivière Corneille.**

A hiker walks along the boardwalk at Niapiskau Island.

MINGAN ARCHIPELAGO NATIONAL PARK RESERVE
(Réserve de parc national de l'Archipel-de-Mingan)

INFORMATION & ACTIVITIES

VISITOR & INFORMATION CENTRES
Havre-St.-Pierre Reception and Interpretation Centre 1010 Promenade des Anciens, Havre-St.-Pierre, QC G0G 1P0. Phone (418) 538-3285 or (888) 773-8888.
Longue-Pointe-de-Mingan Reception and Interpretation Centre 625 Du Centre St., Longue-Pointe-de-Mingan, QC G0G 1V0. Phone (418) 949-2126.

SEASONS & ACCESSIBILITY
Park open from mid-June to early September.

HEADQUARTERS
Mingan Field Unit, 1340 de la Digue St., Havre-St.-Pierre, QC G0G 1P0. Phone (418) 538-3331. www.parkscanada.gc.ca/mingan.

ENTRANCE FEES
$6 per person, $15 per group per day; $29 per person, $74 per group per season.

PETS
None permitted.

ACCESSIBLE SERVICES
Universal access at Havre-St.-Pierre, Longue-Pointe-de-Mingan Reception and Interpretation Centre. The film *The Mingan Islands* subtitled in English and French for visitors with hearing disabilities. Petite Île au Marteau has wheelchair-accessible wharf, picnic area, washrooms, and lookout point.

THINGS TO DO
Hiking along 24 km (15 mi) of trails on four islands. More than 97 km (60 mi) of navigable waters for sea kayaking. For boating, contact **Club nautique de Havre-St.-Pierre** (418-538-1679). For scuba diving, contact local businesses such as **SM Boréale** (418) 538-2865, *www .smboreale.com*), to rent equipment.

SPECIAL ADVISORIES
- Sea conditions may delay return to mainland. If camping, bring a small axe for kindling and food for an extra two days.
- Some areas along the shoreline may present difficult or hazardous conditions. To avoid falling rocks, do not walk beneath overhanging rocks or stop next to the base of overhanging cliffs.
- Rocks can be slippery at low tide. At high tide, water may block the trail.
- Do not climb on the monoliths.
- Check with the park office about sites that are off-limits during seabird nesting season (May–Aug.).
- For water activities, ensure one of the party can interpret marine and tide charts, navigate in fog, and perform first aid. Wear wet suits to avoid hypothermia. In case of emergency, call (888) 762-1422.

OVERNIGHT BACKPACKING
No backcountry camping.

CAMPGROUNDS
Campgrounds are open mid-June to early September. Primitive campgrounds $16. Group camping $5–$6 per person. $11–$14 per reservation. For opening dates, call (418) 538-3331. 42 campgrounds on 6 islands, including 6 oTENTik tents on Quarry Island. Camping permits can be obtained at the visitor centres or at the Park Reserve administrative office in off-season. Reservations accepted up to 6 months in advance: 1-877-737-3783; parkscanada.gc.ca.

HOTELS, MOTELS, & INNS
(unless otherwise noted, rates are for a 2-person double, high season, in Canadian dollars)

Inside the park:
Auberge de l'Île aux Perroquets (418) 949-0005. info@ileauxpperroquets; www.ileauxperroquets.ca. $375.

Outside the park:
Hôtel Motel du Havre 970 boulevard de l'Escale, Havre-St.-Pierre, QC G0G 1P0. (418) 538-2800. info@hotelduhavre.ca; www.hotelduhavre.ca. $83–$110.

For more accommodations visit www.tourism ecote-nord.com.

Twilight on Cap-des-Rosiers, Forillon National Park

▶ FORILLON

QUEBEC
ESTABLISHED 1970
240 sq km/59,305 acres

Depending on your perspective, Forillon marks either the beginning or the end of the Canadian portion of the International Appalachian Trail. Much of the park is pure mountain wilderness with seaside cliffs and remarkable hiking trails. It also boasts a cluster of traditional Gaspé fishing villages, pebble beaches in quiet coves, and rugged cliffs looming along a coastline that wraps around two of the triangular park's three sides. At its northeastern tip, the park pokes into the Gulf of St. Lawrence via a peninsula topped by a lighthouse.

Forillon National Park protects an extensive range of varied little eco-systems: natural prairies and farm fields, seaside cliffs, rivers, lakes, marshes, the seashore itself, and forest. The park shelters a peculiar combination of some 700 kinds of local flora along with plants most often found in Arctic or alpine envi-ronments, such as purple mountain saxifrage, tufted saxifrage, and white dryad.

Historically, this resource-rich area of Quebec was exploited for its supply of wood. People living off the coast in the village of L'Anse-au-Griffon, on the park's northwest side, were involved in the early lumber industry here. Sawmills turned out planks, beams, cedar shingles, barrel staves, even timbers to build wharves and bridges.

Wildlife spotters on the prowl in the park can look for moose, black bears, lynx, red foxes, beavers, porcupines, coyotes, snowshoe hares, mink, and ermines. Bird-watchers are drawn by 253 known species. Along the cliffs, perfect for breeding, seabirds such as black-legged kittiwakes, double-crested cormorants, black guillemots, and razorbills are plentiful. Great blue herons, terns, gulls, and sandpipers inhabit shorelines, and more than two dozen inland raptor species include northern harriers, American kestrels, bald eagles, peregrine falcons, and great horned owls.

How to Get There

Fly into Quebec City from any major North American city, then make the 10-hour drive on Trans-Canada 20 from Quebec City to Rivière-du-Loup and then Rte. 132 to the park. The magnificent route follows the south side of the vast mouth of the St. Lawrence River, skirting the northern edges of the Gaspé Peninsula and passing through its small towns and villages. Stop in the city of Mont-Joli (Rimouski) about halfway to the park, or shorten the drive by flying from Quebec City into Mont-Joli and renting a car there.

A quicker alternative is to fly from Quebec City or Montreal to the town of Gaspé. From there, the park lies just 30 km (19 mi) away on Rte. 132, an extremely pretty coastal drive. You can also reach the park by train.

When to Go

Summer's the season that really shines in Forillon. The coastal scenery is at its finest, wildflowers bloom almost frantically, beaches are easily accessible, and trails are at their peak of natural beauty. In winter, two cross-country skiing trails are maintained by volunteers.

How to Visit

A two- or three-day visit allows you to see all the major attractions. The best way to experience the park is on foot. On the first day, explore a few beaches and do some sea kayaking, take a whale-watching cruise, or go snorkelling.

On the second day, check out the Hyman & Sons General Store, populated by character actors, and the restored homestead and farm of Anse-Blanchette, which are virtually all that remains of the old fishing village of Grande-Grave. Take the late afternoon and evening to spend time in nearby Gaspé, where more than three dozen small hotels and B&Bs can provide cozy, lacy Québécois-style beds. Explore the

FORILLON

American porcupine

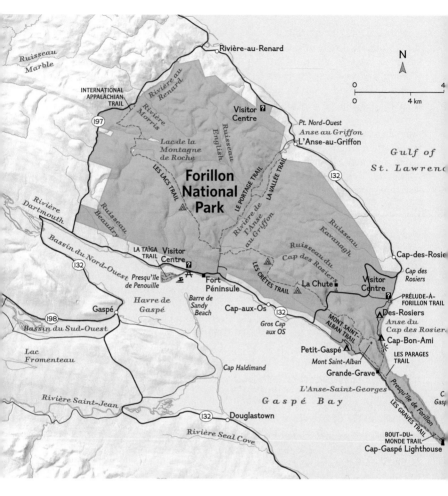

restaurants in town, which also has a few interesting local museums.

If there's time for a third day in the park, fill up the backpack with the day's necessities and squeeze in some wilderness hiking. Or do as the locals do and go for a picnic along the rugged cliffs. Spend some time ranging along the round-pebble beaches, or make your way to the Cap Gaspé lighthouse on Land's End, where the views stretch on and on. The lighthouse is just 13 m (43 ft) high, but it squats on the edge of a 95-m (312 ft) cliff.

WATER ACTIVITIES

Six different kinds of whales and porpoises can be seen in the park's marine environment. Whale-watchers flock to Forillon all summer to see whales from the only vessel licensed to ply these waters. From early June until the beginning of October, the 48-passenger, open-deck *Narval III* (866-617-5500, *www.baleines-forillon.com*) sails from the park's Grande-Grave harbour on 2.5-hour cruises throughout the day. The onboard guides are very good at spotting blue, fin, humpback, and minke whales, as well as white-sided dolphins and harbour porpoises.

From Grande-Grave Harbour, guided sea-kayaking tours are offered from mid-June until September. Encounter seals, paddle at sunset, or make an excursion all the way up the coastline around Forillon peninsula.

For scuba diving, push off from **Petit-Gaspé, Grande-Grave,** or **Anse-St.-Georges** to explore the ocean floor and check out marine Atlantic sealife. Fishing is permitted off the wharves at Grande-Grave and **Cap-des-Rosiers** on the north side of the peninsula.

Almost a half dozen pebbled beaches around the peninsula make for great strolls, and the sand beach at **Penouille,** just down a long spit of land not far from the park's south side visitor reception centre, is a good, sheltered wading and swimming spot, equipped with picnic areas, playgrounds, a snack bar, washrooms, and showers.

Near Penouille beach, you will find the remains of Fort Peninsula, a World War ll fortifiction built to protect the Bay of Gaspé in the unlikely event that Germany managed to invade North America. You can also explore the underground tunnel here, home to unused cannon. Écorécréo Rental Centre offers shuttle service; tours; and paddleboard, bike, and quadricycle rentals.

In the park's South Area, the Recreation Centre has a heated outdoor swimming pool as well as a wading pool.

HIKING & CAMPING

Remote Forillon is a hiker's heaven, with nine mostly interconnecting trails cutting through the park. For a challenge and some great sea views, the **International Appalachian Trail** continues along the **Les Graves Trail.** Beginning at Grande-Grave, this 15-km (9 mi) trek along the coast

FORILLON

Cap Bon Ami, Forillon National Park

A northern gannet from Bonaventure Island fishes off the coast of Forillon.

Forest rapids

Lobster traps on Grande-Grave Wharf

will take you past sea coves and beaches all the way to Cap Gaspé, where you may well see whales and seals around. (Hikers can pick up the International Appalachian Trail again by getting to Sackville, New Brunswick, via bus or car, and then hiking over the Confederation Bridge to Prince Edward Island and points north.)

For a shorter trek, an 8-km (5 mi) portion of the Les Graves Trail starts at L'Anse-aux-Amérindiens. There's a **wilderness camping** area on the **Les Lacs Trail** for overnighters. Other long trails that require carrying camping gear are the 16-km (10 mi) **Les Crêtes Trail,** mountainous and forested, with periodic lookout points and two wilderness camping areas (registration is required). The 10-km (6 mi) **Le Portage Trail** that traverses the park from north to south is used by cyclists and horseback riders as well as hikers; the trail is especially good for wildlife-watching (be sure to use bear bells).

The Les Graves Trail short version, **Mont St. Alban Trail,** and **La Vallée Trail** all run about 8 km (5 mi), and each can be done in a day. The first two concentrate on cliffside views (the first few kilometres of the Mont St. Alban Trail are steep and sometimes a bit tricky to navigate), and La Vallée follows the Anse-au-Griffon River in the woods.

For much shorter excursions, **Prélude à Forillon,** which starts near the interpretation centre, runs just over 0.5 km (0.3 mi), is wheelchair accessible, and offers interpretive material along the way. The 3-km (1.8 mi) **Une tournée dans les parages** ("a walk around the area") is less a hike than a short stroll around local history, passing by **Fruing Beach,** the historic **Hyman & Sons General Store** and **Anse-Blanchette,** and the remains of old houses and barns, once part of the now gone cod-fishing and drying village of Grande-Grave. Exhibits along the way explain the area's history. The short, all-natural **La Chute Trail** blends a charming little waterfall, a maple grove, and a small river cascade into an easy and peaceful 1-km (0.6 mi) ramble through the woods.

The little village of **L'Anse-au-Griffon** still exists just outside the park boundaries on the northwest side, on its traditional fishing harbour. The village can be reached along Rte. 132, which loops all the way around and through the park. Dedicated hikers can reach L'Anse-au-Griffon at the northwest end of the hiking/cycling Le Portage Trail. Pick up the trailhead just off Rte. 132 on the southeast side of the park. Two restored buildings in the village, the **Centre Culturel Le Griffon** and the **Manoir Le Boutillier** (a national historic site), both house elements of local history. The cultural centre has a small café, and there is also a small motel here, the Motel Le Noroît.

GRANDE-GRAVE HERITAGE SITE

Forillon's rich fishing has attracted settlement for 6,000 years, the most recent being the village of **Grande-Grave** ("Grave" refers to a pebble beach where cod was dried) in the late 19th and early 20th centuries. Here, hundreds of workers for two large fishing companies caught cod, and dried and salted it for sale to Europe and the West Indies. Families fleshed out their earnings, and their groceries, with a little farming. Today, visitors can prowl the remains of many buildings that mark the location of the village. Two of the buildings have been restored. The ground floor of the two-storey **Hyman & Sons General Store,** built in 1864 as a home, was turned into a business in 1918.

Today it has been refurbished and refurnished with all the dry goods a period fishing and farming family might have needed. Upstairs, a small permanent exhibition documents life in Grande-Grave, and a projection room adjacent to the main-floor store offers a documentary video.

At Anse-Blanchette, the **Blanchette homestead** has been restored, complete with its barn, fish house, and woodshed. In the barn, you can watch a video, "We Always Looked to the Sea."

FORILLON NATIONAL PARK
(Parc national Forillon)

INFORMATION & ACTIVITIES

VISITOR & INFORMATION CENTRES
L'Anse-au-Griffon Visitor Centre and **Penouille Visitor Centre** open June to September.

SEASONS & ACCESSIBILITY
Park open June to October.

HEADQUARTERS
122 Gaspé Blvd., Gaspé, QC G4X 1A9. Phone (418) 368-5505. www.parks canada.gc.ca/forillon.

ENTRANCE FEES
$8 per person per day; $39 per year.

PETS
Pets must be leashed at all times.

ACCESSIBLE SERVICES
Visitor centres and the Prélude à Forillon interpretive trail are wheelchair accessible.

THINGS TO DO
Sea-kayaking service available June to September. Reservations recommended (418-892-5056). Whale-watching services available from June to October. Reservations recommended (418-892-5500). Scuba diving and snorkelling. Reservations recommended (418-892-5888).

Hiking on the **International Appalachian Trail.** To hike with an interpreter, call (418) 368-5505. Cycling, in-line skating, and horseback riding. For bike rentals call (418) 892-5058.

Swimming, tennis, volleyball, shuffleboard, and a playground are available at the recreation centre. Also fishing, scuba diving, and snorkelling. Beaches at **Cap-Bon-Ami, Petit-Gaspé, Grande-Grave,** and **Des-Rosiers Campgrounds.**

SPECIAL ADVISORIES
- Remain on designated trails. Do not leave waste; there are no trash cans.
- Open fires forbidden in backcountry.
- Snowmobiling is forbidden everywhere in the park except for boundary corridors.
- For water sports, use a buddy system and check the weather and tides before setting out.
- Do not harass, trap, or feed wildlife. No fishing permitted in freshwater.

OVERNIGHT BACKPACKING
Backcountry lean-to camping, $15 per person, available only at **Les Lacs** and **Les Crêtes** campsites along the International Appalachian Trail; registration mandatory.

CAMPGROUNDS
Camping fees $26 for unserviced campgrounds; $29 for serviced campgrounds. 352 semi-serviced campsites and 3 unserviced campgrounds and 3 lean-to dormitories in the backcountry. **Petit-Gaspé** 167 sites (66 with electricity); **Des-Rosiers** 147 sites (42 with electricity); **Cap-Bon-Ami** 41 sites. For reservations, call (877) 737-3783; (866) 787-6221 for the hearing impaired. 8 oTENTik (a cross between a tent and a cabin) basic service packages $100 per night; 7 oTENTiks ready-to-camp packages $120 per night.

HOTELS, MOTELS, & INNS
(unless otherwise noted, rates are for a 2-person double, high season, in Canadian dollars)

Outside the park:
Gîte des Trois Ruisseaux 896 boulevard Griffon, L'Anse-au-Griffon, QC G4X 6B2. (418) 892-5528. www.gites-classifies .qc.ca. $70–$80.
La Maison de la Demoiselle 1796 boulevard Forillon, Cap-aux-Os, QC G4X 6L2. (418) 892-5449. www.gaspesie .net /maison_de_la_demoiselle. $975–$1,300 per week.
Motel le Noroît 589 boulevard Griffon, L'Anse-au-Griffon, QC G4X 6A5. (418) 892-5531 or (855) 892-5531. www.motel lenoroit.com. $70–$80.

▶ **NATIONAL MARINE CONSERVATION AREA**

SAGUENAY–ST. LAWRENCE
QUEBEC

This 1,245-sq-km (481 sq mi) marine park near the village of Tadoussac at the confluence of the Saguenay and St. Lawrence Rivers offers jaw-dropping scenery and whale-watching opportunities from land, boat, and kayak. It was created in 1998 to protect and showcase portions of the St. Lawrence Estuary and the Saguenay Fjord.

Kayaking along the Saguenay River

Jointly managed by the provincial and federal governments, this stunning park features one of the southernmost fjords in the world, measuring 276 m (905 ft) deep in some places. The park is home to some 10 species of marine mammals, including seals, endangered blue whales, and about a thousand endangered St. Lawrence belugas.

The Parks Canada Saint-Fidèle Visitor Centre (418-235-4703, *www .parcmarin.qc.ca*), along Hwy. 138, is open end of June to mid-October and is worth a stop for park tips, a small exhibit, and a picnic area.

Closer to the park is the pretty village of **Tadoussac** (*www.tadoussac .com*), a few hours north of Quebec City along Hwy. 138 and a ferry ride from Baie-Sainte-Catherine. French explorer Jacques Cartier came here in 1535. Pierre Chauvin built the first trading post in 1600, and explorer Samuel de Champlain arrived in 1603. Fur traders and the area's First Nations people traded at Tadoussac. Visitors can find accommodations in local hotels and B&Bs, as well as at Camping Tadoussac and Camping du Domaine des Dunes (*www.domainedesdunes.com*).

From Tadoussac, go to the **Marine Environment Discovery Centre** in Les Escoumins, about 30 km (19 mi) from Tadoussac, to participate in a dive without getting wet. Sit in a theatre and watch a giant screen as biologist-divers equipped with a camera go live beneath the St. Lawrence River. You may see sea stars and other marine life. Visitors can talk to divers underwater through a real-time two-way video link and follow along on the dive.

The centre also has a permanent exhibit about the rich marine life that makes the area so attractive for whales.

A child examines the living treasure at a tide pool.

WHALE-WATCHING: One of the highlights for visitors to the park is being able to see whales. The sociable and highly vocal beluga is often called "sea canary" because its calls are reminiscent of singing. It also emits ultrasonic sounds for echolocation. The returning echo allows it to locate prey, find holes in the ice, and avoid obstacles.

Whale-watching boats and Zodiacs operate from May to October, departing from Tadoussac, Les Escoumins, Les Bergeronnes, Saint-Siméon, Rivière-du-Loup, and Baie-Sainte-Catherine. It can get chilly on the water, so wear long pants and bring a hooded windbreaker, sweater, gloves, and a hat.

Some whale-watching companies offer tours of the Saguenay Fjord.

Regulations adopted in 2002 require that motorized boats and kayaks stay at least 400 m (1,312 ft) from endangered beluga and blue whales and 200 m (656 ft) from other whale species and impose speed limits and flyover height restrictions.

The marine park covers a portion of the St. Lawrence Estuary and Saguenay Fjord, but visitors can whale-watch and experience the park from interpretation and observation points set up on dry land along the park's boundary. Each site focuses on a particular theme related to the marine environment.

MARINE OBSERVATION: At **Cap de Bon-Désir,** 25 km (16 mi) east of Tadoussac, freshwater from the Great Lakes and St. Lawrence River mixes with salt water from the Gulf of St. Lawrence. This makes the St. Lawrence Estuary a rich environment for marine life and Cap de Bon-Désir a good spot to learn about the evolution of navigation on the St. Lawrence and the diversity of marine life. Visitors can whale-watch from land at the end of a 300-m (984 ft) trail and also participate in interpretive activities.

Pointe-Noire Interpretation and Observation Centre sits across from Tadoussac, at the confluence of the Saguenay Fjord and the St. Lawrence Estuary. An exhibit at this interpretation and observation centre explains riptide zones and the formation of plumes. A panoramic trail leads to a lookout. The site also has alignment beacons that guard the mouth of the Saguenay River.

Baie Sainte-Marguerite, 30 km

Sea anemones

in Les Bergeronnes, for example, looks at the park's archaeology and paleohistory. At **Saint-Fulgence,** the fjord's rocky cliffs disappear, only to be replaced by large marshes. There is a 605-m (1,985 ft) spit. The spit and marsh are a unique feature of the fjord. The **Centre d'interprétation des les battures et de réhabilitation des oiseaux** looks at the plants and birds that make their home in the Saguenay's tidal flats.

(19 mi) from Tadoussac, is another good spot for beluga-watching. The whales sometimes stay there for hours. An interactive exhibit at the **Beluga Discovery Centre** shares information with visitors about the habitat in which belugas live.

These and a number of other sites link to form the Saguenay–St. Lawrence Marine Park's Discovery Network (888-773-8888, *www .marinepark.qc.ca*). Other sites focus on the area's history. The **Centre Archéo Topo** *(www.archeotopo.com)*

KAYAKING: Novice kayakers can try half-day excursions in the sheltered waters of **Baie Éternité,** on the south side of the Saguenay River. More experienced paddlers could opt for the 72-km (45 mi) scenic route from **Sainte-Rose-du-Nord** to Tadoussac at the mouth of the St. Lawrence River. For a current list of outfitters, go to *www.marine park.qc.ca*.

Saguenay–St. Lawrence Marine Park, 182, rue de l'Église, Tadoussac, phone (418) 235-4703.

Beluga whale

Lac Wapizagonke, La Mauricie National Park, in autumn

▶ LA MAURICIE

QUEBEC
ESTABLISHED 1970
536 sq km/132,500 acres

Nestled in the Laurentian foothills, La Mauricie National Park presents an untamed yet homelike environment. It is bordered by two wildlife refuges, the Mastigouche and the Saint-Maurice, and the Saint-Maurice and Matawin Rivers. A sprawling network of valleys and a multitude of lakes, streams, and falls all bear witness to its history. Conifers and hardwoods intermingle to form a gigantic forest mosaic. Visitors will be awestruck by the park's strings of lakes, flowering coves, natural beaches, rock cliffs, speckled trouts, loons, and moose.

The view from the top of the Laurentian foothills embraces a huge plateau rising from east to west and undulating as far as the eye can see. Formed from rock dating to the first billion years of the Earth's existence, the land is split among three main valleys running in a northwest direction. Here and there, glaciers have left their traces on the landscape in the form of eskers, erratic boulders, and sand beaches. Tectonic forces in combination with glaciations have, with time, given birth to a multitude of lakes in all shapes and sizes. As the glaciers melted and receded, the Champlain Sea inundated the lowlands, leaving its imprint in the form of clay marine terraces along the Saint-Maurice River.

Following the disappearance of the glaciers, forests slowly returned to the area and today cover 93 percent of the park. The diversity of stands is apparent at a glance: Maple, which is dominant in the southern portion, is gradually overtaken by balsam fir to the north. The park numbers more than a hundred different stands, some of which— including pine, hemlock, and oak— are of exceptional quality.

Owing to the richness and diversity of these forests, moose and black bears are frequently sighted. The eastern wolf, designated a species of special concern, and the wood turtle, a threatened species, are present but more discreet. Lakes and streams sporting picturesque names evoke the age-old presence of the aboriginal peoples and the more recent passage of loggers and fish-and-game-club members.

How to Get There

Nestled in the heart of Quebec, the park is located midway between Montreal and Québec City, less than an hour's drive from Trois-Rivières. To get there, first take Rte. 40 in the direction of Trois-Rivières, and then Rte. 55 N. Turn off Rte. 55 at exit 226 and follow the directions to Saint-Jean-des-Piles, the only entrance open year-round. If you wish to enter the park via the other entrance, take exit 217 and follow the directions to Saint-Mathieu-du-Parc.

When to Go

The Mauricie region is canoeing country par excellence. But no matter the season, it is also a great place for getting out and about in any number of ways—hiking, biking, skiing, and kayaking. In the summertime, dally

about Lac Wapizagonke or take off into the backcountry until you reach Waber Falls. Spring and fall put on a show of colour and offer excellent opportunities for viewing wildlife up close. From January to March, an extensive network of cross-country ski and snowshoe trails is bound to make your outings memorable.

How to Visit

If you have only one day to spend in the park, travel the length of the parkway and stop off at any of the numerous lookouts, where exhibits tell the story of the surrounding landscape. Stroll along an interpretation trail and get acquainted with the local wildlife. Cool off in a falls or on a natural beach.

Extend your getaway at one of the park's three semi-serviced campgrounds or in the comfort of a heritage lodge; interpretation activities are presented by naturalists nearby. Embark on a canoe adventure, paddling in pace with the movements of the sun and the wind. You can choose from a range of itineraries throughout the park lasting one to three days, with stops at primitive campsites. Hiking and mountain-biking trails will afford you both access and insight into the landscapes around you.

CANOEING ON LAC WAPIZAGONKE
a half to full day

At **Lac Wapizagonke,** all the charm, beauty, and richness of the park is on display, making for a 16-km-long (10 mi) natural spectacle. Resembling a river, this lake can be easily reached from the south (4 km/3 mi) or the north (25 km/ 16 mi) via the parkway starting from the

La Mauricie National Park

St.-Mathieu entrance. A broad range of services and activities is available on location: campground, picnic area, snack bar, and canoe and kayak rental outfit, as well as swimming, canoeing, hiking, fishing, and nature interpretation. The entire area is pervaded by a particular spirit.

Serving as point of departure, the **Shewenegan picnic area** boasts an interpretation module offering insights into little-known aspects of the lake. A footbridge crossing over the lake provides access to the easy 2-km (1 mi) **Les Cascades Trail—** so named for the gushing waterfalls that create a continuously cool, calming environment. Spring and fall colours make for a spellbinding experience along the trail.

Once you've completed your walk, you're ready to take off and canoe or kayak for two hours in the direction of the Esker, following in the path of the first aboriginal peoples. Sightings of wildlife are frequent mornings and evenings and include such species as the beaver, moose, loon, and, more rarely, wood turtle. **Esker** is where you stop for lunch, a dip in the lake, or a bit of aural and visual contemplation. Your ears will tickle to the sound of nearby waterfalls and your eyes are sure to delight at the sight of the majestic white pines rising on the Esker point. Close by, a

250-m (820 ft) boardwalk leads to a bog featuring wild orchids and carnivorous plants.

More adventuresome canoers will enjoy paddling out to the **Vide-Bouteille.** The diversity of landscapes along this 9-km (6 mi) return route is nothing short of amazing, and includes sandy beaches, marshy coves, and stream outlets. This outing will take you over a route travelled by the aboriginal peoples. Logging companies later dammed the route and used it to carry timber, while wealthy Americans and Canadians belonging to the Shawinigan Club canoed along it in quest of prize catches.

There is quite a mixture of forests to be seen along the way, including stands of pine, balsam fir, spruce, maple, and cedar. **Île aux Pins** is only to be admired, as no stopping is allowed on it. In fact, since 1987, conservation measures have protected loons. A little marshy cove harbours a number of aquatic plants—water lily, pickerelweed, pond lily—whose names are as evocative as their flowers are lovely to behold. American black ducks, mallard, loons, and common mergansers can be seen swimming, diving, and dabbling, while the peregrine falcon silently wheels and turns above its hunting territory. Le Vide-Bouteille, the stopping point, is home to a large sandy beach and sheer cliff faces that lend themselves well to relaxation and daydreaming. As you paddle your way back, you are likely to be rocked gently by the wind and the current.

If you're keen to add to your experience of Lac Wapizagonke, a series of three roadside lookouts show off the surrounding valley in its full grandeur. The fall colours make for spectacular viewing. Perched at an altitude of 150 m (492 ft), **Le Passage lookout** (km 35) tells the story of the formation of the valley. The **Vide-Bouteille lookout** (km 46) reveals the origin of its peculiar name. **Île-aux-Pins lookout** (km 52) recalls both the presence of an aboriginal camping site and the impact of the great fire of 1923.

WABER FALLS

1 to 2 days

The trip to **Waber Falls** combines canoeing (8 km/5 mi), hiking (9 km/ 6 mi), and swimming, all in a spectacular environment unlike any other. Depart from the Wapizagonke picnic area, located at km 38 on the parkway. A convenience store and a canoe rental outfit are also on site. It is recommended that you get an early start.

Beaver

The outing begins with an hour of canoeing through the islands of Lac Wapizagonke until you reach the Lac Waber portage. Moose and beaver are frequently sighted along the way. Then, during the climb by foot, be sure to stop at **Le Portageur lookout** and take in the view out over Lac Wapizagonke and its islands. A series of ponds lines the trail until

A group of visitors takes a voyage of discovery aboard Rabaska canoes.

Aboriginal petroglyphs dating back centuries

Carnivorous plant

you reach Lac Waber. The sound of a low roar means the falls are not far off. And what a pleasure it is to cool off in the prettiest and, at 30 m (98 ft), the tallest falls in the park.

On your way back, follow the portage trail in the direction of Lac Anticagamac for 2 km (1 mi). Midway, a lookout offers a panoramic view out over the lake, famous for its majestic cliffs, vast aquatic grass beds, unique forest, and richly diverse fauna. **Lac**

Anticagamac and **Lac Wapizagonke** are linked by a 3-km-long (2 mi) portage. In 1997 and 1998, prescribed burning was carried out in this area as part of efforts to restore the white pine.

In order to camp, you'll need to portage your canoe and camping gear. Lac Anticagamac offers a primitive campsite at the foot of some daunting, 100-m (328 ft) cliffs. The evening's program of events includes a sunset, black sky, and a concert of loon song and eastern wolf howls. The next day, take the opportunity to meander through a most unusual aquatic garden, where pickerelweed, watershield, and water lilies can all be seen blooming on a midsummer's day. A diversity of wildlife also wends its way through these teeming grass beds. The northern pike and yellow walleye, species that are absent from the park's other lakes, are attracted by the abundance of food that flows in with the flood waters of the Matawin River. All in all, it is an ideal place for fishing, nature-watching, and photography.

ALONG RIVIÈRE À LA PÊCHE
a half to full day

After a stop at the **Saint-Jean-des-Piles Reception Centre** for some useful information and advice, continue along the parkway for another 5 km (3 mi) until you reach the **Rivière à la Pêche Service Centre.** Recently upgraded, the centre is a meeting point for seasoned hikers, skiers,

and cyclists and offers an array of services, including restrooms and showers, a dining room, and exhibits. It is also the head of a major network of trails, such as the 17-km (11 mi) **Deux-Criques Trail,** the 11-km (7 mi) **Mekinac Trail,** the 5.7-km (3.5 mi) **Lac-Solitaire Trail,** and several others that vary in terms of distance and level of difficulty.

Rivière à la Pêche is the longest watercourse in La Mauricie National Park. It originates in Lac Édouard, flows into Lac à la Pêche and Lac Isaïe, and then empties into the Saint-Maurice River. **Trail No. 3,** a former logging road, runs alongside the river, Lac Isaïe, and Lac à la Pêche over a distance of 15 km (9 mi). It is easily accessible by foot or by mountain bike. The route bears the unmistakable stamp of past logging and log-driving activities. The point of departure is located within view of the oldest white spruce plantations in Canada.

At km 2, the trail crosses over Rivière à la Pêche, the site of some magnificent waterfalls. It then hugs

LA MAURICIE

Hikers stop to admire the view.

LA MAURICIE NATIONAL PARK
(Parc national de la Mauricie)

INFORMATION & ACTIVITIES

VISITOR & INFORMATION CENTRES

Saint-Jean-des-Piles Visitor Reception and Interpretation Centre Hwy. 55, exit 226. **Saint-Mathieu Reception Centre** Hwy. 55, exit 217. Phone (819) 538-3232. Open mid-May to October.

SEASONS & ACCESSIBILITY

Park open year-round. Contact park office for information on snow cover in winter and snowmelt in spring.

HEADQUARTERS

702 Fifth St., P.O. Box 160 Main Station, Shawinigan, QC G9N 6T9. Phone (819) 538-3232. www.parkscanada.gc.ca/mauricie. www.facebook.com/MauricieNP

FRIENDS OF LA MAURICIE

Info-Nature Mauricie 702 Fifth St., P.O. Box 174 Main Station, Shawinigan, QC G9N 6T9. Phone (819) 537-4555. info-nature@cgocable.ca; www.info-nature.ca.

ENTRANCE FEES

$8/adult, $4/youth, $20 per group per day.

PETS

Pets not permitted on beaches, trails, boats, or in the backcountry.

ACCESSIBLE SERVICES

Accessible displays at Saint-Jean-des-Piles Visitor Reception and Interpretation Centre. Dock is wheelchair accessible. **Lac Étienne Trail** is a universal-access interpretive trail with observatories and interpretation panels, tactile exhibitions, and braille text. Campgrounds, beaches, picnic areas, and some hiking trails are also accessible.

THINGS TO DO

Hiking, mountain biking, canoeing, and fishing ($10 permit). Boat rentals, snack bar, beaches, picnic tables and barbecues, launching ramps, and interpretive activities at **Shewenegan** and **Lac-Édouard** picnic areas. Tables and barbecues available at **Wapizagonke, Esker,** and Lac-Bouchard picnic areas. In winter, cross-country skiing ($10 per day) and snowshoeing ($8 per day).

SPECIAL ADVISORIES

• Glass containers not allowed on beaches or Les Cascades Trail.
• Motorboats are prohibited on all lakes.
• Cutting down trees or branches to start or maintain a fire is forbidden.

Lac Isaïe until it reaches a lovely log shelter (km 3.5). Lac Isaïe recently underwent a bit of rejuvenation. Upward of 15,500 sunken logs littering its floor were retrieved as part of efforts to return the lake to full health. These wood fossils offer proof that some impressive hemlock forests were growing here at the time of Jacques Cartier's arrival in Canada in 1534. Today, the richest maple stands in the park are located here. Such species as the great-horned owl and the pileated woodpecker attest to the maturity of this forest. In addition, rare plants such as yellow lady's slipper and maidenhair fern exemplify all the grace and richness of the hardwood forests lining the Rivière à la Pêche route.

A bit farther along the way lies **Lac à la Pêche** (km 6). There is a pretty little shelter at the junction with **Trail No. 7** (km 8), followed by the **Wabenaki** and **Andrew Lodges,** the last living reminders of the Laurentian Fish and Game Club (1883–1970). In the immediate vicinity of the lodges, you can make your way up the river some 500 m (1,640 ft) to cool off in **Parker Falls** before heading back (11 km/6.8 mi).

- Strong winds over some lakes; boaters should check weather conditions.
- Campers should store food, garbage, and odour-producing items appropriately. Bear-proof racks are available near backcountry campsites.

CAMPGROUNDS

Rivière à la Pêche, Mistagance, and **Wapizagonke** semi-serviced campgrounds with 581 campsites total, each equipped with a fireplace and picnic table. Service buildings have washbasins, toilets, and showers. Unserviced campsites with toilets and showers $26; serviced campsites with electricity $29; group camping with showers $6 per person; primitive campsites for canoe camping $16. **Rivière-à-la-Pêche Campground** open mid-May to mid-October. **Wapizagonke Campground** open late June to early September. **Mistagance Campground** open mid-May to early October. Backcountry camping available year-round. For reservations call (877) 737-3783 or visit www.pccamping.ca. Cancellation at least 7 days in advance of reservation date for complete refund. **La Clairière** group campground. For reservations call (819) 538-3232.

This type of accommodation is available in Mistagance campground during the summer season and year-round at the Rivière à la Pêche campground. $120 per night /5 persons max.

oTENTik experience: A cross between a tent and a rustic cabin, Parks Canada oTENTik tents offer a unique blend of homey comfort and a taste of outdoor adventure.

HOTELS, MOTELS, & INNS
(unless otherwise noted, rates are for a 2-person double, high season, in Canadian dollars)

<u>Outside the park:</u>
<u>St.-Jean-des-Piles, QC G0X 2V0:</u>
Aux Berges du St.-Maurice 2369 rue Principale. (819) 538-2112. www.cdit .qc.ca/absm. $69–$99.
La Maison Cadorette 1701 rue Principale. (819) 538-9883. www.cdit .qc.ca/cadoret. $80.

<u>Shawinigan, QC G9N 6T9:</u>
Wabenaki and Andrew Lodges St.-Gérard-des-Laurentides. (819) 537-4555. *www.info-nature.ca.* $71–$75 for 2 nights (Fri. & Sat.); $34 per night during the week.

EXCURSION

FORGES DU SAINT-MAURICE NATIONAL HISTORIC SITE
TROIS-RIVIÈRES, QC

Relive the history of Canada's first industrial community at the site where, from 1730 to 1883, resourceful engineers produced bar iron and cast iron objects for military or domestic use. Stop in at the Grande Maison, explore the blast furnace, and engage in some time travel at the Devil's Fountain. An amazing range of experiences are on tap, including guided tours, exhibits, a sound and light show, a history trail, and archaeological vestiges. (819) 378-5116 or (888) 773-8888. 70 km (45 mi) south of park via Hwy. 55.

History of Canada's National Parks

Individuals interested in the conservation of Canada's wild places, wildlife, and cultural treasures drove the creation of the National Parks system that exists in Canada today. In 1883, hot springs were discovered near modern-day Banff, Alberta. Government officials withdrew the surrounding areas from private development and, in 1885, created the Banff Hot Springs Reservation. In 1887, legislation designated the hot springs and much of the surrounding area as Rocky Mountains Park (now Banff National Park).

East entrance to Rocky Mountains Park, later Banff National Park, circa 1920

In 1886, the Canadian Pacific Railroad convinced the government to set aside park reserves farther west, forming the basis for Yoho and Glacier National Parks. Other reserves followed, including Waterton Lakes National Park, Elk Island National Park, Mount Revelstoke National Park, and a large forest park in Jasper (now Jasper National Park).

By 1911, the unorganized state of the parks led Minister Frank Oliver to create the framework for Canada's park system, the Dominion Parks Branch. He appointed James B. Harkin commissioner. Harkin saw the necessity of both protecting nature through new parks and reserves and making parks relevant to Canadians. He created Kootenay National Park in 1920. He also established parks to protect wildlife, such as Wood Buffalo National Park in the Northwest Territories; migratory birds were protected at Point Pelee, Ontario.

Harkin focused on expanding the system eastward, creating a national park in the Thousand Islands. He became a proponent of "a park in every province," resulting in the creation of the first prairie parks: Prince Albert in Saskatchewan and Riding Mountain in Manitoba. He completed his career by doing the same in the Maritime Provinces, with Cape Breton Highlands in Nova Scotia and Prince Edward Island. Georgian Bay Islands National Park in Ontario was then added.

One of Harkin's priorities was to establish the "absolute sanctity" of the national parks, protecting them from industrial development. This was achieved when Parliament passed the National Parks Act in 1930. It established that "The national parks of Canada are hereby dedicated to the people of Canada for their benefit, education and enjoyment . . . and the parks shall be maintained and made use of so as to leave them unimpaired for the enjoyment of future generations." This dedication clause has stood the test of time.

After Harkin's retirement, Canadian park creation over the next 30 years slowed with only four new parks—Fundy and Kouchibouguac in New Brunswick, Terra Nova in Newfoundland, and Kejimkujik in Nova Scotia.

In the late 1960s, Jean Chrétien, minister for Canada's north and future prime minister, wanted the system to reflect all of Canada. The creation of new parks in this period responded to the growing calls for governments to place a priority on environmental protection. Chrétien reached agreement for La Mauricie and Forillon in Quebec, Pacific Rim on the Pacific Coast, Gros Morne in Newfoundland, Pukaskwa in Ontario, Kluane in the Yukon, Nahanni in the Northwest Territories, and Auyuittuq in the eastern Arctic that is now Nunavut. He was the first recipient of the J. B. Harkin Medal, awarded by the Canadian Parks and Wilderness Society to those dedicated to parks protection.

Over the next 20 years, the focus was on northern Canada. New parks were created in partnership with indigenous peoples. This resulted in 11 new parks: Quttinirpaaq on Ellesmere Island and Sirmilik on northern Baffin Island in Nunavut; in the Northwest Territories at Aulavik and Tuktut Nogait; in the Yukon at Ivvavik and Vuntut; in Ontario at Bruce Peninsula; in Quebec at Mingan Archipelago; in Saskatchewan at Grasslands; in Manitoba at Wapusk; and in British Columbia at Gwaii Haanas.

Parks Canada has since added seven more national parks and national park reserves. Through the creation of these new parks and expanding other parks such as Nahanni, the total area in national parks has increased by more than one third since the year 2000. The new parks this millennium are: Gulf Islands in British Columbia; Ukkusiksalik in Nunavut; Torngat Mountains in Labrador; Sable Island National Park Reserve off the coast of Nova Scotia; Nááts'ihch'oh National Park Reserve in the Northwest Territories; Qausuittuq National Park in Nunavut; and Akami-Uapishk^u-KakKasuak-Mealy Mountains National Park Reserve in Labrador. It also included a six-fold expansion of Nahanni National Park Reserve, referred to as one of the greatest conservation achievements in a generation. A new type of park is being created by Parks Canada, the Rouge National Urban Park on the outskirts of Toronto, Canada's biggest city.

Several of Canada's parks have been awarded UNESCO World Heritage site status, and Waterton Lakes forms an International Peace Park with Glacier National Park in the United States.

International Bridge, Thousand Islands National Park

▶THOUSAND ISLANDS

ONTARIO
ESTABLISHED 1904
24 sq km/5,931 acres

Ten thousand years ago, retreating glaciers scraped sediment from the landscape near what is now Kingston, Ontario, leaving behind a granite chain of more than a thousand mountains. Today, these hills are the 1,000 Islands—a winding necklace of glittering river jewels. Whispering marshlands, rugged rock outcroppings, and a rich diversity of plant and animal life characterize the 24 islands, 129 islets, and eight mainland tracts that compose Thousand Islands National Park.

The Thousand Islands have a long history of community connection. Their strategic seaway location (within the Frontenac Axis that connects Ontario's Algonquin Provincial Park to New York's Adirondack State Park) means they've played host to many people over the years.

The islands are part of a corridor that acts as a funnel for the north-to-south movement of wildlife. They're also the traditional territory of the Haudenosaunee and the Mississauga Anishinaabe. During the late 1600s, explorers, fur traders, and missionaries relied on the islands, which also played a role in the wake of the American Revolution, as demonstrated by the amount of man-made heritage within park parameters.

More recent man-made structures, such as cottage estates and rustic cabins, might pepper an even higher percentage of the islands if local influence hadn't established a national park here at the turn of the 20th century. In 1904, the Mallorys, a local family, donated a small slice of waterfront property to the government on the condition that the land be used for park purposes. Though this sentiment has always resonated throughout the region, in 1997, the park was named one of four national parks with the highest levels of impairment to ecological integrity.

Today, prescribed burns in the park promote the regeneration of the pitch pine, rarely found in Canada. Studies conducted in partnership by Queen's University and Carleton University examine the road mortality of a range of species, including the northern map turtle. The Ministry of Natural Resources monitors the impact of purple loosestrife, an exotic plant that thrives in the park. Local partnerships have proven key to maintaining this small, fragmented site.

How to Get There

From Kingston, take Hwy. 401 E toward Cornwall for 62 km (39 mi). Take exit 675 and turn right at Country Road #5, which will take you to the Mallorytown Landing Visitor Centre.

When to Go

Services are offered mid-May to mid-Oct. Though the visitor centre closes in early September, the park is open year-round and the islands are popular sites for Thanksgiving picnics, as well as a special Christmas Birdcount event. Call ahead for details. Recreational boating slows in fall, making it the best time to visit the islands by canoe or kayak.

How to Visit

If you're only stopping in for a few hours, particularly if you have kids, the Mallorytown Landing Visitor Centre combines play with park history. A short walking trail allows you to stretch your legs while taking in wooded and wetland habitats along the shore.

Also at Mallorytown Landing are picnic shelters and barbecues, exhibitions, playground, bikes, and equipment for geocaching.

For a full-day adventure, the park's extensive Jones Creek Trail System consists of 16 km (10 mi) of looping paths and gorgeous views. Those wishing to overnight on the islands, where all 68 of the park's campsites are located, can do so by renting kayaks in Gananoque and paddling along one of the dozens of routes through the park. Short, beginner trips from the harbour can be completed in 20 minutes. Experienced paddlers can go as far as Cedar Island off Kingston's Cartwright Point.

MALLORYTOWN LANDING VISITOR CENTRE

1.6 km/1 mi return; 3 hours

Heading east on **Thousand Islands Parkway,** a sweeping waterfront road that offers stunning river views, the **Mallorytown Landing Visitor Centre** is on your right. Before the parkway (or any roads, for that matter) existed in the region, local farmers shipped grain from the docks here. Travellers boarded boats to Kingston and Brockville. Today Mallorytown Landing, the original park site, serves as an interpretive centre.

Aquariums feature local fish, turtles, mudpuppies, and frogs. An indoor theatre shows films like

Voices of Akwesasne, a Parks Canada–produced video project that highlights the relationship between the Mohawk people and the park. Roving interpretive programs touch on everything from turtles and the role of prescribed burns to cultural history. You might even see a black rat snake as part of one of the live exhibits. Habitat loss in the 1,000 Islands has contributed to making the snake an endangered species.

The gardens around the centre feature playground equipment and staked placards—part of a program called Leaders of the Landscape—that focus on the environmental stewardship efforts of local residents.

The trailhead for the centre's trio of walking paths lies on the east side of the main building. The 0.8-km (0.4 mi) **Smoky Fire Trail** cuts across the Thousand Islands Parkway and through red pine plantations and rocky lowland forests. You'll also see the former location of the **Andres farm,** a Loyalist settlement cultivated until 1956. Continue along the 1.4-km (0.8 mi) return **Loyalist Trail** and, if you have time, the 2.8-km (1.7 mi) return **Six Nations Trail.** Or return to the visitor centre, experience camping in a waterfront cabin, and enjoy

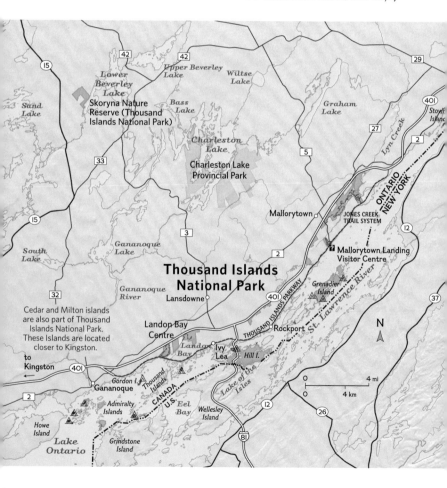

Red fox (*Vulpes vulpes*)

most difficult of the front trail paths. If you'd rather forgo it, take the **Eel Loop** to the right, where you'll pass beneath the canopies of century-old white pine. After Eel merges with **Turtle Loop**, look for a clearing on your left where beavers have harvested the beech and maple trees.

The **Heron Trail,** the rearmost of the four front trails, features a lookout (complete with rustic wooden bench) over the vast **Mud** and **Jones Creek Wetlands**. To go farther, follow Heron downhill. A floating boardwalk crosses the wetlands to connect with the rear system, where five trails carve a semistraight line southwest. Keep your eyes open for wildlife. Turkey vultures, mink, beavers, and coyotes are regularly spotted on the rear trails.

In the spring, **Wolf Trail** is decorated with wildflowers. Come prepared if you're going to hike the whole 16 km (10 mi). **Snipe Trail,** the first loop of the rear system, offers incredible overviews of **Jones** and **Mud Creeks,** but you have to earn them.

a picnic in the massive historical granite gazebo built in 1904 (one of three such structures in the park), where you can read the Mohawk Thanksgiving address etched into the nearby rock.

HIKE AT JONES CREEK
16 km/10 mi one way; a full day

Drive east from Mallorytown Landing. As you approach **Brown's Bay Day Use Area** on the right, you'll notice a sign for the **Jones Creek Trail System** on the left. The land here is one of the mainland tracts that were transferred to St. Lawrence Islands in 2005, a move that doubled the size of the park.

Pull into the small parking lot and self-register at the trailhead. Four trails at the front of the system loop into one another and make for 3 km (2 mi) of easy-to-moderate hiking. The five trails at the rear of the system offer 12 km (8 mi) of more challenging terrain.

A gravel trail leads from the lot to **Bear Loop** on your left. Forested ridges and rock faces make this the

ADMIRALTY ISLANDS
12 km/7.5 mi loop; 1 to 2 days

Gananoque was founded by Loyalist Colonel Joel Stone, who took possession of a 700-acre (283 ha) land grant from the British crown in 1792. Drive past the town's turreted houses, with their wraparound porches and gingerbread accents, to **Gananoque Municipal Marina** at the west end. In addition to kayak rentals, 1000 Islands Kayaking Company (*www.1000islandskayakingco.com*) offers guided half-day, full-day, and multiday adventures to park visitors.

If you do go out alone, maps are provided. There are plenty of

oTENTik camping near Mallorytown Landing.

Black-capped chickadee

options for beginner and experienced paddlers. The **Admiralty Islands** are a cluster situated slightly southwest of the harbour. Their proximity to the mainland (20-min. paddle), combined with the shelter of their many bays, makes this the ideal trip for beginners (though seasoned

paddlers can use the launch as a starting point for longer trips). Put in at the harbour and paddle south to the breakwall. Head west, past **Sisters Island** and **Ormisten Island,** and turn to your left. **McDonald Island** lies directly in front of you. Hug **McDonald's** eastern shore and follow it around to the south side. Just after you pass a stand of cattails you should see the park dock. Seven campsites, three oTENTiks (a cross between a tent and a cabin), composting toilets, and recycling/garbage collection make this one of the busiest islands in the park. Hike the perimeter and move on, or use **McDonald** as a base camp while you explore surrounding islands.

Wanderer's Channel slips southwest between **Lindsay** and **Bostwick Islands** on its way to **Aubrey Island,** which offers more secluded camping. Nearby **Beau Rivage Island** has a perimeter hiking path.

From Aubrey, paddle southeast to round **Bostwick** and **Halfmoon Bay.** To the southeast, **Thwartway**

THOUSAND ISLANDS NATIONAL PARK
(Parc national des Mille-Îles)

INFORMATION & ACTIVITIES

VISITOR & INFORMATION CENTRE
Mallorytown Landing Visitor Centre 1121 Thousand Islands Parkway.

SEASONS & ACCESSIBILITY
Park office open weekdays year-round.

HEADQUARTERS
2 County Rd. 5, RR3, Mallorytown, ON K0E 1R0. Phone (613) 923-5261. www .pc.gc.ca/ti.

ENTRANCE FEE
Fees are paid by self-registration. Parking fees at Mallorytown Landing Visitor Centre. Docking, beaching, camping fees apply on park islands.

PETS
Pets not permitted on beaches and must be on a leash at all times elsewhere in the park.

ACCESSIBLE SERVICES
A 0.6-km (0.4 mi) wheelchair-accessible trail from Mallorytown Landing. Visitor centre is wheelchair accessible.

THINGS TO DO
Boat rentals at local marinas. Boat launching $10 per person per day, $98 per season. **Gananoque Boat Lines** (888-717-4837, *www.ganboatline.com*) runs regular tours of the islands. Sea kayaking along the **1000 Islands Water Trail** in the **Frontenac Arch Biosphere Reserve.** Geocaching. Visitor centre with live animals, hands-on exhibits, and children's activities. Hiking available on **Jones Creek trails,**

16-km (10 mi) trail network, and **Landon Bay,** 6.4-km (3.9 mi) trail network.

SPECIAL ADVISORIES
- Black-legged ticks are abundant. Stay on trails, dress accordingly, and conduct regular tick checks.
- If camping overnight on the islands, pack so animals can't get at the food.

OVERNIGHT BACKPACKING
Campsites on islands are only accessible by boat. OTENTik accommodations (a cross between a tent and a cabin) on park islands and the mainland at Mallorytown Landing. No tent camping on the mainland.

CAMPGROUNDS
Island camping $16 per night; group camping $5 per night. 51 primitive campsites on 12 islands. Reservations for group campsites at Central Grenadier Island. Other services, such as day use and overnight docking, are on a first-come, first-served basis. Call park office for group camping reservations (see above).

HOTELS, MOTELS, & INNS
(unless otherwise noted, rates are for a 2-person double, high season, in Canadian dollars)

Outside the park:
Gananoque, ON K7G 2T6
Glen House Resort 409 1000 Islands Pkwy., P.O. Box 10. (800) 268-4536. www.smugglersglen.com. $109–$319. Smuggler's Glen golf course on-site.

THOUSAND ISLANDS

Island hugs the **Canadian Middle Channel** and features small sandy beaches, perfect for swimming.

Thanks to the microclimate created by the Great Lakes, this area has one of the highest rates of biodiversity in Canada. Explore the phenomenon by moving from island to island.

To the east, the sandstone surface of **Grenadier Island** features a mix of trees. Slightly west, the thin acidic soil carpeting the granite of **Georgina Island** offers ideal growing conditions for pitch pine. Elsewhere, you'll find a mix of Carolinian, boreal, and mixed deciduous hardwood.

EXCURSIONS

BELLEVUE HOUSE NATIONAL HISTORIC SITE
KINGSTON, ON

The lavish home of Sir John A. Macdonald, Canada's first prime minister, has been restored to its pristine 1840s condition. Visit the sprawling period-furnished Tuscan-style villa. Join a guided tour and follow a costumed interpreter who will lead you into this historically significant home where young Macdonald lived with his wife, Isabella, and son. In the magnificent gardens discover heritage plants tended with traditional organic techniques. Open Victoria Day weekend to Thanksgiving.

FORT HENRY NATIONAL HISTORIC SITE
KINGSTON, ON

Built over five years in the 1830s, Fort Henry replaced a crumbling fort from the War of 1812. Visitors can watch (and sometimes participate in) live dramatizations of significant events from the 19th-century history of the fort. Guided tours, musical performances, and military demonstrations by the Fort Henry Guard (university student recruits trained according to British regulations) are scheduled through the season. Open mid-May to mid-September.

FORT WELLINGTON NATIONAL HISTORIC SITE
PRESCOTT, ON

Constructed between Montreal and Kingston during the War of 1812, Fort Wellington was meant to defend St. Lawrence River shipping routes. It was used for military purposes until established as a historic site in 1923. The fort offers crafts, games, and costumes for kids on Tuesdays. Explore the barracks and take part in a live cannon firing. A handful of special events, including Canada Day celebrations, guided tours, and whiskey tastings take place in the summer. Open Victoria Day weekend to Thanksgiving. (613) 925-2896.

KINGSTON FORTIFICATIONS NATIONAL HISTORIC SITE
KINGSTON, ON

The Kingston Fortifications encompass a network of sites in and around Kingston Harbour, including Fort Frederick, Fort Henry, Cathcart Tower, Murney Tower, and Shoal Tower. Together, these sites form a semicircle around the harbour and were meant to serve as defence against American invasion. In 2007, the Kingston Fortifications, along with the Rideau Canal, were designated Ontario's only UNESCO World Heritage site.

MURNEY TOWER NATIONAL HISTORIC SITE
KINGSTON, ON

Built in 1846 on a raised point southwest of Kingston Harbour, Murney Tower has been in operation as a museum since 1925. Managed by the Kingston Historical Society, it houses war and domestic artifacts from the 1800s. Taken together, Murney Tower, Shoal Tower, Cathcart Tower, and Fort Frederick Tower illustrate Kingston's contributions to the defence of British North America in the 19th century. Open mid-May to September.

SHOAL TOWER NATIONAL HISTORIC SITE
KINGSTON, ON

A squat, round-bellied structure, Shoal Tower lies opposite Kingston's City Hall. Along with Murney Tower, Cathcart Tower, and Fort Frederick Tower, Shoal was one of a quartet of defensive towers erected to protect Kingston Harbour. All four towers are examples of the Martello style—short towers with thick walls and roof-mounted artillery. Built in 1847, Shoal protected Kingston's commercial harbour as well as the entrance to the Rideau Canal. The tower is not open to the public.

Mouth of the Rouge River near Rouge Beach in Toronto

▶ NATIONAL URBAN PARK
ROUGE

ONTARIO
ESTABLISHED 2015
*79.1 sq km/30.5 sq mi once fully
established*

When you imagine a national park, a subway car isn't usually part of the picture, but you might see one in Rouge National Urban Park. It is a Canadian first—an urban park created to protect natural, cultural, and agricultural heritage. Located on the edge of Toronto, Markham, Pickering, and Uxbridge, Rouge is close to the country's largest city, yet boasts true biodiversity and opportunities for outdoor adventure.

Once fully established, Rouge National Urban Park will be the largest urban park in North America. The park is located within an hour's drive of 20 percent of the population of Canada. Stand at the edge of the park's Twyn Rivers Drive entrance, and you'll see the repetitive rooflines of a suburban neighbourhood. Turn and follow a footpath in the opposite direction though, and you're faced with panoramic bluffs, tree-lined riverbanks, and waterfront trails.

A portion of this land was once slated for further development as subdivisions. However, local individuals, organizations and levels of government spearheaded efforts to protect the area and, in 1995, it was made a municipal park. In 2012, the federal government committed to including Rouge in the Parks Canada system. As such, it eventually will increase in size from roughly 40 sq km (15.4 sq mi) to 79.1 sq km (30.5 sq mi), encompassing land in Toronto, Pickering, Markham, and Uxbridge.

Rouge is the only park under the Parks Canada umbrella that's accessible by public transit. That isn't the only reason the park is significant, though.

Lands within the Rouge have a long, rich, and diverse history of human presence and habitation extending back 11,000 years. For centuries, the Rouge formed part of an important travel and trade route for First Nations. Its lands provided many resources for hunting, fishing, and eventually farming. Today, the Rouge features a number of significant cultural sites reflective of its rich natural, cultural, and agricultural heritage.

This might have something to do with the area's fertile class-one soil. Family farms began operating here in 1799, and many still do. As Rouge National Urban Park continues to develop, new opportunities to connect visitors with agriculture and food will grow, from community gardens to farm stays, farm markets to educational programs.

Finally, the park's biodiversity includes more than 1,700 species of plants and animals. Visitors to the park can see songbirds, great horned owls, hawks, herons, and egrets, as well as the endangered Blanding's turtle. Over thousands of years, habitat loss had led to a population within the park of just six of these turtles.

However, a joint program between Parks Canada and the Toronto Zoo (which lies within park boundaries) is working to reintroduce juveniles here and thus increase the turtle population.

How to Get There

Rouge Park has multiple access points. To start at the Twyn Rivers entrance from Hwy. 401 heading north, exit Meadowvale Road northbound. Turn right at Sheppard Ave. E. and then left at Twyn Rivers Drive. The park's main parking lot is about 1.5 km (0.9 mi) down the road, on the right. To get there by subway, take the TTC eastbound (line two) to Kennedy Station. Transfer to bus 86A Scarborough towards the Toronto Zoo. Get off at the intersection of Meadowvale Road and Park Road (also known as Zoo Road). Walk 100 metres (328 ft) to the right, down Park Road. It leads to the Parks Canada Welcome Area and Rouge Valley Conservation Centre.

When to Go

Rouge Park is open year-round, with plenty of opportunities for spring, summer, fall, and winter activities, though it should be noted there's currently no trail maintenance during the winter. If you're interested in staying overnight at the onsite campground, plan your trip from May to October. Camping shuts down for the season at the beginning of November.

How to Visit

There are currently 12 km (7 mi) of hiking trails in the park, but this network is scheduled to expand significantly as land transitions to management under Parks Canada. These trails can be hiked all year long, but come winter some of them are better suited to snowshoeing and cross-country skiing.

Glen Rouge Campground, the only campground in the City of Toronto

VISTA AND ORCHARD TRAIL

Vista Trail begins at the Park Road trailhead and runs through a part of the park that's known for its rare Carolinian forests and stunning fall colours. Visitors flock to the area in September and October, when Rouge is one of the best places in the Toronto area to view fall leaves on full, vibrant display.

The Vista is a 1.5-km (0.9 mi) trail that takes roughly an hour to walk, one way. Hikers are treated to stunning views in the first 300 m (984 ft), when a viewing platform offers a full and complete look at Little Rouge Creek Valley. The steep bluffs are a highlight here. As you travel the ridges of the park, note the character of the forest—the way maple and oak dot the park's warm southern slope, while shady hemlock groves cover the cool north slopes.

The trail eventually leads into open fields where meadowlarks and yellow warblers fly overhead and sing from the trees. If you feel like extending the hike, continue on the 1.6 km (0.9 mi) **Orchard Trail.** It begins where Vista ends, at the north trail head at Twyn Rivers Drive. The Orchard Trail loops back to the wetlands at the bottom of Park Road.

When you look out at the landscape from the Vista Trail's viewing platform, it's hard to believe it once hosted a landfill. Beare Hill is all that remains of the waste site, which ceased operating in 1983. These days, the City of Toronto is revegetating the area and planning to turn the former landfill into a municipal park.

There's additional evidence of human impact along Twyn Rivers Drive. There, you'll see the stone walls of **Maxwell's Mill,** one of 14 grist and sawmills that powered local communities by harnessing the water of the Rouge River. Built in the mid-1800s, it's on the City of Toronto Inventory of Heritage Properties. The mill caught fire and burned down in the 1970s; however, its foundation can still be seen.

Elsewhere on Orchard Trail are the overgrown orchards for which the trail is named. Keep quiet and you might see whitetail deer grazing among the forgotten trees, while red-tailed hawks wheel overhead.

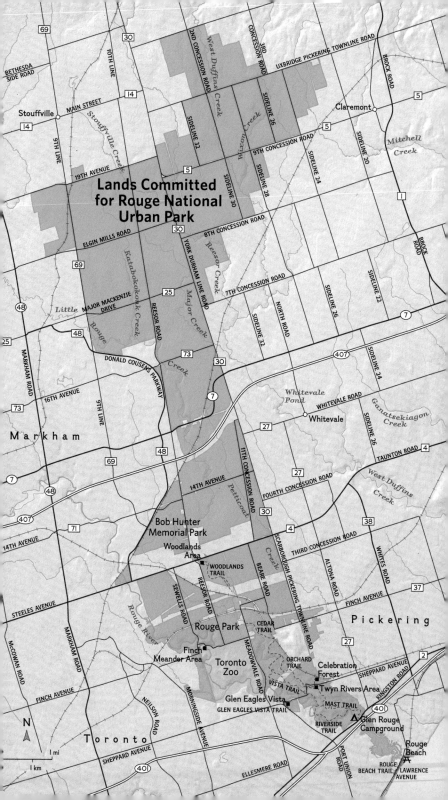

Vista Lookout in the Toronto area of the park

GLEN ROUGE CAMPGROUND AND MAST TRAIL

The only campground within the City of Toronto, **Glen Rouge** is at the south end of the park. On the banks of the Rouge River, it's not far from where the river flows from the Oak Ridges Moraine, a geological landform that runs 1,900 sq km (733 sq mi) into Lake Ontario.

One of the most popular activities in the campground is hiking the **Mast Trail.** Built 200 years ago, this path was initially cut to make way for large trees to be felled, carried out of the woods, and floated down the river to the lake. From there, they were transported to Europe and turned into ships.

Today, the Mast is a maintained 2.2-km (1.3 mi) trail that begins in the campground and ends at Twyn Rivers Drive. Though the hike is short, it's challenging. Following a ridge means there are some steep climbs and descents as the trail leads through Carolinian ecosystems. Mature trees and a lush undergrowth of ferns characterize the vegetation on this hike. Visitors can make the trip on their own, or meet up with an interpreter for one of the guided walks that are regularly scheduled by Parks Canada. They meet at the campground's south trailhead.

The campground, open to tent and RV camping, also offers washrooms, showers, playgrounds for kids, and fire pits. There are additional hiking trails and a sandy beach as well.

ROUGE BEACH AND MARSH

Near Lake Ontario, the park offers beautiful views of the water and of the largest wetland and marshes (roughly 70 hectares/173 acres) in Toronto. Because of this, it's a popular destination for those seeking gorgeous city sunsets.

Rouge Beach is sandy, perfect for swimming and picnicking. There's a 1-km (0.6 mi) trail, the Rouge Beach Trail, that can be used for walking or cycling. Boardwalks and viewing platforms offer clear, uninterrupted views of the waterfront and surrounding wetlands.

If you want to engage in more comprehensive engagement with these wetlands, plan to paddle. Note that there are no onsite canoe or kayak rentals, so you have to bring your own craft.

On-water exploration highlights the unique and distinctly urban nature of Rouge Park. If you put in at Glen Rouge Campground, you start your trip under Hwy. 401, which curves overhead. If you begin your paddle at the beach, the industry of Toronto is visible in the distance.

ROUGE NATIONAL URBAN PARK
(Parc urbain national de la Rouge)

INFORMATION & ACTIVITIES

HEADQUARTERS
3620 Kingston Rd., Toronto (416) 264-2020 (office). 105 Guildwood Plaza, P.O Box 11024, Scarborough ON M1E IN0 (mailing address). www.parkscanada.gc.ca/rouge.

SEASONS & ACCESSIBILITY
Year-round.

ENTRANCE FEE
Free.

PETS
Pets are allowed. Dogs must be leashed.

ACCESSIBLE SERVICES
Parking lots and group picnic areas are wheelchair accessible. Washrooms at **Rouge Beach** and **Glen Rouge Campground** are wheelchair-accessible. So is the marshes pathway at Rouge Beach and Vista Trail.

THINGS TO DO
The park has more than 12 km (7.4 mi) of hiking trails. There is opportunity for swimming at Rouge Beach and paddling canoes and kayaks in **Rouge Marsh** and along the river, starting at Glen Rouge Campground. Those with a valid fishing licence can fish the river. Photography is popular, especially during fall when leaves are vibrant throughout the park's Carolinian forest. Geocaching enthusiasts can search the park during daylight hours for a handful of cache sites.

SPECIAL ADVISORIES
- Watch your step on Mast Trail during wet seasons. Steep grades make for slippery conditions here. Stay on official trails, which are marked with white blazes.
- The beach is open seasonally; lifeguards are on duty from mid-May to Labour Day.

CAMPGROUNDS
Glen Rouge Campground, 7450 Kingston Rd, Scarborough, ON M1B 0B7. (416) 661-6600. info@trca.on.ca. $22–$38.

HOTELS, MOTELS, & INNS
(unless otherwise noted, rates are for a 2-person double, high season, in Canadian dollars)

Comfort Inn 533 Kingston Rd, Pickering, ON L1V 3N7, (905) 831-6200. cn291@whg.com, www.pickeringcomfortinn.com. $99–$150.
Delta Toronto 2035 Kennedy Rd, Toronto, ON M1T 3G2, (416) 299-1500 or (888) 890-3222. www.deltahotels.com/hotels/delta-toronto-east. $139–$196.
Holiday Inn Express Toronto East, 50 Estate Dr., Scarborough, ON M1H 2Z1. (416) 439-9666. whg4701@whg.com, www.ihg.com/holidayinnexpress/hotels/us/en/scarborough/yyzex/hoteldetail. $120–$160.
Monte Carlo Inns Downtown Markham 7255 Warden Ave, Markham, ON L3R 1B4. (905) 752-2700. reservation@montecarloinns.com, www.montecarloinns.com/downtown-markham-suites/downtown-markham. $109–$200.

However, in the 3 km (1.8 mi) of tranquil water between the two spots, paddling the marsh is like gliding through the waters of a savannah. Herons hide in the whispering cattails. A variety of aquatic bird species swim and paddle.

Paddlers wind their way through one of the few remaining marshes along the north shore of Lake Ontario.

Vegetation cover here declined in the second half of the 20th century, with low water levels and considerable carp activity partially responsible for what are now mud flats and open water. Recent recovery efforts have been positive, however: There have been sightings of the provincially rare black tern, Blanding's turtle, and the American bittern.

The Canadian Shield landscape in Georgian Bay Islands National Park dates to the Precambrian era.

▶ GEORGIAN BAY ISLANDS

ONTARIO
ESTABLISHED 1930
14 sq km/3,459 acres

Windswept white pine, rock faces scraped bare, and wide, wild waters number among the most prominent features of Georgian Bay Islands National Park. These characteristics are what drew a collective of painters—known as the Group of Seven—to the area during the 1920s. Their paintings, done in strong, bold brushstrokes, wove the park into the fabric of the Canadian national identity.

A frontcountry park with backcountry scenery, Georgian Bay's vistas and accessibility make it a popular destination. Beausoleil is the park's largest island, with facilities including docks, 105 campsites, 10 waterfront cabins, and five oTENTiks (a cross between a tent and a cabin). It also boasts a network of 11 well-marked and groomed trails, ranging from walking paths to more difficult scrambles across the Precambrian rock of the Canadian Shield.

Beausoleil's size has made it a popular seasonal stopover for centuries. Indigenous people first used the island as a base for hunting and trading as far back as 7,000 years ago. Early voyageurs marked it as a midpoint on their travels between the Severn River and north Georgian Bay.

The southeast side of Beausoleil hosts evidence of a 19th-century Ojibway village, abandoned when the poor quality of the island's thin, acidic soil drove the community west to more arable environs.

While Beausoleil's glaciated ridges proved too rugged to work, they were perfect for recreational properties. Evidence of the Georgian Bay cottage boom of the early 1900s surrounds the park. Thanks to a handful of locals, whose petitions led the government to establish the park in 1929, visitors can still find pristine beauty among the 63 park islands and islets that pepper the shore between Honey Harbour and Twelve Mile Bay. Though all islands are open to the public, Beausoleil is the only one offering trails, docking facilities, washrooms, cabins, camping, and picnic tables.

How to Get There

From Toronto, 166 km (103 mi) south of the park, get on Hwy. 400 N. Take exit 156 and follow the signs for Honey Harbour Road/Regional Road 5. From Sudbury, 240 km (149 mi) north of the park, take Hwy. 69 S to Hwy. 400 S. Then take exit 162 toward White's Falls Road. Turn right at South Bay Road and follow it to Honey Harbour Road/Regional Road 5.

The gateway to the park is located at the Parks Canada Operations Base, across from the Honey Harbour Towne Centre. A sign at the left of the road directs you downhill to the docks, where you can catch the park's *Day Tripper* to Beausoleil (*www.parkscana da.gc.ca/pn-np/on/georg/index.aspx*).

When to Go

During summer, Georgian Bay churns with the chop of powerboats. Even experienced paddlers should wait until the end of August, when visitor numbers drop and boating slows down. During fall, the water is calm, the campsites quiet, and the trails less travelled. Late September to early October is the best time to see the stunning fall foliage for which southwestern Ontario is so well known. The park's paths are quilted with a patchwork of leaves in shades of scarlet and cinnamon.

The park is closed in winter.

How to Visit

For an afternoon visit, book a seat on the *Day Tripper* to **Beausoleil** and hike a leisurely 5.5-km (3.4 mi) loop around the south end of the island. If you have a full day, explore the immense diversity of the park. Though small, Georgian Bay Islands is home to more than 600 plant and animal species. Beausoleil also marks Ontario's north-south transition zone. Cycling or hiking the island's **Huron Trail** highlights the dramatic differences between the two regions.

The park's primitive campsites are considered frontcountry camping due to constant activity on the bay. Mimic a backcountry experience with a weekend trip at the end of September, when you're likely to pass days without seeing anyone. Rent a kayak in nearby Waubaushene, establish a base camp on Beausoleil, and hike out to the **Beausoleil Island Light Range.** If you happen to have your own boat, you may wish to explore the surrounding islands as well.

SOUTH END OF BEAUSOLEIL ISLAND

5.5 km/3.4 mi return; 3 to 4 hours

Unless you have your own boat, you'll need to book transportation in advance. Parks Canada runs the *Day Tripper* out of Honey Harbour.

This modified, open-air barge-style boat makes a 15-minute trip across the azure waters of Georgian Bay to **Beausoleil Island** an average of four times daily. Water taxis are also available through the Honey Harbour Boat Club Marina northeast of the Delawana Inn.

Disembark at Cedar Spring (the main visitor hub of the park and the *Day Tripper*'s southern drop-off point) on the southeast side of the island, where you'll find a picnic area, cabins, oTENTiks, campsites, and washroom facilities. Behind the visitor kiosk is the trailhead for the 1.5-km (0.9 mi) **Lookout Trail**. Follow it through the open meadows that skirt **Papoose Bay** and into cool forests of beech and maple. Lookouts afford views of the bay and the forest canopy from 210 m (689 ft) above sea level.

When the path forks off to the right, keep straight and follow the

Huron Trail south toward **Beausoleil Point.** Midland and Penetanguishene, where William Beausoleil, a Métis settler, lived during the 1800s, lie across the water. From there, take **Georgian Trail** north to **Christian Beach,** where a stretch of shore alternates between sand and cobblestones. If you can, time this trek so you're hiking here later in the day, when sunset stains the horizon and sets the bay ablaze.

Once you reach Christian Beach, follow Christian Trail to the right. This leads through stands of balsam fir and hemlock as the path crosses the island and meets back up with the Heritage Trail loop.

END-TO-END HIKE OF BEAUSOLEIL

13 km/8 mi one way; a full day

Take the *Day Tripper* to Honeymoon Bay at the north tip of Beausoleil, where you can gear up for a day-long hike or choose from among a handful of trails that piggyback off one another as they loop south. To the east, **Fairy Trail** passes **Goblin** and **Fairy Lakes,** both noted hot spots for loon sightings. Jog left to take the **Cambrian Trail** through quintessential Canadian Shield country. Scores of white pine twist up from the rock and cobalt-coloured waves lap the shore as you hike along **Little Dog Channel.**

Cambrian eventually cuts to **Chimney Bay,** where it merges with the Fairy Trail. Walk west for 15 minutes and take the **Massasauga Trail** to **Huron**—the island's longest trail. You'll pass **Camp Kitchikewana,** a YMCA camp that has operated on the island since 1919. Veer left at the **Treasure Trail.** This easy 3.8-km (2.3 mi) hike moves through forest and along the shoreline below

Treasure Bay, where Caspian terns, mallards, and kingfishers dip and dabble. Ospreys also frequent the area, thanks to the conservation efforts of the Georgian Bay Osprey Society. At **Honeymoon Bay,** you can see an example of the platforms this group erects to keep the birds from nesting on power poles.

Farther along the trail is the brush-covered clearing where the Ojibway abandoned their settlement in 1856. Here, gnarled white pine and juniper give way to deciduous species like sugar maple and beech. This is a prime example of "edge effect." Beausoleil Island marks a shift from the hardwood forests of the Great Lakes–St. Lawrence Lowlands to the boreal forests that stretch north toward Hudson Bay.

You'll also notice the granite, so prominent at Honeymoon Bay, disappears as you move south. Twenty thousand to 40,000 years ago, glaciers scoured away the soil and carved depressions into the rock at Beausoleil's north end. The resulting harsh

Fairy Lake

Roasting marshmallows

An autumn bike ride

topography is ideal for the island's sphagnum mosses, lichens, and hardy pines. As you follow Huron south to Beausoleil Point, however, you'll find the land (where layers of rich glacial till were dumped) lies in lush contrast.

GEORGIAN BAY

11 km/7 mi one way; 2 days

The eastern shore of Georgian Bay is the world's largest freshwater archipelago. Plentiful islands and shelter from Lake Huron make it a paddler's dream. However, peak season kayaking is only encouraged for confident paddlers. Canoes are always best left to the shoulder seasons, when there is less motorboat traffic.

Put in at Honey Harbour and stay close to the shore as you follow **Main Channel** north. Pass **Little Beausoleil Island** on the left and slip between **Deer Island** and Beausoleil. Continue along **Main Channel**, between **Frying Pan Bay** and **Tomahawk Island.**

A single campsite with 13 tent pads abuts the docks at Honeymoon Bay. Cook dinner on the wood stove in a nearby pavilion and take in spectacular views of the **North Channel**. At night, store food securely in the animal-proof lockers located in the picnic shelter. In midsummer, when berries are ripening but not edible, opportunistic black bears visit the islands looking for food. You'll also want to protect your cache from bold, smaller mammals like raccoons, squirrels, and chipmunks.

On day two, hike the windy western shore. Trails at the north end are marked by coloured blazes posted on poles according to sight lines. Follow the Fairy Trail to the **Rockview Trail,** but watch your step. The granite is branded with age-old evidence of retreating glaciers, including smiling chatter lines and thick bands of snow white quartz. The rock also acts as prime sunbathing space for the at-risk eastern Massasauga rattlesnake. Though venomous, the Massasauga is a timid snake. If you come across one, keep a wide berth and note its location for Parks Canada staff, who monitor the reptiles.

As Rockview heads south, it meets up with the **Dossyonshing Trail.** Stunning views of **Long Bay, Lost Bay,** and **Turtle Bay** make this 2.5-km (1.5 mi) side trip worthwhile. The Georgian Trail, a short rutted route, passes through wetlands on its way to the **Georgian Island Range Light,** established in 1900.

GEORGIAN BAY ISLANDS NATIONAL PARK
(Parc national des Îles-de-la-Baie-Georgienne)

INFORMATION & ACTIVITIES

VISITOR & INFORMATION CENTRE
Welcome Centre open daily in summer; five days a week in spring and fall.

SEASONS & ACCESSIBILITY
Park open from mid-May (Victoria Day long weekend) to mid-October (Thanksgiving). The park consists of 63 islands accessible by boat from Honey Harbour. Docking is available at **Beausoleil Island,** and private marinas are nearby in Honey Harbour. *Day Tripper* boat service and kiosk on Beausoleil Island open daily in summer; five days a week during spring and fall.

HEADQUARTERS
Administrative Office 901 Wye Valley Rd., Box 9, Midland, ON L4R 4K6. Phone (705) 527-7200. www.parkscanada .gc.ca/gbi.

ENTRANCE FEES
$6 per person per day; $29 per season.

PETS
Pets must be on a leash and attended at all times.

ACCESSIBLE SERVICES
Full access on Beausoleil Island with wheelchair-accessible washrooms, showers, and camping at Cedar Spring Campground. Two of the campsites are fully accessible.

THINGS TO DO
Sailing, boating, and fishing (Ontario sport angling licence required). Beaches for swimming on Beausoleil Island. Also, hiking and cycling on designated trails.

SPECIAL ADVISORY
• Check weather forecasts before sailing.

OVERNIGHT BACKPACKING
8 primitive campgrounds available on a first-come, first-served basis. All camping must be at designated campgrounds.

CAMPGROUNDS
All campsites are tenting only. Maximum 6 people with 2 tents. **Cedar Spring Campground** (main campground) has 45 sites (all reservable), comfort stations with flush toilets, potable water, Visitor Centre. $26 per site per night. Book at res ervation.pc.gc.ca. Primitive (backcountry) campgrounds: 11 primitive campgrounds around **Beausoleil Island** have 5-13 sites each and must be reached by boat. $16 per night. First-come, first-served sites with self-registration. Includes tent pad or platform, picnic table, hibachi, outhouse or composting toilets, picnic shelter. No running water. The park boat shuttle *Day Tripper* is not able to transport campers. Please bring own boat or arrange private water taxi.

HOTELS, MOTELS, & INNS
(unless otherwise noted, rates are for a 2-person double, high season, in Canadian dollars)

Outside the park:
Delawana Resort 42 Delawana Rd., Honey Harbour, ON P0E 1E0. (888) 557-2980. www.delawana.com. $250–$300; two-night minimum.
Christie's Mill Inn and Spa 263 Port Severn Rd. N, Port Severn, ON L0K 1S0. (705) 538-2354 or (800) 465-9966. www.christiesmill.com. $179–$299; two-night minimum.
1875 A Charters Inn B&B 290 Second St., Midland, ON L4R 3R1. (705) 527-1572 or (800) 724-2979. www.chartersinn.com. $149–$199, breakfast included. Private charters to Georgian Bay islands available.

EXCURSIONS

BETHUNE MEMORIAL HOUSE NATIONAL HISTORIC SITE
GRAVENHURST, ON

Visit the childhood home of Canadian humanitarian Dr. Norman Bethune, best known for his role as a prominent surgeon during the Spanish Civil War and the Sino-Japanese War of the late 1930s. This picturesque Victorian house offers private guided tours, interpretive talks, and large expanses of manicured lawn and garden. Many commemorative gifts from visiting Chinese delegates decorate the visitor centre. Open June to October. (705) 687-4261.

MNJIKANING FISH WEIRS NATIONAL HISTORIC SITE
ATHERLEY, ON

Located at Atherley Narrows near Orillia, the Mnjikaning Fish Weirs were used as a fishing site and meeting place by indigenous people more than 5,000 years ago. A system of underwater wooden fences, the weirs were used by the Huron and Anishinaabe until the 20th century. Parks Canada works with the Mnjikaning Fish Fence Circle to preserve and promote the site. No facilities. Open year-round.

▶ NATIONAL MARINE CONSERVATION AREA

FATHOM FIVE
TOBERMORY, ONTARIO

Fathom Five plucked its moniker from Shakespeare's *The Tempest:* "Full fathom five thy father lies; Of his bones are coral made; Those are pearls that were his eyes: Nothing of him that doth fade." A fitting namesake considering the purpose of the park is preservation.

FATHOM FIVE

A diver explores a historic shipwreck in Fathom Five National Marine Conservation Area.

Largely underwater, Fathom Five (114 sq km/28,170 acres) was established in 1971 to protect its unique aquatic ecosystem as well as the many shipwrecks that litter its shoals. In 1987, the park was transferred to the federal government. It is also the sister park to Bruce Peninsula National Park (see pp. 142–147).

The water clarity here, caused by a natural absence of silt and algae, makes for first-rate scuba diving. Visitors can dive the coastal caves or snorkel the skeletal remains of 19th-century schooners that carried supplies between the villages on Georgian Bay. If you prefer to stay dry, book a cruise with one of two private boat companies or rent a canoe or kayak from a local outfitter.

BOAT CRUISES: The Blue Heron Company (855-596-2999, *www .blueheronco.com*), mid-May to mid-October. Bruce Anchor Cruises (519) 596-2555, *www.bruceanchor.com*), mid-May to mid-October.

There are several options for exploring Fathom Five, from jet-boat shuttles to Flower Pot Island to scenic glass-bottom boats and sunset cruises. Departure times are date-dependent, so check the websites for current information. Tickets can be bought onsite or online before departure.

Hop on a Zodiac boat and zip over to **Flowerpot Island**. The 15-minute option goes straight there, while a longer 25-minute tour passes over two shipwrecks—the *Sweepstakes* schooner and the *City of Grand*

▶ NATIONAL MARINE CONSERVATION AREA

Dolomite rock formations on Flowerpot Island

Rapids steamer—before heading to the island. If you'd like more time to observe the wrecks, sign up for a two-hour tour aboard the *Great Blue Heron*. This glass-bottom boat offers eerie, incredible views of the shipwrecks in **Big Tub Harbour** before it completes a circle around the islands.

The *Blue Heron V* allows for the same glass-bottom view of the harbour floor but skips the smaller islands in favour of a long look at Flowerpot Island. You also have the option to disembark at **Beachy Cove** and explore the island's hiking trails and lighthouse, but you must make this decision when you buy your ticket.

During peak season (June–early Sept.), you can sign up for a two-hour sunset cruise along the northern coast of the Bruce Peninsula all the way to Cave Point. Departure times vary, so be sure to call ahead for information.

(Note that while the larger tour boats accommodate strollers and wheelchairs, the Zodiac boats do not, so plan accordingly.)

DIVING: Some of the most incredible sights (and interesting stories) in Fathom Five lie below the waves. Not only is the park home to submerged cliffs, overhangs, and underwater waterfalls, it also acts as the final resting place for more than 20 different shipwrecks. The frigid freshwater temperature here (even during summer it can drop to a mere 4°C/39°F 30 m/98.4 ft down) and the absence of marine ecosystems helps preserve the remains, another part of the reason Tobermory is known as the scuba-diving capital of Canada.

All divers must register and obtain dive tags at the visitor centre on Chi sin tib dek Road before the first dive of each season. Book lessons and rentals in Tobermory. Located in Little Tub Harbour, Divers Den (519-596-2363, *www.diversden.ca*) offers everything from basic open water training to advanced technical certifications, including night diving and peak performance buoyancy up to the Divemaster level. It operates from mid-May through October but is open year-round to answer questions and accept bookings.

Walk-on scuba and snorkelling charters make regular departures for popular sites, including the *W.L. Wetmore* (a storm-wrecked ship off **Russel Island** that's suitable for divers and snorkellers) and the caves at the **Grotto** along the Georgian Bay shoreline. Phone ahead, as schedules vary from spring to fall. If you want to visit a combination of dive sites not included in the standard schedule, ask about tailoring a tour. Dive boats can be booked for full and half days.

Be sure to ask your guide for the history of the wrecks you're diving. The *Newaygo*, a massive steam barge, ran aground in a snowstorm in 1903. The *Arabia,* a barque that foundered off **Echo Island** in the 1800s, lay undiscovered for almost a hundred years. It wasn't until the 1970s, when fishermen in the area noticed their catches coming up with bellies full of corn scavenged from the supplies aboard the ship, that people realized the massive wreck sat 34 m (111.5 ft) down.

G & S Watersports (519-596-2200, *www.gswatersports.net*), located in Little Tub Harbour, also provides diving services.

PADDLING: You can explore the waters of Fathom Five by kayak, canoe, or paddleboard. Check Thorncrest Outfitters (888-345-2925, *www.thorncrestoutfitters.com*) for reasonably priced rentals from mid-June to mid-September. The Tobermory store is located on Hwy. 6, just across the road from the turnoff to Little Tub Harbour. Note that you must arrange any necessary park permits on your own as they are not included in rental fees.

Kayaking is an ideal way to discover the endless coves of Fathom Five's many islands and inlets. First-timers can book a tour of the Tub. This full-day paddle is the perfect introduction to sea kayaking on Georgian Bay and comes complete with certified guides, safety gear, and lunch. More experienced paddlers can head all the way out to Flowerpot Island for an overnight camping trip.

If you intend to do this, be sure to book well in advance (the island's six sites start to fill up as soon as registration opens in early May), and remember to take extra food and water, as weather conditions on the bay can delay departures.

Beachy Cove, on the south side of the island, hosts the only docks on Flowerpot. Campsites are a short walk west on the **Loop Trail.** From here, continue northeast along the trail, past the towering sea stacks that give the island its name. Just beyond the second flowerpot is a large cave with an observation deck. Farther along the path is the stunning **Castle Bluff** light station. The light itself is automated now, but volunteers with Friends of Fathom Five offer tours of the original keeper's house.

During the summer, the island is also staffed with Parks Canada employees who can answer your questions about Fathom Five and Bruce Peninsula.

Flowerpot is the only island with trails and camping, although day use is permitted on all the others. Though the marine park is one of the most ecologically healthy places on the Great Lakes, the food web is in a period of change. A long legacy of invasive species and overfishing, compounded with more recent climate change and coastal development stresses, is transforming the ecosystem. Currently, invasive mussel species are depleting many of the nutrients native species rely on, but natural populations (including lake trout, cisco, and sturgeon) are making a slow, steady comeback.

Fathom Five Parks Canada Visitor Centre, Chi sin tib dek Road, Tobermory, phone (519) 596-2233 ext. 0.

The brilliant blue water of Georgian Bay, Bruce Peninsula National Park

▶ BRUCE PENINSULA

ONTARIO
ESTABLISHED 1987
125 sq km/30,888 acres

The Bruce Peninsula is a 100-km (62 mi) finger of land that cleaves the waves between Lake Huron and Georgian Bay. Though water temperatures here are frigid, the shores seem more lagoon than lake. The sheer limestone face of the Niagara Escarpment—the fossilized edge of a 430-million-year-old saltwater sea—rises 40 m (131 ft) from the tropical turquoise of the bay within the park.

When Bruce Peninsula National Park was formed in 1987, it included lands formerly known as Cyprus Lake Provincial Park (est. 1966). The park was created to protect the spectacular shoreline and rock formations of the Niagara Escarpment. In 1990, portions of the peninsula were designated as part of the Niagara Escarpment UNESCO World Biosphere Reserve. Here, you'll find the northern terminus of the famous Bruce Trail. At 843 km (524 mi), the Bruce is the oldest and longest hiking trail in Canada. It begins in the town of Tobermory and runs all the way to Niagara, connecting 105 parks and protected areas scattered across the most populated part of Canada. The 35 km (22 mi) of the trail that lie within park boundaries show off what the Bruce is best known for—crystal clear waters, karst formations, cobblestone beaches, and rocky cliffs.

Bayside forests, in jewelled shades of emerald and aqua, look lush as any exotic locale.

The thin soil cover (a reminder of the glaciers that scraped the land 15,000 years ago) makes for harsh growing conditions. Regardless, a diversity of plant and animal life thrives here. Pine grows in the dry areas; tamarack in the wet. Sugar maple takes root in deep soil and eastern white cedar grows everywhere. The park is also home to the at-risk eastern Massasauga rattlesnake and Canada's southernmost population of black bears.

How to Get There

The park is located 100 km (62 mi) from Owen Sound. Take Hwy. 6 N through Shallow Lake and Wiarton. The highway ends at the tip of the Bruce Peninsula. Arriving in Tobermory, turn right on Chi sin tib dek Road, which winds through the woods for 1.3 km (less than 1 mi) before reaching the visitor centre.

When to Go

If you're after scenery and solitude, visit the park during the shoulder seasons. In spring, wildflowers carpet the forest floor and the sky fills with migrating birds. Autumn offers stunning fall colour and ideal hiking weather. If you plan on water-based exploration (swimming, diving, and kayaking), consider braving the crowds. Water temperature remains low year-round but reaches its peak, around 22°C (71°F), in summer.

How to Visit

The visitor centre mixes education with exercise. Indoor exhibits are hands-on, offering a comprehensive overview of Bruce Peninsula and Fathom Five. Outside, the Burnt

Point Loop and Lookout Tower allow you to stretch your legs.

For a full-day adventure, park at Cyprus Lake Campground and hike to the bayfront Grotto and Indian Head Cove. Afterward, cross the highway and try one of the lakeside loops at Singing Sands.

If you're going to be around for a few days, plan to go backcountry camping at Stormhaven and High Dump, catch a sunrise at Halfway Log Dump, and hike a section of the Bruce Trail.

VISITOR CENTRE & AROUND

3.5 km/2 mi; 2.5 to 4 hours

Drive toward Tobermory on Hwy. 6. Turn right at Chi sin tib dek Road and follow it to the centre. Your admission fee here acts as a day-use pass for the centre and the nearby tower and trails, as well as Flowerpot Island in Fathom Five (see p. 139).

The **visitor centre** features a permanent multilevel exhibit that showcases the past and present of the national parks on the Bruce Peninsula. See photographs of each of the 42 species of orchid that grow within the parks, catch a screening in the movie theatre, and check out the various artifacts salvaged from Fathom Five, including the original 1897 lantern from the light station at Flowerpot Island.

Outside, at the edge of the parking lot is **Lookout Tower.** This 20-m (66 ft) wooden structure allows for spectacular views of Tobermory's two harbours and the ribbon of escarpment cliffs that edge the shore. The Fathom Five Islands are also visible from here. According to Anishinaabe tradition, the floodwaters from the

Canoeing at Cypress Lake

Yellow lady's slippers

animals, like fishers, that require a great deal of space.

Head back down the tower and follow an 800-m (2,624 ft) trail to a small lookout platform on Little Dunks Bay. This is the trailhead for **Burnt Point Loop**—a 3.3-km (2.1 mi) path dotted with a boulder beach and lookouts where you can see Cove Island, Flowerpot Island, and Bear's Rump Island. Clamber into any one of a dozen nooks in the rocks to take a breather and enjoy the view before looping back through the forest.

breaching of giant beaver dams created the islands 9,100 years ago. Before that, they were part of a land bridge that connected the peninsula to Manitoulin Island.

Look inland, to the south, to see the largest contiguous forest in southwestern Ontario. This entire area was logged in the late 1800s, so much of the surrounding forest is new growth. The wide, uninterrupted cover provides the perfect habitat for

NORTH & SOUTH SHORE HIKES

12 km/7.4 mi return; a full day

From Hwy. 6, take Cyprus Lake Rd. to the heart of the park, Cyprus Lake Campground (about 5 km/3 mi into the woods), and register at the office. Park in the lot at the trailhead. Take **Horse Lake Trail** north. The wide path snakes between towering trees, passing marshlands and **Horse Lake** en route to a boulder-strewn beach. Turn left and follow the white blazes of the **Bruce Trail.** The going is tough here.

The shallow water at **Indian Head Cove** is popular for swimming. Check before swimming, as conditions are often rough with strong undertows. Cliff diving is prohibited. Two minutes west is the **Grotto**—a must-see cave, carved into the rock by centuries of pounding waves. You can climb down into the Grotto, but watch your step. There are no handrails or stairs here. Inside, the cave is otherworldly. Algae and lichens decorate the dolomite ceiling. The water glows a brilliant blue-green where sunlight from an underwater tunnel filters through from the bay.

Back on the Bruce Trail, hike a rugged section west past **Boulder Beach** to **Overhanging Point.** A wave-cut hollow in the soft shale at the base of the escarpment has created a dense, narrow dolostone point that stretches out over the water.

Take the Bruce Trail back to Boulder Beach and turn right to follow **Marr Lake Trail** to **Cyprus Lake Trail.** The 5-km (3 mi) path skirts the perimeter of **Cyprus Lake** where a day-use area allows for swimming and canoeing on the inland lake.

Once you've returned to the parking lot, drive out of the campground and turn right on Hwy. 6. Take the first left, Dorcas Bay Rd., to **Singing Sands.** The view from the south side

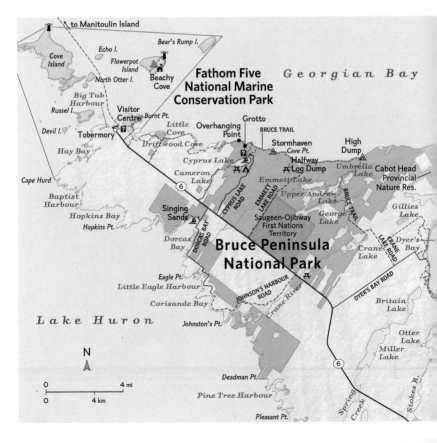

of the peninsula is vastly different from the north. The beaches, dunes, fens, and forests of Singing Sands are dotted with rare and delicate species like the dwarf lake iris and Indian plantain.

The 200-m (656 ft) **Boardwalk Loop** is an easy stroll. If you have the time, try the 3-km (1.8 mi) **Forest Beach Loop.** The slight, sandy hills of the woods here host rare and delicate flowers like the purple fringed orchid. The peninsula is also home to more than 165 species of breeding birds, and bird-watchers may spot warblers, thrushes, and shorebirds. Spend the night at Cyprus Lake Campground.

BACKCOUNTRY OVERNIGHT

13 km/8 mi one way; 2 days

From the trailhead at Cyprus Lake Campground, take **Horse Lake Trail.** Pick up the Bruce Trail and, for stunning views, turn left to follow it to the Grotto. Explore the surrounding area, including Indian Head Cove

and the **Natural Arch.** The Arch has two openings, both above lake level, making it more of a swiss cheese–style hole in the shorescape than an enclosed cave. Then follow the Bruce Trail east to **Halfway Rock Point,** with Flowerpot Island and Bear's Rump Island visible to the north.

Stormhaven lies 2 km (1.2 mi) beyond. One of only two backcountry campgrounds in the park, this terraced dolostone site offers nine tent pads, bear poles to secure food, and a shared composting toilet. Be sure to book your stay well in advance, as these beachfront sites are popular with hikers and kayakers.

After dark, look up as well as around. Bruce Peninsula was designated a Dark Sky Preserve (see pp. 72–73) in 2009. The absence of light pollution in the area makes the park one of only three places (along with nearby Manitoulin Island and the centre of Algonquin Provincial Park) in southern Ontario where you can see the night sky as it appeared two generations ago.

Wake early to catch a stunning sunrise, then continue 8.8 km

A visitor enjoys one of the cross-country skiing trails in Bruce Peninsula National Park.

BRUCE PENINSULA NATIONAL PARK
(Parc national de la Péninsule-Bruce)

INFORMATION & ACTIVITIES

VISITOR CENTRE
Visitor centre Chi sin tib dek Rd., Tobermory. Open Victoria Day weekend to Canada Day and Labour Day to Thanksgiving, Thursday to Monday. Open daily from Canada Day to Labour Day. Closed winter.

SEASONS & ACCESSIBILITY
Park open year-round but with limited services in off-season.

HEADQUARTERS
P.O. Box 189, Tobermory, ON N0H 2R0. Phone (519) 596-2233. bruce-fathom five@pc.gc.ca; www.pc.cg.ca/bruce.

FRIENDS OF BRUCE PENINSULA
Friends of the Bruce District Parks Association www.castlebluff.com.

ENTRANCE FEES
Contact park for current fees.

PETS
Pets must be kept on a leash of 2 m (6.5 ft) or less at all times.

ACCESSIBLE SERVICES
Wheelchair-accessible campsites, an accessible yurt, and trail to Burnt Point Lookout. All-terrain wheelchair available at Cyprus Lake Campground office.

THINGS TO DO
Hiking, swimming, bouldering, canoeing, and kayaking at Cyprus, Cameron, and Emmett Lakes. In winter, cross-country skiing, snowshoeing, and winter camping. Interpretive programs throughout summer; inquire for other times of the year.

SPECIAL ADVISORIES
• Check with park staff for safety tips if kayaking or canoeing in the park.
• Fires only in designated fire pits.
• Use only locally purchased firewood.
• Campgrounds fill up in July and August. Reservations strongly recommended.
• Parking lots fill up in July and August.
• Alcohol permitted at registered campsites only.
• Water from natural sources should be boiled.

CAMPGROUNDS
Cyprus Lake Campground 242 drive-in sites (about 10 are yurts) with picnic tables, fire pits with grills, firewood, potable water taps, and washroom buildings (toilets), $24; $16 per site for winter camping. 3 drive-in group sites, $5 per person, minimum 12 people. Backcountry camping in **Stormhaven** and **High Dump,** 9 sites each with tent platforms and shared primitive composting toilet. Garbage must be carried out. Preregistration required, $10 per person. For reservations, visit www reservations.parkscanada.gc.ca or call Cyprus Office: (519) 596-2263 (May–Oct.), (519) 596-2233 (Nov.–April).

HOTELS, MOTELS, & INNS
For accommodations information visit www.tobermory.com.

(5.4 mi) east along the Bruce Trail to **High Dump.** The trail here moves back and forth between cedar forest and cliffside walkways. Frothy turquoise waves wash over the rocks at the base of dramatic drops. The views from these dizzying lookouts are striking.

The same rules that apply at the campground at Stormhaven also apply at High Dump: Book well in advance, and be sure to bring a camp stove, as fires are prohibited.

For additional information on the Bruce Trail, pick up a copy of the latest edition of the detailed *Bruce Trail Reference,* available from the Bruce Trail Conservancy *(http://brucetrail.org).*

Canada's Boreal Regions

Canada's boreal landscape is home to billions of migratory birds and some of the world's largest populations of wolves, bears, caribou, and moose. Hundreds of First Nations communities exist in these areas that stretch from Labrador in eastern Canada and move across Quebec, Ontario, Manitoba, Saskatchewan, Alberta, and British Columbia. To the north, the boreal taiga and tundra continue until the high Arctic. These taiga and tundra regions continue into Alaska and to the Pacific Ocean.

Forested woodland view along the Beach Trail, Pukaskwa National Park

Here megafauna such as grizzly and polar bears, elk, moose, and woodland caribou live alongside small mammals like beaver, wolverine, otter, and fox. Range areas for boreal taiga caribou herds in the tens of thousands cover millions of acres. Woodland boreal caribou face many risks and are now listed as threatened. Efforts to make sure we keep secure migratory bird habitats mean increases in bird-watching, citizen bird counts, and celebrations of six billion songbirds that migrate through Canada's boreal forest regions each year.

Some of the largest lakes in the world, and rivers that dominate huge continental watersheds, define the Canadian boreal. Tens of thousands of lakes and hundreds of rivers from these regions supply water to most Canadian communities. There is very little private land in these boreal regions; most boreal lands and waters in Canada are publicly owned. Most boreal lands are also historic traditional lands for Canada's indigenous peoples.

The last 35 years have seen dramatic expansion of forestry operations, mineral exploration and new mines, road building, and protected lands in Canada's boreal regions. New national parks and protected areas established by provincial governments are a response to this expansion of resource extraction. Today we are much more aware of what Canada's boreal regions mean to us now and into the future. Canadians have also steadily, over the last 25 years, indicated in national polls their concern for the future of our boreal forests—and preference to keep these regions intact, healthy, and protected.

Natural resource extraction permits and licences have been issued without regional, lands planning, or remedial plans. In fact, development of the oil sands in Canada's west-central boreal region could affect an estimated 13.8 million ha (34.1 million acres) of boreal forest. Today, in part due to the dramatic growth of the oil sands, Canadians are demanding planning *before* resource extraction. They want to see the establishment of national parks and protected lands. Canadians also know that stewardship of the boreal regions is a moral and international responsibility for today and for future generations. Permitting and licensing oil sands operations requires extensive environmental assessment. Companies are required to remediate and reclaim 100 percent of the land after oil sands extraction. The standard for reclamation is a self-sustaining ecosystem with local wildlife and vegetation

During the same 35 years, Canada's constitution was repatriated and its Charter of Rights guaranteed aboriginal rights. Certain court rulings defining aboriginal rights arose from boreal regions and communities. The consultations and negotiations between governments that resulted include maintaining the natural world, stewardship of boreal lands and waters, and establishment of newly protected areas. National parks establishment steps now must include any First Nation or aboriginal community that considers itself affected by a new park proposal.

Climate change is causing everything in Canada's boreal regions to move and shift, even the land, and is adversely affecting boreal communities, species, infrastructure, rivers, and forests. More than 1,500 international scientists led by Nobel Prize–winning authors for the United Nations' Intergovernmental Panel on Climate Change have recommended that at least half of Canada's boreal forest be protected from any industrial activities. Yet permafrost, which normally begins to appear well below 60° N, then gradually expands northward, is now melting. Mackenzie River Valley reports documented the drastic results of this melting, and other studies have shown its impact on northern and Arctic communities.

Canada's boreal forests continue to provide services in the face of climate change. They scrub toxins from the water and air and help maintain river and lake ecosystems. They also store much of the world's terrestrial carbon, making boreal regions the second lung of the world.

Today Canada's boreal lands are a huge laboratory, where both stewardship and monitoring have become urgent in order to protect communities, species, and the economy of these regions. Scientists and concerned citizens are rushing to keep up with the movement of species, changes in range areas, and identification of species that will tell us the most about taking care of boreal regions in the future. Today woodland caribou are the bellwether for the future of Canada's boreal forests.

— GAILE WHELAN ENNS, *Director, Manitoba Wildlands*

CANADA'S BOREAL REGIONS

Explore the secrets of the marshlands by canoe with a park interpreter.

▶ POINT PELEE

ONTARIO
ESTABLISHED 1918
15 sq km/3,707 acres

In May, the skies of Point Pelee National Park fill with feathers. Each year the lush Carolinian forests that stretch between the Mississippi River and the Appalachian Mountains to this, the southernmost tip of mainland Canada, are the stopping point for more than 392 species of migrating birds.

Point Pelee National Park has little of the rugged wilderness that characterizes most Canadian parks. Located south of 42° N latitude, it lies in line with northern California and parts of the Mediterranean. Crickets chirp and hum past dusk, even in October, and the sycamore trees here drip with Virginia creeper. Grape vines twist through the trails, creating an exotic jungle aesthetic. There are very few coniferous trees in Point Pelee, despite the fact that their presence here first piqued mass interest in the region.

In the late 1700s, British naval reserves logged the point's white pine for shipbuilding. Eventually, Lake Erie's ample supply of trout, whitefish, and herring drew fisheries, which gave way to farming and finally hunting. Oddly enough, the latter is what led to the park's creation.

In 1882, while duck hunting, naturalist W. E. Saunders was so bowled over by the diversity of birds at Point

Pelee that he helped found the Great Lakes Ornithological Club—the same organization that played a major role in establishing Point Pelee National Park in 1918.

Pelee, one of few national sites where sport hunting and private ownership were still allowed, quickly became a recreational hot spot. By the 1960s the park had hosted more than 700,000 visitors. A total of 6,000 parking spots couldn't accommodate daily demand. The natural ecosystem was so destroyed that Point Pelee was nearly removed from Canada's list of national parks.

In 1972, a restoration framework was drafted to govern visitor access to the park. Anything alien, including plants, animals, roads, and cottages, was removed. Today, Point Pelee is home to more at-risk species than any other national park in Canada, and there has been 50 percent land restoration since the 1960s.

How to Get There

From Windsor, 60 km (37 mi) northwest of the park, take Walker Rd. to Rte. 3 W. A right at County Rd. 31 followed by a left at County Rd. 20 leads to County Rd. 33. Turn right and continue to the park gates.

When to Go

The first three weeks of May offer an incredible show of song and colour as birds move through the park. Note that Pelee's popularity can mean that parking lots fill by 7 a.m., even on weekdays. Come fall, you can witness the exodus of monarch butterflies, which roost in the hackberry trees, waiting for the winds that will aid them in their journey south to Mexico. During winter, the park trails are open for hiking, showshoeing, and cross-country skiing.

How to Visit

Point Pelee is one of Canada's smallest national parks, but there's plenty to see. If you have just an afternoon to spend, rent a bike at the Cattail Café and ride a section of the 14-km (8.7 mi) multi-use trail. Afterward, catch the shuttle to the tip and stand at mainland Canada's southernmost point.

If you have a full day, rent a canoe at the Marsh Boardwalk and paddle through the cattails. Afterward, enjoy a hike along the DeLaurier Homestead Trail—a 1.2-km (0.7 mi) footpath that winds past farm, field, and forest.

Visitors with a second day can easily hike all of the park's 14 km (8.7 mi) of maintained trails.

CENTENNIAL BIKE & HIKE TRAIL
6 km/3.7 mi one way; 2 to 3 hours

The Centennial Bike & Hike Trail has been extended to the front entrance of the park, with access to the orientation area, marsh boardwalk, and loops in the mid-park. At the entrance you'll find the Marsh Boardwalk Trail and the Cattail Café. Managed by Friends of Point Pelee, a volunteer organization that aids in park programming, the store offers snacks, souvenirs, and rental services.

The Centennial Bike and Hike Trail, a flat, packed-gravel path, loops past the visitor centre back to the Delaurier Homestead. Along the way, duck off onto some of the well-marked side trails to get a true sense of the park's diversity.

In addition to sand dunes, marshes, and savannas, you'll find deciduous forests that include hackberry, black walnut, and shagbark

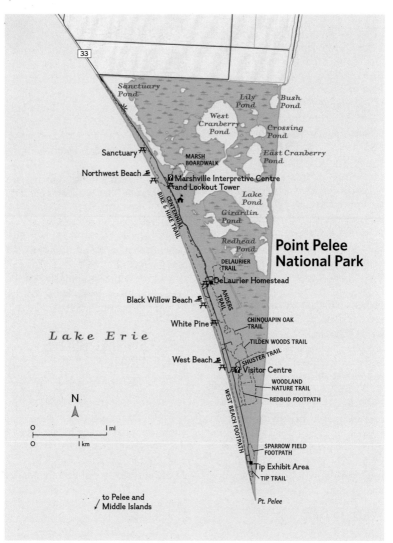

Sanctuary Pond

West Cranberry Pond

Lily Pond

Bush Pond

Crossing Pond

East Cranberry Pond

33

Sanctuary

Northwest Beach

MARSH BOARDWALK

Marshville Interpretive Centre and Lookout Tower

Lake Pond

Girardin Pond

Redhead Pond

Point Pelee National Park

DELAURIER TRAIL

DeLaurier Homestead

ANDERS TRAIL

Black Willow Beach

White Pine

CHINQUAPIN OAK TRAIL

TILDEN WOODS TRAIL

SHUSTER TRAIL

L a k e   E r i e

West Beach

Visitor Centre

WOODLAND NATURE TRAIL

REDBUD FOOTPATH

CENTENNIAL BIKE & HIKE TRAIL

WEST BEACH FOOTPATH

N

0 ———— 1 mi

0 ———— 1 km

SPARROW FIELD FOOTPATH

Tip Exhibit Area

TIP TRAIL

Pt. Pelee

to Pelee and Middle Islands

hickory. Though classified Carolinian (represented in less than one percent of Canada), Point Pelee is somewhat atypical of this zone in that its southern species mix with midwestern and prairie vegetation like sycamore. White pine grows in nutrient-poor exposed soils. The park is home to Canada's only naturally occurring population of the endangered eastern prickly pear cactus.

Watch for wild turkeys, especially early in the morning when they tend to mill around the trees by the path. Previously extirpated from the park, these birds were reintroduced outside park boundaries. Since 2005, they have reestablished themselves in the park itself.

Once you reach the **Visitor Centre,** park your bike and have a look at the interactive exhibits inside. From here, take one of the free open-air shuttles to the tip of land that gave the park its name. French explorers christened the area Pointe Pelée for the bald, sandy spit that reaches out into the water.

Though the beaches at Point Pelee are popular for swimming, the tip is off-limits. Here, east and west waves collide, creating dangerous currents and undertows.

PADDLING THE MARSH
6 km/3.7 mi; 3 to 4 hours

Point Pelee represents five separate habitats, including beach, cedar savanna, dry forest, and wet forest. The fifth and final—freshwater marsh—accounts for two-thirds of the park's total area. As such, the Marsh Boardwalk Trail is one of the park's most popular hikes. For a memorable experience, rent a canoe from the Marsh store. Pick up a map of the marsh area and put in at the docks.

From here, a single canoe route travels 1 km (0.6 mi) east through **Thiessen Channel** to **Lake Pond. West Cranberry Pond** lies directly to the north; **East Cranberry,** which opens up to **Crossing Pond,** is slightly northeast of that. If you are interested in a challenge, paddle southeast on Lake Pond to portage to the south-lying **Redhead Pond.**

Keep your eyes open for wildlife among the swishing reeds and rushes; Point Pelee is home to more than 40 species of fish, reptiles, and amphibians, including painted turtles. The water is also a great place for bird-watching. Geese and ducks eat the roots, shoots, and seeds of surrounding plants. Red-winged blackbirds whistle in the grasses. Marsh wrens weave cattail stalks into nests, feathering them

with the fluff of catkins, and black terns nest on the vegetation mats near the trail.

HIKING
11.5 km (7 mi); a full day

Entrances for seven of the park's eight main trails are on the north-south road that runs from Pelee's main gates to the visitor centre; the eighth is the Centennial Trail, which parallels the main road. Pick up a map when you pay admission.

Follow the **Centennial Trail** to the short, simple **Marsh Boardwalk Trail.** Ascend the 12-m (40 ft) **observation tower** for a view of the wetlands (equivalent to 2,200 football

Monarch butterfly

fields) before strolling the floating boardwalk loop. Look for the small yellow flowers of the carnivorous bladderwort—an aquatic plant whose roots eat water fleas, roundworms, and mosquito larvae via underwater trapdoors.

From here, get back on the Centennial Trail and follow it 2 km (1.2 mi) down the main road

POINT PELEE NATIONAL PARK
(Parc national de la Pointe-Pelée)

INFORMATION & ACTIVITIES

VISITOR & INFORMATION CENTRE
Visitor Centre open daily April to November, and weekends in March and April.

SEASONS & ACCESSIBILITY
Park open year-round. Shuttle service available April to October.

HEADQUARTERS
407 Monarch Ln., Leamington, ON N8H 3V4. Phone (519) 322-2365. www.parks canada.gc.ca/pointpelee.

FRIENDS OF POINT PELEE
1118 Point Pelee Dr., Leamington, ON N8H 3V4. Phone (519) 326-6173. info@ friendsofpointpelee.com; www.friendsof pointpelee.com.

ENTRANCE FEES
Daily: $8 per person, April to October; $6 per person, November to March. Annual: $39 per person, $98 per family or group.

PETS
Dogs are allowed in all areas, including the visitor centre, beaches, and shuttle, but must be leashed at all times.

ACCESSIBLE SERVICES
Call visitor centre to have programs modified to serve people with special needs. Wheelchair-accessible washrooms available at Northeast Beach, Blue Heron, the Tip, and the visitor centre.

THINGS TO DO
Hiking to Canada's southernmost tip, cycling on designated trails. Tour of **DeLaurier Homestead and Trail.** Freighter canoe tour through the marsh operates July to Labour Day weekend in September;

to the entrance of the **DeLaurier Homestead and Trail** on the left-hand side of the road. This 1.2-km (0.7 mi) loop begins near the home of the DeLauriers—a French family that came to Point Pelee in the 1830s. The site, small considering it housed a family 17 members strong, is decorated with artifacts and accoutrements of the time, including the tools Charles DeLaurier used to coop barrels for local fisheries.

Heading southwest, the trail passes through the gnarled remnants of a small and stunted apple orchard. An easy hike through open fields and cedar savanna leads to a swamp forest, where an **observation tower** at the edge of the marsh offers views of eagle-nesting platforms.

From the trailhead, follow the multi-use trail through the Tilden Woods to reach the visitor centre. Highlights include the Chinquapin oak (a southern tree that grows in the cloud forests of Mexico) and the ridged barrier beach of the eastern shore.

At the visitor centre parking lot, connect with the Woodland Nature Trail, cross the main road, and follow the **West Beach Footpath** south. **Pelee Island** is visible from the sandy dunes here. Behind it, lying 30 km (18.6 mi) southwest of the mainland, is **Middle Island**—given to the park by the Nature Conservancy of Canada in 2000. Though inaccessible to the public, Middle Island is managed as a Zone 1 Special Preservation Area, where park staff monitor flora and fauna.

Follow on to the Tip—the southernmost point of mainland Canada—then take a shuttle back.

call (519) 322-2365 ext. 0. Fishing permit $10 per day.

SPECIAL ADVISORIES
• Wear life jacket at all times during canoe cruise tours.
• Winds change rapidly. Check forecasts before visiting the park or arranging canoe or kayak tours.

CAMPGROUNDS
Individual camping is not available in the park. **Campers Cove Campground** family camping resort with 324 campsites on shores of Lake Erie, 239 seasonal, 85 for overnight campers. $39 for water and electricity; $50 for water, electricity, and pull-through site. Cabins available at $67–$75 per night. Wireless internet and general store on-site. Call (519) 825-4632.

White Pine picnic shelter fits 80–100 people, parking capacity for 35 cars, close to beach and trails and enclosed in winter, with electrical outlets, wood-burning stove, and outdoor barbecues (bring charcoal). Firewood must be purchased at the park.

HOTELS, MOTELS, & INNS
(unless otherwise noted, rates are for a 2-person double, high season, in Canadian dollars)

Outside the park:
Comfort Inn 279 Erie St. S, Leamington, ON N8H 3C4. (519) 326-9071. cn276@whg.com; www.choicehotels.ca/cn276. $152. Breakfast and internet included.
Best Western Plus Leamington Hotel 566 Bevel Line Rd., Leamington, ON N8H 3V4. (519) 326-8646. www.bestwestern.com. $190.
Ramada Limited Windsor 2225 Division Rd., Windsor, ON N8W 1Z7. (519) 969-7800. www.ramada.com. $100.
Seacliffe Inn 388 Erie St. S, Leamington, ON N8H 3E5. (519) 324-9266. info@seacliffeinn.com; www.seacliffeinn.com. $120–$160.

POINT PELEE

EXCURSION

FORT MALDEN NATIONAL HISTORIC SITE
AMHERSTBURG, ON

Built in 1796 where the Detroit River drains into Lake Erie, Fort Malden preserves parts of a garrison erected by the British to defend Canada from American attack in the early 19th century. A window into Canada's early military history, the site is also where the historic meeting between Sir Isaac Brock and Shawnee Chief Tecumseh took place. The site offers wheelchair-accessible paths and buildings. Parking, washrooms, and a gift shop are also available. (519) 736-5416.

Ferns and moss cover the Lake Superior shoreline in Pukaskwa National Park.

▶ PUKASKWA

ONTARIO
ESTABLISHED 1971
1,878 sq km/464,064 acres

The very act of getting to Pukaskwa National Park is an extraordinary experience. Whether you approach from the east or west, there are a hundred spots along the highway north of Lake Superior where billion-year-old cliffs plunge to the roadside, where banks of black spruce and jack pine ascend like Vesuvius from the ditches, where you crest a hill and feel a stab to the heart as the world's largest, most majestic, and sometimes most terrifying body of freshwater spreads out before you.

Pukaskwa is one of Ontario's last significant tracts of boreal forest untouched by human development or industry. The vast region of wilderness within its boundaries represents centuries of uninterrupted forest succession dating to the melting of the last glacier some 10,000 years ago. The park's Coastal Hiking Trail runs along the longest undeveloped stretch of shore on the Great Lakes.

While Anishinaabe are known to have inhabited the area for thousands of years, one might well ask how such a sprawling area of wilderness remained largely unvisited by the mining and logging industries during the 19th and early 20th centuries, when almost all similar areas were being consumed by the advance of civilization. Harvesting of white pine and pulpwood occurred in the southern corner of the park during the early 1900s. However, the park at large was simply too rugged and remote for the ongoing cutting and removal of pulpwood or timber. A perceived absence of valuable metals or minerals in the rock discouraged mining. And when the transcontinental railway came through during the mid-1880s, it bypassed what is now Pukaskwa to the north. It bespeaks the ruggedness of the territory—the rock cliffs, marshes, and river chasms—that the stretches of rail in the vicinity of the park were not just the toughest to build and last to be completed by the Canadian Pacific Railway, but in the end cost more than twice as much per hundred kilometres of track as did any 2,000-km (1,243 mi) stretch of rail in western or eastern Canada.

How to Get There

Drive east along Hwy. 17 from Thunder Bay, or west from Sault Ste. Marie, to Hwy. 627, which runs south 10 km (6 mi) east of the town of Marathon. The road will take you through the communities of Heron Bay and Biigtigong Nishnaabeg (formerly know as Pic River First Nation) some 20 km (12 mi) into the public entrance at the park's north end.

Kayakers or canoeists coming from other parts of the lake can enter the park at Hattie Cove or wherever they can locate suitable moorage or beaches. White-water canoeists and kayakers generally enter on the park's eastern boundary, having come from White Lake Provincial Park, where most white-water river excursions into Pukaskwa begin.

When to Go

The most popular time to visit Pukaskwa National Park is June through September, when the days are long,

daytime temperatures generally rise above 20°C (68°F), and most park programs are operational.

How to Visit

Many visitors to the park, especially those with children, will find all the stimulation they seek simply by pitching camp for a weekend or longer at the Hattie Cove Campground, near the park entrance, hiking the day trails, swimming in chilly Lake Superior, or paddling on the inlets of the cove.

During high season, campers can experience local indigenous culture through programs at the Anishinaabe Camp, where a First Nations interpreter will introduce visitors to native life and lore.

Those with a more ambitious agenda will undoubtedly want to venture along the 60-km (37 mi) Coastal Hiking Trail or paddle along the coast of Lake Superior or down the White or Pukaskwa Rivers through the park's remote interior.

COASTAL HIKING TRAIL
120 km/74.5 mi return; 1 to 2 days

Certainly, one of the most compelling of the many recreational opportunities available in Pukaskwa National Park is the hike down the **Coastal Hiking Trail.** This ancient pathway, one of Canada's most renowned and scenic hiking routes, stitches up a primeval line of granite headlands, pebble beaches, and old-growth forest.

Along the trail are 11 primitive campgrounds with a total of 30 campsites (tent pad, privy, bear box, and fire pit) spread more or less evenly along the route. Parts of the trail make for tough hiking up and down the rock outcrops.

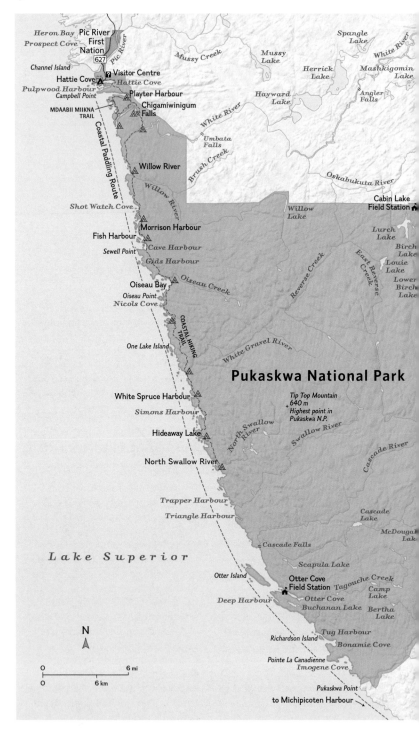

Heron Bay
Prospect Cove
Pic River First Nation
Channel Island
Hattie Cove
Pulpwood Harbour
Campbell Point
MDAABII MIIKNA TRAIL
Coastal Paddling Route
627
Visitor Centre
Hattie Cove
Playter Harbour
Chigamiwinigum Falls
Willow River
Shot Watch Cove
Morrison Harbour
Fish Harbour
Sewell Point
Cave Harbour
Gids Harbour
Oiseau Bay
Oiseau Point
Nicols Cove
One Lake Island
COASTAL HIKING TRAIL
White Spruce Harbour
Simons Harbour
Hideaway Lake
North Swallow River
Trapper Harbour
Triangle Harbour

Mussy Creek
Mussy Lake
Herrick Lake
Hayward Lake
White River
Umbata Falls
Brush Creek
Willow River
Willow Lake
Oiseau Creek
Reverse Creek
White Gravel River
North Swallow River
Tip Top Mountain
640 m
Highest point in Pukaskwa N.P.
Swallow River

Spangle Lake
White River
Mashkigomin Lake
Angler Falls
Oskabukuta River
Cabin Lake Field Station
Lurch Lake
Birch Lake
Louie Lake
Lower Birch Lake
East Reverse Creek

Pukaskwa National Park

Cascade River
Cascade Lake
McDougal Lake
Cascade Falls
Scapula Lake
Tagouche Creek
Camp Lake
Bertha Lake
Otter Cove Field Station
Otter Island
Deep Harbour
Otter Cove
Buchanan Lake
Tug Harbour
Bonamie Cove
Richardson Island
Pointe La Canadienne
Imogene Cove
Pukaskwa Point
to Michipicoten Harbour

Lake Superior

N

0   6 mi
0   6 km

All backcountry users, including hikers, campers, and paddlers, must register with park staff upon arrival and departure. The park limits the number of hikers and canoeists permitted in the backcountry, so if you're planning either a coastal hike or paddle, or an interior river trip, call the park office in advance to book a space.

HATTIE COVE

The interconnected hiking trails close to **Hattie Cove** range up to 3 km (1.8 mi) in length and offer everything from show-stopping views of the lake from atop the local headlands and close-ups of the intricacies of the boreal forest, to sunrise or sunset beach strolls within splashing distance of the pounding surf.

Sharp-eyed hikers are apt to come across any number of small biological wonders in the park, including plants left behind by the Ice Age and nurtured in the park's "Arctic" microhabitats hundreds of kilometres south of their normal range. The encrusted saxifrage produces showy white clusters of flowers in late June along the **Southern Headland Trail.** Inasmuch as Lake Superior produces an "Arctic" effect, it also, in its vastness, holds summer heat and humidity, creating microhabitats alongshore, where blueberries have appeared as late as mid-October.

Pukaskwa National Park is home to a small number of woodland caribou—a species that is considered threatened in Canada. The caribou population has been shown to be declining since Pukaskwa began aerial surveys more than 30 years ago. Experts have predicted that the park's caribou population could disappear by 2020. Parks

Canada is working with surrounding land managers on restoring habitat, so that one day woodland caribou may once again be self-sustaining in the park.

Those who prefer water travel can paddle the inlets around Hattie Cove or, if the wind and water are high, the more peaceful fetches of **Halfway Lake,** within walking distance of the campground at Hattie Cove.

CANOEING & KAYAKING

Canoeing the **White River** is possible during the open-water season but, because of the river's stiff current, requires getting to a point where downstream travel is possible. If you begin in **White Lake Provincial Park** to the east of Pukaskwa, expect to take four days or more to reach Lake Superior, from where it is an hour's paddle north along the coast to the visitor centre at Hattie Cove. The **Pukaskwa River** is also navigable but generally only during spring runoff in May and early June.

Boardwalk trail through the woods

Between early summer and mid-autumn, paddlers enjoy the Coastal Paddling Route from Hattie Cove, down the west side of the **Pukaskwa Peninsula,** and east to **Michipicoten Harbour.** In good weather, the trip can be accomplished in less than a week, but canoeists should be prepared to spend at least one day being wind- or wave-bound at their shoreline campsites.

Lake Superior itself is, of course, a vast part of Pukaskwa's distinction—its vast and icy self-sufficiency; its unpredictability; its tendency to dwarf human endeavour. It is the world's largest lake by surface area, has more shoreline than the west coast of the United States (4,400 km/2,734 mi), and holds about a tenth of the world's accessible freshwater.

When the sun is out, the light above the lake is as bright as sun reflecting off ice. Meanwhile, the light beneath the waves is as mysterious a medium as one is likely to encounter among the Earth's bodies of fresh water. Some would call Lake Superior a mythology unto itself, incorporating thousand-year-old secrets, the ghosts of old ships and drowned seamen, and the gales and cataclysms that put them where they are.

Given the lake's profound ecological and historical significance, every attempt is being made by concerned agencies and individuals to protect and preserve it, as well as the surrounding shoreline and forest. In this, Pukaskwa National Park is leading the way, with its wildlife research and cultural and historical education programs.

Once exposed to the park's extraordinary beauty and significance, visitors tend to include themselves among the growing number not just of Pukaskwa supporters but of wilderness preservationists at large.

PUKASKWA NATIONAL PARK
(Parc national Pukaskwa)

INFORMATION & ACTIVITIES

VISITOR & INFORMATION CENTRE
Visitor Centre located in Hattie Cove at the end of Hwy 627. Open July and August.

SEASONS & ACCESSIBILITY
Park administration building open year-round. Campground comfort stations open May to early September. Interpretive programs July and August.

HEADQUARTERS
P.O. Box 212, Heron Bay, ON P0T 1R0. Phone (807) 229-0801. www.parkscanada.gc.ca/pukaskwa.

ENTRANCE FEES
$6 per adult per day, $29 per adult per season.

PETS
Pets must be leashed.

ACCESSIBLE SERVICES
Two wheelchair-accessible campsites on **Hattie Cove.** All facilities in the kiosk and visitor centre are accessible.

THINGS TO DO
Tour **Anishinaabe Camp** with First Nations interpreter. Hiking on the **Coastal Hiking Trail** to park's backcountry campsites or 18 km (11 mi) round-trip to the White River Suspension Bridge. Day hiking and geocaching in the Hattie Cove Campground. Picnic at one of the park's three beaches. Calm paddling in the inlets of Hattie Cove, **Halfway Lake;** white-water paddling on the **White** and **Pukaskwa Rivers.** Sailing and boating on Lake Superior. Motorboats permitted only in areas accessible from Lake Superior. To register in or out, call (807) 229-0801 ext. 242.

SPECIAL ADVISORIES
- The park is prone to rapid weather changes. Take precautions against hypothermia, dehydration, and overexertion.
- Wear personal flotation device at all times when canoeing or kayaking.
- The Pukaskwa River is navigable only during spring runoff (May–early June).
- Live bait and lead sinkers/lures for fishing are prohibited .
- If travelling by motorboat, note there are no refuelling opportunities in Pukaskwa.
- Keep food contained and out of reach of wildlife, especially bears.

OVERNIGHT BACKPACKING
Backcountry camping at primitive campsites available along the Coastal Paddling Route and **Coastal Hiking Trail.** $10 per person overnight; $69 per year. Contact the park well in advance to reserve. Backcountry hikers and campers must register in and out of the park and complete a mandatory backcountry orientation session. Call (807) 229-0801 ext. 242.

CAMPGROUNDS
Hattie Cove has 67 campsites, 29 electrical ($29), 13 nonelectrical in the south loop; 25 nonelectrical sites including one walk-in site in the south loop ($26). Picnic table and fire pit at all sites; most have a sandy tent pad. Comfort stations with showers and flush toilets. Road to campground closed mid-November to mid-May; opened as snow conditions permit.

HOTELS, MOTELS, & INNS
(unless otherwise noted, rates are for a 2-person double, high season, in Canadian dollars)

Outside the park:
Heron Bay (Pic River), ON P0T 1R0:
Pic River Guest Suite 31 Rabbit Rd. www.picriverguestsuite.com. One mini-apartment, 2 rooms, with kitchenette and private entrance. $110.

Marathon, ON P0T 2E0:
Lakeview Manor 24 Drake St. (807) 229-2248. www.bbcanada.com/3917.html. $115–$140.

PUKASKWA

▶ **NATIONAL MARINE CONSERVATION AREA**

LAKE SUPERIOR
ONTARIO

To understand the evolution of the Lake Superior National Marine Conservation Area, it helps to know that when the Welland Canal that links Lake Erie and Lake Ontario was built in the mid-1800s, bypassing Niagara Falls and allowing large boats to move from the St. Lawrence River into the upper Great Lakes, it inadvertently also allowed sea lampreys to bypass the falls for the first time.

A foggy morning in Lake Superior National Marine Conservation Area

By the mid-20th century, the voracious eel-like fish had severely reduced the lake's population of trout. Meanwhile, many of the 800 rivers and streams that flow into Lake Superior had become polluted and a daily rain of particulate poisons was settling onto the lake from the air.

Although its ecology has drastically altered from what it was before the construction of the canal, Lake Superior is the cleanest of the Great Lakes.

The Ojibwe name for Lake Superior is Gitchi Gummi, meaning "big water." Its size, power, and unpredictability have led many to think of Lake Superior as an "inland sea."

In 1997, Parks Canada began exploring whether there was support for the protection of the marine area within western Lake Superior. In 2007, a 10,880-sq-km (2.6 million acres) section of the lake and its bed was proposed as a national marine conservation area. The Lake Superior National Marine Conservation Area (NMCA) is located in the northern part of the lake, extending from Bottle Point near Terrace Bay (Northwestern Ontario) in the east to Thunder Cape at the tip of Sibley Peninsula in the west, and from the shoreline in the north to the Canada–United States border in the south. It is home to more than 70 fish species and 50 shipwrecks.

Through the establishment process, Parks Canada consults and works with indigenous peoples of Canada in the region, local communities, and stakeholders. Once the Lake Superior NMCA is established, the vast area will be conserved and protected.

National marine conservation areas are established to protect and preserve representative examples of Canada's oceans and Great Lakes. The Lake Superior NMCA will promote opportunities for the ecologically sustainable use of aquatic resources for the long-term benefit of coastal communities in collaboration with partners. What this means is that responsible hunting and fishing can continue in marine conservation areas. Other activities, namely waste dumping, dredging, mining, oil and gas exploration, and development will not be permitted.

ON WATER & ON LAND: The best way to appreciate the near-pristine waters and islands of Lake Superior is by boat, on a fishing trip, or a kayaking venture from one of the public boat launches on beaches in communities along the shoreline. There are areas where the lake is so clear that boaters can see the bottom and sometimes the wrecks of some 17 vessels more than 20 m (66 ft) down. At Silver Islet, the shaft of a 19th-century

silver mine, once the richest on Earth, is visible in the lake bed.

The Lake Superior NMCA offers unparalleled waters for lake trout, whitefish, lake herring, and walleye. The archipelagos within the NMCA offer unique routes for the boating community.

Several communities along the top of Lake Superior offer a range of activities and are able to provide visitors with appropriate supplies for that North Shore experience. The headquarters for **Lake Superior National Marine Conservation Area** is located in Nipigon, Ontario. Call (888) 773-8888 or visit *www.pc.gc .ca/superior* for more information.

LAKE SUPERIOR

Kayaking through a rock arch on Lake Superior

PRAIRIE
PROVINCES

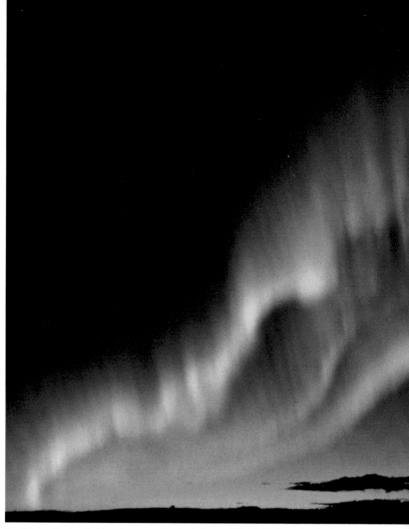

Page 164: top, Meadow Goatsbeard, a common Grasslands flower; middle, 70 Mile Butte, Grasslands National Park; bottom, Horseback riding in Prince Albert's Long Meadow. Page 165: Polar bear and cub, Wapusk National Park

PRAIRIE PROVINCES

The prairie provinces zigzag across a huge landscape that stretches from Manitoba to Saskatchewan and the Northwest Territories. Wapusk protects a fragile subarctic environment on the shores of Hudson Bay where polar bears den. At Riding Mountain extensive wilderness trails lead hikers, bikers, and horseback riders through forests, over hills, and past lakes to a big draw: elk and captive bison. Visitors to Prince Albert seek out free-ranging bison, as well as

Above: A green curtain of the aurora borealis dances across a night sky in Wapusk National Park, where the upper atmosphere pyrotechnics are a common sight in winter due to the park's high northern latitude.

grey wolves, elk, and Grey Owl's cabin. Water sports abound in this park that is one-third water. Grasslands National Park is a semi-arid grassland punctuated by river valleys and badlands. Day hikes and horseback rides yield grand views and sites featuring Paleo-Indian medicine wheels. Wood Buffalo is characterized by forest, salt plains, and karst. It is known for buffalo, endangered whooping cranes, and the world's largest Dark Sky Preserve.

Wood Buffalo

Wapusk

ALBERTA

MANITOBA

Prince Albert

Elk Island

SASKATCHEWAN

Riding Mountain

Grasslands

Polar bears sparring

▶ WAPUSK

MANITOBA
ESTABLISHED 1996
11,475 sq km/2,836,000 acres

Manitoba's Wapusk National Park is one of the few places in the world where, in late February, visitors can watch tiny, three-month-old bear cubs explore, under the watchful eyes of their mothers, their snowy new world for the first time. But no roads or trails lead into this massive park made up of rough subarctic forest, tundra, muskeg, and part of North America's largest expanse of peat bog, which shelters one of the largest known maternity denning areas for polar bears. Wildlife-watching, especially for polar bears, is why people visit.

One of Canada's most accessible northern national parks, Wapusk—Cree for "white bear"—encompasses a good portion of the Hudson James Lowlands, a subarctic ecological transition region between Manitoba's boreal forests to the south and the Arctic tundra of Nunavut to the north. Hudson Bay itself is so vast (822,324 sq km/ 317,500 sq mi) that it creates its own chilly microclimate.

Wapusk National Park is home to polar bears and other wildlife, including many rare birds, black bears, moose, wolves, red and arctic foxes, wolverines, lemmings, and the 3,000-strong Cape Churchill caribou herd, which calves here. While the climate can be inhospitable in winter, the region's indigenous people continue traditional hunting practices in the park, primarily for the caribou. Winter's blank landscape of virtually nothing but snow would have an ill-equipped, unguided traveller lost and frozen within a day.

In summer, Wapusk National Park's peat bogs and marshy wetlands are nearly impossible for visitors to safely navigate. In the tundra, sedge meadows, peat bogs, and ponds cover the landscape, and in the subarctic forest, where the ground is firmer, tiny, stunted trees grow—hundreds of years old, less than 2 m (6.5 ft) in height, with branches only on their south-facing sides, thanks to constant harsh winds. The Hudson Bay shoreline habitat is peppered with salt marshes and flats, rocky beaches, and, because the bay has strong tides, an intertidal zone that stretches some 10 km (6 mi).

Come late October and early November, roughly a thousand polar bears, which have spent their summer shambling around the region's subarctic forest and tundra awaiting the freeze-up of Hudson Bay, move through the park's Cape Churchill area to the new ice. They spend the winter out on the frozen bay, gorging on seals to store up fat reserves for the following year's lean summer.

Visitors can access Wapusk through licensed local operators who provide guided trips into the park. Tours are also available into Cape Churchill Wildlife Management Area, a provincially designated buffer zone surrounding the park that affords additional protection for the polar bear denning area and the delicate ecological system here.

This ecological system attracts and supports some increasingly rare bird species. The habitat along the park's coastline lures more than 200 species of birds—including hundreds of thousands of waterfowl and shorebirds that come to nest or stage and feed en route elsewhere during annual migrations on this major North American flyway. Bird-watchers exploring accessible open tundra and shoreline northwest of the park can spot rare Caspian terns, great grey owls, sandhill cranes, stilt sandpipers, Hudsonian godwits, Ross's and ivory gulls, snow geese, Canada geese, arctic loons, gyrfalcons, and peregrine falcons.

Inexplicably, even grizzly bears have been spotted in the park yearly since 2008.

How to Get There

From Winnipeg, Manitoba, fly north to Churchill using Calm Air. Flights take from 2 to 2.5 hours; some people opt to drive from Winnipeg to Thompson, Manitoba, on Hwy. 6 North—a distance of 700 km (435 mi)—then take a one-hour, less costly plane hop on Calm Air to Churchill. Calm Air flies from Churchill to Thompson on Friday and from Thompson to Churchill on Sunday. Air schedules vary depending on the time of year and passenger demand, however, and in winter Arctic blizzards can disrupt flight schedules, delaying arrivals and departures, sometimes for days.

VIA Rail runs passenger service on the Hudson Bay Line between The Pas and Churchill. Trains arrive in Churchill every Tuesday, Thursday, and Saturday morning with same-day evening departures. Consult with VIA Rail for detailed information. The train should take one night to get there, but can be delayed if the track has been frost

WAPUSK

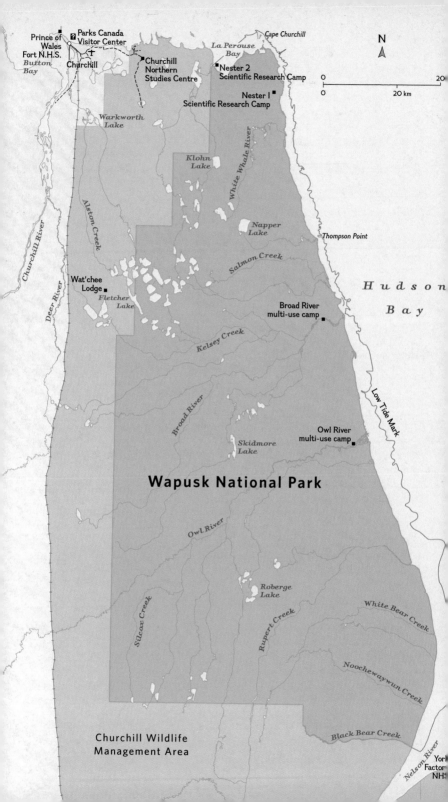

A caribou roams through Wapusk's tundra landscape.

heaved and the train slows to about 15 km (9 mi) an hour, with frequent stops to check the track.

The train offers sleeper cars or economy class. The train also passes through Thompson.

When to Go

The yearly polar bear congregation at the coast happens in late October and early November, while young cubs are visible at denning areas from mid-February to mid-March.

Wapusk National Park is accessible in summer via helicopter for guided tundra hiking as well as wildlife spotting. Birders and wildlife-watchers can also explore the tundra around the town of Churchill, 40 km (25 mi) northwest of the park.

In July, visitors can don dry suits and frolic among hundreds of beluga whales and their calves in the Churchill River estuary. It is recommended that any hiking near Churchill be guided by trained escorts carrying firearms in case of encounters with polar bears. Keeping a vigilant eye out for wandering bears is critical; they sometimes come right into town.

How to Visit

Unescorted travellers are not permitted in Wapusk National Park. Escorting guides, operators, and local hotels usually book up well ahead, so early planning is a must. During "bear season," complete touring packages are the most common way to visit, with all travel details taken care of, from the Winnipeg arrival point on.

Wat'chee Lodge—Wat'chee is Cree for "a hill covered with trees in the middle of the tundra"—one of the few spots in the world where young polar bears can be viewed. The lodge is open from mid-February to mid-March and is reached by night rail from Churchill. Travellers detrain at a stopping point called Chesnaye, where lodge employees meet them with specially equipped all-terrain trucks and take them to the lodge.

BEAR VIEWING, BIG AND SMALL

a full day or weeklong excursion

The polar bear is the big draw for visitors to this subarctic part of Manitoba. Whether on a day excursion or on a weeklong visit or more, the traditional polar bear adventure involves boarding a giant tundra vehicle with massive snow tires roughly 3 m (10 ft) in height. The tires are tall enough to keep a curi-

Heritage Railway Station, Churchill, Manitoba

ous, big bear from rearing up on hind legs for inspection of who's within the vehicle, but not too tall to prevent getting exciting views of the magnificent creatures.

Before heading out to the frozen tundra, visitors should make an effort to visit the **Parks Canada Visitor Centre** in Churchill's Heritage Railway Station. Its staff provide information and interpretive programs. The "Our Land, Our Stories" exhibit offers an introduction to both the park, covering its ecology and the great white bears it protects, and the cultural history of the region.

Healthy adult male polar bears can weigh up to a tonne; adult females weigh about half as much as the males. Polar bears eat almost

their entire year's worth of food in the winter, when they feed on ringed seals caught by waiting at the seals' breathing holes in the Hudson Bay ice. They must put on enough poundage to help them survive through food-sparse Arctic summers, when they subsist on occasional small mammals or wild berries.

Polar bear cubs, born in winter and often as twins, spend the first couple of months of their lives in dens scratched out of the ground above the permafrost by mother bears. The park protects an estimated 500 such dens, perhaps more. The dens are used repeatedly over the years, sometimes by different mothers.

The **Tundra Buggy Lodge** is run by Frontiers North Adventures, the only operator besides Wat'chee Lodge allowed into the national park itself during migration season for bear viewing. The mobile lodge sets up in Wapusk National Park at Cape Churchill for one week in late November. Outfitted with a couple of bunk-bed-style sleeper cars, a lounge, and dining and utility cars— all with open decks in between the cars for better close-up polar bear viewing—the lodge can handle 38 guests at a time.

Similar experiences are offered in the neighbouring **Churchill Wildlife Management Area** in October and November.

For a truly unique opportunity, visitors should look to the **Wat'chee Lodge,** located in the Churchill Wildlife Management Area south of the townsite. Once a navy communications base, the lodge offers its guests day excursions to watch mothers and cubs as the youngsters experience their first tastes of the world outside their birth dens. Watchers must maintain a distance of at least 100 m (330 ft) to avoid distressing the mothers.

WAPUSK NATIONAL PARK
(Parc national Wapusk)

INFORMATION & ACTIVITIES

VISITOR CENTRE
Parks Canada Visitor Centre Churchill, MB R0B 0E0. Phone (204) 675-8863.

SEASONS & ACCESSIBILITY
The park is only accessible via commercial tour operators in Churchill. Contact park office for a list of licensed operators. Peak season for polar bear viewing is October and November.

HEADQUARTERS
P.O. Box 127, Churchill, MB R0B 0E0. Phone (204) 675-8863. www.parks canada.gc.ca/wapusk.

ENTRANCE FEES
Contact tour operators for fees.

PETS
Contact tour operators for regulations.

ACCESSIBLE SERVICES
No facilities in the park; contact tour operators for accommodations. Parks Canada Visitor Centre fully accessible.

THINGS TO DO
Parks Canada tours, hikes, and adventure packages are available at nearby venues. For more information, visit the Parks Canada Visitor Centre, Churchill Heritage Railway Station, which offers an interpretive exhibit, Our Land, Our Stories, or contact the Parks Canada office for tour times, descriptions, and booking. Tour the park with a licensed operator.

SPECIAL ADVISORIES
- Weather is unpredictable and storms are frequent. Dress for extreme cold and wet conditions.
- Temperatures can drop below -40°C (-40°F), and to -62°C (-80°F) with wind chill. Skin freezes in less than 30 seconds of exposure. Wear appropriate clothing and good-quality glasses to avoid frostbite, hypothermia, and snowblindness.
- Open water is very cold. Sea, lake, and river ice may be unstable and unsafe to walk on at any time of year.
- Travel inland restricted to the winter.
- In summer, wear bug-proof jackets and hats and carry insect repellent to avoid biting insects.
- Avoid foxes, as they may carry rabies.
- Watch for polar bear and black bear encounters. Polar bears are a risk especially during ice-free periods from July through November.

HOTELS, MOTELS, & INNS
(unless otherwise noted, rates are for a 2-person double, high season, in Canadian dollars)

Outside the park:
Churchill, MB R0B 0E0
Aurora Inn Box 1030. (204) 675-2071. www.auroramb.ca. $255.
Bear Country Inn 126 Kelsey Blvd., Box 788. (204) 675-8299. www.bearcountry inn.com. $219–$229.
Iceberg Inn 183 Kelsey Blvd., Box 640. (204) 675-2228. www.iceberginn.ca. Call for bear-season rates.
Lazy Bear Lodge 313 Kelsey Blvd., Box 880. (866) 687-2327. www.lazybear lodge.com. $230-$445.

Adventure packages at Lazy Bear Lodge:
Beluga Whale Dream Tour, 2-night package, July–September boat tour to view beluga whales and Prince of Wales fort. $420 all-inclusive without airfare.
Ultimate Arctic Summer Adventure, 6-night package, July–August, tour to view polar bears and beluga whales, and cultural and heritage tour. $3,650 per person including airfare.
Ultimate Polar Bear Tour, 3-night bear-viewing tour, October–November. $2,635 per person, including accommodations, meals, 2 full days on the tundra, and the cultural and heritage tour.

Aurora borealis

◗ RIDING MOUNTAIN

MANITOBA
ESTABLISHED 1929
2,968 sq km/733,409 acres

Encompassing part of a postglacial-age ribbon of high ground that stretches from South Dakota into northern Saskatchewan, Manitoba's Riding Mountain National Park "peaks out" at just under 800 m (2,625 ft) above a sea of surrounding prairie landscape. Within the park, a rich, diverse biosystem with everything from beavers to bison is based on a unique blend of different wilderness areas that offers a plethora of nature-oriented exploration options.

Geologically speaking, some 20,000 years ago a high beach ridge began forming along the western edge of Lake Agassiz, a postglacial inland sea that covered much of north-central North America. In the United States, the ridge is called the Pembina Escarpment or Gorge. The portion of the ridge in Canada is called the Manitoba Escarpment.

Whatever this abrupt rise in the prairie landscape is named, the stretch in Manitoba is a natural island of forests, lakes, and meadows that has been sheltered as a national park since 1930 (though it didn't officially open to the public until 1933) and became the core of the UNESCO-designated Riding Mountain Biosphere Reserve in

1986, one of just 15 such reserves in Canada.

Rich with aspen parkland and grasslands, marshes and small lakes, and spanning deciduous and boreal forests, Riding Mountain is a top wildlife-viewing locale. The park is favoured by hikers, backpackers, horseback riders, and mountain bikers in summer for its extensive series of wilderness trails—more than 300 km (186.5 mi) worth on more than 36 trails—and cross-country skiers and snowshoers in winter, when dozens of trails are groomed for skiers, while snowshoers can explore at will.

Riding Mountain is also one of the few Canadian national parks that was founded during a time when recreation and public enjoyment of nature were the primary raisons d'être for national parks—which is why there's an actual townsite here, Wasagaming, on the shores of Clear Lake, complete with souvenir and clothing shops, restaurants, movie theatre, marina, and a choice of lodges, inns, motels, and cabins for rent. A few of the town's buildings, including the visitor centre, date as far back as the late 1930s; they stand out because of their thick, rough-hewn log structures.

A national parks policy change eventually occurred. Now all Canadian parks serve dual, sometimes potentially conflicting, roles: Protect key Canadian natural treasures from being loved to death, but still allow people to appreciate them as close-up as possible.

How to Get There

The park lies about 4.5 hours northwest by car from Winnipeg—via Trans-Canada 1 (for 98 km/61 mi) then Hwy. 16 (for 182 km/113 mi)

to the park's south gate and, a short distance inside the gate, Wasagaming (known as Clear Lake by locals). The park's more scenic and geographically impressive entrance, the East Gate National Historic Site (see p. 181), is on Hwy. 19, which climbs the slope of the escarpment (take Trans-Canada 1 west to Hwy. 16, aka the Yellowhead Route, just past the city of Portage la Prairie, then head northwest on Hwy. 16 to Neepawa, then north on Hwy. 5, turning west on Hwy. 19).

Park passes can be bought at the north and south park gates.

When to Go

June, July, and August are peak season for vacationers who head to Clear Lake's sandy beaches and deep, cool water, settling into cottages or campsites at one of the park's half-dozen campgrounds (mid-May–mid-Oct.), or booking into the few hotels and B&Bs that edge the park's boundaries. Advance reservations are strongly recommended for campers at the fully serviced Wasagaming Campground; the outlying campgrounds are first-come, first-served.

Most of the public park facilities are closed in winter, except for occasional warming huts on cross-country ski trails, but Parks Canada staff do run a limited winter interpretive program offering, among other things, animal tracking and snowshoeing.

How to Visit

A one-day drive handles both scenic roads in the eastern portion of the national park: Hwy. 10, which runs north and south through the park, and Hwy. 19 to the east. Off Hwy. 10, rounding the north curve of the lake, another road leads to and through

Riding Mountain's lakes provide a variety of recreation.

the national park's signature Lake Audy bison enclosure, where a large elevated, covered exhibit offers information and good views of the bison if the 30-member herd happens to be in this part of the meadow. When travelling through the enclosure, visitors should stay in their vehicles, keep their windows up, and not feed the animals. These beasts are still wild, still unpredictable.

But the park's real attractions are its vast swatches of nature, punctuated by dozens of trails negotiable only on foot, bicycle, or horseback. Dozens of trailheads, designed for long-distance or day hikes, are easily reachable by vehicle; the visitor centre can provide detailed maps. Most visitors should take at least a long weekend to explore the park's natural offerings, and backpackers can hike into remote campsites to spend a couple of nights under the stars.

The best hiking trails lead into the western high meadows and "prairie pothole" areas; the most isolated backcountry campsites are found here. Eastern park trailheads start on Hwy. 19, and western trailheads can be reached via Lake Audy or by driving west outside the park, following Hwy. 45 to gravel

roads 264 or 577, both of which run north to enter more remote areas of the park and reach the narrow, little-travelled trails that make this piece of the park a casual backpacker's heaven.

Most day trails are off-limits to mountain bikers. **Reeve's Raven,** a 11.5 km (7.1 mi) loop on the east side of the park, is a mountain biker's newest challenge that boasts some of the most spectacular views in the park. The Central, Baldy Lake, and Strathclair Trails are easy rides; the Packhorse, Jet, and Baldy Hill Trails are much more hilly and far tougher to handle.

WASAGAMING (CLEAR LAKE)

Wasagaming is "Clear Lake cottage country" and is the busiest part of Riding Mountain, bustling in summer with day-trippers, vacationers, and cottagers. Plenty of short hiking and cycling trails start and end at the edges of the townsite and its adjacent, fully serviced campground with 30 new oTENTiks for a unique blend of comfort with a taste of the outdoors. One of the most popular, the **Ominnik Marsh boardwalk,** is just a five-minute stroll from the visitor centre, and runs just under 2 km (1.25 mi). The visitor centre loans out Marsh Kits with gear to keep kids interested, including binoculars to spot marsh birds and wildlife.

Worth a stop for a little park natural history and orientation, the **visitor centre** is one of the few original log buildings in town, built in the 1930s. Another, the 1937 **Park Theatre,** is North America's largest log cabin theatre; it runs current films, changing them up every few days. The theatre sits on Wasagaming Drive, the town's main street. Most souvenir shops and restaurants are found along this street. (The Whitehouse Bakery is famous

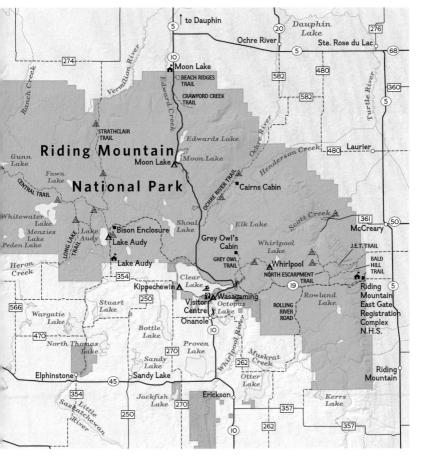

Hikers on the Manitoba Escarpment take in the view.

Bulrushes along Whirlpool Lake and reflections

Juvenile great horned owls (*Bubo virginianus*)

for its irresistible giant, gooey cinnamon buns.)

The 18-hole Clear Lake golf course—considered one of Canada's most beautiful golf courses—is located at the lake's east end and is open throughout the full summer season, as are the tennis courts. Other area golf courses include the new 18-hole Poplar Ridge Golf Course, on Hwy. 354 off Hwy. 10, near the village of Onanole just outside the park's south gate; the nine-hole Lakewood Hills Golf Course in Onanole; and a nine-hole course at the Elkhorn Resort.

Powerboats and pedal boats, canoes and kayaks, and fishing boats (fishing licences can be bought at the visitor centre; catch-and-release is practised here) can be rented at the town's main pier. Dinner and lake cruises are available on the **Martese cruise ship.** Bike rentals are easy to find in town, and horseback riding is available through the **Elkhorn Resort.**

WILDLIFE-WATCHING
predawn & dusk

Riding Mountain National Park is blessed with a bounty of wildlife, much of which can be seen by even casual visitors, much more so by wildlife enthusiasts. Wildlife-watchers favour the park in late April/early May and late September/early October—the former because the wildlife's just waking up from being dug in for the winter and newborns tended through the snowy season are taking early steps into the wild outside world; the latter because it's both the fatten-up-for-winter season as well as the mating season for elk (Manitoba's largest population of elk lives in the park), moose, and other wildlife. In general, the animals are more active in the predawn and dusk hours, and thus are more easily spotted then.

Some wildlife-watchers stay in Wasagaming, at the Elkhorn Resort on the edge of the park near the South Gate entrance, or at Riding Mountain Guest Ranch, where sunset bear-watching is a "specialty of the house."

For optimum wildlife-viewing opportunities, join a guided hike led by local wildlife experts who know the park and daily wildlife movement patterns intimately. On these forays, wildlife-watchers are out on the back roads and trails before sunrise, when morning fog and mists cloak the quiet wetlands, and the only sounds are the flapping of wings or, in autumn, the scraping of elk antlers against trees and the eerie bugle of an elk in search of a mate.

These are the times when a moose could perhaps be spotted trotting along a gravel road or browsing the branches of low-hanging trees and bushes in a marshy meadow. A lone wolf or coyote may stand quietly at roadside, hoping not to be noticed, and beavers are easily visible dragging logs through patches of wetland to shore up lodges and dams in shallow ponds that are dotted with dozing waterfowl.

Lucky observers may catch glimpses of pine marten, fishers, mink, raccoons, coyotes, porcupines, and lynx. White-tailed deer herds, however, are easily spotted throughout the

park, while fresh scat on narrow trails reveals the presence of black bears.

Pre-dusk bird-watchers in Riding Mountain will almost certainly spot bald eagles by **Moon Lake, Whirlpool Lake,** and **Lake Audy;** falcons and hawks overhead; songbirds in the trees; and grouse in the forest undergrowth. Riding Mountain National Park boasts more than 260 species, so bird-watchers may easily find loons, ospreys, white pelicans, pileated woodpeckers, and great blue herons as well.

WHITEWATER LAKE
a half day

Before it became a national park, this area was a forest reserve, supplying firewood to surrounding farms and communities. During World War II, domestic fuel shortages meant it became a firewood source again— only this time, the wood was cut by German prisoners of war who lived in a **park encampment** at Whitewater Lake from 1943 to 1945.

Because it was so remote, the POW camp was neither fenced nor walled. Today, the ruins of building foundations remain and the site is now a campsite that can be reached by foot, bike, or horse via the **Central Trail** to Whitewater Lake. Park interpreters also lead horse-drawn wagons to the site.

GREY OWL HIKE
17 km/10.5 mi return;
a full day

One of the park's most popular day trails is the 17-km (10.5 mi) round-trip **Grey Owl Trail.** Its trailhead is off Hwy. 19, 7 km (4 mi) from Wasagaming. The trail takes hikers to the remote cabin of Grey Owl,

RIDING MOUNTAIN

RIDING MOUNTAIN NATIONAL PARK
(Parc national du Mont-Riding)

INFORMATION & ACTIVITIES

VISITOR CENTRE
Wasagaming, MB R0J 2H0. Phone (204) 848-7228. Visitor information and interpretive programs, theatre, Discovery Room, and Nature Shop. Purchase park passes and fishing licences here, as well as book backcountry camping permits.

SEASONS & ACCESSIBILITY
Open year-round. Wasagaming Campground closed in winter. Visitor centre closed mid-Oct. to mid-May.

HEADQUARTERS
Wasagaming, MB R0J 2H0. Phone (204) 848-7275. www.parkscanada.gc.ca/riding. Open year-round Mon.-Fri., 8 a.m.-4 p.m.

FRIENDS OF RIDING MOUNTAIN
Columbine Ave. in Wasagaming. Box 226, Onanole, MB R0J 1N0. Phone (204) 848-4037. friends.rmnp@pc.gc.ca; www.friendsofridingmountain.ca.

ENTRANCE FEES
$8 per person, $20 per group per day. $40 per person, $100 per group per year.

PETS
Pets must be leashed.

ACCESSIBLE SERVICES
Most facilities are wheelchair accessible, including the Park Theatre, Wasagaming Campground, and Beach Bath House. Accessible wharf and tennis courts.

THINGS TO DO
Hiking, cycling, horseback riding, horse-drawn wagon rides, and fishing. Boating, sailing, swimming, and scuba diving. Interpretive programs ($4 per person) and guided hikes. Visits to the Pinewood Museum. Also, golfing at the Clear Lake Golf Course, (204) 848-4653; and tennis at the Clear Lake Tennis Courts, (204) 848-2649.

In winter, cross-country skiing on the surface of Clear Lake and along the park boundary, snowshoeing, skating, and ice fishing.

who was supposedly a native naturalist, sported braids and buckskins, and became the park's first official naturalist in the company of his pet beavers, Jelly Roll and Rawhide.

Grey Owl fooled everybody with his aboriginal act. He was really an Englishman named Archibald Belaney, who'd come to eastern Canada and "gone native," then moved west and passionately embraced ecological preservation. He quickly became a Canadian legend, preaching preservation of nature and wilderness. Then the national parks system offered him the job of park naturalist at Riding Mountain National Park, which he took. He served as the park's naturalist for six months in 1931, living in a two-room (one for his beavers, one for him) cabin park employees built for him. He then moved on to Prince Albert National Park (see pp. 182–187) in the neighbouring province of Saskatchewan. By then, Jelly Roll and Rawhide were the parents of four kittens; Grey Owl also had rounded up a few other beavers and begun raising them, too. Today, gnaw marks from Jelly Roll and Rawhide are still visible in places on the interior logs of the cabin beside **Beaver Lodge Lake.** The cabin is now a designated federal heritage building.

Mountain bikers are allowed to use the Grey Owl Trail as well, though it's a bit rough in spots.

SPECIAL ADVISORIES

- Boil water before drinking at outlying campgrounds and backcountry campsites.
- In an effort to prevent the introduction of zebra mussels and other invasive species, boaters must have their watercraft inspected and obtain a free permit for as long as the boat stays in park waters.
- Swimming areas unsupervised. Coat skin with mineral or cooking oil to avoid swimmer's itch, a parasite.

OVERNIGHT BACKPACKING

Permit required for backcountry camping. Call (204) 848-7275.

CAMPGROUNDS

Wasagaming Campground, water, sewer and electricity $38; electricity and water $35; electricity only $32; unserviced with toilets and showers $27; oTENTik $100; yurt $90. Reservations (877) 737-3783 or www.pccamping.ca. **Moon Lake, Lake Audy, Whirlpool,** and **Deep Lake** outlying campgrounds, $16. All campsites have a fire box, picnic table, and access to washrooms or pit privies. For group camping, yurt, **Cairn's Cabin,** and backcountry camping, reservations (204) 848-7275.

HOTELS, MOTELS, & INNS

(unless otherwise noted, rates are for a 2-person double, high season, in Canadian dollars)

Inside the park:
Wasagaming, MB R0J 2H0:
Mooswa Resort, Mooswa Drive. (855) 586-3575 or (204) 848-2533. www.mooswa.com. $203–$230.
Idylwylde Cabins 136 Wasagaming Dr., Box 130. (204) 848-2383. www.idylwylde.ca. $142–$308; $940–$1,980 per week.
Lakehouse Boutique Hotel 128 Wasagaming Dr., (204) 848-7366. www.staylakehouse.ca. $159–$169.

Outside the park:
Crooked Mountain Cabins Southeast of Riding Mountain National Park. (204) 636-7873. www.crookedmountaincabins.ca. minimum 2-night stay in spring and fall, weekly rentals only in July and Aug. $150; $1,050 per week.
Elkhorn Resort & Conference Centre/ Solstice Spa Box 40, Onanole, MB R0J 1N0. (204) 848-2808. www.elkhornresort.mb.ca. $109–$259.
Honeycomb Bed & Breakfast 11 Erickson Dr. (204) 848-2345. www.honeycombbbbclearlake.com. $95–$128.

EXCURSION

RIDING MOUNTAIN PARK EAST GATE REGISTRATION COMPLEX NATIONAL HISTORIC SITE
RIDING MOUNTAIN NP, MB

Built in 1933 and 1934 as part of the Canadian federal government's Depression Relief Program, the park's East Gate Registration Complex National Historic Site is the only original national park gate still standing. Built from local logs and a prime example of 1930s rustic design style, the gate, its registration building, and two staff cabins make for a truly traditional picture-postcard photograph.

Kayaking on Waskesiu River

▶ PRINCE ALBERT

SASKATCHEWAN
ESTABLISHED 1927
3,875 sq km/957,500 acres

Typical of its era, Prince Albert National Park was created to serve as a recreational playground—its stewardship value would only be recognized much later. The park spans a slender transition zone between the northern boreal forest and the southern aspen parkland. Its rolling hills of spruce, pine, aspen, and birch shelter pockets of fescue and sedge meadows. Year after year, forestry concerns and encroaching civilization have threatened this ecosystem elsewhere, making Prince Albert today a precious preserve.

Prince Albert is also notable for the bison herd that roams along its southwestern border, a free-ranging herd of wild plains bison that still occupies its ancestral territory. The herd is descended from animals that were relocated here from Elk Island National Park. The herd now boasts more than 200 head.

Numbering many millions before near extirpation at the hands of European settlers, Canada's largest land mammal—a bull can weigh more than a tonne—is still very much a threatened species. The bison are not fenced in here and thus move freely between the park and public lands, much to the consternation of some neighbouring landowners.

When Prince Albert National Park was established, its land was occupied by First Nations, Métis, and Cree, who had settled in the area in the mid-19th century; most of them were then obliged to move east to Montreal Lake. Soon afterward, the park became home to the renowned conservationist writer Grey Owl. Though he purported to be a member of the First Nations, he was in fact an Englishman named Archibald Belaney. The revelation of his true identity after his death was an international scandal. Nonetheless, Grey Owl's conservationist message— "Remember, you belong to Nature, not it to you"—has stood the test of time. His cabin on Ajawaan Lake is one of the country's best known hiking destinations.

How to Get There

Most visitors arrive by automobile via provincial Hwy. 2 and Hwy. 264, the quickest route to the East Gate and the village of Waskesiu Lake. Hwy. 263, a winding and scenic paved road that passes through the South Gate, is an alternate route. For access to the largely undeveloped West Side, visitors can use Hwy. 55. Saskatoon has the closest international airport and passenger rail service. The provincial bus line, STC, serves Waskesiu with daily departures from Saskatoon and Prince Albert. Service runs from early May to early September.

When to Go

The park is at its best between Victoria Day and Labour Day. The extra-long days around the end of June are especially glorious. The aspen and tamarack reach the height of their tangerine colour around mid- to late September, when you will

have the park mostly to yourself. A handful of businesses are open year-round. Call the visitor centre to learn more. Freeze-up and winter arrive quickly and there is usually enough snow for skiing from December through late March. Recreational options are most limited in April, when the lake ice is unsafe and roads and trails are muddy.

How to Visit

Set inside the park, the resort town of **Waskesiu** (Cree for "red deer") offers accommodations, restaurants, shops, and services; hotel accommodations are available year-round. Typical visitors make the town their base for car-supported day trips on the **East Side** of the park, especially along Hwy. 263. Excellent sandy beaches are found on **Waskesiu, Namekus,** and **Sandy Lakes.** There is an extensive trail network for day-use and backcountry hiking, cycling, and skiing on groomed trails. Backcountry paddling routes are limited, but there are many good day-trip options.

Visitors primarily interested in the park's **plains bison herd,** or in horseback- and wagon-riding trips into the park, should contact park staff for suggestions about accommodations and outfitters. In all cases, overnight backcountry stays require a permit from the visitor centre in Waskesiu.

EAST SIDE: KINGSMERE ROAD & GREY OWL'S CABIN
a full day

Kingsmere Road heads north from the townsite of Waskesiu, following the shore of Waskesiu Lake, until it dead-ends at the Kingsmere Lake

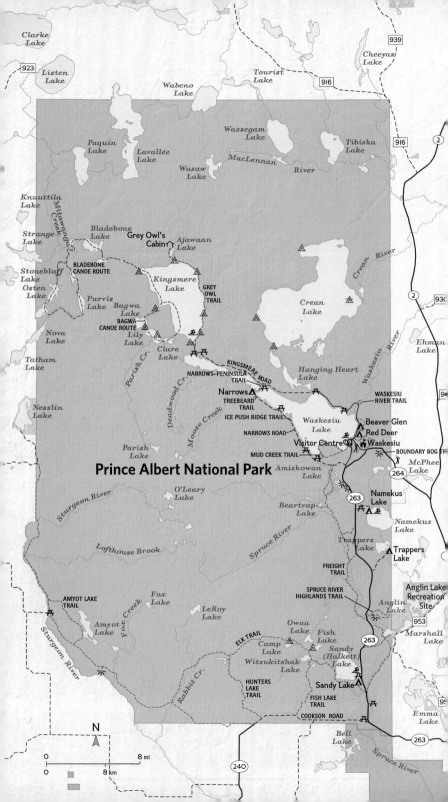

day-use area and boat launch. Along the way are many day-trip possibilities and backcountry entry points. Observant visitors might spot deer, wolves, black bears, grouse, elk, and bald eagles if they drive slowly and pay attention. A wheelchair-accessible trail is located at the **Waskesiu River.**

The **Waskesiu Lake Marina** has powerboats, canoes, and kayaks for rent. The big lake can be treacherous for any craft. Paddling close to shore is safer and more interesting. There are more rentals a little farther west along the Kingsmere Road at **Hanging Heart Lakes Marina.**

This narrower, more protected waterway is inviting to paddlers. Deer and bears often appear on its grassy foreshores. Get an early start, and you can paddle 8 km (5 mi) to glimpse **Crean Lake** before turning back. Or better yet, set up camp at one of the backcountry sites. Pontoon boat trips with an interpreter are available along the route, too.

Farther west, the lovely **Narrows Peninsula Trail** gives views of Waskesiu Lake. Kingsmere Road terminates at the **Kingsmere River,** where a trail leads north and divides into two. One trail leads to Grey Owl's cabin and the other, a half-hour stroll following the winding ribbon of water, brings you to the south shore of **Kingsmere Lake.** In good weather, this beach is a lovely spot to picnic and swim; the lake has a sandy bottom that remains shallow a long way out.

The second trail follows the eastern shore of Kingsmere Lake to **Grey Owl's cabin** on **Ajawaan Lake,** 20 km (12.5 mi) north. The Grey Owl hike has become a kind of pilgrimage. It started in the summer of 1936 when several hundred people made

Hawthorn tree berries (*Crataegus* sp.)

the journey to meet the famous author and his enigmatic wife, Anahareo, who were famous across the British Empire.

To this day the pilgrims keep coming, from all over the world. Grey Owl's personal life was sordid and unhappy at times, but his conservationist message was worthwhile. There is no better way to understand the beauty he wrote about than to hike to the cabin where he worked.

WEST SIDE: BISON HERD
a full day from Waskesiu

In contrast to the paved road and cottage-country developments on the park's East Side, Prince Albert's West Side retains a wild, frontier feel. Yet this hitherto virtually unvisited region is the focus of increasing attention—mostly because of the plains bison herd that inhabits the **Sturgeon River Valley.** The burly animals can often be seen grazing in sedge meadows. Walk 200 m (219 yds) along an accessible trail to the Valleyview Trail

PRINCE ALBERT

Canoeing on Bear Trap Lake

picnic area for a breathtaking vista.

Horseback riding and wagon trips are offered by outfitters along the West Side, who have the advantage of local knowledge in finding bison. The not-for-profit Sturgeon River Plains Bison Stewards *(www.bison stewards.ca)* often has the most current information about the herd.

Always be cautious around bison. Despite their size and power, they are skittish animals. Shy of people, they will generally move away if approached within, say, 100 m (330 ft). Keep your distance and the animals will stay put; push too close and you may find yourself in danger. Bulls in the summer mating season can be aggressive, as can mothers protecting their young. Bison are formidable when riled. Rely on a pair of binoculars for dramatic close-ups.

No road crosses the park, so getting to the West Side from Waskesiu means a long drive around the park's perimeter, mostly on gravel roads. Consider a West Side guest ranch stay to maximize your bison "hunting" time.

The park becomes a snowy wonderland in winter.

PRINCE ALBERT NATIONAL PARK
(Parc national de Prince Albert)

INFORMATION & ACTIVITIES

VISITOR CENTRE
969 Lakeview Dr., Waskesiu Lake, SK S0J 2Y0. Phone (306) 663-4522. panp.info@ pc.gc.ca.

SEASONS & ACCESSIBILITY
Park open year-round. Main campgrounds operate mid-May through September; camping in Waskesiu and backcountry available year-round.

CONTACT INFORMATION
Box 100, Waskesiu Lake, SK S0J 2Y0. Phone (306) 663-4522. www.parks canada.gc.ca/princealbert.

ENTRANCE FEES
$8 per person per day; $30 to $40 per person per year. $20 per group per day.

PETS
Pets must be leashed at all times. Ask staff about dog-friendly beaches.

ACCESSIBLE SERVICES
The Visitor Centre, Beaver Glen, Red Deer Campgrounds, some paths on the Waskesiu River Trail, and the Nature Centre are wheelchair accessible.

THINGS TO DO
Hiking trails of various lengths. Eight beaches on **Waskesiu, Namekus, Sandy** (Halkett), and **Kingsmere Lakes.**

Canoeing in **Spruce** and Waskesiu Rivers and **Amiskowan,** Shady, **Heart,** Kingsmere, or Waskesiu Lakes and the **Bagwa Canoe Route.** Rentals available at Waskesiu Lake Marina (306-663-1999). Powerboating on Waskesiu, **Crean,** Kingsmere, Sandy, and Heart Lakes. Fishing permitted with licence (obtain at visitor centre or marina facilities; check with park on limits).

Exhibits and videos at the Nature Centre in Waskesiu Lake. Cycling on designated backcountry trails. Golf at the Waskesiu Golf Course (18 holes; 306-663-5300). In winter, cross-country skiing and snowshoeing.

SPECIAL ADVISORIES
• Open fires are only permitted in provided fire circles and pits.
• No boats or canoes allowed in buoyed beach areas. Beaches are unsupervised.
• Conditions highly variable on park lakes. Canoeists and kayakers advised to follow the eastern shore of Kingsmere Lake.
• Use bear caches for food, garbage, and toiletries.
• Boil lake water before drinking.

OVERNIGHT BACKPACKING
Overnight backcountry visitors must register at the visitor centre prior to the trip. Fees apply in designated backcountry campsites.

CAMPGROUNDS
In Waskesiu: **Red Deer Campground,** $30–$35 per night for campsites with water, sewer, and electricity; max. 1 RV and 1 tent. **Beaver Glen Campground,** $24–$30 per night with electricity; $20–$25 unserviced campsite with toilets and showers; max. 2 tents or 1 RV and 1 tent. Maximum stay 21 nights; maximum capacity 6 people per site. oTENTiks, $120 per night, sleep up to 6. Reservations (877) 737-3783, www .pccamping.ca.

In outlying areas: **Sandy Lake, Namekus Lake,** and overflow primitive campsites, $15 per night. **Narrows Campground,** unserviced campsite with toilets only, $22 per night, $127 per week, or $475 per month.

HOTELS, MOTELS, & INNS
(unless otherwise noted, rates are for a 2-person double, high season, in Canadian dollars)

Waskesiu Lake, SK S0J 2Y0
Elk Ridge Resort (800) 510-1824. www.elkridgeresort.com. $269–$369, includes wine and cheese, breakfast, and dinner.
Hawood Inn (306) 663-5911. www.hawood.com. $132–$188.

Additional visitor information:
Waskesiu Community Council www.waskesiu.org and Waskesiu Chamber of Commerce www.waske siulake.ca.

Blackfoot Worldview & Land

All societies, in one way or another, lay claim to a territory. Within the territory, a culture arises from a mutual relationship with the land. A culture consists of theoretical concepts, customs, and values. The theoretical concepts we can call paradigms. Paradigms are the tacit infrastructures members of a society utilize for their beliefs, behaviour, and relationships. To understand and appreciate a culture, one has to have a good understanding of that society's worldview.

Plains bison graze in Stoney Plain Meadow.

Thousands of generations of Blackfoot have dwelled in what is known as Blackfoot territory. Blackfoot territory roughly covers an area from the North Saskatchewan River to the Yellowstone River in Montana; from the Continental Divide of the Rocky Mountains to the confluence of the North and South Saskatchewan Rivers and the Cypress Hills in Saskatchewan. Within that territory the mutual relationship of humans, animals, plant life, the land, and the cosmos has resulted in a paradigm albeit not exclusive to Blackfoot.

The Blackfoot paradigm consists of constant flux, energy waves, everything being animate, interrelationships; reality requiring renewal, land, and language as a repository for Blackfoot knowledge. The notion of constant flux means for the Blackfoot that everything is in constant motion: Everything is undergoing a continuous process of change, transformation, deformation, reformation, and restoration. As Gary Witherspoon observes in *Language and Art in the Navajo Universe* (1977), the essence of life and being is movement. The constant flux consists of energy waves (physicists talk about the same thing but in terms of subatomic particles). For the Blackfoot, these energy waves can be referred to as the "spirit."

For the Blackfoot, everything is animate. All is animate because everything consists of energy waves. All existence has spirit, including humans, plants, animals, the land, and the cosmos. The constant flux results in a complex relational network. Consequently, for the Blackfoot everything is interrelated. One will hear in many North American prayers the phrase, "all my relations." In other words, because all have "spirit," all are my relations including the land.

The Blackfoot paradigm incorporates the notion of renewal. There is a tacit belief that in the flux there is a combination of energy waves that makes up for the individual and collective existence of everything. In other words, when the particular combination of energy waves that constitutes a human, animal, rock, and so on dissolves or dissipates, death occurs. One can look at it as a disappearance into the flux. Or, one can look at it as being consumed by the flux. Recognizing that the energy wave combinations that make for our existence can dissipate, Blackfoot attempt to renew or sustain the existing reality through renewal ceremonies.

For the Blackfoot, land is very important. Blackfoot are so closely related to the land that they refer to it as "mother." Just as a mother is the source of human life, so is the land. The land is the source of life. Blackfoot are very respectful to "the mother," the land. In other words, the land is to be treated in the same manner that we treat our biological mothers. The land is important because it is where many observable manifestations of the flux occur. Manifestations such as cosmic events, patterns, cycles—and happenings such as migrations of animals, life cycles of plants, seasonal rounds—and so on are observable and occur on the land.

Language is important because it acts as a repository for the knowing in Blackfoot culture. Blackfoot language mirrors the constant flux because it is about motion, processes, and action, as opposed to English, which is noun oriented, and to a large extent, stagnant. Blackfoot language mirrors the flux because it allows for alliances and relationships between spirits, energies, and powers in ways very different from Indo-European languages such as English.

Short-eared owl (Asio flammeus)

When one comes to appreciate the paradigm of Blackfoot people and applies that paradigm to relationships with the land, one will find that sustainability, conservation, leaving the land as pristine as possible, leaving the land to bring about an ecological balance, and having humans fit themselves into that ecological balance are renewal goals of Blackfoot society. It seems that, in many ways, national parks have the same goals. One can say, if the Blackfoot paradigm were applied to all of our lands in Canada, all of Canada would become a "national park."

— LEROY LITTLE BEAR, *University of Lethbridge*

Enjoy the adventure of backcountry camping.

▶ GRASSLANDS

SASKATCHEWAN
ESTABLISHED 1981
730 sq km/180,387 acres

The prairie was once an ocean of grass where a million bison roamed and where summer wildfire was a rejuvenating force. Then settlement converted nearly the whole into the grid of agricultural townships that define the West today. Grasslands National Park, however, protects one of the largest remnants of pristine prairies along the U.S. border. Here, under the blue dome of prairie sky, great vistas run to the distant horizon—and small miracles are found underfoot.

Grasslands is still growing as area ranchers sell land to Parks Canada. To date park lands total 80 percent of the 905-sq-km (349 sq mi) proposed boundary. The West Block is dominated by the Frenchman River Valley; the East Block is known for the Rock Creek Badlands Wood Mountain Uplands. Both sections contain areas untouched by ice during the most recent glaciation,

and fossils in the poorly consolidated bedrock of the hillsides record the last days of *Tyrannosaurus, Triceratops,* and other dinosaurs that roamed here.

In the valley bottoms you can walk through prairie dog towns that are as large as human towns, and perhaps spot rarities such as the blackfooted ferret, an endangered species. Prickly pear cactus grows profusely on the sun-facing banks; mule deer and antelope browse in the cooler, lightly wooded coulees. Short-horned lizards, prairie rattlesnakes, garters, racers, and bull snakes can all be found, too.

The ancient hills are graced by teepee rings, bison drive lands, and the stone tools of the First Nations people. Weathered remnants of dwellings tell of a much more recent relationship with the land.

How to Get There

A vehicle is a practical necessity for trips into either block of Grasslands National Park. Regina and Saskatoon have the nearest international airports and other major transportation links.

Access to the West Block is via the village of Val Marie at Hwys. 4 and 18, where a stop at the visitor centre is recommended. The closest towns to the East Block are Glentworth and Wood Mountain on Hwy. 18.

In summer, staff at the Rodeo Ranch Museum in Wood Mountain Regional Park and the Rock Creek Campground can provide condition reports on the gravel roads leading into the park off Hwy. 18. From Wood Mountain, head south on Hwy. 18 for 22.4 km (14 mi), then turn west for 6.4 km (4 mi), then south for another 6.4 km (4 mi), and then west for 2.4 km (1.5 mi) until you reach the park entrance.

When to Go

The park is open year-round. The heat of summer can be challenging. Afternoon thundershowers caused by daytime heating can be severe and can make roads impassable. Early morning and late evening, when temperatures have moderated, are good times to visit. Though the visitor centre is closed mid-October to mid-May, the off-season has advan-

tages. Winter temperatures can be very mild by prairie standards. Snowfall is generally quite low, so that hiking is a year-round possibility. The great vistas of Grasslands can be stunning in hoar-frost conditions. Warmer days arrive in early March, and flowers are abundant in May and June.

How to Visit

Grasslands is hypnotically beautiful, and accessible by car in dry weather. However, there are limited services, and some roads become impassably muddy if it rains. The landscape rewards hikers with transcendent natural beauty and the freedom to roam anywhere. But distances are deceiving and good navigation skills are required. Water is currently unavailable in the park, so you must bring your own—2 l (0.5 gal) per person per day at a minimum. Summer conditions are hot and desertlike, and there is little natural shade. A one-day, self-guided Ecotour Road threads through the West Block, with interpretive signs at various stops.

To fully experience the subtle beauty of the park, get out on the trails. Horseback riding is welcome. The park and outside outfitters offer horseback experiences.

WEST BLOCK: 70 MILE BUTTE HIKE

a half day

A lovely introduction to the French-man River Valley, the newly built 70 Mile Butte trail rewards visitors with stunning views from one of the highest points in the West Block. From the visitor centre in Val Marie, travel south on Hwy. 4, then turn east on the 70 Mile Butte Access Road that leads to the trailhead kiosk.

GRASSLANDS

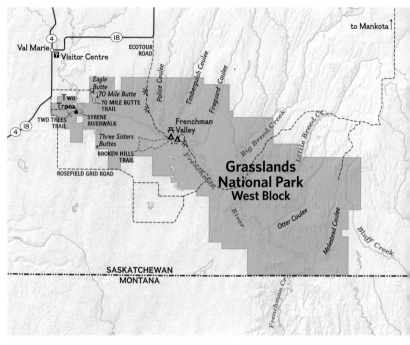

The trail climbs into one of the great landmark uplands of the Frenchman Valley and provides awe-inspiring views from atop the **70 Mile Butte,** rising 932 m (3,058 ft) above sea level. The 5-km (3 mi) loop route is moderately difficult and will take a leisurely morning to complete. Start at dawn to avoid the heat of the day and to see an array of wildlife at their most active.

The butte was a guiding landmark for the First Nations peoples for thousands of years; however, its name comes from the time when the Northwest Mounted Police patrolled the region via horseback. The butte was midpoint of the patrol—112.7 km (70 mi)—between Wood Mountain Post and Eastend Post and provided a reliable landmark.

Constable John George Donkin recorded in his journal of 1886: "These expeditions are fully armed of course and remain out on the prairie

for a week. A transport wagon is attached to each, carrying tent, bedding, rations of tea, biscuit, bacon and oats, a spade, camp-kettles and frying pan, and wood."

The whole perimeter of 70 Mile Butte and the adjacent plateaus has archaeological remnants of native encampments. Make a side trip if your energy and map skills allow, and leave what you find untouched.

EAST BLOCK: RIM HIKE
a half to full day

The **Rim Hike** offers a wonderful overview of the beauty of the East Block. The loop trail can be hiked in an hour or two, or extended to fill a day if side trips are made. To reach its trailhead, follow the directions to access Grasslands from Wood Mountain and park at the Rock Creek Campground and Picnic Area.

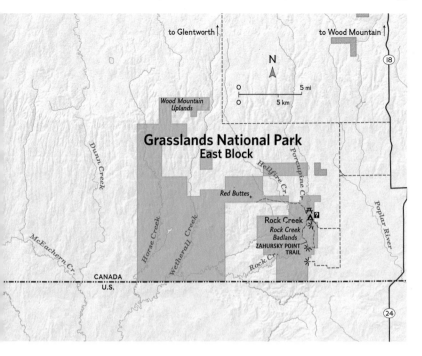

Grasslands National Park
East Block

to Glentworth
to Wood Mountain

N

0 5 mi
0 5 km

Wood Mountain
Uplands

Dunn Creek

Porcupine Cr.

Hellfire Cr.

Red Buttes

Rock Creek
Rock Creek
Badlands
ZAHURSKY POINT
TRAIL

Horse Creek

Wetherall Creek

McEachern Cr.

Rock Cr.

Poplar River

CANADA
U.S.

18

24

In 1911, James McGowan began to homestead in this area. After three generations of ranching, the McGowan family sold their lands to the national park in the 1980s. It is a familiar pattern, for making a living in this area has been a struggle. From 1850 to 1880, bison met their fate, and without the buffalo, Plains Indians and Métis could no longer live off the land. In the following years, cattle replaced buffalo, creating a new economy on the prairies and bringing in huge ranching companies. However, harsh winters, a massive die-off of cattle due to disease, and the Homesteaders Act of 1908 ended the era of open-range ranching.

The government enticed settlers from Europe and eastern Canada to "tame the west" and "break the land." Homesteaders faced many hardships, including drought, frost, insect infestations, and disease. They soon learned that the land was more suited for grazing. Many homesteaders picked up and left after only a few years. A mix of ranching and farming complements the region today.

The land's fundamental low productivity has, more than anything, kept the grasslands intact. The grasses and forbs that thrive here are

Crocus (*Anemone patens*)

A hike through Eagle Butte provides breathtaking views and incredible scenery.

Sharp-tailed grouse (*Tympanuchus phasianellus*)

Black-tailed prairie dog (*Cynomys ludovicianus*)

specialists, and many of them are visible on the Rim Hike. Needle-and-thread or blue grama grass, lichens, and moss phlox are characteristic ground cover plants. Sage is a staple for both antelope and grouse. Crocuses, avens, pin cushion cactus, and pale blue harebell bloom throughout the summer. And an array of wildlife may be spotted, among them mule deer, badgers, jackrabbits, and coyotes.

One of the joys of hiking in Grasslands is the freedom to choose your own route. Exercise your option to descend to **Rock Creek** via a coulee from the rim. Its modest flow supports leopard frogs, crayfish, and many other aquatic species in this rich environment.

The dramatic **Rock Creek Badlands** are visible to the southwest. Just beyond the farthest reach of the last glaciations, these bluffs yielded, in 1874, the first recorded dinosaur remains found in western Canada.

GRASSLANDS NATIONAL PARK
(Parc national des Prairies)

INFORMATION & ACTIVITIES

VISITOR CENTRE
West Block: Junction of Hwy. 4 & Centre St., Val Marie, SK. Near the West Block of Grasslands National Park. East block: Rock Creek Campground.

SEASONS & ACCESSIBILITY
Park open year-round. Visitor centre open daily mid-May to mid-October. Check the website for hours of operation.

HEADQUARTERS
P.O. Box 150, Val Marie, SK S0N 2T0. Phone (306) 298-2257 or (306) 476-2018. www.parkscanada.gc.ca/grasslands.

ENTRANCE FEES
No entry fee.

PETS
Pets must be kept on a leash and at a safe distance from wildlife. Keep pets away from prairie dog towns.

THINGS TO DO
Hiking (day and overnight), backpacking, camping, wildlife viewing, learning about archaeological sites, horseback riding, scenic drives, stargazing, interpretive programs. The "Ecotour Driving Adventure" is one of Saskatchewan's most scenic drives. The "Ranching Roots" experience offers Wild West activities, including lassoing. "Sunset at the Top of **70 Mile Butte**" offers grand views from the highest point in the area. Prairie dog towns and scenic photography.

SPECIAL ADVISORIES
• Portable stoves and campfires banned in the dry seasons. Be prepared to camp without a fire in designated areas when fire ban in effect in the East and West Blocks.
• Vehicles must remain on roads.

OVERNIGHT BACKPACKING
No designated backcountry campsites; backpackers must camp at least 1 km (.62 mi) away from the road. Self-registration. $10 per person per night.

CAMPGROUNDS
Frenchman Valley Campground in the West Block has electrical sites, tipi and oTENTik accommodations, fire pits, picnic tables, potable water, and vault toilets. Close to Coulee Centre, a hub for park programs. $16 per night. To reserve, call (877) 737-3783.
Rock Creek Campground in the East Block offers terraced RV campsites with fire pits, tipis, sheltered tent sites, summer kitchens, picnic tables, potable water, and vault toilets. $16 per night. To reserve, call (306) 476-2018.

HOTELS, MOTELS, & INNS
(unless otherwise noted, rates are for a 2-person double, high season, in Canadian dollars)

Outside the park:
Val Marie, SK S0N 2T0:
Convent Inn Box 209. (306) 298-4515. conventinn@sasktel.com; www.convent.ca. Summer only. $79–$89 for one-person occupancy; $10 per additional guest.
The Crossing at Grasslands Box 31. (306) 298-2295. thecrossingatgrasslands@gmail.com; www.crossingresort.com. $105–$125.
Rosefield Church Guesthouse Box 14. (306) 298-2030. info@rosefield.ca; www.rosefield.ca. $130, two-night minimum.

Mankota, SK S0H 2W0:
The Grasslands Inn Railway Ave. (306) 478-2909. $99.

Sunlight breaks through the fog in Elk Island National Park.

▶ ELK ISLAND

ALBERTA
ESTABLISHED 1913
194 sq km/47,938 acres

Originally established as a sanctuary for elk, Elk Island is recognized today as the cornerstone of bison and elk conservation in Canada. Without this place and the dedication of its people, these iconic creatures would not thrive in Canada today. At Elk Island, visitors join in the legacy of conservation success as they explore and reconnect with the park's gentle wilderness.

Elk Island National Park—Canada's only national park that is fully fenced off from surrounding lands—is an excellent example of Alberta's aspen parkland, meaning an open woodland of leafy trees and conifers that is transitional between the dense boreal evergreen forest of northern Canada and the grasslands of the Great Plains. These days the park is also thought of as a wilderness surrounded by agricultural land.

The park's landscape is a mosaic of hills and hollows, ponds and marshes, meadows and woods. This is knob-and-kettle topography, which is created when irregular masses of glacial ice melt away under a cover of gravel and till. The knobs are the hills; the kettles are the hollows. The topographic relief is about 60 m (200 ft), enough to sustain an ecosystem in which small differences in elevation produce large differences in plant communities. Biodiversity is high here and the species list is long, especially the bird checklist. Both species of bison (plains bison and woodland bison) are represented in the park.

The north and south portions of the park are separated by Hwy. 16 (Yellowhead Hwy.), which provides the main access to the park. All bison seen south of the highway are wood bison; to the north are the plains bison. There are no major north-south differences in the park's elk population.

The Elk Island Parkway takes visitors northward to the park's activity hub, the Astotin Lake Area. At 3.8 km (2.4 mi) long, Astotin Lake is the largest of the 250 water bodies in the park. One of the islands in the lake is named Elk Island, which may account for the park's name.

Birding and viewing the park's wildlife are popular activities year-round. Visitors can walk, ski, or snowshoe 11 maintained trails, most of them loops. One lengthy trail is paved and suitable for wheelchairs or strollers, but it has steeper sections that may be challenging for some wheelchair users.

A boardwalk provides a short interpretive tour of a marsh near the visitor centre. Reserved for non-motorized boating activities, Astotin Lake is popular among canoeists and kayakers. Boat rentals are available on weekends in May through September in the Astotin Lake Area. There is no fishing in the park. Cross-country skiing and snowshoeing are great ways to explore the peaceful serenity of the trails in the winter.

Artificial lighting in the park is minimal. Stargazing and aurora viewing are excellent, especially in winter.

How to Get There

Elk Island National Park is only 45 minutes from downtown Edmonton, Alberta. From Edmonton (closest airport), follow Hwy. 16 (Yellowhead Hwy.) east for 27 km (17 mi) and turn left onto the Elk Island Parkway. The parkway continues northward from the Astotin Lake Area to the northern park boundary, where it becomes Hwy. 831 to the town of Lamont.

When to Go

The warm months are June through August. In July, temperatures in the park typically reach into the 20s°C (70s–80s°F). Wildflowers begin to bloom in May and are at their best from late June to mid-July. The park's aspen groves turn a brilliant yellow in mid-September. By the end of October, the trees have lost their leaves and snow has started to accumulate. Be prepared for very cold days in January, when Arctic high-pressure cells can bring cold snaps of -40°C (-22°F).

How to Visit

Bison and elk roam freely through the park and may be seen nearly anywhere. The **Elk Island Parkway** (see p. 199), the park's main access road, is much better than Hwy. 16 (Yellowhead Hwy.) for observing wildlife. Take this low-speed paved road northward to the **Astotin Lake Area.** Once there, get out of your vehicle and explore.

Families will find much to see and do in the Astotin Lane Area, which has been developed with public recreation in mind. You can enjoy scenic views of the lake on the Lakeview and Shoreline Trails, take in an interpretive program at the interpretive theatre, go for a paddle, or enjoy a picnic. A playground is

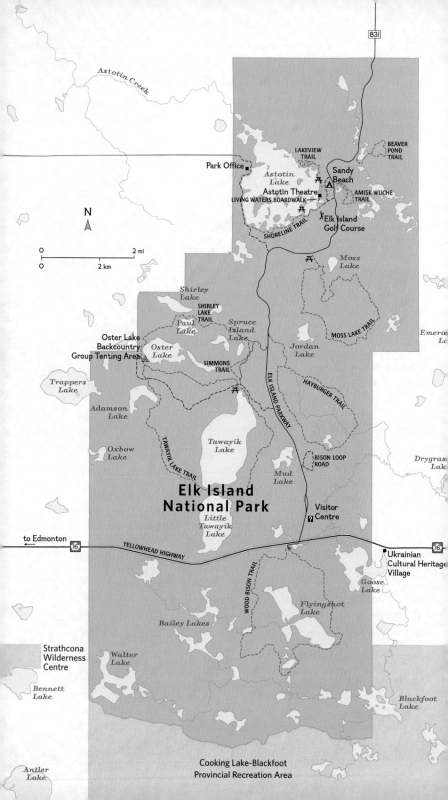

Astotin Creek

831

LAKEVIEW
TRAIL

BEAVER
POND
TRAIL

Park Office

Sandy
Beach

Astotin
Lake

Astotin Theatre
LIVING WATERS BOARDWALK

AMISK WUCHE
TRAIL

N

Elk Island
Golf Course

SHORELINE TRAIL

Moss
Lake

0   2 mi

0   2 km

MOSS LAKE TRAIL

Shirley
Lake

SHIRLEY
LAKE
TRAIL

Spruce
Island
Lake

Paul
Lake

Emerald
Le

Oster Lake
Backcountry
Group Tenting Area

Oster
Lake

Jordan
Lake

SIMMONS
TRAIL

ELK ISLAND PARKWAY

HAYBURGER TRAIL

Trappers
Lake

Drygras
Lak

Adamson
Lake

TAWAYIK LAKE TRAIL

Tawayik
Lake

BISON LOOP
ROAD

Oxbow
Lake

Mud
Lake

Elk Island
National Park

Little
Tawayik
Lake

Visitor
Centre

Ukrainian
Cultural Heritage
Village

to Edmonton 16

YELLOWHEAD HIGHWAY

16

WOOD BISON TRAIL

Goose
Lake

Flyingshot
Lake

Strathcona
Wilderness
Centre

Bailey Lakes

Bennett
Lake

Walter
Lake

Blackfoot
Lake

Antler
Lake

Cooking Lake-Blackfoot
Provincial Recreation Area

also available along with plenty of field space to run and play. The Astotin Lake Campground operates from May to October. Golfers can play a public nine-hole course, and the golf club serves meals and snacks to the general public.

Despite all the facilities at the Astotin Lake Area, most of Elk Island National Park remains wild. Many visitors spend the day walking the trails that wind through the park's complex landscape, identifying bird species and taking photographs of wildlife in natural settings.

The park's bison are wild animals, and visitors need to exercise caution; a distance of at least 100 m (330 ft) should be kept at all times. The same applies for the park's elk, moose, and deer. Males become more aggressive during the mating season (summer for the bison, late summer and autumn for the others), and the females are very protective of their young.

Stay well back when taking photographs. Keep your pets leashed at all times. Black bears and other predators are very rarely seen in the park.

Mountain biking is permitted; however, there is a potential for encounters with wildlife. Exercise caution and stay alert for wildlife, especially bison, whether on trails or on the road.

WILDLIFE-WATCHING ALONG ELK ISLAND PARKWAY

20 km/12.4 mi; at least 1 hour

You will find many pull-offs and viewpoints with interpretive signs along this very popular park-access and wildlife-viewing route. Observe the speed limits, and be especially cautious at dawn, at dusk, and at

night. The parkway is not fenced, and dark-coloured bison may be standing in the road.

Your best chance of seeing the park's plains bison is to turn off the parkway at the **Bison Loop Road,** 2.6 km (1.6 mi) from the start, where the animals tend to congregate. The loop is 1.8 km (1.1 mi) long. Stay in your car during the midsummer mating period, when the male bison can be heard "roaring."

Elk, white-tailed deer, and mule deer prefer the open, grassy areas with woods nearby. During the autumn elk rut, the males "bugle," producing loud whistling sounds that carry to the females and provide a challenge to other males. Give them plenty of room. Moose live in the park, too, mostly in the wooded wetlands. Other species to watch for include coyotes and beavers.

BIRDING

Elk Island has been described as a birder's paradise. The varied wet/dry ecosystems in the park provide habitat for some 250 species of birds, among them the distinctive American white pelican, the double-crested cormorant, and the trumpeter swan. Sandhill cranes frequent the park. Pileated woodpeckers—the largest woodpecker species in Canada—are often seen in aspen and poplar groves.

The short **Living Waters Boardwalk loop** at **Astotin Lake** is an easy-to-reach observation area for wetland birds and waterfowl, including red-necked grebes, cormorants, yellow-headed blackbirds, tundra swans, ducks, and shorebirds.

Any of the hiking trails at the lake will provide rewarding birding, especially the **Lakeview Trail,** 3.5 km

ELK ISLAND

(2.2 mi), one to two hours. The trailhead is located at the north end of the Astotin Lake Area. Birders looking for a longer walk will enjoy the **Shirley Lake Trail,** 10.5 km (6.5 mi), three to four hours, which is well known for views of the park's nesting waterfowl.

HIKING

Trails in the Astotin Lake Area are very popular for short walks. The **Shoreline Trail** around the lake, 6 km (3.7 mi) return, two to three hours, is paved and wheelchair accessible. The easy and varied **Amisk Wuche Trail,** 2.5 km (1.6 mi), roughly a one-hour walk, is very popular with families.

Longer trails take visitors to some of the wilder parts of the park. The **Moss Lake Trail,** 13 km (8 mi), 3.5 to 4.5 hours, explores the area south-east of Astotin Lake, while the **Wood Bison Trail,** 16 km (10 mi), four to five hours, is the only route into the portion of the park lying south of Hwy. 16 (Yellowhead Hwy.). This is the wildest area in the park, and you may, indeed, see wood bison here.

Cross-country skiing is popular at Elk Island.

SKIING & SNOWSHOEING

The winter activity season runs from November through March. Snowshoes can be rented from the visitor centre. Visitors can also bring skates during January and February to skate on Astotin Lake. The park maintains a skating track that whisks skaters from the beach area to and around an island. Bring a headlamp at night for a magical, star-filled experience. Though trails are not track-set, cross country skiers enjoy Elk Island trails.

A bull moose sheds velvet from its antlers in Elk Island National Park.

ELK ISLAND NATIONAL PARK
(Parc national Elk Island)

INFORMATION & ACTIVITIES

VISITOR CENTRE
54401 Range Rd. 203, Fort Saskatchewan, AB T8L 2N7. Phone (780) 922-2950. einp.info@pc.gc.ca; www.parkscanada.gc.ca/elkisland.

SEASONS & ACCESSIBILITY
Park open year-round.

FRIENDS OF ELK ISLAND
Friends of Elk Island Society P.O. Box 72099, Ottewell, Edmonton, AB T6B 3A7. (780) 895-7399. info@elkisland.ca; www.elkisland.ca.

ENTRANCE FEES
$8 per day for adults, $7 per day for seniors, $4 per day for youth, and $20 per day for families. Special rates apply for school and commercial groups (contact the park). Day Passes can be purchased at the South and North Gates, Astotin Lake Campground, visitor centre, and administration office, or at the automated pass machines at the park gates.

PETS
Dogs must be leashed at all times.

ACCESSIBLE SERVICES
Washrooms and some sites at the Astotin Campground are accessible.

THINGS TO DO
Paddling on **Astotin Lake** (boat rentals available). Boat launch at the Astotin Lake Area parking lot. Eleven trails for hiking. Cross-country skiing and snowshoeing on and off trails. Picnicking at **Tawayik Lake Picnic Area** and Astotin Lake.

In summer, interpretive programs offered free of charge with valid park pass. A nine-hole golf course and pro shop are located in the Astotin Lake Area. Golf course (780-998-3161, *www.elkislandgolf.com*) open May to October.

SPECIAL ADVISORIES
• Swimming in Astotin Lake is not recommended.
• Do not feed or chase squirrels or other small animals.

• 24-Hour Emergency Parks Canada (877) 852-3100.
• Fires and camping not permitted on islands in Astotin Lake.

OVERNIGHT BACKPACKING
Must obtain free permits from the visitor centre. Overnight backcountry camping is available at **Oster Lake** by reservation.

CAMPGROUNDS
Astotin Campground, open May to October. 68 unserviced campsites. Flush toilets, showers. For reservations, call (877) 737-3783 or go to www.reservation.parkscanada.gc.ca. Maximum stay is 21 days. Group camping is available at the **Astotin Lake Campground** (minimum 10 campers). Not available on long weekends and must be reserved in advance (780-992-0017). Winter camping area available in the RV loop and is free of charge (park entrance fee still applies). Additionally, winter camping is offered when the Astotin Campground closes, typically after Thanksgiving weekend (October) until early May (weather dependent).

HOTELS, MOTELS, & INNS
(unless otherwise noted, rates are for a 2-person double, high season, in Canadian dollars)

Outside the park:
Lakeview Inn & Suites 10115 88 Ave., Fort Saskatchewan, AB T8L 4K1. (780) 998-7888. www.lakeviewhotels.com. $119–$139.
Prairie Sunset Bed & Breakfast 54140 Range Rd. 224, Fort Saskatchewan, AB T8L 3Y5. (780) 997-0551. reamc@telusplanet.net; www.prairiesunset.com. $105.

Additional visitor information:
Edmonton Tourism
www.exploreedmonton.com

Some 10,000 wood bison roam freely across Wood Buffalo, which was established to protect the species' habitat.

▌WOOD BUFFALO

ALBERTA & NORTHWEST TERRITORIES
ESTABLISHED 1922
44,972 sq km/11,112,832 acres

Wood Buffalo is Canada's largest national park: Covering more territory than Switzerland, it sprawls across northeastern Alberta and juts into the southern part of the Northwest Territories. Designated a UNESCO World Heritage site, it is home to one of the world's last remaining free-roaming wood bison herds, the nesting habitat for endangered whooping cranes, and the world's largest Dark Sky Preserve.

The park's varied landscape includes boreal forest, salt plains, and gypsum karst landforms. The southern portion of the park features the Peace-Athabasca Delta, one of the largest inland freshwater deltas in the world. All four North American flyways converge over the delta each spring and fall. The last remaining flock of migratory whooping cranes nest in a remote corner of the boreal forest every summer.

In 1982, the International Union for the Conservation of Nature recognized Wood Buffalo for protecting the Peace-Athabasca Delta and the whooping crane nesting area. The two areas were designated as Ramsar sites under the Ramsar Convention, which focuses on identifying and protecting critical habitat for migratory birds. The Slave, Peace, and

Athabasca Rivers flow through the park. Opportunities for backcountry hiking and camping include a trip down the Peace River followed by a 14-km (8.75 mi) hike into Sweetgrass Station, which features a restored warehouse and former bison corrals.

The boreal plains near the Northwest Territories town of Fort Smith are the most accessible and popular area of the park. Day hikes take visitors through boreal forests of spruce, jackpine, aspen, and poplar to see salt flats, underground streams, sinkholes, and saline streams. Wood Buffalo is home to such elusive species as black bear, wolf, moose, fox, beaver, and sandhill crane. But seeing these shy creatures is completely left to chance.

How to Get There

The park has two main gateway communities: Fort Smith and Fort Chipewyan. To reach Fort Smith, home to the park's headquarters, take the Mackenzie Hwy. from northern Alberta. Connect to Hwy. 5, an all-weather road of partly hard-packed gravel that starts near Hay River, Northwest Territories. Watch for black bears and bison that sometimes lumber across the highway.

The park office in Fort Chipewyan is only accessible by air or water, except for a few months every winter when an ice road links it to Fort Smith and Fort McMurray. Northwestern Air Lease offers scheduled commercial flights. Flightseeing tours can also be arranged.

When to Go

The best time to visit the park is between the Victoria Day weekend and Labour Day, when the Pine Lake Campground is open. Summer temperatures range from 20°C to 30°C (68°F–86°F). Community

events include the Pine Lake Picnic in mid-July and the Paddlefest Flotilla in early August. Contact the visitor centre for regularly scheduled programs and activities.

The park is open in winter. January and February are the best months for viewing the aurora borealis, due to the long nights. Temperatures hover between minus 25°C and minus 30°C (–13°F and –22°F). The winter road from Fort McMurray, up to Fort Chipewyan and through the park to Fort Smith, is an experience in itself. Driving the winter road requires proper preparation. Contact the park for road conditions and details.

How to Visit

A car provides the best means to see the park. A few pull-offs just past Hay River as well as the **Salt Plains Lookout** give visitors a chance to start experiencing the park before reaching the visitor centre in Fort Smith. Be sure to spend some time exploring **Fort Smith.** It was on the fur-trade route during the 18th and 19th centuries, and the administrative centre of the Northwest Territories until 1967. The town is a mix of First Nations, Métis, and nonaboriginal people. Spend a day hiking the trails at the Salt River Day Use Area and at Pine Lake, then spend the night at the Pine Lake Campground.

HAY RIVER TO FORT SMITH
270 km/168 mi; about 4 hours

Myriad sights lie along Hwy. 5 between Hay River and the northern boundary of Wood Buffalo National Park. Visitors should first stop to see the **Angus Sinkhole and Fire Tower.** Walk around the park's largest sink-

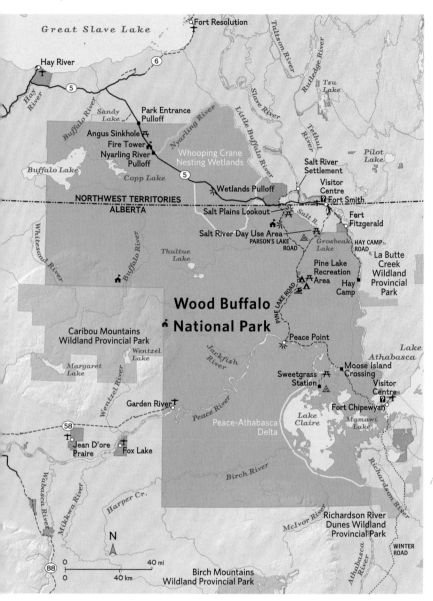

Great Slave Lake

Fort Resolution

Hay River

Tsu Lake

Taltson River

Rutledge River

Slave River

Little Buffalo River

Nyarling River

Sandy Lake

Buffalo River

Park Entrance Pulloff

Angus Sinkhole
Fire Tower
Nyarling River Pulloff

Whooping Crane Nesting Wetlands

Buffalo Lake

Copp Lake

Wetlands Pulloff

Pilot Lake

Tethul River

Salt River Settlement

Visitor Centre
Fort Smith

NORTHWEST TERRITORIES
ALBERTA

Salt Plains Lookout

Salt River Day Use Area
PARSON'S LAKE ROAD

Salt R.

Fort Fitzgerald

Grosbeak Lake

HAY CAMP ROAD

Whitesand River

Thultue Lake

Pine Lake Recreation Area

Hay Camp

La Butte Creek Wildland Provincial Park

Wood Buffalo National Park

PINE LAKE ROAD

Caribou Mountains Wildland Provincial Park

Wentzel Lake

Wentzel River

Margaret Lake

Jackfish River

Peace Point

Lake Athabasca

Sweetgrass Station

Moose Island Crossing

Visitor Centre

Fort Chipewyan

Garden River

Peace River

Peace-Athabasca Delta

Lake Claire

Mamawi Lake

Jean D'ore Prairie
Fox Lake

Birch River

Richardson River

Wabasca River

Mikkwa River

Harper Cr.

Richardson River Dunes Wildland Provincial Park

McIvor River

WINTER ROAD

N

40 mi
40 km

Birch Mountains Wildland Provincial Park

Athabasca River

hole, 100 m (330 ft) wide and 60 m (197 ft) deep. It formed when the top of an underground cave collapsed. Facilities here include interpretive panels, picnic tables, and washrooms. Continue along Hwy. 5 to the **Nyarling River Pull-Off.** The river flows for 26 km (16 mi), but you'd never know: Most of it flows underground. Interpretive panels explain why. Closer to Fort Smith, the **Wetlands Pull-Off and Interpretive Trail** leads to a spot overlooking the boreal landscape typical of where endangered whooping cranes rear their young. Interpretive signs provide information on the Peace-Athabasca Delta and the whooping crane nesting area.

Back in the car, keep an eye out for a sign marking the side road to the **Salt Plains Lookout and Day Use Area.** This viewpoint offers a sweeping perspective of the 370-sq-km (143 sq mi) salt plains. The lookout's high-powered telescopes can help visitors spot wildlife down below. Take the 500-m (0.25 mi) trail down the steep escarpment to the salt plains. There are no marked trails on this fragile, salt-encrusted landscape. Keen-eyed visitors might find delicate salt mounds and animal tracks indicating the passing of bears and bison.

Another lookout, the **Parson's Fire Tower,** lies a few kilometres down the 57-km-long (35.5 mi) dirt **Parson's Lake Road,** which leads from the day-use area deep into the boreal forest and connects with Pine Lake Road. This one-lane trail is not recommended for RVs and is impassable when wet. Keep an eye out for bison; you're on their land. The fire-tower site offers a panoramic view of the surrounding landscape. Return to Hwy. 5 and continue to Fort Smith.

Upon arriving in town, head to the park's visitor centre, which has an exhibit area and various videos on the park. Park staff can answer questions, provide maps, notify you of any bear sightings or fire bans in effect, and advise on backcountry trips and camping. They also offer regularly scheduled guided hikes and activities.

The centre also provides information about the various attractions in town, such as the **Northern Life Museum and Cultural Centre, Slave River Rapids, Thebacha Trail,** and **Fort Smith Mission Historic Park.** You can stock up on snacks at Kaeser's or the Northern Store for your second day in Wood Buffalo National Park.

PINE LAKE ROAD
120 km/74.5 mi; a full day

Just south of Fort Smith, the all-weather gravel Pine Lake Road runs southward from Hwy. 5 to the Peace River. Most people concentrate their visits on the Salt River and Pine Lake Day Use Areas.

The **Salt River Day Use Area** sits just inside the park's border. In early May this area is a mass of wriggling bodies: Hundreds of red-sided garter snakes emerge from their winter snooze underground to mate before slithering off to their summer feeding grounds. This is the species' most northerly hibernaculum. Park interpreters are on hand to answer questions during this mating period. The snakes return each September to hibernate. The day-use area is also the starting point for several hikes.

The **Karstland Interpretive Trail** is an easy 750-m (0.5 mi) loop that wanders past active sinkholes and good examples of karst topography. Access the 7.5-km (4.5 mi) **North Loop Trail** from the day-use area or start at the trailhead 2.4 km (1.5 mi) beyond it, on the west side of Pine Lake Road. The hike offers a gentle climb to the top of an escarpment with a scenic view of **Salt Pan Lake.**

The 9-km (5.5 mi) **South Loop Trail** starts at the Salt River on the east side of Pine Lake Road. The hike wanders over bridges and along a saline creek to the trail's highlight—the salt flats at **Grosbeak Lake.** This unique landscape features strangely shaped rocks and glacial erratics that have been formed by salt and frost. Look for animal tracks in the iron-rich mud, such as lumbering bear paws crossing the delicate prints of a sandhill crane. For a 20-minute shortcut to Grosbeak Lake, start at the far end of the trail located

WOOD BUFFALO

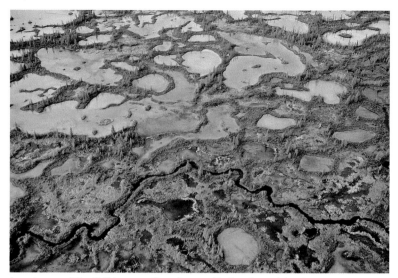

A remote corner of Wood Buffalo serves as the nesting ground for the endangered whooping crane.

2.4 km (1.5 mi) past the Salt River Day Use Area on the east side of Pine Lake Road. Canoeing from bridge to bridge is also possible on the Salt River during spring runoff.

Continue along Pine Lake Road to the **Pine Lake Day Use Area.** A sandy beach borders this startlingly aquamarine lake. Blue-green algae at the bottom of the lake reflect back the sun's rays, giving the lake its brilliant colour. This is a good place to swim and picnic or paddle around in a canoe or kayak.

Visit one of the park's **Dark Sky Observation Sites,** also accessed via the Pine Lake Access Road. Here there is a dark-sky circle (platform) made for enjoying the night skies. August is a great time to see the stars as the days are growing shorter. The easy 3-km (2 mi) **Lakeside Trail** connects the day-use area with the secluded Kettle Point Group Camp (a small campground on the eastern shore of the lake), which can also be accessed via the gravel Kettle Point Access Road off Pine Lake Road. About midpoint along the Lakeside

Trail, the 6-km (3.5 mi) **Lane Lake Trail** veers off and passes a chain of sinkhole lakes, ending at Lane Lake. The trail can also be picked up where it crosses Kettle Point Access Road.

Beyond Pine Lake, the road continues to the **Peace Point Reserve** on the Peace River.

The salt plains cover some 370 sq km (143 sq mi).

WOOD BUFFALO NATIONAL PARK
(Parc national Wood Buffalo)

INFORMATION & ACTIVITIES

VISITOR CENTRES
Fort Smith Visitor Reception Centre 149 McDougal Rd., Fort Smith, NT X0E 0P0. Phone (867) 872-7960.
Fort Chipewyan Visitor Reception Centre MacKenzie Ave., Fort Chipewyan, AB T0P 1B0. Phone (780) 697-3662.

SEASONS & ACCESSIBILITY
Park open year-round. Fort Smith Visitor Reception Centre open daily late May to Labour Day; weekdays rest of the year. Fort Chipewyan Visitor Reception Centre open weekdays year-round and most weekends in the summer.

HEADQUARTERS
Box 750, Fort Smith, NT X0E 0P0. Phone (867) 872-7960. www.parkscanada.gc .ca/woodbuffalo.

ENTRANCE FEES
No entry fee.

ACCESSIBLE SERVICES
Day-use area and two campsites wheelchair accessible at Pine Lake Campground. Kettle Point Group Camp is wheelchair accessible. Most interpretive exhibits are wheelchair accessible.

THINGS TO DO
Canoeing on **Pine Lake** for easy day paddling or on the **Peace, Athabasca,** and **Slave Rivers** for backcountry paddling. Paddling on the **Buffalo, Little Buffalo,** and **Salt Rivers** in spring. Canoe rentals available in Fort Smith. Fishing in some of the larger rivers (fishing permit $10 per day, $35 per year).

Hiking on seven frontcountry trails (easy–moderate) or two backcountry trails (moderate–challenging). Interpretive exhibits at **Angus Fire Tower** and Day Use Area, **Nyarling River** pull-off, **Wetlands** pull-off, **Salt Plains** Viewpoint and Day Use Area, **Salt River Day Use Area,** and the visitor centres. Taiga Tour Company is a licensed outfitter offering guided tours; call (867) 872-2060.

SPECIAL ADVISORIES
- Fish stocks are poor and difficult to reach, even in the larger rivers. Visitors should obey the daily catch-and-possession limit for grayling, whitefish, northern pike, goldeye, and walleye.
- Hikers should contact the Visitor Reception Centre at Fort Smith or Fort Chipewyan for trail updates and safety information on bear sightings or restrictions. Registration and check-out are mandatory for backcountry camping.
- Wear clothing layers that protect from bug bites. Mosquitoes are most prevalent in June and July.

OVERNIGHT BACKPACKING
Registration required for backcountry camping. Backcountry camping permitted off main trails. Backcountry camping at serviced sites including **Sweetgrass Station** and **Rainbow Lakes;** $10 per person per night, $69 per person per season. There is no fee for camping in the wilderness where there are no designated campsites. Paddle or hike to Sweetgrass Station starts at Peace Point; paddling downstream takes 10 to 12 hours.

CAMPGROUNDS
Pine Lake Campground and **Kettle Point Group Camp** open Victoria Day weekend to Labour Day. **Pine Lake** has fire pits, tent pads, picnic tables, water (boiling required), firewood, outhouses, and a playground; $16 per night. **Kettle Point** has a log shelter, tenting area, beach, fire circle and firewood, picnic tables, outhouses, and playground; $5 per person. Reservation fee $39. Call (867) 872-7960.

HOTELS, MOTELS, & INNS
(unless otherwise noted, rates are for a 2-person double, high season, in Canadian dollars)

Outside the park:
Fort Smith, NT X0E 0P0:
Pelican Rapids Inn & Suites 152 McDougal Rd. (867) 872-2789; www.pelican rapidsinn.com. $162.

Additional visitor information:
Fort McMurray, Alberta
www.travelinalberta.com/FortMcMurray .cfm

ROCKIES

Page 208: top, White-water rafting in Yoho National Park; middle, a mother grizzly bear and her two cubs, Banff National Park; bottom, Iceland poppies *(Papaver nudicaute)*, Banff. Page 209: Castle Mountain and boreal forest

ROCKIES

From Waterton in Alberta to Mount Revelstoke in British Columbia, these parks offer a photo-ready landscape of peaks, glaciers, rivers, lakes, and waterfalls. Waterton Lakes boasts scenic drives, horseback riding, boat cruises, and hiking through habitat for moose, elk, and deer. Banff is renowned for its historic hot springs, turquoise Lake Louise, and more than a thousand glaciers. In Jasper, visitors take the tramway to the top of Whistler's Mountain for

reflected in lake, Banff. Above: The sun descends behind cedar trees and mountains near Athabasca Pass.

a view of six mountain ranges, hikers follow trails grooved by wildlife and early First Nations peoples, and professional cavers explore a huge cave system. Hikers and skiers at Elk Island find plains and wood bison, elk, and moose, or soak in the springs at Kootenay. Yoho attracts fossil hunters to the renowned Burgess Shale fossil beds, and hiking is popular at Glacier. The subalpine meadows of Mount Revelstoke brim with wildflowers.

Vermilion Range and Floe Lake, Kootenay National Park

▶ KOOTENAY

BRITISH COLUMBIA
ESTABLISHED 1920
1,406 sq km/347,430 acres

"Kootenay" is an old spelling of the Ktunaxa (pronounced "k-тоо-nah-ha") First Nations. Comprising the southern corridor of Hwy. 93 in the Canadian Rockies west of Banff, this park features a fully developed hot spring and other popular geological attractions. New growth after major forest fires has been allowed to occur naturally, providing outstanding examples of ecological succession.

Since Kootenay is a narrow park with a highway down the middle, you can view much of its spectacular mountain scenery from the road. The park protects much of the headwaters of the Kootenay River and all of its tributary, the Vermilion, which Hwy. 93 follows closely for 56 km (35 mi) from the Continental Divide to the confluence. Travellers along the highway enjoy first-hand views of a textbook glacial river, complete with milky blue water, gravel outwash flats, and big daily changes in flow. Farther on, the road passes through narrow, winding Sinclair Canyon, a stream-cut feature that contrasts with the glaciated landscape.

At 3,377 m (11,079 ft) high, Deltaform Mountain is the highest peak in Kootenay. The lowest point lies at only 880 m (2,887 ft) in Sinclair Valley. This presents impressive topographic relief of 2.5 km (1.5 mi), in which all the elevational life zones of the Canadian Rockies are represented, from the grassy, juniper-clad lower slopes of the trench—the driest place in the region—through open montane woods to dense subalpine forests, windswept alpine tundra, high-elevation glaciers, and icy summits atop enormous cliffs.

How to Get There

From Calgary (closest airport), take Trans-Canada 1 west for 143 km (89 mi) to the junction with B.C. Hwy. 93 between Banff and Lake Louise (not the junction farther west, just past Lake Louise). Follow B.C. Hwy. 93 west for 10 km (6 mi) to the park.

From the south, take Hwy. 93/95 to the village of Radium Hot Springs, where B.C. Hwy. 93 branches east into the park. From the west, turn off Trans-Canada 1 at Golden and take Hwy. 95 south 102 km (64 mi) to Radium Hot Springs, then turn east onto B.C. Hwy. 93.

When to Go

Some spring wildflowers appear early in April near the park's west gate, but for better roadside displays wait until July, the warmest month. Daytime temperatures are typically comfortable through most of the park in July and August; nights are usually cool. The west gate area in the Rocky Mountain Trench can be hot.

B.C. Hwy. 93 is kept open all winter, plowed and sanded because it is a main highway. Still, the road can be icy after a snowstorm. Marble Canyon is particularly beautiful in the snow, and the Radium Hot Springs pools are open year-round. The highway can be very busy on Friday evenings and Sunday afternoons, when Calgary weekenders drive to and from their vacation properties in the Rocky Mountain Trench.

How to Visit

A popular approach is to see the park from east to west along B.C. Hwy. 93, a distance of 106 km (66 m) from the junction with Trans-Canada 1 to the village of Radium Hot Springs. Once you've turned off the highway, allow 1.5 hours of driving time through the park and another hour or two for stops at **Marble Canyon** and the **Paint Pots,** plus additional time if you're planning to picnic and take a dip in the hot springs. There are eight picnicking sites along the road. Sandwiches and beverages are available in summer at Kootenay Park Lodge *(www.kootenayparklodge.com),* km 41.

KOOTENAY PARK HIGHWAY
104 km/65 mi; 1.5 hours

Originally named the Banff-Windermere Hwy., B.C. Hwy. 93 was the first auto route to reach entirely across the central Canadian Rockies. It opened in 1922 as a rough gravel track after British Columbia ceded land for the park. The federal government, in exchange, provided money for road construction.

No fuel is available along this road. If you are headed west, the last chance for fuel in summer is at Castle Mountain Chalets (turn right at the junction with Trans-Canada 1; http:// castlemountain.com). In winter, fill up at Banff or Lake Louise. Fuel is always available in the village of Radium Hot Springs at the end of the tour.

Turn west onto B.C. Hwy. 93 from Trans-Canada 1 between Banff and Lake Louise. As you crest **Vermilion Pass,** elevation 1,640 m (5,382 ft), you cross from Atlantic to Pacific drainage and from Alberta into British Columbia. In 1968, a forest fire in this area restarted ecological

KOOTENAY

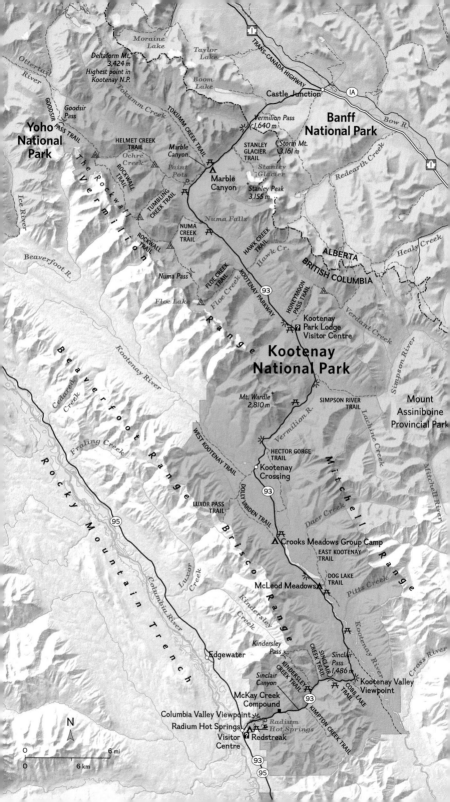

succession, allowing lodgepole pines and shrubs to replace the previous climax forest of spruce and sub-alpine fir.

Soon the road enters a much larger and more recently burned area, in which 162 sq km (40,031 acres), nearly 11 percent of the park, were consumed by fire in 2003. Here the succession is even younger, with small pines growing rapidly through a carpet of fireweed. All these fires were started by lightning. Rather than replanting the forest or trying to influence its species makeup by using chemicals, Parks Canada has allowed regrowth to occur naturally. The result is one of the better and more accessible examples of ecological succession in the Rockies.

Past Marble Canyon, long, bright green avalanche paths scar the steep mountain slopes. Snowslides every winter keep the trees cleared out of these paths, but alders and other shrubs survive by bending to let the snow move by. Ahead looms the **Rockwall,** a continuous line of Cambrian limestone cliffs about 600 m (1,969 ft) high. Watch for blue-white glaciers at the heads of side drainages.

At **Mount Wardle,** where white mountain goats often pick their way along the rocky slopes to natural mineral licks on the right (north) side of the highway, the **Vermilion River** punches through the Rockwall. The road climbs over a knoll and descends to the wide, gentle valley of the **Kootenay River,** a major tributary of the Columbia.

Hwy. 93 follows the Kootenay southwestward for 28 km (17 mi) through forests of lodgepole pine between the craggy **Brisco Range** on the right (west) and the slabby **Mitchell Range** on the left. The road climbs up to the **Kootenay Valley**

Oxeye daisies flourish in Kootenay.

Viewpoint, an excellent vantage point with interpretive signs.

The route then turns west and crosses wooded **Sinclair Pass** (1,486 m/4,875 ft). Soon you enter **Sinclair Canyon,** the steep, winding stream course of Sinclair Creek. Cliffs of brilliantly red Ordovician rock indicate that you are approaching Radium Hot Springs. The road passes right by the pool, then squeezes through the canyon's narrowest point to emerge into the **Rocky Mountain Trench,** a 1,500-km-long (932 mi) valley that marks the western edge of the Rockies. Past the park gate you're in the village of Radium Hot Springs, which offers food, fuel, and accommodation.

KOOTENAY

MARBLE CANYON

45 minutes

Marble Canyon is located along B.C. Hwy. 93, 17 km (11 mi) west of the junction with Trans-Canada 1, and 87 km (54 mi) east of Radium Hot Springs village. Glacially blue **Tokumm Creek** rushes through a gorge 35 m (115 ft) deep and very narrow, with a waterfall and natural bridge at its upper end. The Cathedral dolostone is similar to limestone but with magnesium as well as calcium. A short **interpretive trail** provides guardrail-protected views into the

KOOTENAY NATIONAL PARK *(Parc national Kootenay)*

INFORMATION & ACTIVITIES

VISITOR & INFORMATION CENTRE
Kootenay National Park and Radium Hot Springs Visitor Centre 7556 Main St. E, Radium Hot Springs, BC V0A 1M0. Phone (250) 347-9505. Open May to October. www.parkscanada.gc.ca /kootenay.

SEASONS & ACCESSIBILITY
Open year-round. Book accommodations months in advance if planning a trip in July or August. Services offered at Radium Hot Springs Chamber of Commerce (250-347-9331) late October to early May.

HEADQUARTERS
Radium Hot Springs Administrative Building Phone (250) 347-9615.

FRIENDS OF KOOTENAY
Friends of Kootenay National Park Box 512, Radium Hot Springs, BC V0A 1M0. Phone (250) 347-6525. friendsofkootenay@gmail.com; http://friendsofkootenay.ca.

ENTRANCE FEES
$10 per adult per day, $68 per year.

PETS
Keep pets on a leash.

ACCESSIBLE SERVICES
Wheelchair accessibility at Visitor Centre; Kootenay Park Lodge at Vermilion Crossing; Radium Hot Springs Pools; Redstreak, McLeod Meadows, and Marble Canyon Campgrounds; Redstreak Theatre; Olive Lake Area picnic site and interpretive panels; and Sinclair Canyon and Kootenay Valley Viewpoints.

THINGS TO DO
Canoeing, rafting, climbing and mountaineering (for conditions, call 403-762-1473), cycling and mountain biking, fishing (permit $10 per day, $35 per year), hiking, wildlife viewing, photography, camping. Swimming in the Radium Hot Springs, call (250) 347-9485 or (800) 767-1611.

SPECIAL ADVISORIES
- To avoid attracting bears and other predators, never leave coolers, pets or pet bowls, dishes, cooking stoves,

gorge. You may see American dippers here, small brownish grey birds that hop into the torrents to eat small water insects.

PAINT POTS
1 to 2 hours return

An easy and very popular interpretive trail (1 km/0.5 mi) leads to three small **ponds** (the "pots") fed from deep below by acidic water containing iron, zinc, manganese, and lead. Iron oxide in the springwater has permeated the silty soil here, and these redochre deposits have attracted paintpigment collectors since prehistoric times. From the early 1900s into the 1920s, the locality was mined. Water

flows from the Paint Pots into the Vermilion River, staining the rocks along one bank red for some distance downstream. The trailhead lies along Hwy. 93, about 20 km (12 mi) west of the junction with Trans-Canada 1.

RADIUM HOT SPRINGS

Radium Hot Springs lies along Hwy. 93, 3 km (2 mi) east of the village of Radium Hot Springs. The water in the large soaking pool averages 39°C (102°F), comfortably warm in any weather. Open year-round, the Parks Canada facility here also includes a cool pool for swimming, lockers, and Pleiades Massage and Spa *(www.hotsprings.ca)*.

garbage bags, wash basins, or toiletries unattended or in your tent.
- Watch for black ice when driving in winter.
- Be alert for rockfalls in steep terrain in the Rocky Mountains. Do not walk on or beneath overhanging ice or snow.
- Avoid stopping in avalanche zones.
- Stay far away from all wildlife—at least three bus lengths from elk, deer, moose, and mountain goats; 10 bus lengths from bears, wolves, cougars, and lynx.
- Bring clothes and gear for a variety of trail conditions.

OVERNIGHT BACKPACKING
Primitive camping $10 per night. Five campgrounds along the rock wall: **Floe Lake, Numa Creek, Tumbling Creek, Helmet Falls,** and **Helmet Ochre Junction.** Tent pads, food lockers, and bear poles at each site.

CAMPGROUNDS
Four campgrounds, 391 campsites available in peak season (July–Aug.). Campsite day use, fire permit, and dump station $9 per day each. **Redstreak** open May to mid-October. Water, sewer, and electricity $38, electricity only $32, unserviced with washroom (toilets and showers) $27. **McLeod Meadows** open June to September. Unserviced with washroom (toilets only) $22. **Marble Canyon** open June to September. Unserviced with washroom (toilets only) $22. **Crook's Meadow** group campsite open May to October, $6 per person. Minimum 20 people, maximum 60.

HOTELS, MOTELS, & INNS
(unless otherwise noted, rates are for a 2-person double, high season, in Canadian dollars)

outside the park:
Best Western Plus Prestige Inn Radium Hot Springs 7493 Main St. W, Radium Hot Springs, BC V0A 1M0. (250) 347-2300. www.prestigehotelsandresorts.com. $130–$350.
Windermere Creek Bed and Breakfast Cabins 1658 Windermere Loop Rd., Windermere, BC V0B 2L2. (250) 342-0356 or (800) 946-3942. www.windermerecreek.com. $139–$159.

EXCURSION

KOOTENAE HOUSE NATIONAL HISTORIC SITE
INVERMERE, BC

A stone monument and interpretive signs mark the location of the first fur-trading post in the Rocky Mountain Trench, built in 1807 by David Thompson of the North West Company and used for only five years. The site is located a short distance north of Invermere on Wilmer Rd., 0.7 km (0.4 mi) north of the intersection of Wilmer Rd. and Toby Creek Rd.

Moraine Lake in Banff National Park

▶ BANFF

ALBERTA
ESTABLISHED 1885
6,641 sq km/1,641,027 acres

Simplicity marks the origin of Banff—Canada's first national park. In 1883, on the slopes of the Canadian Rocky Mountains, three railway workers discovered a natural hot spring, and from there the park was born. Nowadays, Banff is one of the world's premiere destinations, spanning a region of unparalleled majestic mountain scenery. Every year, millions of visitors make the pilgrimage to Banff to take in its stunning views and arsenal of activities.

Banff—the birthplace of the world's first national park service—is part of UNESCO's Canadian Rocky Mountain World Heritage site. Located in the heart of the Canadian Rockies, the park boasts a wealth of postcard-perfect mountains. These monoliths range from 45 to 120 million years old, with the highest entirely in the park, Mount Forbes, coming in at 3,612 m (11,850 ft).

The park encompasses Banff, the highest town in Canada at an elevation of 1,384 m (4,540 ft); the hamlet of Lake Louise (1,540 m/5,052 ft), the highest permanent settlement in Canada; several national historic sites (see pp. 226–227); Castleguard Caves, the largest cave system in Canada; more than a thousand glaciers; glacier-fed lakes such as Lake Louise as well as Moraine, Bow, and

Peyto Lakes; hundreds of hotels, restaurants, and retail shops, and a 27-hole championship golf course.

In 2010, the park marked its 125th anniversary, commemorating some of the finest unspoiled ecosystems in the world. An integral part of the celebrations was the creation of the **Banff Legacy Trail,** a nonmotorized, paved trail for the likes of walking, cycling, and in-line skating. The 26-km (16 mi) trail connects users from the nearby town of Canmore through the park. Incorporating scenic views, it runs primarily along Trans-Canada 1 and the wildlife fence from the park's East Gate to the Bow Valley Parkway.

How to Get There

Banff National Park is located 129 km (80 mi) west of Calgary. Calgary's international airport is serviced by major national and international carriers with multiple flights arriving daily. From the airport, rent a car and take Trans-Canada 1 west from Calgary straight into the park, through Banff and Lake Louise. A direct bus service from the airport or downtown Calgary is also available to Banff and Lake Louise, as are shuttle services through tour operators.

When to Go

Open year-round, Banff offers amazing wildlife viewing and sightseeing, plus plentiful shopping and dining options, any time of the year. Summer is popular for hiking, paddling, mountain biking and cycling, photography, and climbing. The best time for viewing seasonal colour is fall, when the larch trees—the only coniferous trees to lose their needles in winter—turn yellow.

In winter, the mountain landscape makes for incredible downhill and cross-country skiing. In fact,

three major downhill ski resorts operate within the park. Lake Louise Ski Area, Sunshine Village, and Mount Norquay combine to offer a large skiable terrain, not to mention the backcountry trails available throughout the park. The ski season, which runs from November to May, is one of the longest in North America. Visitors can also enjoy wildlife tours, ice walks, snowshoeing, and dogsled and horse-drawn sleigh rides.

Weather in the Canadian Rockies can change quickly. A single day can have a mix of sunshine, snow, wind, and rain, so dress in layers. Summers are warm with low humidity. Temperatures average a high of 21°C (70°F) and daylight lasts until 11 p.m. Autumn brings cool nights and crisp air. Winters can be frigid. In January, the average daytime high is minus 7°C (19°F), but by April it is 9°C (49°F).

How to Visit

Visiting the park by car or tour bus is most common. In the town of Banff you can also catch the ROAM bus, a publicly accessible and environmentally friendly hybrid outfitted with wildlife information. Pick up a map or bus schedule at the Banff or Lake Louise visitor information centres. GPS guides are also available.

To get the most out of the park, plan to spend a day in the town of Banff and the rest of your vacation outdoors, immersing yourself in the mountains, hiking or skiing.

TOWN OF BANFF
a full day

Start with a stroll down **Banff Avenue,** the main road into town and home to a bevy of retail shops

BANFF

and restaurants. At the end of Banff Avenue make your way to Cave and Basin National Historic Site where you can peer down into the cave that started the national park service.

But don't just stick to the main drag. Venture off the beaten path to the **Whyte Museum** *(www.whyte.org)* on Bear Street (one block west) to learn about the area's cultural history, or succumb to the delicious tastes of Rocky Mountain cuisine at the Bison Restaurant & Lounge. Dine at the full-service restaurant or grab a delectable sandwich to go. If you have time, enjoy a cultural performance at **The Banff Centre** *(www.banffcentre.ca)* on Tunnel Mountain Drive (up the hill on Buffalo St.).

If you prefer to stay outdoors, try a horseback ride. Saddle up with Warner Guiding & Outfitting *(www.horseback.com)* on Banff Avenue for a Rockies trail ride. You can follow backcountry trails to a beautiful alpine lake or take a more daring weeklong trip into the backcountry and camp along the way.

At the end of Banff Avenue, after crossing the bridge, follow Mountain Avenue to take a dip at **Banff Upper Hot Springs.** Canada's First Nations were the first to enjoy these waters, believed to be a place to cure illness and maintain health. Open year-round, this historic bathhouse gives you the chance to literally soak up the alpine scenery while relaxing in the natural springs after a long day of riding, hiking, or skiing.

Farther up Mountain Avenue, enjoy the best views of the park on the **Sulphur Mountain Gondola,** located five minutes from the town. You can hike up, but most visitors prefer the short gondola ride to the top of the mountain (an elevation of 2,282 m/ 7,486 ft), where you'll come upon a panoramic view of six mountain

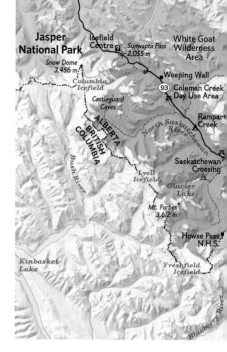

ranges. Keep your eyes peeled for birds and wildlife, such as the Rocky Mountain bighorn sheep. At the top, grab a bite at one of the restaurants. The most popular trail here is the **Banff Skywalk Trail** (1 km/0.6 mi), a self-guided interpretive walkway to **Sanson Peak.**

BOW VALLEY PARKWAY TO LAKE LOUISE

56 km/35 mi; a half to full day

Head west from Banff on the **Bow Valley Parkway** (Hwy. 1A), the slower, more scenic alternative to Trans-Canada 1. To give animals the space they need to thrive, particularly throughout spring, there are nightly travel restrictions. Visit *www.pc.gc.ca /banff* for up-to-date information. Along the way, there are plenty of interpretive pull-outs, viewpoints, and picnic spots to choose from.

Drive about 18 km (11 mi) then detour at **Johnston Canyon,** where you can see the steep cliffs carved

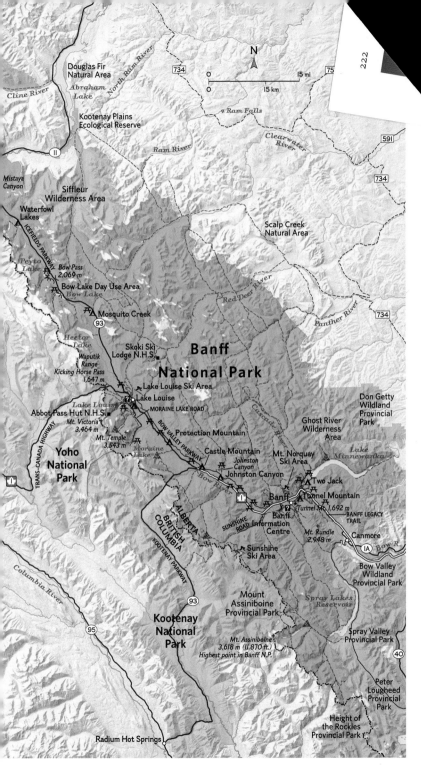

N

734

75

0 ——— 15 mi

0 ——— 15 km

Cline River

Douglas Fir
Natural Area

Abraham
Lake

North Ram River

734

Ram Falls

Kootenay Plains
Ecological Reserve

Ram River

Clearwater River

591

Mistaya
Canyon

Siffleur
Wilderness Area

734

Waterfowl
Lakes

Scalp Creek
Natural Area

Peyto
Lake

Bow Pass
2,069 m

Bow Lake Day Use Area

Bow Lake

Red Deer River

ICEFIELDS PARKWAY

93

Mosquito Creek

Panther River

734

Hector
Lake

Waputik
Range

Skoki Ski
Lodge N.H.S.

Banff
National Park

Kicking Horse Pass
1,647 m

Lake Louise Ski Area

Don Getty
Wildland
Provincial
Park

Lake Louise

Lake Louise

MORAINE LAKE ROAD

Ghost River
Wilderness
Area

Abbot Pass Hut N.H.S.

Mt. Victoria
3,464 m

Protection Mountain

BOW VALLEY PARKWAY

Cascade R.

Lake
Minnewanka

TRANS-CANADA HIGHWAY

Mt. Temple
3,543 m

Moraine
Lake

Yoho
National
Park

Castle Mountain

Johnston
Canyon

Johnston Canyon

Mt. Norquay
Ski Area

Two Jack

Bow River

Tunnel Mountain

1

ALBERTA

BRITISH COLUMBIA

Banff

Banff
Information
Centre

Tunnel Mt. 1,692 m

BANFF LEGACY
TRAIL

Canmore

KOOTENAY PARKWAY

SUNSHINE ROAD

Mt. Rundle
2,948 m

1A

Bow R.

Columbia River

Sunshine
Ski Area

Bow Valley
Wildland
Provincial
Park

93

Kootenay
National
Park

Mount
Assiniboine
Provincial Park

Spray Lakes
Reservoir

95

Mt. Assiniboine
3,618 m (11,870 ft.)
Highest point in Banff N.P.

Spray Valley
Provincial
Park

40

Peter
Lougheed
Provincial
Park

Radium Hot Springs

Height of
the Rockies
Provincial Park

Fairmont Chateau Lake Louise

by rushing white water. In summer, from one of the viewpoints you can feel the spray from the waterfalls. It's a 20-minute hike to the **Lower Falls** and 40 minutes to the **Upper Falls.**

LAKE LOUISE & MORAINE LAKE

Approximately 5 km (3 mi) up Lake Louise Drive, off Hwy. 1, you'll find the glacial lake itself. Walk or ride a horse along the lake, marvelling at its emerald colours, or try one of the many hiking trails, such as the classic **Plain of Six Glaciers** (4–5 hr round-trip). The popular **Lake Agnes Trail** (2.5–3 hr return) takes you past **Mirror Lake** to a backcountry teahouse at the top. Continue beyond (1.6 km/1 mi) to **Little Beehive** for a stunning view of the lake from above. For the more seriously adventurous, scramble up **Fairview Mountain** from **Saddleback Pass.** You can also rent a canoe and paddle your way across the lake, or hike the lovely trails surrounding the lake.

The **Fairmont Chateau Lake Louise,** a historic luxury resort hotel built in the early 20th century by the Canadian Pacific Railway, stands steps from the lake and is worth exploring. You may wish to stop in for its charming high-tea service or for a luxurious high-end spa treatment.

Another place worth a visit is

Moraine Lake, a beautiful glacially fed lake situated in the Valley of Ten Peaks, which is part of the Continental Divide, the geographic point where waters flow either west to the Pacific Ocean or east to the Atlantic Ocean. The 13-km (8 mi) road from Lake Louise ends with a breathtaking view of Moraine Lake.

There are a few trails to explore around Moraine Lake. The easiest is the short **Rockpile Trail.** The view of the lake from the top of the rock pile is one of the most familiar sights in Canada; you may recognize the scene from older Canadian $20 bills. The 3.2-km (2 mi) **Consolation Lakes Trail,** with an elevation change of 90 m (295 ft), starts along the same trailhead.

The landscape around Lake Louise and Moraine Lake is not only highly attractive, it is also excellent grizzly bear habitat. To protect bears and people, visitors must hike in tight groups of four or more on some trails at some times of the year. Find more information at trailhead information kiosks or at the information centres.

ICEFIELDS PARKWAY
230 km/142 mi; a full day

From Lake Louise, proceed west along Trans-Canada 1. After 2 km (1.5 mi), exit and follow the signs for Hwy. 93 N, the **Icefields Parkway**—one of the world's most spectacular drives. Stretching between Banff and Jasper, this stunning stretch of road winds through mountain passes, around glassy turquoise lakes, centuries-old ice fields, hanging glaciers, waterfalls, and alpine meadows.

The parkway is open year-round, but, especially in winter, it makes sense to check ahead for road condi-

Rocky Mountain bighorn sheep

Canoes resting on the dock at Moraine Lake

Skiing the Rocky Mountains

tions in case heavy snowfalls have caused closures. You also need to have snow tires and gas up beforehand as there are no services along the parkway from November to March. The summer months are a peak time for road cyclists. As a motorist, keep an eye out for them, or grab a bike and join them on the scenic ride. The drive takes about three hours, but plan for at least five hours to experience the breathtaking mountain panoramas and discover some of the parkway's hundreds, if not thousands, of hidden and not-so-hidden treasures.

Be on the lookout for bighorn sheep, elk, moose, or even black bears. Chances of seeing wildlife on the parkway are very good in spring or fall, so take things nice and slow, have your camera at the ready, and do your best to be safe. Pull over carefully off the highway, and never

BANFF NATIONAL PARK *(Parc national Banff)*

INFORMATION & ACTIVITIES

VISITOR & INFORMATION CENTRES

Banff Visitor Centre 224 Banff Ave., Banff AB T1L 1K2. Phone (403) 762-1550. banff .vrc@pc.gc.ca. **Lake Louise Visitor Centre** next to Samson Mall, Village of Lake Louise AB T0L 1E0. Phone (403) 522-3833. ll.info@pc.gc.ca.

SEASONS & ACCESSIBILITY

Park open year-round.

HEADQUARTERS

Box 900, Banff, AB T1L 1K2. Phone (403) 762-1550. www.parkscanada.gc.ca/banff.

FRIENDS OF BANFF

Friends of Banff National Park, 214 Banff Ave., Banff, AB T1L 1C3. Phone (403) 760-5331. info@friendsofbanff.com; www .friendsofbanff.com.

ENTRANCE FEES

$10 per adult per day, $20 per group per day; $68 per person, $136 per group per year. Student, youth, senior rates.

PETS

Pets must be on a leash at all times and are not permitted to overnight in or outside the shelters.

ACCESSIBLE SERVICES

A variety of accessible services and facilities. Contact Information Centres.

THINGS TO DO

Hiking, walking, scenic drives, and wildlife viewing are enjoyed year-round. Summer is great for geocaching, horseback riding, fishing, kayaking, canoeing, and interpretive programs. **Lake Minnewanka, Lake Louise,** and **Moraine Lake** offer canoe rentals. The **Upper Hot Springs** bathhouse and outdoor spring-fed pool are open year-round.

Snowshoeing, ice climbing, cross-country skiing, and ice skating in winter. Equipment rentals are available in both Banff townsite and Lake Louise townsite. For the best trails to visit in the winter, stop in at a visitor centre.

SPECIAL ADVISORIES

- Visit Lake Louise and Moraine Lake before 11 a.m. or after 5 p.m. to avoid congestion in peak season (July–Aug.).
- Be prepared for sudden changes in temperature, especially at higher elevations.
- When boating, be aware the water temperature is seldom over 10°C (50°F). Small boats should stay close to shore, as capsizing could lead to hypothermia.
- Boaters should be ready for sudden strong winds and waves on the larger lakes, particularly in the afternoon.
- Water should be filtered and treated or boiled before drinking.
- Horseback riding and fishing permits required.

approach or disturb wildlife. If you plan to backtrack to Banff instead of proceeding to Jasper, try to leave enough travel time to drive back in daylight.

Designed for sightseeing, the parkway parallels the Continental Divide through the main ranges of the Canadian Rockies. The drive takes you through the Rockies' highest passes, the uppermost being **Bow Summit** at a lofty elevation of 2,069 m (6,787 ft) at km 40.

Nearby, you'll also find one of the world's best mountain panoramas, at **Peyto Lake viewpoint.** On a typical sunny day, snowcapped peaks pierce the bright blue sky from every direction.

At km 19, stop to stretch your legs at the viewpoint for **Hector Lake,** formed in a glacial basin. From there you'll enjoy stellar views of **Mount Balfour** and the **Waputik Range** to the southwest. **Crowfoot Glacier** (km 33) once resembled a crow's foot with three large toes. The crow's lower toe has since melted away.

OVERNIGHT BACKPACKING

Fifty backcountry campgrounds, 2 trail shelters, 3 alpine huts, and 4 backcountry lodges. **Bryant Creek** and **Egypt Lake** public trail shelters available year-round, $7 per person per night. Mandatory Wilderness Pass for backcountry use $10 per person per night. Reservations for campsites and shelters can be made up to 3 months in advance. Call (403) 762-1556. Paddlers must camp at designated roadside or backcountry campgrounds.

CAMPGROUNDS

Tunnel Mountain Village I, unserviced with toilet and showers $27. **Tunnel Mountain Trailer,** full service $38. **Two Jack Main**, unserviced with toilets $22; six-person tent, six sleeping pads, stove and propane, lantern, campground orientation $70. **Two Jack Lakeside,** unserviced with toilet and showers $27; oTENTik accommodations (a cross between a tent and a cabin, with electricity and hot showers) $120. **Johnston Canyon**, unserviced with toilets and showers $27. **Castle Mountain,** unserviced with toilets $22. **Lake Louise Trailer,** full service $32. **Lake Louise Tent,** unserviced with toilet and showers $27. **Mosquito Creek,** unserviced with dry toilet $18. **Waterfowl Lakes,** unserviced with toilets $22. **Rampart Creek,** unserviced with dry toilet $18.

Winter camping: available at Tunnel Mountain in Banff and at Lake Louise. Firepits $9 available at some sites.

Winter camping at Tunnel Mountain in Banff and at Lake Louise. Visit reservation .pc.gc.ca/Banff for complete listing information.

HOTELS, MOTELS, & INNS

(unless otherwise noted, rates are for a 2-person double, high season, in Canadian dollars)

Banff, AB:
Blue Mountain Lodge B&B 327 Caribou St. (403) 762-5134. www.bluemtnlodge .com. $155–$189, including breakfast.
The Fairmont Banff Springs 405 Spray Ave. (403) 762-2211 or (866) 540-4406. banffsprings@fairmont.com; www.fairmont.com/banffsprings. $350–$600.
Mount Royal Hotel 138 Banff Ave. (403) 762-3331 or (877) 442-2623. www .brewster.ca/hotels/mount-royal-hotel. $259–$269.
Rimrock Resort Hotel 300 Mountain Ave. (403) 762-3356. www.rimrockresort.com. $348–$523.

Lake Louise, AB TOL 1EO:
Fairmont Chateau Lake Louise 111 Lake Louise Dr. (403) 522-3511 or (866) 540-4413. www.fairmont.com/lakelouise. From $450.

Additional visitor information:
Banff Lake Louise Tourism (403) 762-0270. info@banfflakelouise; www.banfflakelouise.com.

BANFF

Nearby **Helen Lake** is the place for a gratifying day hike with meadows bursting with alpine flowers, noisy marmots, and a chance to scramble on rocky faces.

At km 71, **Mistaya Canyon** requires a 10-minute trek along the trail. You'll find amazing canyon views, but watch your step and keep your distance from the edge as you gaze upon the rushing waters and eroding rock walls.

Back along the parkway, keep veering northwest until you come upon the **Coleman Creek day-use area** at km 99. It offers a pleasant picnic rest stop, where you might spy mountain goats perched on the cliffs above. Farther along, at km 106, you'll see the **Weeping Wall,** a very popular place with ice climbers, where meltwater from Cirrus Mountain pours over the steep rock face as a series of graceful waterfalls.

At km 126 sits a major highlight of the Icefields Parkway—the **Athabasca Glacier,** which is part of the huge Columbia Icefield (see pp. 234–235).

EXCURSIONS

ABBOT PASS REFUGE CABIN
NATIONAL HISTORIC SITE
BANFF NP, AB

Built in 1922 by Swiss guides, the alpine shelter is one of 24 shelters managed by the Alpine Club of Canada. For generations, climbers have travelled to the stone cabin as a base for ascents up Mount Lefroy and Mount Victoria or as a destination in itself. The steep ascent to the hut should only be attempted by skilled mountaineers. Winter visits are not advised.

BANFF PARK MUSEUM
NATIONAL HISTORIC SITE
BANFF, AB

Discover how natural history was interpreted in Canada during the Victorian era. Western Canada's oldest natural history museum displays more than 5,000 specimens, from bees to bears. Admire the stately 1903 log masterpiece and the oldest surviving federal building in any Canadian national park. Though the building was refurbished in 1985, the original exhibits still reflect museum interpretation practices from 1914. Located in downtown Banff at 91 Banff Ave. (403) 762-1558.

CAVE AND BASIN NATIONAL
HISTORIC SITE
BANFF, AB

Commemorating the birthplace of Canada's national parks system, this site received a face-lift as part of the 125th anniversary of the park in 2010. Naturally occurring warm mineral springs, along with the pungent smell of sulphur, greet visitors inside the cave and outside in the emerald-coloured basin area. Walking trails and wetlands surround the site. Check out the Story Hall with interactive programs, exhibits, and a giant four-screen visual experience. Open year-round. (403) 762-1566.

HOWSE PASS NATIONAL HISTORIC SITE
BANFF NP, AB

This traditional aboriginal transportation route over the Continental Divide links the North Saskatchewan and Columbia River systems. David Thompson traversed it in 1807 and Canadian fur traders used it until 1810 to explore and establish posts west of the Rockies. Joseph Howse, the Hudson's Bay Company employee after whom the pass is named, first crossed it in 1809. It is located on the British Columbia–Alberta border, hiking 26 km (16 mi) west from the Icefields Parkway (Hwy. 93 N).

SKOKI SKI LODGE NATIONAL HISTORIC SITE
BANFF NP, AB

A throwback to the early days of ski tourism, the lodge exemplifies Banff's rustic design tradition. Opened for business in 1931, Skoki was built as a destination for backcountry skiers by a group of local ski enthusiasts, using timbers cut in the vicinity. Accessible only by ski- or hike-in, it was the first such facility to operate on a commercial basis in Canada. Contact the site for up-to-the-minute information on operating hours. (888) 997-5654. www.skoki.com.

SULPHUR MOUNTAIN COSMIC RAY STATION NATIONAL HISTORIC SITE
BANFF NP, AB

A cosmic ray station was built at the top of Sulphur Mountain as part of the International Geophysical Year in 1957–1958. Today, a plaque commemorates 22 years of discovery and a time when geophysicists studied cosmic rays and space particles entering the atmosphere from a station perched above the town of Banff. A thrilling gondola ride brings you to the summit to enjoy the view of six mountain ranges and uninterrupted views of breathtaking Bow Valley. From the upper terminal take the easy Banff Skywalk Trail to the station.

BANFF

Painting the Canadian Rockies

Linking the country from east to west, Canada's national parks and the Canadian Pacific Railway (CPR) established a sense of national identity in the 19th century. But it was the inspired work of early visual artists that ultimately brushed the finishing touches on Canada's unique character. As Canada celebrates the 150th anniversary of Confederation, contemporary artists continue to connect the country through current interpretations of protected places and iconic Canadian landscapes.

Marmaduke Matthews, *Bow River*, circa 1887, oil on canvas, Whyte Museum of the Canadian Rockies

In 1885, the CPR completed their ribbon of steel across Canada through the Canadian Rockies. The same year, a reserve was set aside around the hot springs at Banff, forming the basis of Banff National Park, Canada's first national park. Other mountain parks at Yoho and Glacier soon followed, although it would be decades before Canada's parks were expanded into a truly national system.

William Cornelius Van Horne, the CPR's general manager, saw art as a means to promote mountain tourism and western settlement. By providing travel, lodging, and other benefits to artists, he encouraged them to paint the mountain landscapes.

Much of the visual narrative of Canada's history is told through the eyes, minds, and hands of these early artists. Painted views of the Canadian Rockies were used by the CPR and the Government of Canada to lay claim, populate the country, and encourage economic development of Western Canada through to the Pacific.

Some of the first artists to travel to the Rockies in the late 1880s were John Fraser, Frederic M. Bell-Smith, Marmaduke Matthews, and Thomas Mower Martin. All were influenced by European landscape traditions and the Sublime Movement in American art. They primarily used watercolour to paint romantic views that reflected the grandeur of Canadian landscapes and popularized the West.

Banff and the other mountain parks continued to draw artists throughout the 20th century, including Belmore Browne, Aldro Hibbard, Carl Rungius, and Charlie Beil. Born in Banff in 1905, Peter Whyte attended the School of the Museum of Fine Arts, Boston, where he met fellow artist and his future wife, Catharine Robb. Married in 1930, Peter and Catharine Whyte travelled internationally and were cosmopolitan in their outlook, however their love of the mountains led them to live, build a studio, and make art in Banff.

From their mountain home, Peter and Catharine Whyte graciously hosted and painted with the best landscape artists of the day. The artwork they produced and the friendships that were made further positioned the Rocky Mountains, Banff National Park, and the town of Banff as iconic locations that are synonymous with Canadian identity. Ultimately, in 1968, Peter and Catharine founded the Whyte Museum of the Canadian Rockies, which after 50 years continues to explore the culture shaped by this mountain landscape.

With the inception of the Banff School of Fine Arts in 1935, Banff National Park continued to be a magnet for artists. Many great Canadian landscape artists taught and studied at the Banff School, now known as The Banff Centre. Inspired by the mountain parks, Walter J. Phillips, A. C. Leighton, Janet (Holly) Middleton, and Takao Tanabe taught here, and in turn inspired the work of their students, contemporaries, and followers.

A member of the Group of Seven, A. Y. Jackson taught at the Banff School. Also Group of Seven artists, Arthur Lismer, Lawren Harris, and J. E. H. MacDonald all painted in the mountain parks. Lismer visited once in 1928, while Harris and MacDonald spent several summers in the parks in the 1920s. MacDonald became a close friend of Peter and Catharine Whyte's. Contemporary artists continue to paint the parks today. Their paintings are modern interpretations that capture the mystery and beauty of the parks across Canada.

Catharine Robb Whyte, *Mount Temple and Larches*, circa 1937-1945, oil on canvas, Whyte Museum of the Canadian Rockies

The national parks will continue to inspire the artists who capture the beauty of these places and contribute to our national identity. For those who may have a chance to visit only once in a lifetime, artists' works provide another way to experience when peaks and people meet, the gift of Canada's national parks.

— *Whyte Museum of the Canadian Rockies* (*adapted from original by* MICHALE LANG)

PAINTING THE CANADIAN ROCKIES

Spirit Island on scenic Maligne Lake in Jasper National Park

▶ JASPER

ALBERTA
ESTABLISHED 1907
11,228 sq km/2,774,500 acres

The largest national park in the Canadian Rockies, Jasper is wild in every sense of the word. Its landscape covers an expansive region of rugged backcountry trails and mountainous terrain juxtaposed against fragile protected ecosystems as well as the world-renowned Columbia Icefield. It's also chock-full of wildlife, home to some of North America's healthiest populations of grizzly bears, moose, and elk along with thousands of species of plants and insects.

The park comprises rough-and-tumble mountains, valleys, glaciers, forests, alpine meadows, and rivers along the eastern slopes of the Rockies in western Alberta. More than 980 km (615 mi) of hiking trails offer day and overnight trips. A number of spectacular mountain drives also beckon.

Established in 1907, Jasper protects what's left of the wildlife that was once commonplace in the West. While other areas have seen a dramatic decline in wildlife, strong populations of plants and animals persevere here. The park's elevation range, geology, geography, and climate serve as a safe habitat for a variety of species.

Due in part to the incredible diversity of wildlife found here, Jasper is part of the UNESCO Canadian Rocky

Mountain Parks World Heritage site, one of 17 World Heritage sites in Canada. It is home to nearly 70 species of mammals whose health and survival depend on the park. That's why it's crucial that visitors don't approach or feed the wildlife.

How to Get There

The town of Jasper is situated at the intersection of Hwy. 16 (Yellowhead Hwy.) and Hwy. 93 N (Icefields Pkwy.). It is straight west 362 km (225 mi) on Hwy. 16 from Edmonton and west from Calgary along Trans-Canada 1, then north on Hwy. 93 from Lake Louise, 412 km (256 mi) in total. Major national and international carriers service both Edmonton and Calgary's international airports, with multiple flights arriving daily. Renting a car at the airport is the easiest way to make the trip, but rail travel to the park is also available through VIA Rail *(www.viarail.ca)* and the Rocky Mountaineer *(www.rockymountaineer .com)*. Shuttle services are available through tour operators.

When to Go

The park is open year-round, but the weather and scenery are generally spectacular in late summer and early fall. Forest-fire season in North America also winds down in the fall, so the air is clearer—especially important for photo enthusiasts.

Wildlife viewing can happen any time of year, but your best bets are early in the morning or late in the evening during the slow seasons (fall and spring), particularly for bears, elk, and sheep. The best time to watch the annual elk rut, when males bugle and compete with each other for females, is August to September along the Athabasca River. Camping is very popular in summer. Most campgrounds are open until Labour Day weekend; some stay open later in the fall. There are winter campgrounds as well. Skiing and snowboarding at Marmot Basin typically runs from November to April.

How to Visit

Within the park, travel by car is most convenient. Drive with care and be prepared to avoid a collision with wildlife at all times. Be especially cautious at dusk and dawn, when many animals are most active and visibility is poor.

You can hike and bike along an extensive network of trails. Many of the backcountry trails were established first by wildlife, then by early travellers including First Nations people, fur traders, explorers, and adventurers.

There are nearly 1,000 km (621 mi) of trails and 84 backcountry campsites in the park. Licensed commercial services include three backcountry lodges, several horse outfitters, and numerous hiking/ interpretive guides. The Alpine Club of Canada *(www.alpineclubofcanada .ca)* manages four alpine huts.

Plan to spend at least a half day in the town of Jasper and several days exploring the park.

MUNICIPALITY OF JASPER
a half to full day

Start your visit by talking to the knowledgeable staff at the information centre. Acquaint yourself with the town using the accessible **Jasper Discovery Trail,** an 8-km (5 mi) loop that borders Jasper and offers unique town vistas. Easy to navigate, the trail incorporates interpretive signs that inform trail users about special features of the area, including both cultural and natural heritage tidbits.

For a bird's-eye view of the town of Jasper and the surrounding area, head for the 2,277 m (7,472 ft) **Jasper Tramway** (April–Oct.; *www.jaspertram way.com*). You'll soar up Whistlers Mountain, the large rounded mountain just outside the town, into the alpine tundra for dramatic views of six mountain ranges, glacier-fed lakes, and the Athabasca River. Perfect for the whole family, it's the longest and highest guided aerial tramway in Canada. A tour guide accompanies you in your enclosed cabin on the seven-minute ascent.

As you reach the **Upper Station,** the mountains loom overhead, enticing you to hit the boardwalks adorned with interpretive exhibits. Watch for wildlife in this alpine life zone, the park's most fragile area. You can venture off the boardwalks to hiking trails leading to the breathtaking summit of the mountain, but be careful not to disturb the flora and fauna. Bring extra clothes in case of sudden weather changes.

Next, take a detour out of town to **Mount Edith Cavell** for impressive views of the mountain and of Angel and Cavell Glaciers. Travel south, following Hwy. 93A for 5 km (3 mi). After crossing the Astoria River, turn right onto Cavell Road, open from June to mid-October. Although it is paved, the road comprises several narrow switchbacks rendering it unsuitable for motor homes or buses. In winter, the road is closed until mid-February, even to skiing, for caribou conservation purposes. Continue 4 km (3 mi) up the road to the lush **Astoria Valley Viewpoint.**

Cavell Road ends at the Mount Edith Cavell parking lot. Here you will find two interpretive trails and

a few climbing routes. On the **Path of the Glacier Loop** (1–2 hr return), glacial debris from the Little Ice Age litters the trail, which takes you toward the north face of the mountain, across a rocky landscape left behind by glaciers. The trail ends at a viewpoint above **Cavell Pond,** which sometimes plays host to fallen icebergs and provides a good view of both glaciers. The moderately steep **Cavell Meadows Loop** (3–6 hr) guides you to alpine meadows flecked with flowers and striking views of powder blue **Angel Glacier.** Be alert, as you will likely see wildlife on your trip—birds, squirrels, deer, goats, marmots, pika, and maybe a caribou. Take as many pictures as you like, but do not feed or approach the animals.

MALIGNE VALLEY ROAD

45 km/29 mi; a half to full day

A side trip to Maligne (pronounced MAH-leen) Lake is a must-do when

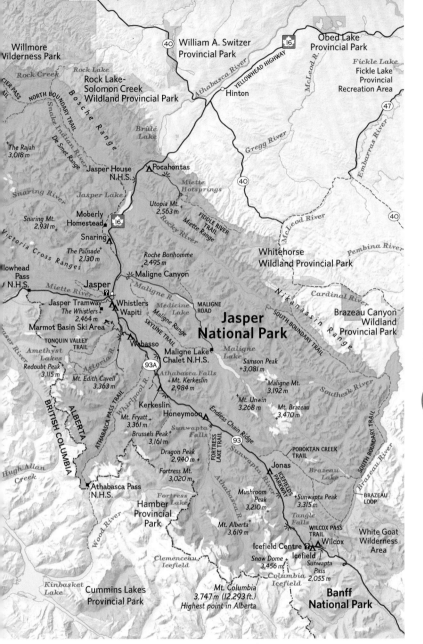

Willmore
Vilderness Park

William A. Switzer
Provincial Park

Obed Lake
Provincial Park

Fickle Lake

Rock Creek
Rock Lake

Rock Lake-
Solomon Creek
Wildland Provincial Park

Fickle Lake
Provincial
Recreation Area

NORTH BOUNDARY TRAIL

Brûlé
Lake

Hinton

McLeod R.

Athabasca River

YELLOWHEAD HIGHWAY

Gregg River

The Rajah
3,018 m

Jasper House
N.H.S.

Pocahontas

Miette
Hotsprings

Snaring River

Jasper Lake

Utopia Mt.
2,563 m

FIDDLE RIVER TRAIL

McLeod River

Pembina River

Snaring Mt.
2,931 m

Moberly
Homestead

Snaring

Rocky River

Miette Range

Whitehorse
Wildland Provincial Park

Victoria Cross Ranges

The Palisade
2,130 m

Roche Bonhomme
2,495 m

Nikassin Range

Cardinal River

Brazeau Canyon
Wildland
Provincial Park

owhead
Pass
N.H.S.

Miette River

Jasper

Maligne Canyon

Maligne R.

MALIGNE
ROAD

Jasper
National Park

SOUTH BOUNDARY TRAIL

Jasper Tramway
The Whistlers
2,464 m

Whistlers
Wapiti

Medicine
Lake

Maligne Range

SKYLINE TRAIL

Marmot Basin Ski Area

TONQUIN VALLEY
TRAIL

Wabasso

Maligne Lake
Chalet N.H.S.

Maligne
Lake

Samson Peak
3,081 m

Southesk River

aser River

Amethyst
Lakes

Astoria R.

Athabasca Falls

Mt. Kerkeslin
2,984 m

Maligne Mt.
3,192 m

Redoubt Peak
3,115 m

Mt. Edith Cavell
3,363 m

ATHABASCA PASS TRAIL

93A

Whirlpool R.

Kerkeslin
Honeymoon

Endless Chain Ridge

Mt. Unwin
3,268 m

Mt. Brazeau
3,470 m

BRITISH COLUMBIA

ALBERTA

Mt. Fryatt
3,361 m

Sunwapta
Falls

Athabasca River

POBOKTAN CREEK
TRAIL

Jonas

Brazeau
Lake

SOUTH BOUNDARY TRAIL

BRAZEAU RIVER

Brussels Peak
3,161 m

Dragon Peak
2,940 m

93

FORTRESS LAKE TRAIL

Sunwapta River

ICEFIELDS PARKWAY

BRAZEAU
LOOP

Hugh Allan
Creek

Fortress Mt.
3,020 m

Athabasca Pass
N.H.S.

Fortress
Lake

Hamber
Provincial
Park

Wood River

Mushroom
Peak
3,210 m

Sunwapta Peak
3,315 m

Tangle
Falls

WILCOX PASS
TRAIL

White Goat
Wilderness
Area

Mt. Alberta
3,619 m

Icefield Centre

Wilcox

Clemenceau
Icefield

Snow Dome
3,456 m

Icefield

Sunwapta
Pass
2,055 m

Kinbasket
Lake

Cummins Lakes
Provincial Park

Mt. Columbia
3,747 m (12,293 ft.)
Highest point in Alberta

Columbia
Icefield

Banff
National Park

visiting Jasper. Go east on Hwy. 16
and turn right across the Moberly
Bridge, 2.5 km (1.6 mi) east of the
town of Jasper, and follow the signs.
This stretch of road is home to a
number of natural wonders, including a deep canyon (which can be

explored from the bottom in winter),
a lake that disappears down sinkholes,
and Jasper's most picturesque lake.

Have your camera at the ready
while you drive this winding road, as
many kinds of animals are commonly
seen here. As always in the park, be

on the lookout for bears, elk, deer, moose, sheep, and goats. Stay a safe distance away and remain in your vehicle if you do come upon wildlife.

At km 6, watch for the Maligne Valley Overlook on your left; the sign can be easy to miss. Take this exit for an exceptional panorama of the vast glacier-carved **Athabasca Valley,** the town of Jasper in the valley bottom, and, across the valley, **Pyramid Mountain.**

At km 7, turn left into the **Maligne Canyon day-use area.** Created by Maligne River erosion between the Maligne and Athabasca Valleys, the canyon is up to 50 m (160 ft) deep at various places. Take a self-guided tour along the canyon's interpretive trail to learn about the geological history of the area. Cross the four bridges running across the gorge, each with its own special view. A short hiking loop takes you to the upper reaches of the canyon, while a longer trail follows the gorge. Stay on the trail and resist the temptation to climb past the railings for that perfect picture. Canyon walks, including winter ice walks, are available through various tour operators.

Continue on Maligne Road to km 20 to see **Medicine Lake,** which is not your average mountain lake. In summer, glacial meltwaters flood the lake, sometimes to overflowing. But in fall and winter, the lake disappears. With no visible channel draining the lake, it's unclear where the water goes—a veritable disappearing lake phenomenon.

In fact, the lake drains from the bottom like a bathtub. After Maligne River fills the lake, the water drains out through sinkholes in the bottom. It then streams through an underground cave network formed in the limestone rock, surfacing again downstream in the area of Maligne Canyon. It is one of the largest known underground river systems in North America and may be the world's largest inaccessible cave system. Thousands of gallons of water drain every second. During the summer runoff, enough water flows into the lake to surpass the drainage. By September, the runoff drops off, and the lake rapidly drains.

At the end of Maligne Road (km 45), you'll come to **Maligne Lake,** considered to be one of the most scenic spots in Canada. The largest natural lake in the Canadian Rockies at 22.5 km (14 mi) long, Maligne Lake is a popular site for interpretive boat cruises. From May to October, try the 90-minute boat tour to the famed **Spirit Island** in the middle of the lake for 360-degree views of the lake and mountains (the island is accessible only by boat).

Surrounded by snowcapped mountains, Maligne Lake stretches to the meltwater channels of **Coronet Glacier.** Amid the forest of spruce and lodgepole pine, you may once again catch a glimpse of wildlife, including harlequin ducks along the Maligne River. Endless hiking and cross-country skiing trails make the valley a popular year-round getaway. Snowshoeing and guided fishing are also available.

COLUMBIA ICEFIELD AREA & ATHABASCA GLACIER

a full day

Located off the Icefields Parkway (Hwy. 93), the **Columbia Icefield** is the largest reservoir of snow and ice in the Rockies and feeds three of the continent's major river systems. Straddling the borders of Alberta and British Columbia, the ice field

Exploring the narrows of Maligne Canyon

Kayaking Maligne Lake, the largest natural lake in the Canadian Rockies

Bald eagle perched atop a fir tree in the shadow of Sirdar Mountain

JASPER

comprises 260 sq km (64,250 acres) of crystal-blue glacial ice and snow. And, almost three-quarters of the park's highest peaks are located nearby, fashioning a mantle of alpine majesty. A remnant of the last ice age, this frozen giant continues to gradually sculpt the scenery.

A 4.8-km (3 mi) tongue of the ice field, the **Athabasca Glacier** is the most accessible and visited glacier in North America, flowing within 1.6 km (1 mi) of the highway. Its ice is in continuous motion, creeping forward bit by bit every day. Spilling down the valley like a frozen river, the glacier has actually been receding for the last 125 years. As the climate has warmed, the glacier has lost half its original volume and retreated more than 1.6 km (1 mi).

To experience the glacier up close, try a guided ice walk, where you can set foot upon the glacier itself. There are also specially designed Ice

Explorer vehicles that can take you for a glacial expedition. See firsthand what glacier ice looks, feels, and even tastes like as you tread cautiously through ice-carved landscapes. Do not attempt to walk on the glacier on your own; glaciers can be hazardous.

Finish off with a visit to the **Columbia Icefield Centre and Glacier Gallery** (late April–mid-Oct.), located across from the Athabasca Glacier, to learn more about this frozen alpine world. Displays in the gallery show how glaciers are formed and explain the ecology and history of the area.

JASPER NATIONAL PARK *(Parc national Jasper)*

INFORMATION & ACTIVITIES

VISITOR & INFORMATION CENTRES

Jasper Information Centre 500 Connaught Dr., Jasper, AB T0E 1E0. Phone (780) 852-6176. **Icefields Information Centre** Icefields Pkwy. Phone (780) 852-6288. 103 km (64 mi) south of the town of Jasper. Open April to October.

SEASONS & ACCESSIBILITY

Open year-round. Some seasonal restrictions for facilities and trails.

HEADQUARTERS

Box 10, Jasper, AB T0E 1E0. Phone (780) 852-6176. www.parkscanada.gc.ca/jasper.

FRIENDS OF JASPER

Friends of Jasper National Park P.O. Box 992, 415 Connaught Dr., Jasper, AB T0E 1E0. Phone (780) 852-4767. friends@incentre.net; www.friendsofjasper.com.

ENTRANCE FEES

$10 per person, $20 per group per day; $68 per person, $140 per group per year with Canada Parks Discovery Pass.

PETS

Dogs must be leashed at all times; not allowed on some trails.

ACCESSIBLE SERVICES

For information on accessible facilities, call the Jasper Information Centre (wheelchair accessible). Glacier Gallery in the Icefield Information Centre and Miette Hot Springs are accessible.

THINGS TO DO

Hiking, horseback riding, skiing, backpacking, and mountain biking. Rafting, canoeing, and swimming. Bathing in a pool with water from the Miette Hot Springs. Fishing permits $10 per day, $35 per year.

SPECIAL ADVISORIES

- If you encounter bears, slow down and make noise to alert them to your presence. Bear bells will not be enough.
- Never leave coolers, pet bowls, dishes or pots, food items, cooking stoves, garbage bags, or toiletries unattended.

CAMPGROUNDS

84 backcountry campsites. Reserve online at parkscanada.gc.ca/jasperbackcountry or call (877) 737-3783. **Pocahontas,** unserviced with toilets only, $22 per night. **Whistlers,** with water, sewer, and electrical services $38; electrical services only, $32; unserviced with toilets and showers $28; walk-in campground with toilets and showers $22. **Wapiti,** with electrical services $32; unserviced with toilets and showers $28. **Wabasso,** unserviced with toilets $21. **Snaring, Kerkesling, Honeymoon Lake, Jonas, Icefield Tent, Icefield RV,** and **Wilcox** primitive campgrounds $16. Snaring overflow space $11. **Marmot Meadows** group camping $6 per person. **Whirlpool** group camping $5 per person. Serviced (hook-up) sites fill up quickly; arrive early. Cottage tents with space for four adults and two children, electric wall lights, and baseboard heaters. Reserve (www.pccamping.ca or 877-737-3783) in advance of peak season (June–Sept.). Fire, campsite day-use, and dump station permits $9 per day each.

HOTELS, MOTELS, & INNS

(unless otherwise noted, rates are for a 2-person double, high season, in Canadian dollars)

Jasper, AB T0E 1E0:
Jasper offers a wide range of year-round accommodations, ranging from camping, bungalows, cabins, and B&Bs to hostels, motels, hotels, and lodges.

Additional visitor information:
Tourism Jasper, (780-852-7176), www.jasper.travel. **Hostelling International Canada,** (778) 328-2220, www.hihostels.ca., or **Jasper Home Accommodation Association,** www.stayinjasper.com.

EXCURSIONS

JASPER HOUSE NATIONAL HISTORIC SITE
JASPER, AB

Built in 1813, the trading post served as a meeting and provisions place for fur traders and explorers journeying through the Athabasca and Yellowhead Passes throughout much of the 19th century. Originally named Rocky Mountain House, it was renamed after its first postmaster, Jasper Hawes. The Hudson's Bay Company moved the fur-trading post upriver in 1829, but by 1850 the post had declined. It closed permanently 50 years later. Today, access to the field where the house stood is via Hwy. 16, 40 km (25 mi) from Jasper.

JASPER PARK INFORMATION CENTRE NATIONAL HISTORIC SITE
JASPER, AB

A shining example of rustic architecture in Canada's national parks, the facility introduced a tradition of local building materials, namely cobblestone and timber. Completed in 1914, the centre originally housed park administrative offices, a museum, and living quarters for the park superintendent. The first major building in the townsite, it helped define the character of Jasper's early development. It continues to be a park contact point. 500 Connaught Dr. (780) 852-6162.

JASPER

Pedaling the Kootenai Brown Trail

Prince of Wales Hotel on the cliffs overlooking Waterton Lake

▶ WATERTON LAKES

ALBERTA
ESTABLISHED 1895
505 sq km/124,788 acres

The deepest lake in the Canadian Rockies (135.3 m/444 ft) and the first oil well in western Canada (1902) are both found in Waterton. It has international significance as the Canadian portion of Waterton-Glacier International Peace Park, the world's first, and a UNESCO World Heritage site.

Waterton sits in the extreme southwestern corner of Alberta, sharing boundaries with British Columbia and Montana in the United States. It's "where the mountains meet the prairies," as locals like to say. Indeed, lush native grassland rolls right up to the colourful peaks, which have been carved from sedimentary rock well over a billion years old.

With its grand scenery, sunny weather, easily seen wildlife, and wind-raked trees, Waterton is a photographer's paradise. All three of the Waterton Lakes lie along the entry road. Other paved routes provide quick access to park highlights. One of the hiking trails is world famous, while mountain bikers will find several trails open to them, too.

How to Get There

The closest international airport is located at Calgary, 254 km (158 mi)

away. From Calgary, take Hwy. 2 to Fort Macleod (164 km/102 mi), then turn west along Hwy. 3 for 97 km (60 mi) to Pincher Creek, where Hwy. 6 runs southward for 50 very scenic kilometres (31 mi) to the park gate. Hwy. 5 continues another 8.6 km (5.3 mi) to the "townsite" of Waterton Park, as Parks Canada describes the in-park community, summer population about 2,500. From east or west, take Hwy. 3 to Pincher Creek.

From the United States, you can enter the park directly. Take Mont. 17 north to the Chief Mountain border crossing and continue into Alberta on Hwy. 6. Be sure to inquire in advance of your visit for the Canadian post's hours of operation and seasonal closures.

When to Go

Waterton is open year-round. However, few services are available in the park between October and May, when some roads are subject to closure and the townsite population drops to less than 40.

Spring arrives in early May. The park is busiest in July and August, when daytime temperatures reach well into the 20s°C (over 70°F) and may hit the mid-30s°C (90s°F).

Low-elevation wildflowers are at their best in June, while the high country above tree line is most colourful in mid-July. Aspen groves paint the valley floors and lower slopes brilliantly yellow in September, and brilliant golden larches highlight backcountry trails.

How to Visit

You'll want a full day to tour the park's three parkways, so get an early start. Morning light on the mountain front is a spectacle best appreciated from the Waterton Valley viewpoint along

the Chief Mountain Highway (Hwy. 6) in the eastern part of the park.

Return to the townsite for brunch and enjoy a breezy stroll along the shore of Upper Waterton Lake. The M.V. International and other passenger vessels cruise the lake. Since the waves may get bigger as the day goes by, morning is a good time to take the two-hour-plus cruise-boat ride down the lake and back.

Then head up scenic Red Rock Parkway to Red Rock Canyon. The canyon is aptly named, very photogenic, and great fun for the kids.

End your day by taking the Akamina Parkway to Cameron Lake to see stately peaks resplendent in the afternoon sun. The lake offers a smashing view of craggy peaks at the far end, just across the international boundary, plus rare botanical delights along the shoreline.

ENTERING THE PARK

60 km/37 mi; 1 hour

Travelling along Hwy. 6, Waterton comes into view at the Pine Ridge Viewpoint, 36 km (22 mi) south of Pincher Creek, well before you reach the park. Pull off and get out the camera, because this is one of the world's great vistas, 75 million years in the making.

Imagine the mountains creeping toward you at about 1 cm (0.4 in) per year, and gaining elevation as they go. Multiply by 40 million years, add 60 million years of landscape sculpture through erosion—the last three million years by glaciers—and this is what you get.

As you pass the park-boundary sign, watch for a turnoff on your right. This narrow road loops through the Bison Paddock, a grassy fenced-off area where bison graze.

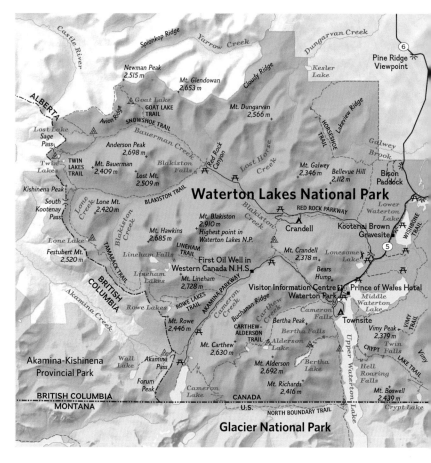

You can get photos of the animals in a natural setting, with lofty peaks in the background, but stay in your vehicle. Bison are dangerous.

The paddock is rolling kame-and-kettle topography, where part of the Waterton Valley's Ice Age glacier melted away under a cover of gravel some 15,000 to 20,000 years ago. The hills (kames) mark spots where the glacier was thin; the hollows (kettles, some with ponds in them) indicate thick spots. The low ridges are eskers, sinuous deposits of gravel left by streams flowing under the ice.

Farther on, **Lower Waterton Lake** occupies a depression in the land-scape, an enormous kettle. You will often see birds, such as osprey, ducks, eagles, and even white pelicans, on the water.

When you reach the townsite, stop at the park's **visitor information centre.** The **Peace Park Native Plant Garden** here reflects the region's exceptional botanical diversity. Also, it's only a short distance (0.4 km/0.25 mi) across the highway and up the access road to the charming **Prince of Wales Hotel,** a national historic site. Go around to the south side of the building, where the view of **Upper Waterton Lake** is most impressive. So is the wind,

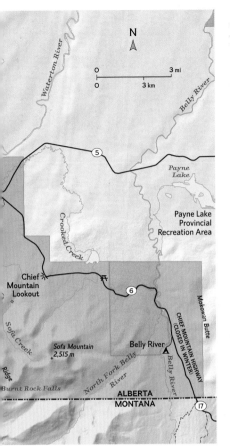

especially when the females have young, so give them plenty of room.

RED ROCK PARKWAY TO RED ROCK CANYON
14 km/8.7 mi; 1 to 3 hours

From the townsite, travel north on Hwy. 5 for 2.9 km (1.8 mi) to the turnoff. The road follows the valley of **Blakiston Creek,** showcasing "where the mountains meet the prairies." The grassy meadows and light tree cover beside the road, open from the first weekend in May to late October, allow open views of the mountains on either side. Much of the rock is ancient argillite—like shale, but harder—in countless layers. Bears wander in the berry patches on the hillsides along the parkway.

The big peak seen well up the valley is **Mount Blakiston,** at 2,910 m (9,548 ft) the highest point in the park. A dark line low on the cliffs is the **Purcell Sill,** molten basalt that squeezed between the layers long before the Rockies began to rise.

The road ends at **Red Rock Canyon,** a shallow gorge stream-cut into red argillite and white sandstone of the distinctive Grinnell formation. The brick red colour in the rock is from hematite, which is oxidized (rusted) iron. A short, paved trail loops around the gorge, and interpretive signs add to the appeal. Another walk of 2 km (1.2 mi) from the parking lot takes you to the viewing platforms at **Blakiston Falls** and back.

AKAMINA PARKWAY TO CAMERON LAKE
16 km/9.6 mi; 1 to 2 hours return

Cameron Lake, elevation 1,660 m (5,440 ft), can be a chilly place in

which the seven-floor hotel has been battling ever since it opened in 1927. Though tied down with steel cables, the building still shudders in the gales.

Once in town, follow the signs to **Cameron Falls,** where Cameron Creek splashes over limestone of the Waterton formation. Dating to 1.5 billion years, this is the oldest sedimentary rock in Alberta.

You may see bighorn sheep right in the townsite. Mule deer, too. They make great photo subjects, but keep in mind that they are still wild animals. Don't feed or touch them. The deer are known to attack people,

WATERTON LAKES

Elk wander the plains of Waterton Lakes National Park.

the morning. By afternoon the temperature is comfortable, while at lower elevations the day is becoming overly warm, so the lake makes a fine destination in hot weather.

The road starts where Hwy. 5 enters the townsite. From the initial switchbacks you get views of **Upper Waterton Lake.** Across the water lies **Mount Vimy** (2,379 m/7,950 ft), named during World War I for a battle won at great human cost to Canadian forces.

At 7.8 km (4.8 mi) you come to **First Oil Well in Western Canada National Historic Site** (see p. 246). Natural oil seeps here attracted drillers, who struck petroleum in 1902. The boom town of **Oil City** sprang up nearby, but it soon died when the flow tapered to practically nothing. Still, this was the first producing oil well in western Canada, and the hydrocarbons were found in extremely old rock, a rare situation.

At road's end, **Cameron Lake** stretches 2.5 km (1.6 mi) to the southwest, where the craggy visage of **Mount Custer** (2,708 m/8,883 ft) lies just across the international boundary in Montana.

The road opened in 1927, and much lakeside development followed. However, Parks Canada has removed it all, restoring the natural ambience. Commerce is limited to a canoe-rental concession. If you walk the shoreline trail in July or August, watch for showy red monkey-flowers and other species seldom seen north of Waterton. Botanical guidebooks and other useful publications are available at the Waterton Natural History Association shop in town.

HIKING & MOUNTAIN BIKING

If you're looking for a good workout, the hiking trail to **Bear's Hump** climbs 240 m (790 ft) in only 1.2 km (0.8 mi). Despite its steepness, this is the most popular trail in the park. The view from the top stretches from the town, toy-like below, to the far end of **Upper Waterton Lake.** Start at the visitor information centre on the north edge of town. Allow one to two hours return, and bring water.

For adventurous hikers, Waterton Lakes National Park offers the world-renowned **Crypt Lake Trail.** Give yourself a full day, and bring pepper spray; the area is famous for grizzly sightings. Begin by taking the water shuttle across Upper Waterton Lake. From the dock to Crypt Lake you gain 675 m (2,215 ft) over 8.7 km (5.4 mi), including a cleverly engineered route through the cliffs below the lake. You'll climb an iron ladder, stoop through a short cave passage (enlarged for easier negotiation), and run your hand along a fixed cable while crossing an exposed ledge.

The lake sits in a glacial bowl at tree line, and the south end of the lake is in the United States. Be sure you get back to the dock for pickup at the appointed time, or you'll be hiking an additional 14 km (9 mi) out to Hwy. 6 then hitchhiking to town.

The most popular trail to tree line and above is the well-graded path to **Carthew Summit,** elevation 2,311 m (7,582 ft). Be prepared for rough weather. Starting at Cameron Lake, the trail climbs steadily for 650 m (2,135 ft) in 8 km (5 mi) to the airy pass, with a view down the other side to the two sky blue **Carthew Lakes,** each a classic glacial tarn sitting in a bedrock basin scooped out by the ice that once flowed down this valley.

Return the way you came or head down to the lakes and into the forest, passing by **Alderson Lake** to finish at **Cameron Falls** in the townsite, 12 km (7.5 mi) away, for a total hike of 18 km (11 mi). Since this is a one-way walk, it's handy to have two cars. Alternatively, shuttle service to Cameron Lake is available. Inquire at Tamarack Outdoor Outfitters (214 Mountainview Rd., 403-859-2378, *www.hikewaterton.com*) in the townsite.

For a shorter hike with its own reward, do the first 4.2 km (2.6 mi) of the trail and stop at **Summit Lake,** surrounded by subalpine meadows full of showy white beargrass, the park's signature wildflower. The species blooms from early June to mid-July.

Of the park's several approved mountain-biking routes, perhaps the most pleasant is the **Snowshoe Trail** in the western part of the park. Start at the end of the **Red Rock Parkway.** A wide dirt track, closed to motor vehicles, continues up **Bauerman Creek** for 8.2 km (5 mi) at an easy to moderate grade. This is a fine ride for beginning trail cyclists,

Harnessing the wind at Bear's Hump

keeping in mind that it does entail small creek crossings. Another outing popular with cyclists is the new **Kootenai Brown Trail,** 6.5 km (4 mi) of paved pathway paralleling Hwy. 5 between the park gate and the townsite.

WATERTON LAKES NATIONAL PARK
(Parc national des Lacs-Waterton)

INFORMATION & ACTIVITIES

VISITOR CENTRE
Visitor Information Centre Phone (403) 859-5133. In the entrance parkway 6 km (4 mi) from the park entrance. Open mid-May to mid-October.

SEASONS & ACCESSIBILITY
The park is open year-round, but most park facilities are closed from late fall to early spring. Peak season in the park is July and August; it's important to book accommodation well in advance. No services on weekends from mid-October to mid-May.

HEADQUARTERS
Box 200, Waterton Park, AB T0K 2M0. Phone (403) 859-2224. www.parks canada.gc.ca/waterton.

FRIENDS OF WATERTON LAKES
Waterton Natural History Association Box 145, Waterton Park, AB T0K 2M0. Phone (403) 859-2624. wnha@tough country.net; www.wnha.ca. Heritage Centre, 117 Waterton Ave.

ENTRANCE FEES
$8 per person per day; $39 per person per year. $68 per person with Parks Canada Discovery Pass.

PETS
Pets must be kept on a leash at all times or in a kennel with a secure top.

ACCESSIBLE SERVICES
There are wheelchair-accessible sites (serviced and unserviced) and washrooms at Townsite Campground. The Visitor Centre and a Linnett Lake trail are accessible.

THINGS TO DO
Boating, canoeing, and kayaking. Canoes, rowboats, paddleboats, and stand-up paddleboards available for rent at **Cameron Lake.** Powerboating on **Upper** and **Middle Waterton Lakes** and waterskiing on Middle Waterton Lake.

Hiking trails: 12 short hikes (20 min.–2 hr), 10 half-day hikes, eight full-day hikes, and one multiday trail.

Visit the **Heritage Centre,** 111 Waterton Avenue, operated by the Waterton Natural History Association. Heritage Interpretation Programs offered by Parks Canada at many locations.

Self-guided tours available at **First Oil Well** in Western Canada (see below) and **Prince of Wales Hotel** national historic sites inside the park. Educational program

EXCURSIONS

FIRST OIL WELL IN WESTERN CANADA NATIONAL HISTORIC SITE
WATERTON LAKES NP, AB

A small iconic derrick shelters the head of the first producing oil well in western Canada. Petroleum was struck at 312 m (1,024 ft) in 1902. Initial production of 300 barrels per day soon dwindled to nearly nothing, however, and other wells fared little better. Instead, one of them went out of control and created the first oil spill in western Canada. From the townsite, head north. Turn onto the Akamina Parkway to Cameron Lake, and follow it for 7.8 km (4.8 mi). (403) 859-5133.

at **Bar U Ranch,** two hours north of the park (late May–mid-Oct.).

SPECIAL ADVISORIES
- Keep food and cooking waste in your vehicle to avoid attracting wildlife.
- Weather is highly variable, and winds average 32 kph (20 mph).
- When boating on Waterton Lakes, watch out for floating logs. Wash boats, motors, trailers, and other equipment before bringing them to the park to avoid the transfer of invasive species to the park's aquatic systems.
- Hunting, snowmobiling, paragliding, parachuting, hang gliding, or use of personal watercraft are forbidden.

OVERNIGHT BACKPACKING
Nine backcountry campsites. Wilderness Use Permit required for backcountry camping. For reservations, call warden office, (403) 859-5140, from April to mid-May and visitor information centre for the remainder of the year.

CAMPGROUNDS
Townsite Campground, 238 campsites, appropriate for RVs. With hot showers, flush toilets, food storage, and kitchen shelters $38 per night; with electricity only $32 per night; unserviced with toilets and showers $27. **Crandell Mountain Campground,** 129 unserviced sites with piped water, flush toilets, kitchen shelters, some fire rings and firewood, food storage, recycling bins, and a dump station $22. Includes a campsite with five teepees ($11 reservation fee; $55 per night per teepee). **Belly River Campground,** primitive camping, $16; group camping by reservation for groups of minimum 25 people ($5 per person). Call (403) 859-2224. Winter camping at **Pass Creek,** call (403) 859-5133. Privately operated campgrounds at **Waterton Springs,** (403) 859-2247, and **Crooked Creek,** (403) 653-1100.

HOTELS, MOTELS, & INNS
(unless otherwise noted, rates are for a 2-person double, high season, in Canadian dollars)

Waterton, AB T0K 2M0:
Crandell Mountain Lodge Box 114, 102 Mountview Rd. (403) 859-2288 or (866) 859-2288. reservations@crandellmountainlodge.com; www.crandellmountainlodge.com. $169.
Prince of Wales Hotel P.O. Box 33, Park entrance road. (403) 236-3400 (in Canada) or (406) 892-2525 (in U.S.). Booking: (844) 868-7474. www.princeofwaleswaterton.com. $249–$315.
Waterton Lakes Lodge Resort P.O. Box 4, 101 Clematis Ave. (403) 859-2150. reservations@watertonlakeslodge.com; www.watertonlakeslodge.com. $199–$224.

BAR U RANCH NATIONAL HISTORIC SITE
LONGVIEW, AB

Bar U Ranch, one of the more successful ranches in Canadian history (1882–1950), brings the Old West to life through its historic buildings, informative exhibits, and reenactments of daily life. Visitors learn everything from driving horses to throwing a lasso. You can also savour cowboy coffee over a campfire while listening to stories, poetry, and music. (403) 395-2212. Located 200 km (125 mi) north of Waterton, Hwy. 22.

A view of Emerald Lake from the entrance to Emerald Lake Lodge

▶ YOHO

BRITISH COLUMBIA
ESTABLISHED 1886
1,313 sq km/324,449 acres

A Cree exclamation of awe, "Yoho" applies perfectly to this park's big peaks, expansive glaciers, and impressive waterfalls. Add Yoho's famous fossils and it's easy to see why this park in the Canadian Rockies is part of a UNESCO World Heritage site. Although many of its highlights are accessible by road, Yoho is also a hiker's dream and a railway buff's delight.

Yoho National Park protects the upper watershed of the Kicking Horse River, a steep, unruly tributary of 53 km (33 mi). Much of the water comes from the Yoho River, ice cold and milky with rock flour from its source at the Wapta Icefield. Many other glaciers feed the Yoho and the Kicking Horse, which thunders over Wapta Falls before rushing through a steep-walled canyon to the Columbia River.

Trans-Canada 1 and the Canadian Pacific Railway follow the Kicking Horse through the heart of the park. Precipitous peaks sporting epaulettes of glacial ice rise more than 1.6 km (1 mi) above the transportation corridor. The highest point in the park is South Goodsir Tower, with a summit elevation of 3,562 m (11,686 ft). A side road leads to world-class Takakkaw Falls. Swollen with glacial meltwater on summer afternoons, the falls plunges 380 m (1,250 ft) to the floor of the Yoho Valley. Other roads lead to appropriately named Emerald Lake.

Among this spectacular terrain lies the Burgess Shale, a layer of half-billion-year-old rock that holds paleontology's most valuable fossils. Specimens are on display at the park information centre.

How to Get There

From Calgary (closest airport), follow Trans-Canada 1 west for 200 km (125 mi) to the community of Field, near the centre of the park. From the south, take Hwy. 95 to Golden, then turn east onto Trans-Canada 1 and follow it 57 km (35 mi) to Field.

When to Go

Yoho is accessible and enjoyable year-round. The western valley floors green up in May, and by mid-June the side roads are open. By mid-July the higher trail passes are snow free, and later in the month the alpine wildflowers reach their peak. In late September, subalpine larch rewards visitors with a showy band of gold at tree line. Winter in Yoho, which lasts from November to March, offers Nordic skiing, snowshoeing, ski touring, and world-renowned waterfall ice climbing.

How to Visit

Give yourself a full day to take in the roadside views and enjoy some easy walking. Emerald Lake makes a fine morning destination, with a stop at Natural Bridge en route. Take a stroll around the lake, then head back to Trans-Canada 1, catch some lunch in Field, and keep going east to the Yoho Valley Road for a drive to jaw-dropping Takakkaw Falls, at its best in the late afternoon.

DRIVING ACROSS THE PARK

46 km/28 mi; 1 to 2 hours or 70 km/44 mi to Golden; 2 hours

If you want to drive across Yoho, begin your journey on Trans-Canada 1, at **Kicking Horse Pass,** elevation 1,647 m (5,404 ft). Located 10 km (6 mi) west of Lake Louise at the eastern park boundary, the pass marks the Continental Divide as well as the boundary between Alberta and British Columbia. All water in the park flows to the Pacific.

Ahead of you, the peak on the left is 3,126-m (10,256 ft) **Cathedral Mountain.** Past small **Wapta Lake,** you descend the **Big Hill,** originally a railbed that had by far the steepest grade (4.5 percent) on the Canadian Pacific Railway (CPR). Pull off at the **Spiral Tunnels Viewpoint** to learn how the CPR reduced the grade to 2.2 percent by cutting two semicircular tunnels into the mountain.

Near the base of the hill you will cross the **Kicking Horse River.** Look low on the cliffs to the right to see small entrances to the **Kicking Horse Mine.** The limestone and dolomite rock contains a lead-and-zinc ore deposit that was mined from 1888 to 1952. Having acquired a major tributary from the **Wapta Icefield**—50 sq km (20 sq mi) of glacial ice straddling the divide—the river rushes across gravel flats in many shallow, shifting channels, more evidence of its Ice Age character.

At the turnoff for Field, stop at the **visitor centre** operated jointly by Parks Canada and Travel Alberta *(www.travelalberta.com).* On display are fossils of trilobites and much stranger creatures from the Burgess Shale, science's window on the Cambrian world. Fuel and snacks

YOHO

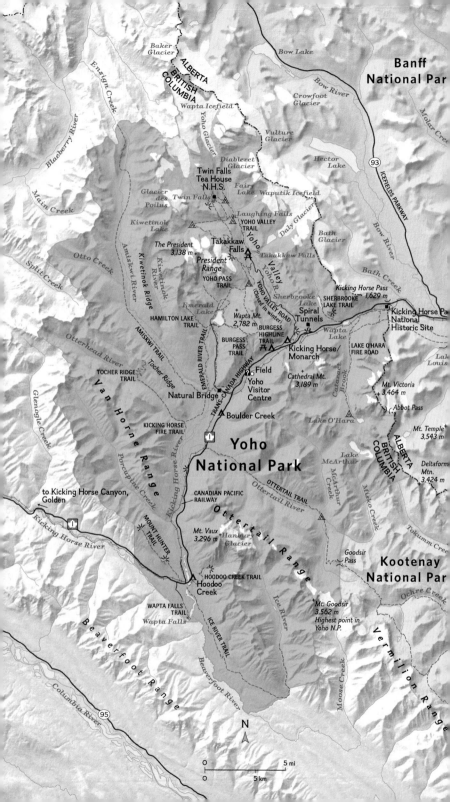

are available at Yoho Trading Post, opposite the visitor centre, during the summer.

West of Field, you cross the Kicking Horse River again as it pours into a gorge cut in Cambrian slate. The next time you see the river, however, it will be flowing more placidly westward through a wide U-shaped glacial valley between the big limestone peaks of the **Ottertail Range** on the left and the gentler peaks of the **Van Horne Range** on the right. The colour of the water is powder blue from dilution by clear tributaries.

Outside the western park boundary, the highway turns west and climbs away from the river again. Some 15 km (9 mi) ahead lies **Kicking Horse Canyon,** viewed spectacularly as you drive over the **Park Bridge.** At this point, you might as well continue another 13 km (8 mi) to the town of **Golden** in the **Rocky Mountain Trench**—a great valley between the western edge of the Canadian Rockies and the eastern edge of the older Purcell Mountains. Straight-walled and more than 1,500 km (930 mi) long, this is one of the world's great topographic features, seen by the *Apollo* astronauts as they orbited the moon.

NATURAL BRIDGE & EMERALD LAKE
9.1 km/5.7 mi one way; a half day

About 1.6 km (1 mi) southwest of Field, turn west off Trans-Canada 1 and follow the branch west then north toward Emerald Lake. The opening stretch has some long road cuts in limy Cambrian slate about 510 million years old. If you drive slowly, you may be able to spot the small, wavy-looking folds in the rock. Heat and extreme pressure hardened and deformed these originally flat-lying layers of seabed mud during the building of the Rockies 55 to 100 million years ago.

At **Natural Bridge,** km 2.4, the Kicking Horse River splashes through a bedrock slot roofed in one spot by the slate. A footbridge across the water provides excellent views.

At road's end, **Emerald Lake** itself is dammed by a rockslide heap, now overgrown with tall conifers and home to Emerald Lake Lodge. One look at the water reveals its namesake deep-green glacial colour, photogenic at any time of day.

Directly across the lake lies the glacier-mantled President Range, where the highest summit, **The President,** stands a lofty 3,048 m (10,000 ft). To the right, across the forested gap of **Yoho Pass,** is the high ridge between **Wapta Mountain** and **Mount Field,** site of the Burgess Shale fossils discovery in 1909 (see p. 253). Farthest right is **Mount Burgess** itself, whose craggy image once graced the Canadian $10 bill.

The trail around the lake offers 5.2 km (3.2 mi) of easy walking. Enjoy the fragrant spruce and fir forest at this elevation (1,300 m/ 4,300 ft). You may see three-toed woodpeckers, grouse, red squirrels, a marten, or perhaps a black bear.

YOHO VALLEY & TAKAKKAW FALLS
13.5 km (8.4 mi) one way; 2 hours

Leave your trailer behind for this drive because it entails two very tight switchbacks near the start. Otherwise the road is easy. En route, note the avalanche tracks on the mountainsides. Sliding snow rumbles down these ski-run-like swaths nearly every winter.

From the parking lots, walk toward the bridge for ever-improving

YOHO

Crossing Little Yoho River

Kicking Horse River at Natural Bridge

A rarely seen mountain lion

views of the falls. "Takakkaw" is another Cree exclamation, this one along the lines of "Magnificent!"

Once across the fast-flowing, green-grey Yoho River, you'll find that the path gets rougher and steeper as you approach the roaring spectacle. The water free-falls for about 254 m (833 ft) out of its 380 m (1,250 ft) total drop over a cliff of Cambrian limestone. Out of sight above is the water's source: the **Daly Glacier,** which is part of the **Waputik Icefield,** 15 sq km (6 sq mi).

In late afternoon, with the sun behind you, a standing rainbow makes the scene magical. Closer yet, the waterfall's wind blast turns most people around. That's a good thing because anyone venturing nearer risks being hit by one of the boulders that come crashing down in the torrent.

LAKE O'HARA

11 km/7 mi (accessible only by bus—reservations required—or on foot); a full day

Justifiably popular for its well-built hiking trails and great scenery, Lake O'Hara is subject to daily visitor quotas and not accessible to cars or tour buses. Public transport to the lake runs mid-June until late September. Reservations are required. Visit *www.parkscanada.go.ca/LakeOhara* for more information.

The bus drops you by the shore, elevation 2,042 m (6,699 ft) and not far below tree line, so be prepared for cool temperatures and cold rain. Upon arrival, you may wish to stroll over to Le Relais Day Shelter, operated by the Lake O'Hara Trails Club, to get the latest information on trail conditions. Le Relais also offers snacks, trail maps, and guidebooks.

The 2.8-km (1.7 mi) **Lakeshore Trail** loop is mostly level, with one climb and descent. **Linda Lake** (3.5 km/2.2 mi one way) is a forest walk with gentle grades, perfect for kids. **Lake Oesa** (3.2 km/2 mi one way) climbs steeply into the rough and spectacular terrain below the continental divide. **Opabin Plateau** (5.9 km/3.7 mi loop) is a moderate hike through treeline meadows.

BURGESS SHALE

9 to 22 km/6 to 14 mi return; a full day

Workers building the Canadian Pacific Railway in the early 1880s discovered what they called "stone bugs" (trilobite fossils) in the Field area that attracted the attention of paleontologist Charles Walcott, Secretary of the Smithsonian Institution. In 1909, Walcott found bizarre soft-bodied forms in what he named the Burgess Shale. The quarry he opened returned to repeatedly, collecting many Cambrian species previously unknown to science, became a World Heritage site in 1980. In 1988, all of Yoho was included in the much larger Canadian Rocky Mountain Parks World Heritage site.

The Burgess Shale is famous enough to tempt fossil thieves, so Parks Canada has restricted access to Walcott Quarry and Mount Stephen fossil sites to groups led by authorized guides only. Getting to either place entails a steep hike to higher elevations, where the views are as wonderful as the ancient animal remains in the rock. Contact Parks Canada at *www.reservations.pc.gc.ca* or the Burgess Shale Foundation at (800) 343-3006.

HIKING TRAILS & THE RAILWAY

If you enjoy a two-hour walk, do not miss **Wapta Falls,** west of Field. If you are a fit day hiker, explore the Emerald Basin or Hamilton Lake trails in the Emerald Lake Area. Or spend the day on the aptly named **Iceline Trail,** which takes you through rugged, recently glaciated terrain high on the west wall of the Yoho Valley. Backpackers can include this trail on an overnight circuit, tenting at a secluded backcountry campground in the **Little Yoho Valley.** Mix strenuous exercise and fascinating science on a hike to one of two Burgess Shale locations (see above).

If you love railways, stop at the **Lower Spiral Tunnels Viewpoint,** partway up the long Trans-Canada 1 grade east of Field. Watch the freights enter the tunnels then emerge going the opposite direction on the mountainside.

YOHO

YOHO NATIONAL PARK *(Parc national Yoho)*

INFORMATION & ACTIVITIES

VISITOR CENTRE
Yoho National Park Visitor Centre
Trans-Canada 1, Field, BC V0A 1G0.
Phone (250) 343-6783. Open May–mid-
October.

SEASONS & ACCESSIBILITY
Park open year-round. Reservations
required for Lake O'Hara camping
(reserve up to three months in advance,
250-343-6433) and day use (make reservations for the entire season, 250-877-
RESERVE, www.reservation.pc.gc.ca).

HEADQUARTERS
P.O. Box 99, Field, BC V0A 1G0. Phone
(250) 343-6783. www.parkscanada
.gc.ca/yoho.

FRIENDS OF YOHO
P.O. Box 100, Field, BC V0A 1G0. Phone
(205) 343-6393. info@friendsofyoho.ca;
www.friendsofyoho.ca.

ENTRANCE FEES
$11 per adult per day; $68 per adult per
year. $20 per group per day; $136 per
group per season.

PETS
Leashed pets permitted but not at
Lake O'Hara.

ACCESSIBLE SERVICES
Multiple disabled-access facilities.

THINGS TO DO
Guided tours of **Burgess Shale fossil
beds** and exhibit at the visitor centre.
White-water canoeing and kayaking on
the **Kicking Horse River.**
  Contact the visitor centre for climbing
and mountaineering route descriptions,
and the Association of Mountain Guides
for guided tours (403-678-2885, www
.acmg.ca). Also mountain biking on designated trails, fishing (permits $10 per day,
$34 per year), and hiking. Guided hikes to
Mount Stephen Fossil Beds $50 to $55
per adult, to **Walcott Quarry** $63 to $70.

SPECIAL ADVISORIES
• Never leave coolers, pets or pet bowls,
dishes, cooking stoves, garbage bags,
wash basins, or toiletries unattended.
• Watch for black ice when driving.
• Be alert for rockfalls. Do not walk on
or beneath overhanging ice or snow.
• Avoid stopping in avalanche zones.
• Never feed or approach wildlife.
• Prepare for a variety of trail conditions.

OVERNIGHT BACKPACKING
Primitive camping $10 plus $12 reservation
fee. Four campgrounds in Yoho Valley:
Laughing Falls, Twin Falls, Little Yoho,
and **Yoho Lake,** and **McArthur Creek
Campground** in Ottertail Valley (links to
the Rockwall in Kootenay). Tent pads and
bear poles at all sites.

CAMPGROUNDS
Call visitor centre for availability. Campsite
day-use permit and fire permits $9 per day.
Takakkaw Falls (35 sites) and **Monarch**
(44 sites), walk-in primitive campgrounds,
$18. **Hoodoo Creek,** 30 sites, unserviced
campground with washroom (toilets only),
$22. **Kicking Horse,** 88 sites, unserviced
campground with washroom (toilets
and showers), $27.

HOTELS, MOTELS, & INNS
*(unless otherwise noted, rates are for a
2-person double, high season, in Canadian
dollars)*

Field, BC V0A 1G0:
Cathedral Mountain Lodge Yoho Valley
Rd. (250) 343-6442. info@cathedral
mountain.com; www.cathedralmountain
.com. $279–$379.
Emerald Lake Lodge 1 Emerald Lake Dr.
(250) 343-6321. www.crmr.com.
From $399.
Truffle Pigs Bistro & Lodge 100 Center St.
(250) 343-6303. oink@trufflepigs
.com; www.trufflepigs.com/lodge.
$175–$200.

Lake Louise, AB T0L 1E0:
Lake O'Hara Lodge Lake O'Hara, P.O.
Box 55. (250) 343-6418 or (403) 678-
4110. www.lakeohara.com. $655–$945.

Additional accommodations:
Field, BC www.field.ca

EXCURSIONS

TWIN FALLS TEA HOUSE NATIONAL HISTORIC SITE
YOHO NATIONAL PARK, BC

Built by the Canadian Pacific Railway to serve its hiking and horseback-riding hotel guests, the log-cabin "teahouses" of the Canadian Rockies are still welcome sights along the trail. The 1908 teahouse at Twin Falls, 8.5 km (5.3 mi) up the Yoho Valley from the trailhead at Takakkaw Falls, is a worthy choice to commemorate them all. (403) 228-7079.

KICKING HORSE PASS NATIONAL HISTORIC SITE
YOHO NP, BC

In 1881, the Canadian Pacific Railway chose this pass instead of a much easier route across the Rockies farther north. The length of the line was reduced by 122 km (76 mi), but construction and day-to-day operation proved to be very costly. The site commemoration is found at the Spiral Tunnels Viewpoint along Trans-Canada 1 between Lake Louise and Field.

YOHO

Migrations

A female wolf—captured and radio-collared near Banff, Alberta, in 1992—got everyone thinking about large-scale migration and the role of national parks. Fitted with a satellite transmitter, Pluie, as the wolf came to be known (French for the rain that poured down that June morning), recovered and set off on an epic journey that challenged every boundary drawn on a map.

Wolves are found throughout most of Canada and play an integral part in keeping the ecosystem in balance.

As an ecological imperative, migration is well understood. Animals move in order to find mates, avoid predators, escape diseases, find seasonal foods, recolonize areas swept by fire and flood, and search out safe places to rear their young. Indeed, migration patterns are the reasons behind the establishment of many Canadian national parks over the last 125 years. Point Pelee National Park in southern Ontario, for example, protects a major stopover point for 380 species of migratory birds, and Ivvavik National Park, set aside in 1984 in the northern Yukon, protects the calving grounds of the 120,000-member Porcupine caribou herd. But these are just pieces in a much larger conservation puzzle that, like the individual words in a beautiful poem, hold little value when removed from the larger whole.

What was so impressive about Pluie's journey was its scale: Driven by urges as old as the world itself, she moved from Alberta to Montana to northern Idaho to south-central British Columbia and back again, crisscrossing hundreds of roads, ranches, forests, meadows, rivers, and mountain ranges in the process. Her movements encompassed more than 120,000 sq km (46,332 sq mi), the equivalent of 20 Banff National Parks. It took two years for her to complete her zig-zag journey, and the message it left scrawled across biologists' maps has reverberated through the conservation community ever since: Think Big; Be Bold; Act Now.

Such slogans can't be found directly within Canada's National Parks Act but they exist between the lines, which is why Parks Canada signed a memorandum of agreement with the U.S. Park Service in 1999. Dubbed Y2Y for short, the Yellowstone to Yukon Conservation Initiative puts forth a bold new vision for conservation in North America: Establish and manage national parks and other protected areas not as stand-alone entities but as components in a much larger system of core reserves linked by wildlife corridors.

The focus of Y2Y is the Rockies and the wide-ranging species—like elk, caribou, grizzly bears, wolves, and wolverines—that still roam its many folds. But there are other, equally important reserve network proposals cropping up all over the continent, including Adirondacks to Algonquin (A2A) in the east and Baja to Bering Strait (B2B) along the Pacific Coast.

The role of Canadian national parks within these reserve networks is to preserve the connections critical to the continuation of migratory life. This involves look-ing both inside and outside park boundaries. The most visible example is the construction of wildlife overpasses and under-passes across Trans-Canada 1 in Banff National Park, but one can also point to the sixfold expansion of Nahanni National Park (2009) and the addition of a 3,500-sq-km (1,313 sq mi) Marine Conservation Area to Gwaii Haanas National Park Reserve (2010).

Much remains to be done. As temperatures rise due to climate change, not only will animals need to move across borders, but plants will too. Entire forests will need to migrate, seed by seed, to find the cooler environments they require to survive.

The need for continuity and con-nectivity in our landscapes is more important than ever. As visi-tors to national parks, we need to take the lessons and inspirations offered by the animals we're lucky enough to see and apply them in our everyday lives. How much wood, oil, gas, and other raw materi-als we consume and where they come from has a direct impact on the wildlife corridors between national parks.

We need to think big. We need to be bold. And yes, we need to act now.

— KARSTEN HEUER, *wildlife biologist and author of* Walking the Big Wild

MIGRATIONS

Illecillewaet Valley and the Selkirk Mountains

▶GLACIER

BRITISH COLUMBIA
ESTABLISHED 1886
1,349 sq km/333,345 acres

Experience the Columbia Mountains—what used to be called the Interior Ranges—of British Columbia in Canada's Glacier National Park. Glacier protects the heart of the Selkirk Mountains, the highest range in the Columbias. Trans-Canada 1 crests the Selkirks at historic Rogers Pass, while the Canadian Pacific Railway punches through far below in the longest standard-gauge train tunnel in the Americas.

Glacier National Park is best known for its deep valleys, thick coniferous forests, and spectacular mountain scenery, all seen by millions annually as they travel Trans-Canada 1 through Rogers Pass. Pyramidal Mount Sir Donald, elevation 3,284 m (10,774 ft), stands nearly 2 vertical km (1.4 mi) above the pass. From the highway you can also see the Illecillewaet Névé (ill-uh-SILL-uh-wet neh-VEIGH), a famous ice field and the best known glacier in the park. The park protects the headwaters of the Illecillewaet, Beaver, and Incompapleux Rivers. The highest point is Hasler Peak at 3,377 m (11,079 ft).

How to Get There

The park is located between Golden and Revelstoke along Trans-Canada 1.

The closest major international airport is at Calgary, 330 km (205 mi) east of Rogers Pass. The highway can be busy in summer, and only half the distance is four-lane divided highway, so budget four to five hours of travel time from Calgary.

When to Go

Trans-Canada 1 is open year-round through the park. From December into May, however, expect short-duration road closures—typically two hours or less—through Rogers Pass for avalanche control. While the valleys at lower elevations may green up in May, and June brings a fine wildflower display, the park receives so much snow that trails at and above tree line can be blocked by snow into July. Alpine wildflowers are at their best in mid-August.

Temperatures at Rogers Pass are often cool in summer (mid-20s°C/mid-70s°F); however, extended hot spells of 30°C (86°F) occur every year. If you're camping or planning to spend the day outside, be prepared for rain and mosquitoes.

How to Visit

It's possible to cover the distance between Golden and Revelstoke in less than two hours, but you'll miss plenty. There are several must-see places along the 45 km (28 mi) of highway through the park, including the Rogers Pass Discovery Centre, the Hemlock Grove Boardwalk Trail, and the summit of Rogers Pass. Your time in the park will be extended by an hour or two, but your travel experience will be much richer.

This park has much to offer hikers, mountaineers, and skiers. Easy loop trails with interpretive signs show off Glacier's big trees and impart railway lore. Steeper, longer trails lead to the high country, where the landscape is Ice Age and so is the weather. Most of the park's trails can be hiked in a day, and many provide access to classic Selkirk Mountains climbing routes. Several trails have backcountry campsites, but the only multiday backpacking trek in the park is the Beaver River-Twenty Mile-Copperstain route.

Experienced cavers can explore the Nakimu Caves system with the approval of the superintendent, and a number of guided caving tours are offered during the summer months.

In winter, skiers willing to head up the slopes under their own steam—there are no lifts in the park—can enjoy the park's outstanding wilderness ski routes.

GLACIER

ROGERS PASS
a half day

Centrally located along Trans-Canada 1, the summit area of the pass has the park's only visitor centre. The pass is named for American Albert Bowman Rogers, a retired Army major, civil engineer, and surveyor who was responsible for establishing the route of the Canadian Pacific Railway (CPR) across the country's western mountains. Following a suggestion from an earlier surveyor, Rogers discovered the avalanche-prone pass in 1881.

The railway was built through in 1885. After the deaths of about 100 railway workers and countless snowslide delays, however, the CPR gave up on the Rogers Pass in 1911 and blasted the 8-km (5 mi) Connaught Tunnel under it. In 1988, the company completed the Mount Macdonald Tunnel. At 14.7 km (9.1 mi) long, it is the longest standard-gauge tunnel in the Western Hemisphere.

Trans-Canada 1 was completed through the pass in 1962. Several concrete snowsheds (strong-roofed structures that allow snow to slide harmlessly over the road), plus the most thorough avalanche forecasting and control program in the world, have succeeded where the railway could not. Still, the road closes 30 times each winter, on average, for crews to shoot the snow down with artillery before it avalanches on its own.

Try to reach the **Rogers Pass Discovery Centre** well before it closes for the day. Designed to resemble a historic railway snowshed, it offers a multimedia experience, including landscape models, interactive exhibits, and lively theatre programs.

Travelling across the pass in winter, when the highway has been plowed through very deep snow, gives an appreciation of what it takes to keep this nationally important transportation corridor open. Parks Canada's excellent 25-minute film *The Snow War* tells the full story of people versus avalanches in the park. You can view it at the visitor centre.

SHORT SELF-GUIDED TRAILS

Step into the wilderness on one of seven interpretive trails along the highway. The **Hemlock Grove Boardwalk Trail** is located in the western part of the park. A wheelchair-accessible loop of 400 m (0.25 mi), this pleasant stroll takes you through a typical Glacier forest of old-growth western hemlock.

The **Loop Brook interpretive trail**, located 6.4 km (4 mi) west of Rogers Pass, is at Loop Brook Campground. The path threads its way among stone trestle supports built by the CPR to elevate the rails along portions of two adjoining semicircles.

Inquire at the visitor centre about other interpretive trails.

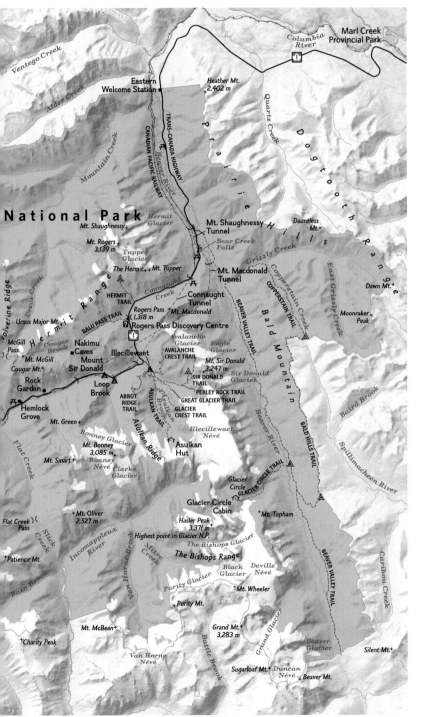

GLACIER

Marl Creek
Provincial Park

Columbia
River

Ventego Creek

Alden Creek

Heather Mt.
2,402 m

Eastern
Welcome Station

Quartz Creek

Dogtooth Range

Mountain Creek

TRANS-CANADA HIGHWAY

CANADIAN PACIFIC RAILWAY

Beaver River

Prairie Hills

National Park

Hermit
Glacier

Mt. Shaughnessy
Tunnel

Dauntless
Mt.

Mt. Shaughnessy

Mt. Rogers
3,139 m

Tupper
Glacier

Bear Creek
Falls

Grizzly Creek

Dawn Mt.

East Grizzly Creek

The Hermit   Mt. Tupper

Connaught
Creek

Connaught
Tunnel

Mt. Macdonald
Tunnel

COPPERSTAIN CREEK

COPPERSTAIN TRAIL

Moonraker
Peak

HERMIT
TRAIL

BEAVER VALLEY TRAIL

Wolverine Ridge

Hermit Range

Ursus Creek

BALU PASS TRAIL

Rogers Pass
1,318 m   Mt. Macdonald

Rogers Pass Discovery Centre

Avalanche
Glacier

Eagle
Glacier

Bald Mountain

McGill
Pass

Cougar
Brook

Nakimu
Caves

Illecillewaet

AVALANCHE
CREST TRAIL

Mt. Sir Donald
3,247 m

Sir Donald
Glacier

Baird Brook

Mt. McGill

Cougar Mt.

Mount
Sir Donald

SIR DONALD
TRAIL

Rock
Garden

Loop
Brook

ABBOT
RIDGE
TRAIL

ASULKAN TRAIL

PERLEY ROCK TRAIL

GREAT GLACIER TRAIL

GLACIER
CREST TRAIL

BALD HILLS TRAIL

Spillimacheen River

Hemlock
Grove

Mt. Green

Asulkan Brook

Beaver River

Bonney Glacier

Mt. Bonney
3,085 m

Asulkan Ridge

Illecillewaet
Névé

Asulkan
Hut

Flat Creek

Mt. Smart

Bonney
Névé

Clarke
Glacier

Glacier
Circle

GLACIER CIRCLE TRAIL

Flat Creek
Pass

Mt. Oliver
2,527 m

Glacier Circle
Cabin

Mt. Topham

BEAVER VALLEY TRAIL

Caribou Creek

Stick Creek

Incomappleux
River

Van Horne Brook

Mitre
Creek

Hasler Peak
3,371 m

Highest point in Glacier N.P.

The Bishops Glacier

Patience Mt.

The Bishops Range

Black
Glacier

Deville
Névé

Bain Brook

Purity Glacier

Mt. Wheeler

Grand Glacier

Purity Mt.

Mt. McBean

Grand Mt.
3,283 m

Beaver
Glacier

Silent Mt.

Charity Peak

Van Horne
Névé

Battle Brook

Sugarloaf Mt.

Duncan
Névé

Beaver Mt.

LONGER HIKES

Illecillewaet Campground, located 3.5 km (2.2 mi) west of Rogers Pass, is the jumping-off point for several steep but popular day-hiking trails to exceptional viewpoints. Trail maps and current information are posted at the trailheads. Purchase guidebooks and maps at the visitor centre.

All of Glacier is bear country, so hikers should take precautions—make noise, hike with others, keep your dog on a leash, and never approach a bear. The **Balu Valley** is prime grizzly habitat, and hikers are sometimes required to walk in groups of four or more. You may find that other trails have been restricted or closed to prevent disturbance of grizzly bears.

BEAVER RIVER BACKPACKING

42 km (26 mi); 3 days

The trailhead for the **Beaver River Trail** is located 10 km (6 mi) east of Rogers Pass along Trans-Canada 1. Expect the wet and muddy trail conditions typical of the backcountry in the Columbia Mountains.

The thickly forested trail functions as a valley-floor trunk route for a tougher side trip up on the high country via Caribou Pass. Note that as of 2016, the Beaver River cable car has been decommissioned and the Glacier Circle Trail is no longer maintained. Check at the visitor centre for up-to-date information about these routes.

CAVING

A cluster of limestone caves is found 5 km (3 mi) northwest of Rogers Pass, near Balu Pass. First described in 1902 and known collectively as the **Nakimu Caves,** the passages total more than 5 km (3 mi). Despite being cold, wet, and dangerous, some of the caves were developed for public tours early in the history of Rogers Pass, when the CPR was maintaining its Glacier House hotel not far away.

After the CPR abandoned Glacier House in 1927, the caves were rarely visited. Nowadays, Parks Canada strictly controls access. The caves can only be reached by a circuitous 9-km (5.6 mi) route that avoids the grizzly bear habitat in the Cougar Valley. Persons wishing to enter the caves should inquire at (250) 837-7500 or revglacier.reception@pc.gc.ca.

BACKCOUNTRY SKIING

In an average winter, 9.3 m (31 ft) of snow falls at Rogers Pass, 15 m (49 ft) at higher elevations. With 2 m (6.5 ft) of snow lying on the ground at the pass in February and March, and 3 m (10 ft) or more higher up, it is no wonder that backcountry skiers are attracted to the park. They need to be highly skilled and well equipped, because the weather is often stormy and avalanche danger is a constant concern.

A winter permit system allows backcountry users to enter restricted areas affected by the highway avalanche control program when artillery gunfire is not anticipated. This avalanche control work is conducted to keep the transportation corridor open and does not make the slopes safe for recreation. Anyone travelling into the backcountry in winter must be able to assess avalanche terrain and conditions. Before taking off in winter, check the park website for the most up-to-date information on conditions and permit requirements.

GLACIER NATIONAL PARK *(Parc national des Glaciers)*

INFORMATION & ACTIVITIES

VISITOR CENTRE
Rogers Pass Discovery Centre Phone (250) 837-7500. Opening hours vary by season.

SEASONS & ACCESSIBILITY
Park open year-round. Contact visitor centre for facility openings if planning to visit in spring or fall.

HEADQUARTERS
P.O. Box 350, Revelstoke, BC V0E 2S0. Phone (250) 837-7500. www.parks canada.gc.ca/glacier.

ENTRANCE FEES
$8 per adult per day; $20 per group per day. Annual passes available.

PETS
Leash all pets. No pets in Balu Pass.

ACCESSIBLE SERVICES
Illecillewaet Campground, Abandoned Rails Trail, and the summit of Rogers Pass Picnic Area accessible June to October. Hemlock Grove Boardwalk is barrier-free with interpretive panels, accessible picnic area, and toilets. All-terrain wheelchair for loan at the Illecillewaet Campground welcome station. Tactile topographical map, low-level viewing scope available year-round at Discovery Centre. Barrier-free facility at Heather Hill welcome station.

THINGS TO DO
Day hikes from Illecillewaet Campground. Backpacking trails. Ski touring in **Rogers Pass,** mountain climbing, and tours of **Nakimu Caves.** For more activities, visit the Discovery Centre. Check website for weather conditions.

SPECIAL ADVISORIES
• Challenging or complex avalanche terrain. A valid winter permit is required to enter restricted areas in the park. For avalanche bulletins call (250) 837-6867.
• Skiers should wear avalanche transceivers and be prepared for self-rescue.
• Compass and navigation skills necessary to hike Bald Hills Trail.
• Rain forest park: be aware of extremes in temperature and precipitation.

OVERNIGHT BACKPACKING
Wilderness pass required (available at Discovery Centre and Illecillewaet Campground). Backcountry campsites: **Caribou Pass, 20-mile, Sir Donald,** and **Hermit.** Open fires not permitted. For information about winter camping and random camping, visit the Discovery Centre. Four backcountry huts: **Sapphire Col Hut, Glacier Circle Cabin, Asulkan Hut,** and **Wheeler Hut.** Contact Alpine Club of Canada (403-678-3200) for reservations.

CAMPGROUNDS
Illecillewaet (60 sites), **Loop Brook** (20 sites), and **Mount Sir Donald** (15 sites) **Campgrounds.**

HOTELS, MOTELS, & INNS
(unless otherwise noted, rates are for a 2-person double, high season, in Canadian dollars)

Outside the park:
Canyon Hot Springs P.O. Box 2400, 7050 Trans-Canada 1, Revelstoke, BC V0E 2S0. (250) 837-2420. www.canyonhotsprings .com. $95–$295.
Heather Mountain Lodge Box 401, Golden, BC V0A 1H0. (250) 344-7490 or (866) 344-7490. www.heathermountain lodge.com. $154.
Purcell Mountain Lodge P.O. Box 1829, Golden, BC V0A 1H0. (250) 344-2639. www.purcellmountainlodge.com. Accessible by helicopter only. $1,755–$2,410 for three nights (includes helicopter travel and meals).

GLACIER

Meadow wildflowers in Mount Revelstoke National Park

▶ MOUNT REVELSTOKE

BRITISH COLUMBIA
ESTABLISHED 1914
262 sq km/64,741 acres

The park is best known for its scenic parkway linking the town of Revelstoke with the summit of Mount Revelstoke, which is a surprisingly gentle parkland of timberline woods and flowery meadows. Short self-guided trails loop through the area, while longer ones reach northeastward toward the park's wilderness peaks and glaciers.

From base to top, Mount Revelstoke rises through 1,500 m (5,200 ft) of topographic relief. Park staff describe the elevational life zones in the park as, lowest to highest, "rain forest, snow forest, and no forest." You can see all three in one short visit.

The panorama from the summit of Mount Revelstoke, summit elevation 1,938 m (6,360 ft), takes in dozens of peaks in the Selkirk and Monashee Ranges of the Columbia Mountains. On a clear day, the view

alone is worth the 26-km (16 mi) drive up the switchbacking Meadows in the Sky Parkway.

At the summit, the park's other great attraction spreads out before you: carpets of wildflowers. Nowhere else in the mountains of western Canada can you step out of your car into subalpine meadows as richly floral as these. Through the course of the summer, which can be condensed to the single month of August in a year with lingering snow, the display changes colour week by week. White anemones, yellow glacier lilies and buttercups, red paintbrush species, and blue lupines put on quite a show.

How to Get There

Trans-Canada 1 runs along the southern edge of the park. The only other road in the park, the Meadows in the Sky Parkway, is accessible from the town of Revelstoke. From Calgary, the closest international airport, follow the Trans-Canada 1 west for 380 km (236 mi) to the turnoff for the Meadows in the Sky Parkway at Revelstoke.

When to Go

The park's low-elevation trails are typically snow free in mid-May, and most facilities are open by Victoria Day. In a typical year, the Meadows in the Sky Parkway is open all the way to the top of Mount Revelstoke by mid-July, but the road cannot be fully opened until the deep summit-area snowpack has melted, which can be as late as the first week in August. Lower elevation sections of the parkway open earlier than the summit portion. The road always closes at Thanksgiving.

From December to May, cross-country skiers and snowshoers can enjoy the parkway track-set trail. Go 11 km (6.8 mi) up the parkway to the Caribou Cabin, where backcountry visitors can spend the night. Register by calling (250) 837-7500 or at revglacier.reception@pc.gc.ca.

How to Visit

If you wish to see the park's high-country wildflowers at their best, visit in the first or second week of August. Weekend traffic on the Meadows in the Sky Parkway can be heavy, so go in mid-week if you can.

The park's wild and extremely rugged northeastern wilderness attracts experienced backcountry travellers. Mountaineers are drawn to the glaciers and granite summits found there. At the other elevational extreme, self-guided loop trails along the Illecillewaet River show off old-growth rain forest and a valley-floor wetland.

MEADOWS IN THE SKY PARKWAY
26 km/16 mi one way; 1 hour

Completed in 1927, the Meadows in the Sky Parkway is the premier attraction in Mount Revelstoke National Park. In addition to taking visitors to the summit of **Mount Revelstoke,** this road also provides access to the historic fire lookout tower there. The parkway opens at 7 a.m. and closes at 10 p.m. in June and July (visitors can stay in the park until 8:30), with shorter hours during the rest of the summer and fall.

The parkway is paved, with grades any standard vehicle can handle, but it is narrow and there are 16 switchbacks. Trailers and buses are not permitted, and Class A motorhomes are not recommended because the summit parking lots are very small. You can drop your trailer off before reaching the first switchback. Leave it in the parking lot at the **Nels Nelsen Historic Area,** worth visiting for its own sake. Nelsen was a world-champion ski jumper, and the early days of the sport in British Columbia are commemorated here at what was for many years Canada's premier ski-jumping hill. The interactive exhibit at the top of the jump provides a view of the valley and a fun way to imagine what it is like to fly without wings.

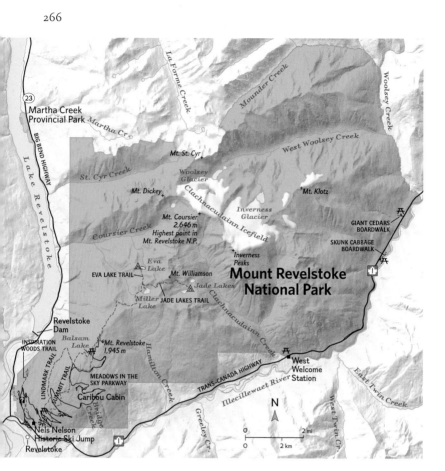

If you are planning to drive the road early in the summer, check with Parks Canada to see whether it is open. Deep snow can keep the upper section closed well into July. There is no fuel available on the parkway, so be sure you have enough to make the climb and return to Revelstoke.

To start the drive, take the Trans-Canada 1 bypass around Revelstoke. The turnoff for the parkway is 1.2 km (0.75 mi) east of the intersection of Victoria Road and the highway. The first half of the route is a steady climb through heavy forest, including western redcedar and hemlock, two species characteristic of the wet Columbia Mountains ecosystem. Higher up the views expand, with scenic pull-offs. At km 19, you pass the **Caribou Cabin,** an overnight stop for ski tourers ascending the parkway in winter.

The summit is particularly photogenic at sunset, but you'll want to be back through the gate at the lower end before closing time, which varies seasonally (check website for details: *www.pc.gc.ca/eng/pn-np/bc/revelstoke /visit/visit2.aspx*).

HIKING

From mid-July to mid-September, a free shuttle service runs the last kilometre (0.6 mi) from the parking lot at the end of the parkway at Balsam Lake to the summit area

(10 a.m.–4:30 p.m.). Or walk the pleasant **Summit Trail** to get there.

Bring a sweater with you. It's cool up there, nearly 2 km (more than 1 mi) above sea level. You'll also want mosquito repellent, water, and a jacket to keep the rain and wind off. Maps and other essentials can be found at the Parks Canada Office in Revelstoke or the Revelstoke Tourism Info Centre.

Give yourself about four hours to explore the easy interpretive trails that loop through the summit area, especially the popular **First Footsteps Trail,** a 1-km (0.6 mi) loop from **Heather Lake.** The trail features sculptural pieces that evoke the long First Nations history in the Columbia Mountains, and it passes by the **Icebox,** a deep cleft in the rock that holds snow all summer. The **Koo Koo Sint interpretive loop** develops the story of early fur-trade explorer David Thompson. Another trail takes you to the **Historic Firetower,** which has been restored to its original look.

Day hikers can make it to **Eva Lake** and back in a few hours, while backpackers eager to spend the night outdoors can camp at Eva Lake or at the more distant Jade Lakes.

Those using wheelchairs should contact the park in advance for permission to take their vehicles to the shuttle drop-off at Heather Lake. The trail from there to the **Parapets Viewpoints** is fully accessible.

BOARDWALK TRAILS IN THE ILLECILLEWAET VALLEY

En route to or from the park, consider stops at the Giant Cedars Boardwalk Trail or Skunk Cabbage Boardwalk Trail. These short, low-elevation interpretive paths present a striking ecological contrast to the subalpine plant community atop Mount Revelstoke. Both offer picnic areas and flush-toilet washrooms.

Near the eastern park boundary, 30 km (19 mi) from Revelstoke, watch for the turnoff to the **Giant Cedars Boardwalk Trail.** As you follow this short loop through peaceful

MOUNT REVELSTOKE

Visitors at Heather Lake

old-growth forest, it's hard to believe that a major highway lies close by. Interpretive signs provide information about British Columbia's interior wet belt. The trees here were seedlings when Christopher Columbus reached the shores of North America.

Located 2 km (1.2 mi) closer to Revelstoke, the **Skunk Cabbage Boardwalk Trail** takes you into a classic Columbian forest marsh, where yellow skunk cabbage, with its enormous leaves, predominates. If you arrive in May, the skunk cabbage may look quite different. Large yellow flower sheaths protect the musty-scented blooms, which come before the leaves. Birds banded here have been tracked to their winter homes in tropical South America.

Woodland caribou

Alpine lily

The serene summit of Mount Revelstoke in winter

MOUNT REVELSTOKE NATIONAL PARK
(Parc national du Mont-Revelstoke)

INFORMATION & ACTIVITIES

VISITOR & INFORMATION CENTRE
Parkway Welcome Station On the parkway. Open from mid-May to late October.

SEASONS & ACCESSIBILITY
Many facilities not accessible in winter. Lower Meadows in the Sky Parkway, Giant Cedars, and Skunk Cabbage open mid-May to late October. Upper parkway open mid-June to early October. Park open for skiing and snowshoeing December to April.

HEADQUARTERS
P.O. Box 350, Revelstoke, BC V0E 2S0. Phone (250) 837-7500. www.parkscanada .gc.ca/revelstoke.

ENTRANCE FEES
$8 per person, $20 per group per day; $29 to $39 per person, $74 to $98 per group per year.

PETS
Pets must be on a leash at all times.

ACCESSIBLE SERVICES
West Welcome Station, Monashee picnic area, Balsam Lake day-use area, and Heather Lake day-use area are wheelchair accessible.

THINGS TO DO
Hiking on self-guided trails (**Giant Cedars, Skunk Cabbage, Meadows-in-the-Sky**); cycling on the **Meadows in the Sky Parkway,** and trails at the foot of Mount Revelstoke.

Stand in "Nels Knickers" at the Nels Nelsen historic ski jump and have your photo taken as a 1920s ski-jump Olympian.

Join the annual Eva Lake Pilgrimage, a guided hike and trail run for the whole family, or enjoy an evening of stargazing and meteor-watching at the summit.

SPECIAL ADVISORIES
• Open fires not permitted except in Monashee Lookout fireplace.

• Rain forest park: be aware of extremes in temperature and precipitation.

OVERNIGHT BACKPACKING
Eva Lake and **Jade Lakes** backcountry campsites, with tent pads, outhouses, and food storage poles. Wilderness pass required (available at Parkway Welcome Station and park headquarters).

CAMPGROUNDS
There are no frontcountry (vehicle accessible) campgrounds. **Blanket Creek Provincial Park,** 63 campsites (30 reservable), open May to September. Call (800) 689-9025. **Martha Creek Provincial Park,** 25 vehicle-accessible campsites and three tent pads, open May to September. First-come, first-served. **Caribou Cabin,** open in winter only, is ski- or snowshoe-accessible. Call park office to reserve. **Canyon Hot Springs** serviced (power and water) and nonserviced sites.

HOTELS, MOTELS, & INNS
(unless otherwise noted, rates are for a 2-person double, high season, in Canadian dollars)

Revelstoke, BC V0E 2S0:
Courthouse Inn Revelstoke
312 Kootenay St. (250) 837-3369 or (877) 837-3369. info@courthouseinnrevelstoke.com; www.courthouseinnrevelstoke.com. $149–$189.
Coast Hillcrest Hotel 2100 Oak Dr. (250) 837-3322. www.hillcresthotel .com. $219–$239.
Inn on the River (B&B) 523 Third St. W, P.O. Box 1284. (250) 837-3262. www .innontheriverbc.com. $150–$250.

For additional accommodations:
See Glacier National Park (p. 263).

PACIFIC RIM

Page 270: top, Hiking on the West Coast Trail in Pacific Rim; middle, A herring boat at twilight in the Gulf Islands; bottom, Hiking above Kathleen Lake in Kluane. Page 271: Winter in Kluane National Park.

PACIFIC RIM

The four national park reserves in the Pacific Rim region stretch from Yukon's Kluane, with its giant ice fields, south to the Gulf Islands, where small islands between Vancouver Island and the mainland bask in the sun. Kluane National Park and Reserve offers spectacular views of mountains and glaciers. Gwaii Haanas National Park Reserve and Haida Heritage Site, ranging across forested islands almost 500 miles north of Vancouver, allows

Above: Relaxing at East Point, Saturna Island, in Gulf Islands National Park Reserve, a couple enjoys the sunrise over Boundary Passage, which separates the island from the San Juan Islands in the United States.

visitors to see the villages and archaeological sites of the Haida people as well as unique subspecies of wildlife and vegetation. A sliver of land and islands west of Vancouver Island, Pacific Rim National Park Reserve boasts a pristine beach, waterways for kayakers, and a challenging rain forest hike. Gulf Islands encompasses meadows, hills, and headlands with rare vegetation; its waters are home to seals, sea lions, and killer whales.

East Point, Saturna Island, orca and audience

▶ GULF ISLANDS

BRITISH COLUMBIA
ESTABLISHED 2003
37 sq km/9,1443 acres (31 sq km/7,760 acres on land; 6 sq km/1,482 acres on water)

Nurtured by a unique Mediterranean climate, Gulf Islands National Park Reserve supports a stunning diversity of rare birds, plants, and marine life spread across 15 islands and numerous islets and reefs in the northern reaches of the inland Salish Sea.

There's no gate or interpretive centre at this national park reserve: Much of the nearly 37-sq-km park reserve is spread over 699 sq km (270 sq mi) of sheltered ocean separating mainland Vancouver from the city of Victoria on Vancouver Island, and some of it is under water. Much of the park is located on the larger southern Gulf Islands, including Saturna, North and South Pender, and Mayne.

The abundant marine life, climate, and physical beauty of this archipelago—protected in the rain shadow of two mountain chains—have attracted people for more than 5,000 years.

First were the Coast Salish, thriving on the bountiful shellfish, plants, and game; Spanish explorers followed, adding their names to the waterways and islands. The British joined the Hawaiians and other

Europeans as pioneer farmers, clearing great swaths of the forest to plant apple orchards and to graze sheep.

The latest wave of settlers—mostly artists, seasonal cottagers, and retirees—have created enormous new development pressures across the southern Gulf Islands in the later part of the 20th century and into the 21st, threatening the endangered ecosystems found only in this microclimate, including the multitude of rare life-forms associated with the meadows and rocky outcrops occupied by the Garry oak, British Columbia's only native oak. The demand for waterfront property has also threatened the last critical habitats for fish, sea lions, and killer whales.

In 2003, Canada's federal government gathered together a patchwork of existing ecological reserves, provincial parks, and newly acquired lands under the banner of a national park reserve.

How to Get There

There is regular car/passenger ferry service (BC Ferries) to the larger southern Gulf Islands throughout the year from Swartz Bay (near Victoria) and the Tsawwassen ferry terminal accessible from Vancouver. The rest of the parklands and marine protected waters open to the public are only reachable via private means—passenger ferry, water taxi, boat, or kayak.

When to Go

The dry, warm season between June and early October is the best time for most activities in the park reserve. Services and some park access are limited in the winter months.

How to Visit

In the absence of visitor centres, the Parks Canada website provides maps and information about hiking routes, boating, and other activities.

If you have only one day, take a car ferry to Saturna Island, the biggest and least developed of the southern Gulf Islands with national park reserve land on them. Home to about one-third of the park's total land area, it offers short trails, day-use areas, and some of the most commanding views in the region. Accommodations are limited. Most overnight options require booking ahead. For a truly rugged experience, the park reserve offers a seven-site backcountry campground at Narvaez Bay that operates on a first-come, first-served basis.

For a very popular but no less spectacular view of the park, spend a second day exploring Sidney Spit on Sidney Island, wandering the beautiful sandy beaches, forests, and meadows.

Note: There are no garbage cans throughout the park. Pack out what you pack in. Bring your own drinking

GULF ISLANDS

Bald eagle (*Haliaeetus leucocephalus*)

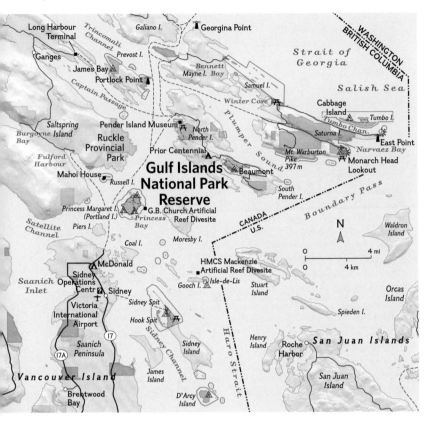

water, too, as it is in short supply during summer across the Gulf Islands.

SATURNA ISLAND

a full day

Largely undeveloped and home to just 350 people, **Saturna Island** provides visitors with a glimpse of what the Gulf Islands were like a hundred years ago.

To stand atop **Mount Warburton Pike**—at 401 m (1,316 ft) the highest peak in the park—take East Point Road from the ferry terminal for about 2 km (1.25 mi), turning right onto Harris Road for about five minutes; a left turn onto Staples Road, a steep winding gravel route, will take you to the top, named for a British

explorer and author who bought several large parcels on the island in the 1880s to farm sheep.

On a clear day you can see from Victoria's Oak Bay to the Olympic Mountains and the San Juan Islands in the east. Directly across Plumper Sound is **South Pender Island.** From this vantage point falcons, eagles, and feral goats are common sights—the latter have roamed wild on Saturna Island for more than a century, descendants of livestock kept by early settlers.

Now backtrack to the junction of East Point Road and Narvaez Bay Road, turn right, and follow Narvaez Bay Road to its end, where there is parking for a short trail down to stunning Narvaez Bay, named for Spanish explorer José María Narváez, who captained the naval schooner *Santa Saturnina* (thus the island's name) through these waters in 1791.

One of the most beautiful little bays in the park, **Narvaez Bay** penetrates for almost 2 km (1.25 mi) into the island's southeast shore. Walk down the former driveway past the bike rack for about 1 km (0.5 mi), through to the field at the bottom—turn left and walk down to the campsites and the bay. Narvaez Bay is remote and secluded, except for the odd sailboat that anchors in its protected clear green waters. Be cautious on the cliff edges and rocky promontories, particularly if it is wet.

The easiest way to get to the **Monarch Head lookout** at the head of the bay is to walk about 40 m (130 ft) up Narvaez Bay Road from the parking lot and take the trail on the left (two large rocks mark the trail). Follow the trail until it comes out into a small clearing, then follow

the signs up another former logging road; the route is steep, but it only takes about 10 minutes to hike up to the lookout. From atop the bluff, watch for killer whales and porpoises in **Boundary Pass,** amid the busy shipping lane and boat traffic using the nearby international border.

Exploration of the western Saturna parklands begins with a hike to **Boat Passage** in **Winter Cove,** a picturesque, sheltered spot that is a popular day-use area, especially with private boaters. From Narvaez Bay Road, turn right on East Point Road, then left on Winter Cove Road. Take the first right, which will take you into the national park at Winter Cove. Here a gravel-groomed trail (about 1.6 km/1 mi round-trip) loops through Douglas fir and red alder forests to the water. Try to time your visit close to low tide. That's when the currents pushing between the point and Samuel Island create fast-flowing rapids.

To get back to the parking lot, follow the loop trail that parallels

GULF ISLANDS

As dusk falls, kayaks lie at rest on the southwest side of Princess Margaret Island. Sea kayaking is one of the best ways to explore the Gulf Islands, offering an intimate experience with nature.

the shoreline around two saltwater lagoons and follow the boardwalks back to the trailhead.

East Point, on the far eastern tip of the island, is home to an automated light station and restored fog alarm/heritage centre. It also offers close proximity to an offshore marine oasis that regularly attracts killer whales, sea lions, and seals.

Follow East Point Road for 10 km (6.2 mi) (it eventually becomes Tumbo Island Road), much of it with ocean views, to the road's terminus. Walk through an open grassy field to the restored **1938 Saturna fog alarm building**—the island's most photographed building.

A local historical group hosts a heritage centre here, detailing local island history and the nautical feats of the Spanish explorers who "discovered" the island.

A five-minute walk takes you to the tip of East Point, where on a clear day, spectral Mount Baker rises in the east—an active volcano almost 3,353 m (11,000 ft) high in Washington's nearby North Cascades—looming above all else. Arrive at low tide, when the flow of water rushing through **Tumbo Channel** is at its greatest—and behold the water accelerating so fast that it is audible.

The unusual concentration of marine life here is the result of the upwelling and collision of nutrient-rich currents: Just offshore, the waters of Boundary Pass, the Strait of Georgia, and Washington's Puget Sound collide.

The aptly named **Boiling Reef,** situated in the midst of this aquatic chaos, is a resting place for seabirds and a haul-out for seals (year-round) and sea lions (fall to spring). Resident and transient killer whales, which patrol these waters between spring and fall, often appear along the cliff immediately below the light station, seemingly so close one could jump on their backs as they swim by.

SIDNEY & HOOK SPITS

1 to 2 days

At the northern end of Sidney Island, in Haro Strait, you will find Sidney Spit and Hook Spit, the main attractions of this 4-sq-km (990 acres) chunk of park reserve.

Through time Sidney Island has been used by humans for First Nations clam harvesting, as a brick factory, then later a provincial and now federal park. Most of the island is still in private hands.

A private 12-m (40 ft) passenger ferry travels the 3.7 km (2 nautical mi) between the town of Sidney, on Vancouver Island, and Sidney Island from May to September (call for times; Alpine–Sidney–Spit Ferry 250-474-5145).

There is pay parking at the Sidney Pier Hotel or Port Sidney Marina, from which you can walk in two minutes to Beacon Pier dock; remember to pack snacks and water.

The ferry lands at a day-use area situated at the base of **Sidney Spit**—a thin, white arm of sand that reaches more than 2 km (1.2 mi) into Haro Strait; you can walk its entire length, right to the light beacon at the point.

Hook Spit—a second spit that is equally long—is located to the west, curling into a hook creating a lagoon. This inner lagoon is off limits, primarily to protect resting and feeding birds. The eelgrass beds beyond the lagoon are sensitive and can be damaged by anchors.

Hiking is permitted on the outside of Hook Spit, provided

visitors stay out of the vegetated area and walk along the beach. The inner lagoon side of the spit is a special preservation area; there is no access.

Because the lagoon is situated on the Pacific flyway, migratory birds use it as a stopover for their spring and fall migrations; in all, at least 150 species of resident and migratory birds can be seen here—including bald eagle, great blue heron, purple martin, and multiple species of grebe and cormorant.

To explore the spit, take the 2-km (1.2 mi) loop trail (about 40 minutes to complete) that can be picked up directly from the day-use area at the ferry dock and follow it through Douglas fir and arbutus forests heavily thinned by the island's very large population of fallow non-native deer. These small, reddish-coloured deer (the males often display impressive palmated antlers) were likely brought to the island in the early 1900s, where they have thrived ever since without predators.

Each winter since 2005, the park closes for several months to facilitate a First Nations hunt for the invasive deer on Sidney Island.

Follow the trail along the eastern edge of the island; a staircase leads down to a beautiful eastward view facing the United States at **East Beach.** Continue on the trail; at the campground the route loops back across toward the lagoon, where you will approach a large clearing. It is a gathering point for large herds of deer. (Remember: It is a federal offence to disturb the deer.)

Pink seablushes and purple camas carpet a meadow.

GULF ISLANDS

Steller sea lions

GULF ISLANDS NATIONAL PARK RESERVE
(Réserve de parc national des Îles-Gulf)

INFORMATION & ACTIVITIES

HEADQUARTERS
Sidney Operations Centre 2220 Harbour Rd., Sidney, BC V8L 2P6. Phone (250) 654-4000 or (866) 944-1744. www.parkscanada.gc.ca/gulf.

SEASONS & ACCESSIBILITY
Sidney Operations Centre open weekdays, year-round.

ENTRANCE FEES
No entry fee.

THINGS TO DO
Kayaking, powerboating, and whale-watching. Road cycling, hiking, beach walking, geocaching, and self-guided tours.

You can picnic in **Winter Cove** or **East Point** on Saturna Island, **Sidney Spit** on Sidney Island, or **Roesland** on North Pender Island.

Free interpretive programs are offered during summer months. Check website for locations and schedules.

SPECIAL ADVISORIES
- Bring water supplies and containers for packing out garbage.
- No bike lanes or paved shoulders for cyclists on Saturna, Mayne, or Pender Islands. Cycling on park trails is not allowed.
- Visitors should remain on designated hiking trails.
- Consult the Canadian Hydrographic Service website (www.charts.gc.ca) for tide tables.

CAMPGROUNDS
Backcountry campgrounds with tent pads or tent platforms and pit or composting toilets are open year-round (fee May–Sept.) on **Cabbage Island;** at **Narvaez Bay** on Saturna Island; **D'Arcy Island; Isle-de-Lis; Portland Island; James Bay** (Prevost Island), accessible by water only; and **Beaumont** (South Pender).

Frontcountry campgrounds can be reserved and are open May 15–September 30. They include Sidney Spit (29 sites), accessible by boat or walk-on ferry; McDonald Campground in Sidney (49 sites); and Prior Centennial Campground (17 sites) on Pender Island.For group camping reservations, contact the park office at (866) 944-1744.

Mooring buoys at **Sidney Spit, Beaumont,** and **Cabbage Island** are $10 per night, 14-day maximum stay. Vehicle-accessible camping is available at McDonald and Prior Centennial Campgrounds. Reservations can be made by contacting the Parks Canada Reservation System at (877) 737-3783 or www.reservations.pc.gc.ca.

Camping fees are $14 per party or $5 per person for backcountry campsites. Call park office for special rates and group campsite reservations. Visit park website for updated fees.

HOTELS, MOTELS, & INNS
(unless otherwise noted, rates are for a 2-person double, high season, in Canadian dollars)

Outside the park:
Saturna Island, BC V0N 2Y0:
Saturna Lodge 130 Payne Rd. (250) 539-2254. innkeeper@saturna.ca; www.saturna.ca. $145–$160.

Sidney, BC:
Beacon Inn at Sidney 9724 Third St., Sidney by the Sea, V8L 3A2. (250) 655-3288 or (877) 420-5499. info@beaconinns.com; www.thebeaconinn.com. $160–$200.
Cedarwood Inn & Suites 9522 Lochside Dr., V8L 1N8. (250) 656-5551 or (877) 656-5551. info@thecedarwood.ca; http://thecedarwood.ca. $139–$239.
Sidney Waterfront Inn & Suites 9775 First St., V8L 3E1. (250) 656-1131 or (888) 656-1131. stay@sidneywaterfrontinn.com; www.sidneywaterfrontinn.com. $156–$217.

EXCURSIONS

GULF OF GEORGIA CANNERY NATIONAL HISTORIC SITE
RICHMOND, BC

In Steveston, Canada's largest commercial fishing harbour, the historic cannery, built in 1894, has been transformed into an interactive museum dedicated to Canada's west coast fishing industry. Experience how European, Chinese, Japanese, and First Nations fishermen and workers caught and processed mountains of Pacific salmon through interpretive tours, exhibits, images, and a restored (and still noisy) canning line. Open daily. (604) 664-9009.

FISGARD LIGHTHOUSE NATIONAL HISTORIC SITE
COLWOOD, BC

Perched at the tip of a causeway jutting into the sea, Fisgard Lighthouse has been a homeward beacon to mariners plying the turbulent waters of the Juan de Fuca Strait since 1860. Explore the museum housed in the former keeper's residence next door—one of the oldest homes in the city of Victoria—where visitors can enjoy colourful interactive exhibits. Abundant wildlife and stunning views of Washington's Olympic Mountains complete the experience. (250) 478-5849.

FORT RODD HILL NATIONAL HISTORIC SITE
COLWOOD, BC

Next door to Fisgard Lighthouse, this intact 1890s British artillery fort, operative until 1956, was designed to protect the Royal Navy base at Esquimalt Harbour and the city of Victoria from naval attack. Visitors can explore underground magazine complexes, walk the original ramparts of three gun batteries, and examine artillery pieces. Interpretive displays, special programs (including the "Firepower" demo on summer weekends), and reenactments May–September. (250) 478-5849.

▶ NATIONAL MARINE CONSERVATION AREA (PROPOSED)

SOUTHERN STRAIT OF GEORGIA
BRITISH COLUMBIA

Shielded by the rainshadow of Vancouver Island, the proposed Southern Strait of Georgia National Marine Conservation Area Reserve could protect a vast stretch of seabed and water column that is home to abundant fish and marine mammals, all in close proximity to British Columbia's big cities of Vancouver and Victoria.

Sculpin close-up

Beginning in 2003, the province of British Columbia and Canadian federal governments collaborated to create a national marine park in the southern portion of the Strait of Georgia to protect the waters that separate the Vancouver mainland from the southeast coast of Vancouver Island. Its proposed boundary abuts the Gulf Islands National Park Reserve (pp. 274–280).

Rich subtidal life rings the islands and reefs, giving way to lush kelp forests. These waters are home to five species of Pacific salmon, which make their seasonal migrations to natal streams situated throughout this region. Also here

is the Pacific octopus, the world's biggest, which can weigh 60 kg (132 lbs), with arms stretching more than 7 m (23 feet). Seasonal schools of herring mass through mid-water depths, above bottom-dwelling six-gill sharks and multiple species of rockfish that can exceed a century in age. The glass sponge reefs located around **Mayne** and **Galiano Islands** are 9,000 years old.

The reserve owes its fecundity to the upwelling of nutrient-rich waters and the freshwater discharge from the **Fraser River.** Beneath the surface is a dizzying variation of seabed topography that provides nursery habitat for the mosaic of life.

BOATING & SAILING: This area is a year-round motor and sail-boater's paradise with 250 annual days of sun and less than 20 cm (8 in) of rain per year. Traffic is heaviest in the boating lanes between the biggest southern Gulf Islands and their harbours and marinas—**Ganges Harbour** (on **Saltspring Island,** the largest of the southern Gulf Islands and the only island with a town), **Montague Harbour** on **Galiano Island, Winter Cove** on **Saturna Island,** and the beach destination of **Sidney Spit.**

SALTWATER FISHING: Whether you hire a charter fishing company or fish from the shore or your own vessel, angling is second only to boating in recreational popularity here. Chinook salmon, the biggest of the five Pacific salmon, are the prize catch here and the best time to catch them is July to October, when larger adult Chinook migrate through these waters (runs of pink, sockeye, coho, and chum salmon can be found during these months, too).

Licences must be purchased. British Columbia fishing regulations, published annually in hard copy and online (*www.pac.dfo-mpo .gc.ca/fm-gp/rec/index-eng.html*), spell out area-specific closures and rules that are strictly enforced. Half- and full-day guided charters are offered from **Gabriola Island** by Silver Blue Charters (250-247-8807, *www .silverbluecharters.com*) and **Pender Island's** Saltwater Moon Charters, *www.gulfislandsfishing.com.*

KAYAKING: Bennett Bay Kayaking (250-539-0864, reservations@ben nettbaykayaking.com, *www.ben nettbaykayaking.com*) offers hourly and multiday kayak rentals as well as guided kayak tours from **Mayne Island,** which takes paddlers along scenic shorelines frequented by seals, sea lions, bald eagles, and killer whales.

MARINE MAMMAL WATCHING: There are at least 15 species of marine mammals found in these waters, including harbour seals, Steller and California sea lions, two species of porpoise, and four species of whale. By far the most visible is the southern resident population of killer whales that chase the annual migrations of Chinook salmon across the Strait of Georgia. Humpbacks are seen here between mid-March and late October on their annual migration from their Mexico and South Pacific winter breeding grounds toward Alaska. These whales are famous for their aerial displays, and female humpbacks can often be seen escorting young calves. Remember to follow the Be Whale Wise guidelines: Boats cannot approach or be positioned closer than 100 m (3,238 ft) to any whale; when within 400 m (1,310 ft) of the nearest whale, speed must be reduced to less than seven knots. A gathering spot for marine mammals—including porpoises, killer whales, sea lions, and seals—is **East Point,** just off of **Saturna Island,** an underwater reef and upwelling point for nutrients that attracts a variety of marine mammals and fish.

There are many whale-watching businesses based out of Victoria, Vancouver, and smaller coastal towns. Wild Whales (604-699-2011, *www.whalesvancouver.com*) leaves from Granville Island in Vancouver, while Eagle Wing Tours operates out of Victoria (800-708-9488, *www .eaglewingtours.com*).

SOUTHERN STRAIT OF GEORGIA

Taking a moment to capture the view

▶ PACIFIC RIM

BRITISH COLUMBIA
ESTABLISHED 1970
510 sq km/126,024 acres

Few people forget the first time they walk out onto seemingly infinite Long Beach, a 16-km (10 mi) strip of undeveloped coastline set against a backdrop of lush emerald rain forest and distant mountains. One of Canada's most visited tourist attractions, the beach attracts surfers, beachcombers, and marine life enthusiasts.

Skirting the western fringe of Vancouver Island, Long Beach is the northernmost of three park units, a 141-sq-km (34,800 acres) chunk of beach-fronted coastal temperate rain forest and, since 2000, a core protected area of the Clayoquot Sound UNESCO World Biosphere Reserve. Unknown to the world before 1959, when a road was punched across the width of Vancouver Island, the beach became an end-of-world refuge for draft dodgers, hippies, and surfers until 1970, when the beach settlements were evicted for the new national park reserve. Much of the laid-back vibe of that earlier era remains. The shoreline stretches roughly between the town of Tofino in the north and Ucluelet in the south.

Directly to the east of Ucluelet are the Broken Group Islands—an archipelago of more than a hundred tiny, rugged islands at the centre of Barkley Sound, a popular kayak destination.

Only about 16 sq km (3,950 acres) of land is found across the 107 sq km (26,440 acres) of ocean park area; this maze of waterways and channels is accessible by watercraft only.

The southernmost area is the 264-sq-km (10,130 acres) West Coast Trail, the 75-km (47 mi) backcountry hiking path through pristine rain forest between Port Renfrew and Bamfield. The trail was established in 1907 as an emergency rescue path for shipwrecked mariners after 120 people died when the *Valencia* ran aground on a reef near Pachena Point during a gale.

The unifying elements of these three units are water, rain forest, and the native Nuu-chah-nulth people and culture. Present in the Pacific Rim area for thousands of years, these master mariners and whale hunters utilized the natural resources for trade and sustainability and often battled the waves of Spanish then British (and later Americans) who descended on the coast in the late 18th century to exploit furs, timber, and whale oil. Today seven of 15 Nuu-chah-nulth nations maintain at least 22 small treaty settlement lands and reserves within the park and nine at the border of the park; they are active partners in park administration and interpretive programs.

How to Get There

Long Beach is the only one of the park's three units that can be explored by car—and you will need one. From Victoria: travel northwest on Hwy. 19, take the Hwy. 4 exit about 34 km (21 mi) past Nanaimo. (*Hwy. 4 is beautiful but challenging: It has steep grades, little room for passing, and traffic congestion in the summer.*) Budget three hours for the drive from Nanaimo. From Vancouver, take a ferry from West Vancouver's Horseshoe Bay ferry terminal to Nanaimo and proceed to Hwy. 4. A right turn at the Tofino–Ucluelet junction leads to the Long Beach area. The highway runs through the park for 22.5 km (14 mi), with the town of Tofino at its end.

When to Go

For most activities at Long Beach, visit between June and Labour Day. (Book ahead for accommodation during this time.) For storm-watching and advanced surfing, the winter is best—fearsome winter gales can rip this coastline, conjuring waves 8 m (26 ft) high, and dropping up to 48 cm (19 in) of rain in a single day. The West Coast Trail is open between May and late September.

How to Visit

Most visitors stay for longer than a day, basing themselves in Tofino or Ucluelet. If a day is all you have, focus on **Long Beach**—roughly between the Tofino–Ucluelet junction and Tofino. Long Beach is where rain forest hikes, beach and tide-pool exploration, and a surf lesson will easily fill a day.

Spend a second day whale-watching and exploring the northern reaches of the park: Walk the sand dunes and tidal pools in **Schooner Cove** and look for wildlife in the sheltered, kayak-friendly **Grice Bay.** End the day with a dinner and walkabout in **Tofino** or **Ucluelet** (just beyond the northern and southern park boundaries), the best bases of operations for any park visit.

For a longer adventure (3–7 days), the **West Coast Trail** requires both advanced backcountry experience and substantial advance planning. The best way to see the **Broken Group Islands** is by boat. The Port Alberni–based M.V. *Frances Barkley,* a

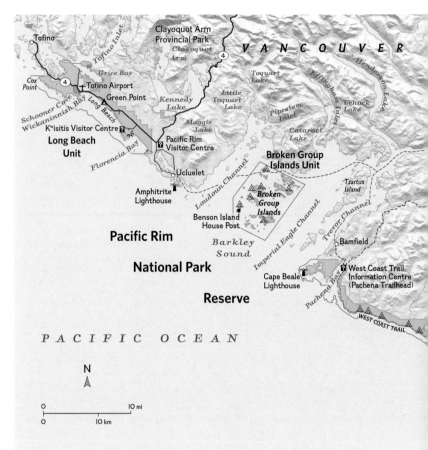

120-foot passenger ferry, offers day trips through the islands June through mid-September *(www .ladyrosemarine.com/index.html)*.

PACIFIC RIM HIGHWAY

Tofino–Ucluelet Jct. to North Long Beach; about 15 km/9 mi; at least a day

Start at the **Pacific Rim Visitor Centre** at the Tofino–Ucluelet junction for maps, suggestions for tours and activities, and tide tables, then drive 5 km (3 mi) to the Wick Rd. turnoff to the Kʷisitis Visitor Centre, which stands about 3.5 km (2 mi) away at the end of the road.

Wickaninnish Bay and **Beach** are named after the great Clayoquot chief of the late 18th century, who traded local sea otter pelts, then in great demand in Asia, with the Americans and British. The Kʷisitis Visitor Centre offers exhibits, films, and interpretive information about Nuu-chah-nulth culture and history, rain forest ecology, and the diversity of marine life found on the coast.

To explore the sand dunes at **Wickaninnish Beach,** set out northwest along the beach in front of the visitor centre and walk for some 10 to 15 minutes toward **Combers Beach.** The dunes here are the highest in the

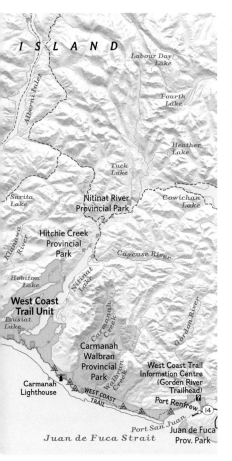

and black oystercatchers. (While exploring, watch your footing and incoming waves, as well as the tide.)

The warmest the water ever gets is about 14°C (57°F). The best way to get in the water (and best vantage point of the entire beach) is on a surfboard. There are many private surf schools between Tofino and Ucluelet that provide friendly instruction as well as a wet suit and board rental. Instructors take students to relatively shallow waters with smaller swells (3-m/10-ft swells are common in summer). Many beginners succeed in standing up on their first day.

Step back from the shore at the **Shoreline Bog Trail;** the trailhead is about 300 m (1,000 ft) south of the Florencia Bay turnoff. This 800-m (2,625 ft) boardwalk trail loops through one of the wettest areas of the park—coastal bog, which accounts for about 5 percent of the forested Long Beach area. Rain forest species like western redcedar and hemlock grow grudgingly in this acidic soil; shore pine does better, with some hundreds of years old, their grey limbs topped with vivid green tufts.

Drive back to Hwy. 4 and turn left; drive about 4 km (2.5 mi) to the **Rainforest Trail** (about 6.4 km/ 4 mi northwest from the Pacific Rim Visitor Centre). This interpretive loop trail consists of two 1-km (0.6 mi) loops on either side of Hwy. 4, leading beneath a canopy of breathtaking 800-year-old redcedars, 300-year-old hemlock, and amabilis fir.

GRICE BAY TO TOFINO

about 12 km/7.5 mi; at least a full day

Pacific Rim National Park Reserve lies along a migratory route for Pacific grey and humpback whales, and its coastal waters are also

PACIFIC RIM

area, towering to 27 m (88 ft), running a length of about 3 km (2 mi). In summer, even if the winds that rip the beach are cool, the dunes are always several degrees warmer. (Be prepared for rain, even in summer.)

To explore the intertidal zone, walk 10 minutes southeast from the centre: Walk out on the rocks as far as the tide allows. Time your exploration for low tides. The difference between low and high tide can be as much as 4 m (14 ft). Tide-pool denizens include big purple and yellow ochre sea stars, sea palm algae, and giant green sea anemones, as well as raucous seagulls, harlequin ducks,

Salal (*Gaultheria shallon*)

frequented by killer whales. Pacific grey whales and humpbacks are a common sight from March to late October; transient killer whales can be seen year-round. Harbour sea lions, seals, and porpoises are year-round residents as well.

Boarding a private whale-watching boat for what is usually a three-hour tour is the best way to see any combination of the marine mammals. The park visitor centres can provide information on the tours and a listing of companies that offer them.

Back on dry land, **Schooner Cove** is the most northerly beach in the national park, easily accessed at low tide by a 1-km (0.6 mi) hike from the Schooner Cove parking lot (4.8 km/3 mi north of Green Point Campground on Hwy. 4). The hike down to the beach winds through a mixed cedar/hemlock forest, passing a small salmon stream along the way.

Emerging at the beach at low tide, turn right and walk north up and around the jutting point of land. About 1 km (0.6 mi) up the beach, a series of small rocky islets lie just

offshore; they make for interesting tide-pooling at low tide.

Walk to the far north end of this 2-km-long (1.25 mi) beach, where a system of sand dunes stretches about 470 m (1,500 ft) behind the beach.

The tidal mudflats at **Grice Bay** offer a glimpse of a more protected marine environment—and a spectacular stopover for the enormous number of migratory waterfowl travelling the Pacific flyway, one of four major migratory routes for North American birds. From the Schooner Cove parking lot, follow the highway north to the turnoff for the Grice Bay public boat launch.

There are no hikes or trails along this sensitive shoreline. The best way to bird-watch is from a canoe or kayak, or with a spotting scope from the boat launch. The absence of large waves and rocky reefs makes this a sheltered spot for a relaxing paddle—but not during low tide, when the shallow bay transforms into a mudflat.

Winter provides the best opportunities to see the greatest numbers and diversity of birds. Huge numbers of Canada geese, trumpeter swans, and ducks by the thousands descend on the flats, including mallards, buffleheads, and goldeneyes. (April and May are also a good time to see ducks and a variety of sandpipers in the thousands.) Great blue herons favour the tidal shallows as a summer hunting ground; bald eagles are regulars; and the bottom-feeding Pacific grey whales come into the bay to feed on ghost shrimp, although their presence is not consistent year to year.

End your day in **Tofino.** The quality (and laid-back friendliness) of the indie coffee shops, bakeries, art galleries, and resort restaurants is widely renowned. A walk through the downtown core takes half an hour.

PACIFIC RIM NATIONAL PARK RESERVE
(Réserve de parc national Pacific Rim)

INFORMATION & ACTIVITIES

HEADQUARTERS
2040 Pacific Rim Hwy., P.O. Box 280, Ucluelet, BC V0R 3A0. Phone (250) 726-3500. www.parkscanada.gc.ca/pacificrim.

SEASONS & ACCESSIBILITY
Pacific Rim Visitor Centre, K^{w}isitis Visitor Centre, Pachena Bay Information Centre, and Green Point Theatre Programs open seasonally. West Coast Trail closed October to May. See park website for up-to-date seasons and hours of operation.

ENTRANCE FEES
Fees vary. See park website for current information.

PETS
No pets permitted at walk-in sites.

THINGS TO DO
Birding and fishing (licence required). Nightly presentations from late June to early September at indoor theatre in **Green Point Campground. Long Beach:** Walking along 10 km (6 mi) of trails and kayaking in **Grice Bay.** Consult Fisheries & Oceans Canada for tide timetables (www.lau.chs-shc.gc.ca). **Broken Group Islands:** Boating and kayaking. **West Coast Trail:** Hiking.

SPECIAL ADVISORIES FOR BROKEN GROUP ISLANDS
- Boaters need to be wary of strong winds, particularly westerlies during the afternoon, due to daytime heating.
- Boaters should know how to navigate through fog and should carry a marine VHF radio and Canadian Hydrographic Service Chart #3670 for navigation.
- If you want to eat shellfish you catch, you need a valid Tidal Fishing Licence and should check the daily PSP warnings.

OVERNIGHT BACKPACKING
West Coast Trail: 3 to 7 days. May to September. Reservations recommended. Check park website for more information on reservations and limitations.

CAMPGROUNDS
94 drive-in sites, 20 walk-in sites, 5 equipped camping sites, and 1 group walk-in site at **Green Point Campground** located on Hwy. 4. Flush toilets, picnic tables, garbage cans, and firewood for sale. Open mid-March to mid-October. For reservations, call (905) 566-4321 or (877) 737-3783 or visit www.pccamping.ca for reservations. For group walk-in site, fax request to (250) 726-3520. Maximum stay 7 nights. Backcountry camping on **West Coast Trail** ($128 overnight use fee) and **Broken Group Islands** ($10 per person per night May–late Sept.). Frontcountry camping $32 (serviced), $24 (unserviced), $70 (equipped).

HOTELS, MOTELS, & INNS
(unless otherwise noted, rates are for a 2-person double, high season, in Canadian dollars)

Outside the park:
Bamfield, BC V0R 1B0:
Marie's Bed & Breakfast 468 Pachena Rd. (250) 728-3091. mariesbedand breakfast2@gmail.com; www3.telus.net/marie/ $90.

Ucluelet, BC V0R 3A0:
Pacific Rim Motel 1755 Peninsula Rd. (250) 726-7728. info@pacificrimmotel.com; www.pacificrimmotel.com. $85–$160.

Festivals in Canada's National Parks

Festivals have been around for centuries and, in early days, were most often associated with religious celebrations. They are now more likely to celebrate some unique aspect or common set of values of a particular community.

A Stoney Indian brave performs a ceremonial dance at a festival in Banff.

This is true of festivals that occur in and around Canada's precious protected areas as well, where people come not only to appreciate nature but also to celebrate their common traditions and culture.

Loggers Days & Edge of the World Music Festival

On the Queen Charlotte Islands, or Haida Gwaii, the locals say, "When you've reached the edge of your world, ours begins." Perched off the west coast of British Columbia, Canada's most remote archipelago is rich with unique natural endowments and is steeped in culture.

Gwaii Haanas National Park Reserve is unique in Canada for being the first national park to be cooperatively managed by a joint board of First Nations and the Canadian government. First settled around 13,000 years ago, the early inhabitants of the islands developed a culture that was informed by the abundance of the land and sea. They became known as the Haida, a linguistically distinct group with two main clans, the Eagles and the Ravens. When Europeans arrived in the area, they too stamped their cultural presence. The depth of the cultural heritage of Gwaii Haanas illuminates two of its festivals. Loggers Days, held in July, speaks to the strong roots of the islands' logging industry, and in the languid days of August, local musicians with names like Honey Brown and Crabapple Creek Electric Jug Band headline the aptly named Edge of the World Music Festival.

Banff Mountain Festival

Straddling the Canadian Rockies, Banff National Park is probably Canada's most famous national park, as well as a UNESCO World Heritage site. Rugged mountains, glaciers, and ice fields; flower-filled alpine meadows; impossibly turquoise alpine lakes; steaming mineral hot springs; mysterious canyons; and silt-laden rivers dominate the landscape. Home to elk, bighorn sheep, bears, wolves, and cougars, the park is also home to adventurers. Climbers, kayakers, trekkers, and skiers flock to the pristine wilderness in all four seasons.

There is one month—a month almost *between* seasons—when the flow of mountain enthusiasts reaches stampede proportions. November is Banff Mountain Festival month, when more than 10,000 people come to celebrate mountain culture, mountain traditions, and the spirit of adventure. This annual festival pays tribute to the common values of mountain people from around the world: love of nature, concern for the environment, and a healthy appetite for vertically induced adrenalin. Often referred to as a "tribal gathering," the festival features film, literature, photography and mountain art, mountain-inspired crafts, music, and vertical dance that blend creative mentality with a spirit of adventure. The result is an amazingly vibrant sense of energy. For nine action-packed days, Banff theatres and lobbies are crammed with those who come to be inspired, and to connect with like-minded people. The town of Banff swarms with festival-goers clad in fleece and down, and the surrounding canyons and peaks enjoy a resurgence in activity, from ice climbing to hiking to skiing.

Festival of Birds

Southern Ontario's Point Pelee National Park marks its unique position in the world of birds with its annual spring Festival of Birds, when birders from around the globe flock to the park to experience the melodious avian migration in Canada's southernmost mainland.

Bird-watcher, Point Pelee National Park

Over the course of three-plus weeks, bird-watchers can partake in guided hikes and birding workshops, all while adding numerous species to their life lists.

— BERNADETTE MCDONALD, *author of* Tomaz Humar

Even with some figures weathering in the moist climate of the Haida Gwaii, the long-standing mortuary poles at SGang Gwaay still impress with their artistry.

▶ GWAII HAANAS

BRITISH COLUMBIA
ESTABLISHED 1988
1,474 sq km/364,233 acres

Unique in the Parks Canada system, this entity consists of the park reserve, the heritage site, and the marine conservation area reserve (see pp. 299–301), encompassing everything from the seafloor to the mountaintops. Gwaii Haanas, "islands of beauty" in the Haida language, is world renowned for its cultural heritage and natural splendour. It boasts an unparalleled biological richness, more than 600 archaeological sites, and a cultural history that dates back more than 12,000 years.

At its southernmost end lies the ancient village of SGang Gwaay, a UNESCO World Heritage site home to around two dozen cedar totem poles that represent family and clan crests like eagle and bear; carved more than 100 years ago, many of them honour past chiefs.

Gwaii Haanas is located in the southern end of the archipelago of Haida Gwaii (formerly known as the Queen Charlotte Islands), 120 km (74.5 mi) west of Prince Rupert and 770 km (478.5 mi) north of Vancouver. Efforts to protect what is now Gwaii Haanas began in the 1970s, when logging of the region began. In 1985, the Haida designated

Gwaii Haanas as a Haida Heritage Site and blocked logging roads on Lyell Island to protest the destruction of the area. Their efforts paid off in 1988 with the establishment of the park reserve. In a unique arrangement, the Council of the Haida Nation and the government of Canada co-manage the site. In August 2013, the Gwaii Haanas Legacy Pole was raised in celebration of the 20th anniversary of the Gwaii Haanas Agreement and the 25th anniversary of the South Moresby Agreement.

Before European contact in the late 1700s, the Haida are estimated to have numbered between 10,000 and 30,000 people, scattered throughout many permanent villages on Haida Gwaii. Smallpox—a European import—devastated the Haida, killing almost 95 percent of the population, and by 1900 fewer than 600 Haida remained, congregated in the villages of Skidegate and Masset. Today, the Haida number around 4,500 and the people are still tied to their land and waters, using the Gwaii Haanas area to harvest food and run a cultural youth camp.

Although there are no permanent residents in the old village sites, hereditary chieftainships of the villages are still passed down through the generations and all areas remain of great significance to the lives of the Haida. Today, Haida Gwaii Watchmen (cultural guardians) can be found in five key village sites during the summer months.

What makes Gwaii Haanas remarkable is not only its cultural significance but also its biological richness: Many species are different from those on mainland British Columbia. Some common species are not found here at all while some have evolved into their own subspecies (Haida Gwaii has its own subspecies of black bear—the largest found anywhere).

How to Get There

Gwaii Haanas is very remote—there are no services or designated hiking trails and only limited facilities. Gwaii Haanas is accessible only by BC Ferries from Prince Rupert or by a two-hour flight from Vancouver, with airports in Sandspit (southern end) or Masset (northern end). Most licensed Gwaii Haanas operators leave from the village of Queen Charlotte or Sandspit. A wide range of accommodations are available in the towns. The visitor centres at the Sandspit Airport and in the village of Queen Charlotte can provide information about tour operators. Tour operators offer a variety of experiences and transportation options, from flight-seeing to day trips by motorboat to multiday kayak and sailing expeditions.

Only a limited number of visitors are allowed to visit Gwaii Haanas each day. All visitors must first attend an orientation session, a legal requirement. Orientations for independent travellers are provided at the Haida Heritage Centre at Ḵay Llnagaay in Skidegate. Orientations for visitors travelling with a licensed tour operator are given by their guide on the trip.

Independent visitors travelling by kayak or motorboat most often launch from Moresby Camp, accessible from the logging road on Moresby Island north of the Gwaii Haanas boundary. Check in at the visitor centres for up-to-date road conditions and procedures for travelling on active logging roads.

When to Go

The best time to visit Gwaii Haanas is between May and the end of September. June enjoys about 18 hours of daylight and the summer months tend to have calmer waters. Fall and winter both have unpredictable weather with storms that may prevent boats or planes from travelling. May and June are best for seeing large concentrations of whales and dolphins, although these animals can occasionally be seen any time of year.

How to Visit

Because of its remoteness and the fact that travel by air and water is often weather dependent, it is necessary to be flexible when planning a trip to Gwaii Haanas. Many sites can be visited within a day on a floatplane or boat, but some require more time. Many kayakers have floated and paddled weeks away, immersed in a place so far removed from their home. Independent travellers not only need time but also skills in navigation and water safety—even in good weather, help is hours away at best.

A highlight for many visitors is their interactions with the Haida Gwaii Watchmen. The Watchmen (elders, adults, and youth) live at the old village sites during the summer months. The mandate of this program is to protect culturally sensitive sites and educate visitors about the cultural heritage of Gwaii Haanas. The Watchmen can also provide information about safety and marine forecasts. Because only 12 people are allowed onshore at any one time, it is necessary to radio ahead on VHF radios to request permission to come ashore. There is no camping permitted at the village sites (except **Windy Bay**). Composting toilets are available at all Watchmen sites.

Skedans and **Tanu**, although not formally within the national park reserve boundaries, are within the Haida Heritage Site.

K'UUNA LLNAGAAY
a half day

K'uuna Llnagaay ("village at the edge" or "grizzly bear town") also known as Skedans, is the most northern and most accessible of the old Haida village sites. It is one of the few remaining villages with standing poles (in various stages of decay) and remnants of longhouses. The village is on the eastern tip of Louise Island and can be visited easily as a day trip by boat or floatplane.

The Watchmen cabin can be found behind the village facing the opposite side of the peninsula. Skedans is also home to the largest red alder tree measured in British Columbia; it has a circumference of 7.1 m (23 ft) and can be found at the western end of the village trail.

T'AANUU LLNAGAAY
a half day

T'aanuu Llnagaay ("eelgrass town"), also known as Tanu, is named for the eelgrass that grows in the shallow water around the village. It has also been called Klue's Village after the original village chief—a name that can be found on some of Emily Carr's work after she came here to paint in 1907. The village follows the shoreline of two beaches separated by a rocky shoal. Many of the logs on the ground were actually the posts and beams of old longhouses. There are no standing poles here but if you look closely, you may find carvings barely visible as they have been polished smooth over time and half buried in furry moss. The Watchmen cabin is at the northeast end of the village.

GANDLL K'IN GWAAY-YAAY
a half day

Gandll K'in Gwaay-Yaay ("hot water island"), also known as Hotspring Island, is well known for the healing and spiritual properties of its natural thermal pools. It has been a sacred place for the Haida for thousands of years. At one time, a village stood on the east side of the island, but it isn't visible today. The best place to come ashore is on the northeast side of the island, where a trail takes you through lush forest to the Watchmen cabin. Two cabins are located adjacent to the Watchmen cabin—these are privately owned by Haida families.

In October 2012 a magnitude 7.8 earthquake disrupted the island's thermal flow. None of the permanent pools are currently usable for bathing, though thermal activity and flow rates continue to recover. The Watchmen create an intertidal pool to catch some of the hotter seeps and can use it at lower tides. Visitors can learn about Haida art and culture firsthand from artists and Haida Gwai Watchmen.

HLK'YAH G̲AWG̲A
a full day

Hlk'yah GawGa—also known as Windy Bay—is popular with kayakers and other independent travellers. It is located on the exposed eastern coast of **Lyell Island** at the site of what was once a major village called Hlk'yah Llnagaay, or "peregine falcon town." The village is not visible today. This island is also where the Haida stood their ground, blocking logging roads in their fight to protect what is now Gwaii Haanas. The longhouse-style cabin named **Looking Around and Blinking House** honours this victory and provides

A bat star edges across sea lettuce.

camping-style accommodation for one night for kayakers. A trail winds through an old-growth forest of huge Sitka spruce and western redcedar; some of the trees are more than a thousand years old and reach 70 m (230 ft) in height. Look carefully at the trees: Some bear ancient test holes, made to see if the tree would make a good canoe or standing pole.

SG̲ANG GWAAY
1 to 2 days

SG̲ang Gwaay is the southernmost Haida village site on the small island of SG̲ang Gwaay, which is also known as Anthony Island. The name SG̲ang Gwaay refers to the wailing sound made when the wind pushes through the rocks at a certain tide level. The village was also named Nan Sdins Llnagaay (Ninstints) after one of the village chiefs. SG̲ang Gwaay has the park reserve's most impressive array of longhouse remains and standing poles; it was declared a UNESCO World Heritage site in 1981. Although 11 of the best preserved poles were removed in 1957 to southern museums, about two dozen poles stand in various stages of decay, and there are posts and pits from several longhouses.

Because of a protected bird colony and a ban on air traffic, visitors who fly to SG̲ang Gwaay actually land in nearby Rose Harbour and then take an inflatable boat the rest of the way. The boats drop anchor at the north end of the island, where visitors disembark. A boardwalk trail winds through a lush forest, leading visitors to the village. After passing the Watchmen cabin, visitors are suddenly confronted with a row of monumental mortuary poles dating from the mid- and late 1800s. Many

Views from Gandll K'in Gwaay-yaay

people sense that spirits still remain, making this village site a spiritual experience for some. At low tide, canoe runs are visible on the beach—these are areas that have been deliberately cleared of rocks (making it easier to bring canoes to safety).

Because of its distance and extra issues of accessibility, SGang Gwaay is often visited as part of a multiday trip and accommodations are available at Rose Harbour. However, flight operators are able to offer the trip as a one-day excursion.

Haida artist at work, giving Hotspring Island (Gandll K'in Gwaay-yaay) visitors a close-up view

Not only is the marine life abundant, it is easy to see. At low tide, most of the channel's 293 species are visible in the roughly half-metre-deep (1–2 ft) water.

BURNABY NARROWS
a half day

Burnaby Narrows is a 50-m-wide (164 ft) shallow channel of water between Moresby and Burnaby Islands. It has one of the highest levels of living biomass of any intertidal zone in the world. The bat star, for instance, which can be found in almost every brilliant colour, is found in quantities up to 74 per square metre. Though a starfish wasting disease has had a negative impact on the species, it is expected to recover.

IKEDA COVE
a half day

Ikeda Cove, on the southeast coast of Moresby Island, is named for the Japanese fisherman who discovered copper here and later operated a mine between 1906 and 1920. The remnants of a small former mining town can still be seen set against the lush rain forest.

GWAII HAANAS NATIONAL PARK RESERVE, NATIONAL MARINE CONSERVATION AREA RESERVE, AND HAIDA HERITAGE SITE *(Réserve de parc national, réserve d'aire marine nationale de conservation, et site du patrimoine haïda Gwaii Haanas)*

INFORMATION & ACTIVITIES

VISITOR INFORMATION
Queen Charlotte Visitor Centre 322 Wharf St., Queen Charlotte. Phone (250) 559-8316. www.qcinfo.ca.
Haida Heritage Centre at Kay Llnagaay, 60 Second Beach Rd., Skidegate, Queen Charlotte, BC V0T 1S0. Phone (250) 559-7885. www.haidaheritagecentre.com.

HEADQUARTERS
60 Second Beach Rd., Skidegate (Haida Heritage Centre). P.O. Box 37, Queen Charlotte, BC V0T 1S0. Phone (250) 559-8818. www.parkscanada.gc.ca/gwaii haanas.

ENTRANCE FEES
Backcountry/Excursion fee $18 per adult.

PETS
Pets not allowed at Haida Gwaii Watchmen village sites. Dogs must be on a leash when on shore.

THINGS TO DO
Kayaking, boating, and saltwater fishing (licence required). Electrical hookups for boats available in Queen Charlotte, Sandspit, and Masset.
Information about Haida villages from Haida Gwaii Watchmen at **K'uuna Llnagaay** on Louise Island, **T'aanuu Llnagaay** on Tanu Island, **SGang Gwaay Llnagaay** on SGang Gwaay island, **Hlk'yah GawGa** on Lyell Island, and **Gandll K'in Gwaayaay** on Hotspring Island.
For information contact the Haida Gwaii Watchmen Program, P.O. Box 1413, Skidegate, Haida Gwaii, BC V0T 1S1. Phone (250) 559-8225.

SPECIAL ADVISORIES
• Hikers should have good compass and orienteering skills.
• Hike in groups and make loud noises to avoid making contact with bears.
• No maintained hiking trails.
• Emergency assistance at operations stations on Ellen and Huxley Islands, Haida Gwaii Watchmen sites, and Rose Harbour residences. Canadian Coast Guard (800) 567-5111.
• Ferry reservations needed from Prince Rupert to Skidegate. BC Ferries (888) 223-3779. www.bcferries.com.

CAMPGROUNDS
No designated campsites. Beaches above high tide line recommended. Consult tide timetables before selecting campsite. Practise no-trace camping.

HOTELS, MOTELS, & INNS
(unless otherwise noted, rates are for a 2-person double, high season, in Canadian dollars)

Outside the park:
Masset, BC V0T 1M0:
Copper Beech House 1590 Delkatla. (250) 626-5441 or (855) 626-5441. cbh@copperbeechhouse.com; www.copperbeechhouse.com. $120–$145.

Queen Charlotte City, BC V0T 1S0:
Dorothy and Mike's Guest House 3127 Second Ave. (250) 559-8439. doromike@qcislands.net; www.qcislands.net/doromike. $85–$125.
Premier Creek Lodging 3101 Ocean View Dr. (250) 559-8415 or (888) 322-3388. premier@qcislands.net; www.qcislands.net/premier. $40–$110.

Sandspit, BC V0T 1T0:
Northern Shores Lodge 455 Alliford Bay Rd. (250) 637-2233. $125.

▶ NATIONAL MARINE CONSERVATION AREA RESERVE

GWAII HAANAS
BRITISH COLUMBIA

Setting a global precedent, Gwaii Haanas National Park Reserve, National Marine Conservation Area Reserve, and Haida Heritage Site is the first protected area to extend from the seafloor to the mountaintops. It is a victory recognizing that for the Haida, the land, sea, and people are interconnected and inseparable.

A colourful sunflower star lurks in the shallows of an inlet.

Gwaii Haanas extends approximately 10 km (6.2 mi) offshore and encompasses 3,400 sq km (1,313 sq mi) of the Hecate Strait and Queen Charlotte Shelf. It is the first national marine conservation area reserve established under Canada's National Marine Areas Conservation Act. The designation aims to protect the ecological and cultural resources of the area so that ecologically sustainable use can continue. The area supports the Haida's traditional harvest of marine resources as well as commercial fisheries that include herring roe, halibut, salmon, rockfish, geoduck clam, and red sea urchin.

These nutrient-rich waters support some of the most abundant, diverse, and colourful intertidal communities found in any temperate waters. From ocean abyss to continental slope to shallow shelf to rugged islands, this marine area is one of biological richness and is home to more than 3,500 marine species, including species at risk and 20 species of whales, dolphins, and porpoises. Above the waters, the area provides nesting for more than 370,000 pairs of seabirds.

As a protected region, safeguarded from large-scale fishing and petroleum interests, Gwaii Haanas offers visitors an unparalleled opportunity to appreciate and enjoy the beauty and abundance of the oceans.

▶ NATIONAL MARINE CONSERVATION AREA

DIVING: This rich and colourful underwater world teems with kelp forests, sea stars, anemones, sea urchins, and a vast array of fish species and offers spectacular diving opportunities. The best diving is in spring when the area boasts crystal clear waters; in the summer, warm waters create algae blooms that can compromise visibility.

Because of the area's remoteness and the logistical difficulty of transporting tanks and refilling them, it is easiest to join a guided dive trip. Diving in Gwaii Haanas is not for beginners—divers should be experienced cold-water dry suit divers and bring their own suits. (Note: The closest hyperbaric chamber is in Vancouver, which could take several hours to reach even by air.)

SNORKELLING: While diving might be reserved for only the experienced, snorkelling offers a way for everyone to enjoy the underwater beauty of Gwaii Haanas. The thermal springs at **Hotspring Island** make the underwater plant life extra colourful and **Burnaby Narrows** offers unparalleled snorkelling in an incredibly rich area of biodiversity.

KAYAKING: There are several ways to enjoy kayaking in Gwaii Haanas. Kayakers who are experienced and self-reliant and have the gift of time may choose to spend days or weeks exploring the protected area. Those less experienced but still ambitious may choose to participate in a guided kayaking trip.

Even novice kayakers may still have the chance to paddle in paradise, as many of the boating tour operators carry kayaks with them on their voyages.

BOATING & SAILING: There are 11 buoys spread throughout the area. In some places, boats may need to anchor without buoys. The general anchoring policy for the park is that a vessel is permitted to stay in any one place for up to three nights, but after that it must move locations, weather permitting.

SALTWATER FISHING: The Haida people have since time immemorial used these waters to harvest food and continue this practice today. Unless you are Haida, a licence is required for all saltwater fishing in Gwaii Haanas and these can be obtained online from Fisheries & Oceans Canada (*www.pac.dfo-mpo.gc.ca /fm-gp/rec/licence-permis/index-eng. htm*). Freshwater fishing within Gwaii Haanas is prohibited. In addition, there are some areas within the protected area that are closed to all fishing or have fishing restrictions.

MARINE MAMMAL-WATCHING: Marine mammals inspire awe, spark our imaginations, and fill our hearts. It can be hard to control excitement but please use caution in areas of marine mammal activity, show courtesy by slowing your speed, and keep a distance of at least 100 m (330 ft). It is never safe to swim with or feed the marine life.

At the southern tip of Gwaii Haanas near **Cape St. James** is a large sea lion rookery with a large breeding colony of Steller sea lions. A new rookery has been established on the Garcin Rocks near the east entrance

Dusk over the islands

of Houston Stewart Channel. There are also several other haul-outs in the area, one located near **Hemming Head,** just north of the Gwaii Haanas boundary. Sea lions are particularly vulnerable during the breeding and pupping season (May–July). Female sea lions (cows) give birth high on the rocks to protect their young from being swept away by waves and drowning. Use caution and leave at the first sign of agitation. Any disturbance that causes the mother to change spots risks her pup falling into a crack in the rocks or into the ocean and drowning.

More than 20 species of whales, dolphins, and porpoises can be seen in the Gwaii Haanas Marine Conservation Area, including orcas (killer whales), humpbacks, minkes, and grey whales. Humpback whales, known for their acrobatics, arrive each April to feed on herring. They have spent the winter in either Mexico or Hawaii and pass through on their migration. Humpbacks can be seen throughout the spring and summer. Grey whales also pass through each spring on their way to their summer feeding grounds in the Bering Sea. Large aggregations can sometimes be seen east of Juan Perez sound or Skincuttle Inlet.

There are some guidelines to keep in mind when encountering these majestic sea creatures: Travel parallel to whales and dolphins and never travel through them with the intent of having them ride your bow. When approaching, do so from the side instead of from the front or behind.

In the spring, thousands of dolphins, killer whales, salmon, and halibut can be found in the nutrient-rich waters near Hotspring Island.

Gwaii Haanas National Park Reserve, National Marine Conservation Area Reserve, and Haida Heritage Site, Queen Charlotte, BC V0T 1S0. Phone (250) 559-8818. gwaiihaanas@pc.gc.ca.

Approximately 70 km (43.5 mi) long and some 5 km (3 mi) wide at its terminus, Lowell Glacier ends at Lowell Lake, through which the Alsek River flows.

▶ KLUANE

YUKON
ESTABLISHED 1972
21,980 sq km/5,431,000 acres

They say the Yukon's soul resides in Kluane, and the giant peaks, glaciers, and abundant wildlife in Kluane National Park and Reserve make it clear why. Vast ice fields form the park core—crowned by Mount Logan, Canada's highest peak at 5,959 m (19,551 ft) high—and glaciers spill into broad valleys populated by grizzly bears, Dall sheep, and mountain goats.

Kluane's landscape is in flux. The geologically active St. Elias Mountains stretch from Alaska to northern British Columbia, breached just once by the Tatshenshini-Alsek River flowing to the Pacific Ocean. Dynamic forces like surging glaciers, silt-laden rivers, and forest fires constantly reshape the land. The rain shadow of the St. Elias Mountains creates a dry continental climate in much of the park, while some areas are heavily influenced by moist Pacific air masses. The result is highly changeable, sometimes turbulent weather: Picture icy winds howling out of the ice fields or wildflowers peeking out from under a summer snowfall.

Kluane National Park and Reserve's grandeur is about size as much as it is about beauty. It's one of Canada's largest parks, covering an area four times the size of Prince

Edward Island. Combined with three adjacent parks—Tatshenshini-Alsek Provincial Park in British Columbia and Wrangell–St. Elias National Park and Preserve and Glacier Bay National Park and Preserve in Alaska—it forms the largest international protected region in the world, a UNESCO World Heritage site. Mount Logan is believed to be the most massive mountain in the world. It towers over a dozen 4,600-m (15,000 ft) peaks, all enveloped by the planet's largest nonpolar ice fields.

North America's most genetically diverse population of grizzly bears make their home in Kluane, as do snowshoe hares, lynx, wolves, and moose. This wild, remote region is also part of the homelands of the Southern Tutchone people, who travel, hunt, and live in the area. Along with Parks Canada, two First Nations—and possibly a third in the future—share in park management.

How to Get There

From Whitehorse, drive 160 km (100 mi) west on the Alaska Highway to Haines Junction, where the visitor centre and park headquarters are located. Paved highways follow the park boundary: From Haines Junction the park can be explored northwest along the Alaska Highway or south along the Haines Road. In both directions, the road skirts along the base of the Kluane Front Ranges. Flight-seeing and air charters into the park operate out of Haines Junction airport, Burwash Landing airport, and the Silver City airstrip at Kluane Lake.

When to Go

Summer is an energetic time of long sunny days, while fall is colourful but chilly. Winter is cold, bright, and snowy, and spring is notable for late-season skiing and early wildflowers. Kluane receives up to 30,000 visitors per year—with most coming in the summer—so you can find uncrowded wilderness experiences anytime of the year. Backcountry hiking and rafting trips occur from June to September. Climbing season in the ice fields is late April to late June.

How to Visit

Most people explore Kluane's frontcountry from the road, where wildlife is often visible and well-maintained trails lead into nature. Haines Junction is a good base for a lengthy stay in the area. The town has a full range of tourist services, including the Kluane National Park and Reserve Visitor Centre, which is housed within the **Da Kų** Cultural Centre. The park visitor centre is the place to learn about the park and register for backcountry trips.

The best way to experience Kluane is through hiking, canoeing, river rafting, cultural experiences, nature walks, and other outdoor pursuits. The Kathleen Lake Campground and day-use area 27 km (16.5 mi) south of Haines Junction is one hub of activity: Its setting is spectacular and it's the easiest place to access the park. A second hub is the **Tachäl Dhäl Visitor Centre,** about 70 km (43 mi) north of Haines Junction on the Alaska Highway, surrounded by hiking trails, great wildlife viewing, and eye-popping scenery.

Discovering some of Kluane's gems involves some effort and adventure, requiring overnighting in the Kluane backcountry. Wilderness tour operators guide multiday hiking trips on several major routes, and rafting companies lead expedition-style trips down

KLUANE

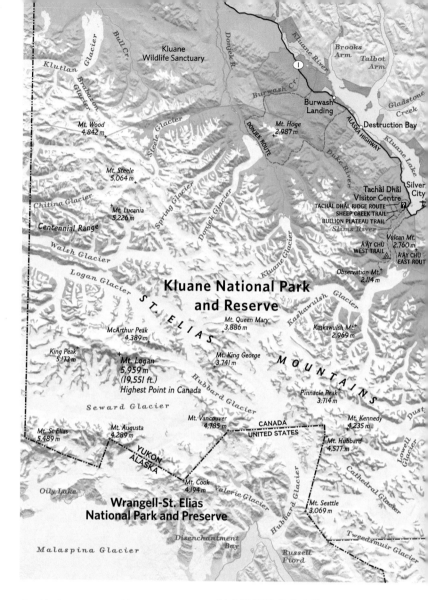

Kluane
Wildlife Sanctuary

Klutlan Glacier
Bull Cr.
Brabazon Glacier
Donjek R.
Kluane River
Burwash Cr.
Brooks Arm
Talbot Arm
Gladstone Creek

Mt. Wood
4,842 m

Steele Glacier

Mt. Hoge
2,987 m
DONJEK ROUTE
Burwash Landing
Destruction Bay
ALASKA HIGHWAY
Kluane Lake

Mt. Steele
5,064 m

Chitina Glacier

Mt. Lucania
5,226 m
Spring Glacier
Donjek Glacier
Duke River

Tachäl Dhäl
Visitor Centre
Silver City
TACHÄL DHÄL RIDGE ROUTE
SHEEP CREEK TRAIL
BULLION PLATEAU TRAIL
Slims River

Centennial Range

Walsh Glacier

Logan Glacier

Kluane Glacier

Vulcan Mt.
2,760 m
Ä'ÄY CHÚ
WEST TRAIL
Ä'ÄY CHÚ
EAST ROUTE

Observation Mt.
2,114 m

Kluane National Park
and Reserve

S·T· E L I A S

Kaskawulsh Glacier

Mt. Queen Mary
3,886 m

Kaskawulsh Mt.
2,969 m

McArthur Peak
4,389 m

King Peak
5,173 m

Mt. Logan
5,959 m
(19,551 ft.)
Highest Point in Canada

Mt. King George
3,741 m

M O U N T A I N S

Hubbard Glacier

Pinnacle Peak
3,714 m

Seward Glacier

Mt. Vancouver
4,785 m
CANADA
UNITED STATES

Mt. Kennedy
4,235 m

Dust.

Mt. St Elias
5,489 m

Mt. Augusta
4,289 m

YUKON
ALASKA

Mt. Hubbard
4,577 m

Lowell Glacier

Cathedral Glacier

Oily Lake

Mt. Cook
4,194 m
Valerie Glacier

Hubbard Glacier

Mt. Seattle
3,069 m

Wrangell-St. Elias
National Park and Preserve

Malaspina Glacier

Disenchantment Bay

Russell Fiord

Tweedsmuir Glacier

---

the Alsek River. In addition to great
scenery, abundant wildlife, and
adventure thrills, many of these trips
include views of Kluane's prized
glaciers. Flight-seeing tours offer
an alternative means of seeing the
grand rivers of ice.

If you plan to go walking or hiking, be bear aware. The park visitor
centres have good information about
travelling in bear country.

HAINES ROAD

*64 km/40 mi to Klukshu; at least 2 days
with day hikes*

Kluane is big, and summer's
extended daylight makes it easy to
put in long days. Before setting out
on **Haines Road** from Haines Junction, gas up and stock up on food,
so you can be ready to explore in
any direction.

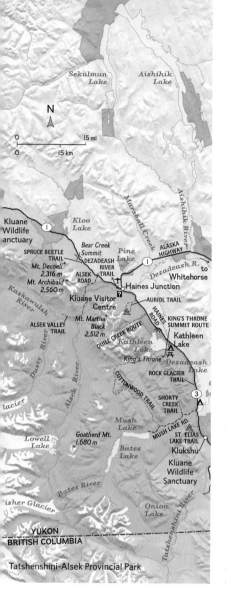

Crocus (*Anemone patens*)

Driving south out of town on the Haines Road, the **Kluane Ranges** parallel the road and fill your view on the right. Just 7 km (4 mi) south of Haines Junction is one of the park's most pleasant and accessible hikes. The **Auriol Trail** is a moderate 15-km (9 mi) loop trail that winds up through spruce and aspen forest into subalpine meadows. It's a popular day hike with great views, and back-packers can camp in the basic camp-site near the midpoint.

Located 27 km (16.5 mi) south of Haines Junction, **Kathleen Lake** is a focal point for activities in Kluane. Parks Canada maintains a campground, day shelter with picnic tables, outhouses, boardwalk, boat launch, and trails. Many people start hikes here or launch canoes from the curving pebble beach. Wheelchair-accessible **Kokanee Trail** is an easy 0.5-km (0.3 mi) stroll a short distance along the shore. The trail to **King's Throne** also starts at the lake. The 5-km (3 mi) steep ascent to an enchanting alpine cirque is hard, but the wildflowers and views are worth the effort.

Haines Road has plenty of other diversions. **Rock Glacier Trail** (0.6 km/0.4 mi) leads to a fine example of a rock glacier, with interpretive panels and segments of boardwalk along the way. An alternative to the Kathleen Lake Campground is the Yukon Campground at **Dezadeash Lake,** outside the park. Depending on the month, you might see spawning salmon and traditional fish traps at **Klukshu,** a Southern Tutchone village at the park's edge.

Top: Hiking on Sheep Mountain Trail. Middle left: Winter in Kluane. Middle right: Remnants of the gold rush town of Silver City at Kluane Lake. Bottom: Dall sheep, in full winter coat.

ALASKA HIGHWAY

61 km/38 mi to Kluane Lake; at least a full day

North of Haines Junction, the **Alaska Highway** provides the means to explore the **Tachäl** Region of Kluane National Park and Reserve. The park is harder to access along here, but some key attractions and the stunning scenery make the drive memorable. Spruce bark beetles have infested these forests, leaving large stands of dead trees while the forest regenerates damaged areas back to their full beauty.

The 2-km (1.25 mi) interpretive **Spruce Beetle Trail,** 17 km (10.5 mi) north of Haines Junction and outside the national park boundary, reveals the extensive devastation—and subsequent rejuvenation—of the boreal forest.

Beyond **Bear Creek Summit,** the highest point on the Alaska Highway between Whitehorse and Fairbanks, the mountain vistas just get more breathtaking. **Kluane Lake** and the **Tachäl Dhäl Visitor Centre,** where more park features are clustered, lie about 75 km (46.5 mi) from Haines Junction, roughly an hour's drive from the town. Dall sheep are often visible on the mountain flanks rising above the centre, which sits in the middle of the **Ä'äy Chù Delta.**

Chilly, dusty outflow winds often blast down this valley from the Kaskawulsh Glacier. Knowledgeable park staff are on hand to share information about sheep or to answer questions about Kluane's natural and cultural history. You can also plan park explorations here or register for trips into the backcountry.

Hiking options in this portion of the park range from an easy 1-km

(0.6 mi) walk to **Soldiers Summit,** to moderate day hikes to **Sheep Creek** or **Bullion Plateau,** to a very challenging multiday trek up the **Ä'äy Chù River.**

BACKCOUNTRY ADVENTURES

4 to 10 days

Seen from the road, Kluane National Park and Reserve looks like an iceberg. Only its tip is visible. Beyond that imposing front range of mountains lie giant peaks, broad valleys, glacial rivers, and the vast St. Elias Icefields.

To get a sense of this grand landscape, take a flight-seeing tour or embark on a multiday wilderness trip. People come from around the world to participate in extended backcountry trips—backpacking and river rafting are the two main activities—into the park.

A multiday rafting trip on the Alsek River is a life-changing journey down one of the world's wildest river systems. The **Alsek River** is designated a Canadian Heritage River, and a float down it through this raw, primordial landscape featuring calving glaciers and grizzly bears will reveal why. This icy river delivers a thrilling ride and the backdrop is spectacular, even when the weather is grim.

Adventurous visitors can plan independent hikes into Kluane National Park and Reserve or hire a commercial guide. The 85-km (53 mi) **Cottonwood Trail** is a popular four- to six-day loop that starts at either Kathleen Lake or the south end of Dezadeash Lake. The Cottonwood is the longest true trail in the park and, even though it is well maintained, it challenges

KLUANE

KLUANE NATIONAL PARK AND RESERVE
(Parc national et réserve de parc national Kluane)

INFORMATION & ACTIVITIES

VISITOR CENTRES
Kluane National Park and Reserve Visitor Centre at Haines Junction open daily mid-May to late September. Phone (867) 634-7207.

Tachàl Dhäl Visitor Centre open daily mid-May to early September. Phone (867) 841-4500.

SEASONS & ACCESSIBILITY
Road access to parking areas from Haines Junction, which is 160 km (100 mi) west of Whitehorse, Yukon, via the Alaska Highway, or 250 km (155 mi) north of Haines, Alaska, via the Haines Road. Topographic map available at visitor centre. Road access at **Kathleen Lake** and **Tachàl Dhäl.** Most park access is by foot, raft, or mountain bike.

HEADQUARTERS
P.O. Box 5495, Haines Junction, YT Y0B 1L0. Phone (867) 634-7250. www.parks canada.gc.ca/kluane.

ENTRANCE FEES
No entrance fee for daily use. $30 per landing. Backcountry permits $10 per night.

ACCESSIBLE SERVICES
Wheelchair-accessible boardwalk on Kokanee Trail (0.5 km/0.3 mi one way) along the shore of Kathleen Lake.

THINGS TO DO
In summer: Mountain biking on **Mush Lake Road, Alsek Trail,** and **Ä'äy Chù East Road.** Rafting or kayaking down the **Alsek River** (pre-booking of Alsek trips is mandatory). Mountaineering in the **Icefield Ranges** (application and waivers required). Flight-seeing tours over ice fields, motorized boating on Kathleen and Mush Lakes, fishing (permit required; $10 per day and $35 per year). Hiking on trails (easy–moderate) and routes (advanced). Ask for schedule of interpretive programming.

In winter: Skiing on **St. Elias Lake, Shorty Creek, Cottonwood, Auriol,** and **Dezadeash River Trail.** In February and March, cross-country skiing, snowshoeing, snowmobiling in designated areas.

CAMPGROUND
Kathleen Lake Campground: 39 sites open mid-May to mid-September; first-come, first-served. Outhouses, bear-proof storage lockers, and firewood for sale. $9 per day for campfire permit; $16 per night for campsite or $5 per person per night for group sites.

HOTELS, MOTELS, & INNS
For information, contact the Village of Haines Junction, Box 5339, Haines Junction, YT Y0B 1L0. (867) 634-7100. vhj@yknet.ca; www.hainesjunctionyukon.com.

even the most experienced hikers with a tough traverse across two alpine passes.

Another long-distance trek, the 45-km (27.4 mi) Ä'äy Chù Trail hike takes approximately three days to complete. At Canada Creek, experienced hikers can step off the trail and continue to Observation Mountain. Only hikers with good orienteering and backcountry skills should attempt this route. The reward is a view overlooking **Kaskwulsh Glacier.**

Registration is mandatory on overnight hiking trips in the park. Register at a visitor centre and receive safety information and updates on current conditions. Kluane has a significant population of grizzly bears; bear awareness and good practices are key to safe travels in bear country.

EXCURSIONS

CHILKOOT TRAIL NATIONAL HISTORIC SITE
CHILKOOT, BC

The Chilkoot Trail is a 53-km (33 mi) scenic hiking trip from Dyea, Alaska, through the Coast Mountains to the Yukon River headwaters in Canada. Canada's largest national historic site, the Chilkoot Trail commemorates the historic gateway to the Yukon once tread by Tlingit First Nations traders and Klondike gold rush prospectors. Hikers should be well equipped, self-sufficient, and in good physical condition for the rugged three- to five-day wilderness trek. Daily departures are limited, and hikers must have a permit. Call Parks Canada well in advance to reserve your hike. (800) 661-0486 or (867) 667-3910.

S.S. KLONDIKE NATIONAL HISTORIC SITE
WHITEHORSE, YT

The S.S. *Klondike* was the largest paddle-wheeler to ply the upper Yukon River in the decades before roads reached Dawson City and the Klondike's rich gold fields. This carefully restored boat is now a national historic site on the riverbank in Whitehorse with a superb view of the Yukon River. Parks Canada operates this popular attraction. The site welcomes visitors from mid-May to mid-September from 9:30 a.m. to 5 p.m. Phone (867) 667-4511 between mid-May and mid-September. During the off season, call (867) 667-3910 or (800) 661-0486.

KLUANE

FAR NORTH

Page 310: top, Arctic blueberries at Ford Lake, Ukkusiksalik; middle, Beaufort Sea, near Firth River, Ivvavik; bottom, Narwhals resting in a hole in the sea ice, near Sirmilik. Page 311: A helicopter below a mountaineer in the Cirque of

FAR NORTH

Although remote and isolated, Canada's northernmost parks are accessible. These parks are best suited to skilled and experienced adventurers or those with a guide or outfitter. Pristine land, abundant wildlife, and the warm welcome of indigenous peoples await visitors. In Vuntut or Ivvavik, celebrate the annual migration of 100,000 caribou. In Nahanni and Nááts'ihch'oh, canoeists and kayakers negotiate mighty waters, while in Tuktut

the Unclimbables, Nahanni. Above: A hiker pauses to take in the view near Black Fox Creek Valley, Vuntut.

Nogait, paddlers reach the Arctic Ocean. Aulavik attracts visitors to its archaeological sites and wildlife. Ski tour on glaciers in Quttinirpaaq, 800 km (497 mi) from the North Pole. The waters of Sirmilik provide food for seals and polar bears. A boat is the best way to see Ukkusiksal. In Auyuittuq, top-notch mountaineers tackle high peaks. Thaidene Nëné, Qausuittuq, and Lancaster Sound round out the Far North portfolio.

A migrating Porcupine caribou herd

▶ VUNTUT

YUKON
ESTABLISHED 1993
4,345 sq km/1,073,673 acres

Vuntut National Park may be one of the most remote and least visited national parks in Canada, but it's far from unpopulated. Vuntut is the domain of the Porcupine caribou herd and half a million migratory birds, and is also the cultural homeland of the Vuntut Gwitchin people. In the Gwitchin language, *Vuntut* means "among the lakes," a fitting moniker for this Arctic landscape, which is dotted by fertile wetlands, winding rivers, and rolling mountains.

Vuntut National Park was established through a land claims agreement in 1995, and is thus a relatively recent addition to Canada's national parks system. It realized the vision the Vuntut Gwitchin people of North Yukon have of preserving the land and their way of life, and they work together with Parks Canada to manage the park.

The Gwich'in people live in about 15 communities across northeast Alaska, the North Yukon, and the Northwest Territories, and are united by their language and a culture founded on a dependence on the Porcupine caribou herd. A number of nations make up the Gwich'in people throughout their vast territory; the Vuntut Gwitchin

First Nation in Old Crow is one of these.

Vuntut lies north of Old Crow, a fly-in community of 300 at the confluence of the Old Crow and Porcupine Rivers. Wetlands are protected in the Old Crow Flats part of the park, but Vuntut also plays a significant role in a much larger protected area. Vuntut's neighbouring national parks include Ivvavik to the north (see pp. 356–361) and the Arctic National Wildlife Refuge across the international boundary to the west.

Caribou is an important species in this northern ecosystem, and Old Crow is located on the migration path of the Porcupine caribou herd. The annual migration of this herd is the largest of any land animal on Earth, and a portion of the herd ranges in Vuntut National Park at various times of the year. Caribou are important to the local communities not only as a source of food but for their role in Gwitchin culture. Historically, Gwitchin hunters built caribou fences to capture the animals, and the remains of several of these fences are important heritage sites in Vuntut National Park.

Hundreds of thousands of nesting or migrating waterfowl visit the Old Crow Flats complex of shallow lakes each year, and moose and muskrat thrive in the wetlands. The park is also home to grizzly bears, wolves, wolverines, raptors, and many small mammals. Parts of Vuntut remained unglaciated in the last Ice Age and served as a refuge for plants and animals trying to survive in the barren environs.

How to Get There

Access to this remote wilderness park is challenging and very expensive. Contact Parks Canada staff well in advance to plan your adventure. The closest road, the Dempster Highway, is about 175 km (109 mi) away. The park is most commonly accessed in the summer by air or boat, and in the winter by air or overland.

Vuntut National Park is 190 km (118 mi) north of Old Crow via river and 50 km (31 mi) north of Old Crow by air. Boats may be available for hire in Old Crow. Departing from Old Crow, motorboats can reach the park boundary only at high water.

Helicopter access to good hiking areas is extremely expensive. Air North flies from Whitehorse to Old Crow, Dawson City, and Inuvik several times a week. An aircraft landing permit is required; there are no defined landing sites in the park.

When to Go

Summer is short north of the Arctic Circle, and June, July, and August are the most pleasant months for a visit to Vuntut National Park.

VUNTUT

Anglican church in the village of Old Crow

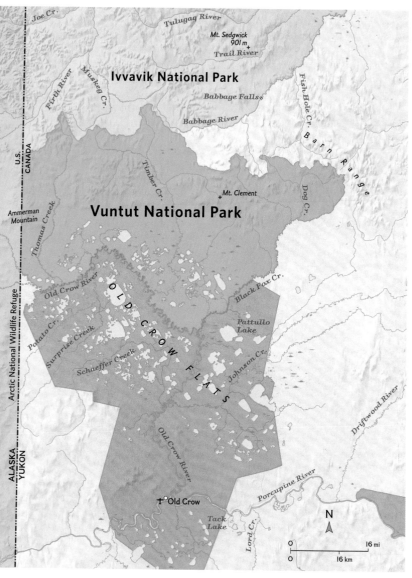

Joe Cr.

Tulugaq River

Mt. Sedgwick
901 m

Trail River

Ivvavik National Park

Firth River

Muskeg Cr.

Babbage Falls

Fish Hole Cr.

Babbage River

Timber Cr.

Barn Range

U.S.
CANADA

+ Mt. Clement

Dog Cr.

Vuntut National Park

Ammerman
Mountain

Thomas Creek

Old Crow River

O
L
D

C
R
O
W

F
L
A
T
S

Black Fox Cr.

Arctic National Wildlife Refuge

Potato Cr.

Surprise Creek

Schaeffer Creek

Pattullo
Lake

Johnson Cr.

Driftwood River

Old Crow River

ALASKA
YUKON

Porcupine River

+ Old Crow

N

Tack
Lake

Lord Cr.

0 ———— 16 mi

0 ———— 16 km

Unfortunately, insects also peak in the summer. Many families from Old Crow go out to seasonal camps in the spring and fall to partake in traditional activities like hunting, trapping, fishing, and berry picking, so even though a visit to the community is special at any time of the year, you'll see more and enjoy a richer cultural experience if you visit between March and September. Your best chance to see caribou near Old Crow is April–May or Sept.–Oct.

How to Visit

Vuntut National Park is a destination for experienced, self-sufficient adventurers. Fewer than 25 people visit the park each year (not including locals); it's complete wilderness. Although Parks Canada staff can assist with planning your adventure, there are no facilities or services—in short, you're left mostly to your own devices. Those who make the effort, though, have an adventure unlike any other. The park is a pristine and unspoiled rich cultural landscape.

Visitors to Vuntut can enjoy exceptional wildlife viewing—with 500,000 birds and 100,000 caribou passing through. Walk in the footsteps of generations of Vuntut Gwitchin people. Hardy souls may wish to backpack through the park's distinctive unglaciated mountains, canoe the Old Crow River, or plan a winter ski trip.

Try to make time to visit Old Crow and stop by the new visitor centre, which stands in the middle of the traditional village. A few of the residents of Old Crow also offer tours, accommodation, and excursions to view wildlife or partake in cultural activities.

OLD CROW

Old Crow is the Yukon's most northerly and isolated community. While the climate may be harsh, the local people are friendly and hospitable, and the village is known as one of the most authentic destinations in the North. It's also a "dry" community, meaning that alcohol is prohibited.

If you visit in the summer you'll experience round-the-clock daylight, while for a few months in winter it's cold and dark, day and night. But

Lichen in Vuntut National Park

VUNTUT

Wetlands of Old Crow Flats—breeding habitat for several aquatic mammals

Camping near Black Fox Creek

A former Hudson's Bay Company fort on the Porcupine River

whenever you visit Old Crow, you can expect a memorable cultural adventure.

There are only a couple of places to stay in Old Crow, so it is wise to book well ahead. There are no campgrounds in Old Crow. If you are tenting, call Parks Canada to explore camping opportunities in the area.

The airport is at the edge of town. A crowd from the village greets the daily incoming flight, and even if you haven't arranged to be met planeside, often someone will help you sort

out your arrangements.

Most people simply walk and ride snow machines or ATVs. Stroll around the rustic village to see the log homes, smokehouses, and caribou antlers that serve as a reminder that Porcupine caribou are in the blood of this tiny North Yukon community.

To learn more about Vuntut Gwitchin culture and history and the caribou that migrate through Old Crow, visit the impressive **John Tizya Visitor Centre**—part museum and part welcome centre. Don't miss artifacts like traditional bone and stone tools and photographs of Gwitchin elders and youth out on the land. Fur-lined audio sets play recordings as part of an interpretive display. Like most large public buildings in Old Crow, the minimalist-modern visitor centre is elevated on posts to protect both the building and the permafrost. Excavating a conventional foundation would cause the permafrost to melt and the building to sink. Parks Canada has an office in the visitor centre.

VUNTUT NATIONAL PARK
(Parc national Vuntut)

INFORMATION & ACTIVITIES

VISITOR CENTRE
John Tizya Visitor Centre Old Crow. (867) 966-3261. www.oldcrow.ca.

SEASONS & ACCESSIBILITY
Open year-round. Some park services are seasonal. No road access. Park access is challenging and expensive. Air North offers scheduled service to Old Crow from Whitehorse and Dawson City in the Yukon and Inuvik in the Northwest Territories. Call (867) 668-2228.

HEADQUARTERS
Yukon Field Unit-Parks Canada Room 205, 300 Main St., Whitehorse, YT Y1A 2B5. Phone (867) 667-3910. vuntut.info@pc.gc.ca; www.parkscanada.gc.ca/vuntut.

ENTRANCE FEES
Access fee $25 per day, $147 per year.

PETS
Permitted; must be on a leash.

ACCESSIBLE SERVICES
None.

THINGS TO DO
No facilities or developed trails in the park. All park waters closed to sportfishing. Caribou Days is a three-day festival to celebrate Gwitchin culture and the Porcupine caribou herd as they begin their migration. For more information, visit www.oldcrow.ca.

SPECIAL ADVISORIES
• Be aware of bear-encounter procedures.
• Firearms not permitted.
• Dense concentrations of blackflies and mosquitoes late June–July.
• Snow can fall at any time of the year, and temperatures can swing by as much as 16°C (60°F) in a few hours.
• Search and rescue operations limited.
• No removal of natural or cultural objects.

OVERNIGHT BACKPACKING
Registration and deregistration required, in person at the office in Old Crow or via phone.

CAMPGROUNDS
None.

HOTELS, MOTELS, & INNS
(unless otherwise noted, rates are for a 2-person double, high season, in Canadian dollars)

Outside the park:
Old Crow, YT Y0B 1N0:
Porcupine Bed & Breakfast P.O. Box 55. (867) 966-3913. bluefish_kennels@hotmail.com. $130.

Ch'oo Deenjik Accommodations P.O. Box 25. (867) 966-3008. choodee@northwestel.net; http://choodee.oldcrow.ca. $160.

VUNTUT

Hiking near Black Fox Creek

A white Arctic landscape

▶ QAUSUITTUQ ᖃᐅᓱᐃᑦᑐᖅ

NUNAVUT
ESTABLISHED 2015
11,008 sq km /2,720,136 acres

A stronghold for the endangered Peary caribou, wild and remote Qausuittuq National Park occupies much of the northern half of Bathurst Island, a mid-size landmass in the central high Arctic. Along the fabled Northwest Passage, the new park includes satellite islands off the north and west coasts. Interior tablelands rise to a height of 396 m (1,300 ft). Coastal bluffs plunge into an ocean rarely free of floating ice. Small wetlands sustain a healthy population of muskoxen, a holdover species from the last ice age. The second northernmost park in Canada, Qausuittuq's Pleistocene-like landscape has seen virtually no visitors other than a handful of scientists and Inuit.

Qausuittuq (pronounced kow-soo-ee-took) means "place where the sun does not rise," and is also the Inuktitut name for the nearby hamlet of Resolute. Summer visitors to the park won't experience the winter dark season, which begins in November and ends in February. Inuit originally came to Resolute from Nunavik in northern Quebec. In 1953 they were relocated by the Government of Canada to the shores of Cornwallis Island, where the government promised good hunting and assurances that they could return to Nunavik if they didn't like it. Their presence helped reinforce Canadian Arctic sovereignty, but the early years were very difficult. Eventually, caribou were discovered on nearby Bathurst Island, where the national park is located. Caribou are a favourite food of many northern people, and Bathurst Island became their supermarket. Since then, the Inuit have come to terms with life here, but the name Qausuittuq still carries a hint of those early difficulties.

The first European to see Bathurst Island was British explorer William Parry in 1819. Later expeditions, both British and American, flocked to the area in search of Sir John Franklin's missing expedition, which had vanished in 1845 while searching for a way through the Northwest Passage.

H.M.S. *Resolute*, in the 1850s, was one of these search vessels. After being abandoned in the ice, the *Resolute* was eventually found by American whalers and returned to England. When it was dismantled, some of the wood was made into a desk, which Queen Victoria gave to U.S. President Rutherford B. Hayes. It still serves as the President's desk in the Oval Office of the White House. Stone cairns built by men from the H.M.S. *Resolute* are found in Qausuittuq, allowing visitors to experience one of the high Arctic's great attributes: its living history.

Peary caribou, named after explorer Robert Peary, are a small, whitish offshoot of the barren-ground caribou that became a distinct subspecies some 120,000 years ago. They are seen only on high Arctic islands.

Some southern caribou herds number in the thousands, but Peary caribou typically occur in groups of a dozen or less. They roam throughout this Arctic region, swimming among the closer islands or walking over the frozen sea.

Peary caribou particularly like Bathurst Island and breed at the northern end, within the park. Qausuittuq is one of the few places where you can stand on a hill and look down on several small herds of this rare creature.

Although muskoxen and Peary caribou numbers were traditionally healthy on Bathurst Island, twice in the late 20th century harsh conditions decimated their numbers. Freezing rain in the fall, which coated the vegetation with an impenetrable glaze for months, was particularly destructive. By the mid-1990s, populations on Bathurst Island had dropped to under 300 caribou and less than 100 muskoxen. They have since recovered to about 1,500 caribou and 1,900 muskoxen.

The park is bounded on the south by Polar Bear Pass National Wildlife Area, a protected corridor that requires special permission from Environment Canada to visit.

Qausuittuq gets just 130 mm (5 in) of precipitation annually, putting it well within the definition of a desert. So while snow covers the ground most of the year, there isn't a lot of it. When it first falls, high Arctic snow tends to be the soft powder that is typical farther south, but it is quickly transformed by wind and cold into a squeaky, hard surface. Skis are useful, but snowshoes are generally unnecessary here.

QAUSUITTUQ

How to Get There

Nunavut has no highways. Its longest road is about 35 km (20 mi) long. An adventure in Qausuittuq begins with a flight to Resolute, longtime hub for high Arctic science and adventure undertakings. Visitors must first fly to Iqaluit from Ottawa or Montreal and then fly with First Air from Iqaluit to Resolute. Charter flights to reach the park are available from Kenn Borek Air. Two hotels are available to accommodate visitors, and they both offer shuttles to and from the airport.

Every summer, several cruise ships pass through Resolute on their way through the Northwest Passage or as part of their exploration of the eastern Arctic. You may wish to contact northern cruise ship companies to determine if they intend to make any stopovers at Qausuittuq. Note that Arctic cruise ships set tentative itineraries, but their true routes depend on weather and sea-ice conditions, which are unpredictable. Companies can never guarantee that a particular shore landing will happen.

For the truly hardy, and weather conditions permitting, there might be opportunities to snowmobile from Resolute to the park with Inuit guides. Not long ago, marathon-loving skiers used to shuffle every spring from Resolute to Bathurst Island and beyond as part of an adventure race. If you wish to undertake this kind of adventure, it would be best to contact a guiding company to determine its feasibility. The presence of a national park near Resolute will be sure to create future opportunities for access.

The routinely icy park sees few visitors.

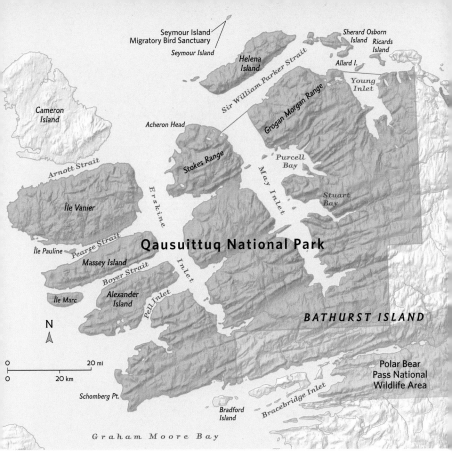

When to Go

The brief summer in Qausuittuq lasts from mid-June to mid-August. Even at this time of year, snow can fall at any time—the average July temperature on Bathurst Island is just 5°C (40°F)—but these two months typically allow visitors to hike on dry tundra and to enjoy the magical midnight sun. At this time of year, lingering fog can cause delays of a day or more on charter flights and even flights into and out of Resolute. Be sure to leave a few extra days on either end of your itinerary to make room for changeable Arctic weather.

The month of May offers the year's best weather, with stable cloudless skies and the high sun beating warmly off the snow during the day. But this is still winter-style camping, and nights can be frigid when the weak northern sun dips near the horizon. Days can feel either sweltering or require parkas, face masks, and mitts if a stiff wind blows.

How to Visit

Summer backpacking or day hiking from a base camp is the best way to appreciate all the subtleties of an Arctic landscape. Without snow, explorers' cairns and the centuries-old circles of rocks indicating where Inuit and their ancestors weighed down their skin tents become apparent.

Peary caribou and purple saxifrage on Ellesmere Island

In moist seepage areas at the foot of slopes or near some of Qausuittuq's small river valleys, hardy flowers like Arctic poppies and purple saxifrage provide welcome food for the Peary caribou. Seashells on hilltops remind visitors how the land has rebounded significantly since the tremendous weight of the glaciers lifted. None of this is visible when snow blankets the land.

While visiting in independent parties is possible, would-be hikers should consider joining an organized tour or hiring an Inuit polar bear guard. In some Arctic parks, such as Quttinirpaaq on Ellesmere Island, polar bears rarely, if ever, venture along the popular inland hiking routes. But three-quarters of Qausuittuq is within 10 km (6 mi) of the ocean. Polar bears, which are abundant in the region, can turn up anywhere. As in other northern parks, only local Inuit and professional guides can carry a firearm, for last-resort protection, in Qausuittuq. Currently, non-lethal deterrents such as bear spray, cracker shells, and flares are not available in Resolute and may not be transported there on passenger aircraft. Qausuittuq officials hope to make these available once the management plan for the new park is complete.

QAUSUITTUQ NATIONAL PARK
(Parc national du Qausittuo ᖃᐅᓱᐃᑦᑐᖅ ᒥᕐᖬᔪᐊᕐᕕᐊᖨ ᓄᓇᒋᐊ)

INFORMATION & ACTIVITIES

VISITOR & INFORMATION CENTRE
None at press time.

SEASONS & ACCESSIBILITY
Open year-round. In early April, -30°C (-22°F) is common. By late May, the sun is high even at midnight, and daytime temperatures can warm to about 5°C (41°F). Park is accessible by charter aircraft from Resolute. Notify Parks Canada of upcoming trip and upon arrival.

HEADQUARTERS
P.O. Box 278 Iqaluit NU X0A 0H0. (867) 975-4680. www.pc.gc.ca/eng/progs/np-pn/cnpn-cnnp/qausuittuq/index.aspx.

ENTRANCE FEES
$25 per person per day, $147 per person per year.

PETS
Yes.

ACCESSIBLE SERVICES
None.

THINGS TO DO
Backpacking, hiking, backcountry skiing, and wildlife viewing.

SPECIAL ADVISORIES
- Spot-type personal locator devices do not work well this far north. Devices made by Inreach or Solara, which run off the Iridium satellite network, are recommended. Likewise, Iridium is the only functional satellite phone in the high Arctic.
- Visits from curious bears are not uncommon, especially when campers are sleeping. These can quickly escalate into predatory situations. Travel with armed outfitters or experienced Inuit polar bear guards is recommended.
- Stiff winds are common. Tents should be sturdy and well staked down.
- Qausuittuq is almost 1,600 km (1,000 mi) from the nearest hospital, in Iqaluit.
- Contact Parks Canada in advance for pre-trip information, to register, and to book the mandatory orientation. During orientation, a detailed itinerary must be provided.
- Weather may delay flights to the North. Allow for flexibility in scheduling.
- Practice proper food management when camping to avoid problems with wildlife.
- Be able to recognize and prevent the onset of hypothermia.
- When hiking, avoid rock walls and cliffs with bare, freshly broken rock.
- Visitors should be experienced in recognizing avalanche hazards and have good route-finding and self-rescue skills.
- Water should be fine-filtered and treated or boiled before drinking.
- Be cautious on riverbanks when crossing rivers and streams. Cross major waterways early in the day (2 a.m.-7 a.m. if possible), and if water levels are high, wait for them to drop.

CAMPGROUNDS
No designated campsites. Contact park for camping recommendations.

OUTFITTERS, GUIDES, AND TOUR OPERATORS
Contact Parks Canada (867) 975-4673, nunavut.info@pc.gc.ca, for an up-to-date list. Visit Nunavut Tourism at nunavut tourism.com for additional options.

HOTELS, MOTELS, & INNS
(rates are for a 1-person single, Canadian dollars; hotels offer airport shuttle service)

<u>Outside the park:</u>
<u>Resolute, NU X0A 0V0:</u>
South Camp Inn (867)252-3737. www.atcosl.com/en-ca/atco-lodge/south-camp-inn/. $275.
Qausuittuq Inn (867) 252-3900. Qausuittuq@innsnorth.coop; www.innsnorth.com. $226.

General tourism information: Resolute hamlet office (867) 252-3616. nunavuttourism.com.

QAUSUITTUQ

Travelling on Sea Ice with Paniloo Sangoya

Sirmilik means "land of glaciers" in Inuktitut, which refers to its northern location and the many glaciers that extend from the summit of the mountains down the recently shaped valley to the ocean. Inuit inhabiting the area have lived here since A.D. 1000 and have traditionally travelled vast distances to harvest terrestrial and marine life. Today, they still travel extensively, and in the absence of roads, sea ice remains the best means of reaching some of these areas.

A dogsled with Inuit guide

We asked Paniloo Sangoya, Inuit Elder from Mittimatalik (Pond Inlet), to share his knowledge of Arctic travel and, in particular, sea ice travel. At this high latitude, winter presides and the temperatures get cold in early September.

> *In November, the sea ice is almost always formed. For that reason, we say Tusaqtuuq in Inuktitut to refer to the time of year when people could visit again. After a summer separated from each other and without communication, the sea ice allowed people to travel again and meet.*

Paniloo says sea ice travel presents unique challenges as the seasons progress. Depending on the amount of snowfall, recent and current temperatures, wind direction and strength, moon cycles, salinity of the water, and solar radiation, the density and thickness of the ice can be drastically different. Dark ice indicates water-saturated, thin, unsafe ice, but Paniloo says that even white ice can be treacherous.

> *Even though the ice is white, it can also be thin ice if the patch used to be qinuaq. What I called qinuaq is the white ice, well-formed ice*

but still thin. It always has to be tested with a harpoon. I fell through ice that looked like that, all nice and white and it turns out that the wind had broken it up, it was white while being very thin, not dark . . . looking exactly like the rest of the ice. Because I had failed to notice the edges, I ended up falling in . . . only the harpoon can expose the thin ice. The harpoon is your best companion.

Even in the high Arctic, in areas of strong current, the water never freezes in winter. These areas are called *polynia* and Paniloo says that you can find polynia in front of Igluluarjuit, Tunnuujaqtalik, and Iqalugaarjuit, and in these places you simply need to know that the ice is never safe. Open water in winter is also found at the floe edge where the ice extends and recedes with the season—the newly formed ice is thin, layered, and can break away. Although this ice is a valuable hunting area for narwhals, seals, and polar bears, the conditions at the floe edge can be extremely hazardous.

In springtime, the ice changes, large cracks open up and turn into leads, the snow starts to melt, and water accumulates. Depending on the strength and structure of the ice, the water drains differently.

At the beginning of July when we lived at Qaurngnak, we went to Pond Inlet to get some provisions for the summer. The sleds were heavily loaded when coming back, the melt pools were deep, and we had to go slow. Nowadays, you don't encounter deep melt pools—the pools are very shallow.

The ice is not very solid anymore and the water doesn't accumulate in deep pools. The time of breakup is also earlier.

Back then, on August 1st—the Commissioner's holiday—although the ice had shifted, we travelled on the sea ice trying very hard to go west, trying to make it through. We couldn't do this now, the ice breaks up sooner and it is all open water at the beginning of August . . . Today, the ice is snowlike: When you check the ice with a harpoon, it bores down quite a bit.

Paniloo and other elders are concerned that changes in climate are greatly affecting the characteristics of the sea ice.

If the conditions continue to change and the sea ice stops forming or becomes more hazardous, we would have no means to travel in winter.

The travel routes are everywhere; they traverse every fjord, the coastline, and span thousands of kilometres. Sea-ice travel is important to the Inuit, and knowledge of the environment is critical in informing their travel, and yours, if you are to fully appreciate the richness, diversity, and beauty of these Arctic national parks.

— MICHELINE MANSEAU, *Ecosystem Scientist, Parks Canada, and Professor, Natural Resources Institute, University of Manitoba*
— GARY MOULAND, *Manager Resource Conservation, Nunavut Field Unit, Parks Canada*
— *Interview conducted by* SAMSON ERKLOO *and translated by* MORGAN ARNAKALLAK

A view of the majestic Nahanni National Park Reserve

▶NAHANNI

NORTHWEST TERRITORIES
ESTABLISHED 1972
over 30,000 sq km/413,000 acres

In the summer of 1928, American adventurer Fenley Hunter paddled up the South Nahanni River hoping to find a huge waterfall that seemed largely the stuff of Dene legend at the time. Hunter thought he would never make it. Halfway upstream he wrote: "The Nahanni is unknown and will remain so until another age brings a change in the conformation of these mountains. It is an impossible stream, and a stiff rapid is met on average every mile, and they seem countless."

The subsequent decades have proved Hunter wrong. Multiday canoeing, kayaking, and rafting trips on the South Nahanni, and to a lesser extent on the Flat and Little Nahanni Rivers, are now the main attractions in Nahanni National Park Reserve. The park is pure wilderness that rolls out of the ice fields, mountains, alpine tundra, and boreal forest along the Continental Divide separating the Yukon and Northwest Territories.

Nahanni National Park Reserve is co-operatively managed with the Dehcho First Nations with the **Nahʔą Dehé** Consensus Team. Nahanni is in Dehcho First Nations Territory and is a gift they have chosen to share with Canada and the world.

For experienced paddlers, the South Nahanni is what Everest is to mountaineers—remote, breathtaking, and mystical. The river may not be the most difficult in the world, but neither is it for the faint of heart. It plunges through a series of four spectacular canyons, churning up rapids, boils, and whirlpools with names such as Hell's Gate, Tricky Current, and Lafferty's Riffle, which can be challenging. Here, grizzly bears, black bears, moose, mountain caribou, trumpeter swans, and upland sandpipers are among the 42 species of mammals and 180 species of birds found in the park.

Nahanni is rich with legends of lost gold, murder, and headless men, along with airier lore of tropical gardens and Dene spirits that dwell in the vents of the river valley's tufa mounds and hot springs. Undisturbed by roads or seismic lines, Nahanni was, along with Yellowstone, one of the first parks to be listed as a World Heritage site.

While river trips are recommended only for skilled paddlers or those travelling with licensed outfitters, visitors of all ages can fly into Virginia Falls, which is twice the height of Niagara.

How to Get There

You can get to Nahanni by flying to Fort Simpson via Yellowknife, and then to the river by floatplane from Fort Simpson. Alternatively, you can make the 18-hour, 1,470-km (913 mi) drive from Edmonton to Fort Simpson in two days along the Mackenzie Highway. For those driving north from Edmonton, High Level in Alberta is the best stopover. Twin Falls Park, 72 km (45 mi) north of the Alberta/Northwest Territories border, offers good camping.

Note: One can drive to Fort Simpson via the Alaska and Liard Highways.

When to Go

In spring, the South Nahanni floods up until early June and sometimes later. The risk of severe weather toward the end of August makes it unwise to go any later, so the best time is between June and August.

How to Visit

Take a day trip from Fort Simpson, Fort Liard, or Muncho Lake in northern British Columbia; trips involve a 90-minute to two-hour flight to **Nálįcho (Virginia Falls)** and the surrounding area. Air charter service information can be found at *www .pc.gc.ca/pn-np/nt/nahanni/visit / visit3.aspx#air.*

A Parks Canada interpreter is usually on hand at **Nálįcho (Virginia Falls)** to give visitors a briefing about the area and what they can see. You can then take a very easy 30-minute hike to the **Nálįcho (Virginia Falls) viewpoint,** which offers a breathtaking view of **Sluicebox Rapids** and the waterfall. The more demanding portage trail around the falls takes about an hour. While it might be sweltering at the top of the falls, the temperature drops by at least 10 or 15 degrees down below in the mist.

You can also plan canoe, kayak, and raft trips—they'll take from eight days to three weeks. Parks Canada highly recommends that people go with a registered, licensed outfitter (see p. 333). Starting points are the **Moose Ponds**—in Nááts'įhch'oh National Park Reserve (21 days), **Island Lakes** (14–18 days), **Gahnįhthah Mįe (Rabbitkettle Lake)** (10–14 days), and Nailicho (7–10 days).

The ending points are **Blackstone Territorial Park** for campers and **Lindberg Landing** (250-233-2344) for those who want a cozy cabin. (Deregistration takes place at the Nahanni National Park Reserve

NAHANNI

Office in Nahanni Butte.) Both are located on the **Liard River** near its confluence with the South Nahanni.

Advance reservations and permits are required. Visitors must register and check out at the beginning and end of their trip.

CHALLENGING WHITE-WATER ROUTES

Apart from the Moose Ponds route, which has about 50 km (31 mi) of very challenging, continuous white water, experienced paddlers have little to be concerned about until they get to Virginia Falls. Immediately downstream of the falls, however, is some challenging white water: **Canyon Rapids** followed by **Figure Eight Rapid** (Hell's Gate), **Wrigley Whirlpool, George's Riffle,** and then **Lafferty's**

Riffle. Spray covers are recommended. The difficulty of these rapids depends entirely on river water levels.

HIKES & HIGHLIGHTS ALONG THE NAHANNI

The **Cirque of the Unclimbables** was named by Arnold Wexler and a group of American rock climbers in 1958. When they saw this cluster of peaks and sheer rock walls, they were haunted by what was before them. It looked like the spires of Yosemite, which Ansel Adams had made famous during his photography expeditions in the 1920s.

When Wexler and his colleagues got over the shocking head-on view of the 2,740-m-high (9,000 ft) fins of wind- and ice-polished granite standing tall and angular and facing one

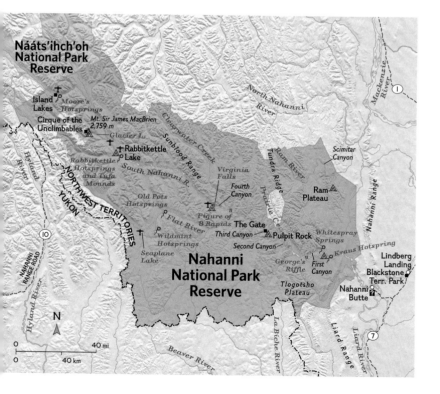

another in a half circle, the adjoining mountains suddenly looked small and terribly ordinary. Turning toward his partners, Wexler declared most of the peaks "unclimbable."

Most trips into the Unclimbables begin at **Glacier Lake,** a designated landing spot in the park. It is also possible (but not easy) to get to the Unclimbables from **Brintnell Creek** along the South Nahanni, an easy day's paddle from Island Lakes. The trail from here is indistinct at best.

From Brintnell Creek, hike upstream for 1 km (0.6 mi) until you get to a snye (a side channel) coming off the South Nahanni. Watch out for a heavily blazed pine tree. The trail eventually makes an abrupt left turn. Follow the trail over rolling hills until it nears Brintnell Creek, then follow the north bank of the creek west to Glacier Lake. Count on losing the trail a number of times along the way. Allow a day to get to Glacier Lake, and another half day to get to the **Fairy Meadows,** which is located at the foot of the Unclimbables.

Continue along to **Gahnjhthah Mje (Rabbitkettle Lake)** and its famous tufa hot springs, the largest in Canada. Some of these terraced mounds of calcium carbonate precipitate are 27 m (89 ft) high and 70 m (230 ft) in diameter. Yamba Déja is said to inhabit one of the vents. It is this spirit, so the Dene legend goes, that went down to Nahanni Butte and drove away two giant beavers that would drown boaters with a slap of their enormous tails.

From the campground at Rabbitkettle, one can hike to the **Secret Lakes**—a series of small, deep lakes nestled in the sides of the mountain valley. There are two 10-km (6 mi) routes in the area; ask the staff based at **Gahnjhthah Mje** for advice on which to take. Note

Paddling Glacier Lake near Mount Harrison Smith

that **Gahnjhthah Mje (Rabbitkettle Lake)** is a hot spot for grizzly bears and black bears, so tread cautiously.

Downriver the **Sunblood Mountains** trailhead (8 km/5 mi one way) is located across the river from the **Nájlịcho (Virginia Falls)** Campground. To get there safely, paddle upstream a few hundred metres and cross the river to the sign that marks the beginning of the trail. Follow this trail to an open scree ridge and continue to the peak of Sunblood.

Marengo Falls (4 km/2.5 mi one way): There are two ways to get to this small waterfall that drops 30 m (98 ft) over a series of limestone ledges. Parks Canada interpreters will be happy to point you to the two routes from **Nájlịcho (Virginia Falls)**. All you'll need is a GPS or map and compass.

THIRD CANYON

In **Third Canyon,** the river takes a sharp turn before cutting a narrow, steep-sided slit through rock streaked red with iron, known as **The Gate.** Passing through this stretch of water in 1927, author/adventurer Raymond Patterson wrote, "The whole thing was like a great gateway through which I glided silently, midget like. I have seen many

NAHANNI

NAHANNI NATIONAL PARK RESERVE
(Réserve de parc national Nahanni)

INFORMATION & ACTIVITIES

OFFICES

Nahanni National Park Reserve office Fort Simpson. Phone (867) 695-7750. Open daily June to October; weekdays rest of year.
Nahanni Butte (867) 602-2025. Duty officer on call 24 hours a day June–September. (867) 695-3732.

SEASONS & ACCESSIBILITY

Park open year-round, peak season May to August. Parks accessed usually by chartered floatplane from licensed company. Park permits required for landing at **Nájlįcho (Virginia Falls)** and **Gahnjhthah Mįe (Rabbitkettle Lake).** Floatplanes accessible from Fort Simpson, Fort Liard, and Yellowknife, NT; Fort Nelson and Muncho Lake, BC; and Watson Lake, YT. Licensed charter companies include Simpson Air, Ltd. (867) 695-2505; South Nahanni Airways (867) 695-2007; Wolverine Air (867) 695-2263; Air Tindi (867) 669-8200; Alpine Aviation (Yukon) Ltd. (867) 668-7725; Kluane Airways/Inconnu Lodge (250) 860-4187; Liard Tours/Northern Rockies Lodge (250) 776-3482.

HEADQUARTERS

10002 100 St., P.O. Box 348, Fort Simpson, NT X0E 0N0. Phone (867) 695-7750. www.parkscanada.gc.ca/nahanni.

ENTRANCE FEES

Backcountry excursion and camping permits are $25 per person per day, $147 per person per year. Reservation requests, member list form, and emergency contact and equipment list forms must be provided to park office.

PETS

Pets permitted but not recommended; must be on a leash at all times.

ACCESSIBLE SERVICES

None.

THINGS TO DO

Most visitors start their trips from **Nájlįcho** (typically 7-10 days) or **Gahnjhthah Mįe (Rabbitkettle Lake;** 10-14 days). Other starting locations include **Island Lakes** (14-18 days; flat, with Class II rapids), the **Little Nahanni River** (6-7 days to paddle to Rabbitkettle Lake and join South Nahanni; Class II-IV rapids), or **The Moose Ponds** (in Nááts'ihch'oh National Park Reserve) 21 days; Class II-IV white water. Alternate routes include **Seaplane Lake/Flat River** (4-5 days; Class II-V rapids) and **Glacier Lake.** Permits required. River guide pamphlets available for $5. Reservations must be confirmed with park office.

Canoeing in the **South Nahanni River** between June and September.

Hiking in the **Cirque of the Unclimbables; Glacier Lake** (accessed from South Nahanni River north of park boundary);

---

beautiful places in my lifetime, but never anything of this kind."

Just past Big Bend, where the Funeral Range ends and the Headless Range begins, is where the headless bodies of the McLeod brothers, Willie and Frank, were found after they went missing in 1903 while searching for gold said by Indians to be piled high in the region. A note carved in a sled runner that read, "We have found a prospect," resulted in a mini gold rush and murderous incidents that are why the Nahanni has been called the "Valley of the Vanishing Men."

Prairie Creek (4 km/2.5 mi one way) is a large alluvial fan that shouldn't be missed. Stay to the left of Prairie Creek's channels when you begin the hike; when Prairie Creek exits the mountains, climb over a saddle to the west of the gap to get to a floodplain flanked by the vertical canyon walls.

Secret Lakes (6–10 km/4–6 mi, one way); **Sunblood Mountain** (8 km/5 mi, one way); **Marengo Falls** (4 km/2.5 mi, one way); **Scow Creek/Headless Range** (8 km/5 mi, one way); **Prairie Creek** (4 km/2.5 mi, one way); **Sheaf Creek–Tlogotsho Plateau** (10 km/6 mi, one way); **Dry Canyon Creek** (10 km/6 mi, one way); **Ram Creek** (15 km/9 mi, one way); **Lafferty Creek** (10 km/6 mi, one way). Heli-hiking provided by licensed outfitter Solitudes Excursions.

Fishing permitted in all park waters at any time of year with five-fish limit for daily catch-and-possession. Fishing permits are $34 per year.

Licensed river outfitters include: Black Feather—The Wilderness Adventure Company (705) 746-1372 or (888) 737-6818; Nahanni River Adventures (867) 668-3056; Nahanni Wilderness Adventures (403) 678-3374.

SPECIAL ADVISORIES
- Open fires not permitted.
- Campsites forbidden on heli-pads at park control cabins.
- Solid experience in white-water paddling or rafting, self-rescue skills, and knowledge of travelling and camping in remote wilderness environments recommended.

CAMPGROUNDS
Nájlicho Campground by reservation. Maximum group size 12 people, 2-night stay, $25 per person per day or $147 per person per year. Collection box at kiosk at Virginia Falls. Travel time to campsite is 2 to 3 days paddling time if starting from

Gahnjhthah Mje (Rabbitkettle Lake); 6 to 7 days if starting from Island Lakes; 10 days if starting from the Mooseponds. Travel time depends on weather conditions and off-river hiking time. Canoe racks, food caches, and composting toilets available.
Gahnjhthah Mje (Rabbitkettle Lake) campgrounds are off the shores of the lake 300 m (984 ft) north of staff cabin, and on an island in the South Nahanni River across from portage landing. Both campgrounds have food caches and outhouses. No camping permitted at portage landing.
The Gate (Pulpit Rock) is a designated campsite. Composting toilet available.
Kraus Hotsprings is the former homestead of Mary and Gus Kraus. Hot springs along river's edge. Check-in station, food cache, and outhouse. Use of soap prohibited.

HOTELS, MOTELS, & INNS
(unless otherwise noted, rates are for a 2-person double, high season, in Canadian dollars)

Outside the park:
Fort Simpson, NT X0E 0N0:
Deh Cho Suites 10509 Antoine Dr., Box 60. (867) 695-2309 or (877) 695-2309. $175–$195.
Maroda Motel 9802 100th St. (867) 695-2201. www.nahanni-inn.com $115–$170.
Nahanni Inn PO Box 258. (867) 695-2201. www.nahanni-inn.com. $115–$170.
Willows Inn 10301 99 St. 867-695-2077. www.janor.ca. $195–$210.

Nahanni Butte, NT X0E 0N0:
Nahanni Butte Inn and General Store P.O. Box 149. (867) 602-2023. $175 per person.

NAHANNI

The dry gravel fan of **Dry Canyon Creek** (10 km/6 mi one way) is at the far eastern end of **Deadmen Valley.** Hike along gravel beds of the steep-walled canyon to the **Nahanni Plateau.** Note that the canyon can flood in a thunderstorm.

OTHER RIVERS

Lafferty Creek joins the South Nahanni near the bottom of First Canyon. Some boulder walking and scrambling is necessary to get through this area. **Kraus Hotsprings** is the site of an old homestead. Here, weary paddlers can soak their bones in one of the warm springs percolating up through the gravel. The challenging **Little Nahanni River** flows out of the park through Nááts'ihch'oh National Park Reserve.

High-country hiking

▶ NÁÁTS'IHCH'OH

NORTHWEST TERRITORIES
ESTABLISHED 2014
4,850 sq km/1,198,461 acres

Nááts'ihch'oh National Park Reserve is located in the heart of the Mackenzie Mountains, one of the wildest mountain ranges on Earth. Home to caribou, grizzly bears, Dall sheep, and trumpeter swans, the park is drained by rivers and is sprinkled with hot springs. Nááts'ihch'oh and its downstream neighbour, Nahanni National Park Reserve, together form one of the world's largest and most spectacular national park complexes, covering a total of 35,000 sq km (8,640,000 acres). The sheer scale of the area is part of its allure, and given the challenges of getting here the two parks are best seen together.

Nááts'ihch'oh contains the headwaters of the legendary South Nahanni River. The park's name comes from Nááts'ihch'oh (Mount Wilson) on the park's northwestern boundary, which in North Slavey means "the mountain that is sharp like a porcupine." The Shúhtaot'ine, Mountain Dene, believe it is a place of strong spiritual power. It is part of the homeland of indigenous people who have resided here for millennia and continue to use the area for spiritual purposes and to hunt moose, sheep, and caribou. Their willingness to share this land with all Canadians made this national park possible.

Nááts'ihch'oh and Nahanni are separately administered because they are in different land claim areas. Nááts'ihch'oh is part of the traditional lands of the Sahtu Dene and Metis of Tulita and Norman Wells, and part of a broader area known as the Sahtu Settlement Area, while Nahanni is within the Dehcho First Nations territory.

When the fur trade came to the region in the 19th century, members of these indigenous groups collected pelts in the mountains in winter. Each spring they would build 14-m (46 ft) boats made of spruce wood frames wrapped with raw moose hides that were sewn with sinew. Loaded with their families, dogs, meat, and furs, these boats would be launched into the strong current to follow the rivers down to trading posts on the Mackenzie River. The process of building one of these vessels is the subject of director Raymond Yakeleya's 1982 National Film Board documentary *The Last Moose Skin Boat*. The boat made for the film is on display in the Prince of Wales Northern Heritage Centre in Yellowknife.

The region is now a magnet for river paddlers from across Canada and around the world. To make the entire three-week run down the length of the South Nahanni River from the west end of Nááts'ihch'oh to the east side of Nahanni is every experienced wilderness paddler's dream.

Despite its forbidding name, the Broken Skull River on the east side of the park offers lively but not too difficult paddling as it flows from Nááts'ihch'oh into Nahanni and features side hikes to hot springs along the way.

Very challenging white-water paddling is found on the Little Nahanni River, which flows from Flat Lakes through a part of Nahanni and Nááts'ihch'oh National Park Reserves, leaving the parks for a period before its confluence with the South Nahanni River in Nááts'ihch'oh. The Little Nahanni was the setting of a remarkable canoe adventure involving famous Canadian canoeist Bill Mason, his daughter Becky, and friends. In 1983 they were descending the river when a forest fire started. After some deliberation they kept going. The fire burned closer, with trees shooting up in flame and embers coming down like firecrackers.

"The burnt trees were falling in the river," remembers Becky Mason. "It was so hot we were worried about going up in flame ourselves so we doused ourselves with river water. We paddled through the fire for a couple of hours." Fortunately, they outran the blaze.

There are also good hiking opportunities in Nááts'ihch'oh park's high country. The tree line is very low and the alpine tundra lends itself to wandering among dramatic mountains.

The protection of this vast parkland was enabled by a successful national campaign led by First Nations, Métis, conservation groups, and river paddlers whose goal was to protect the entire South Nahanni watershed. First came a massive six-fold expansion of Nahanni in 2009 and subsequently Nááts'ihch'oh was legislated in 2014. Alan Latourelle, then CEO of Parks Canada, said, "We are creating the Banff and Jasper of the 21st century." Fully 86 percent of the South Nahanni River watershed is now protected under the Canada National Parks Act.

NÁÁTS'IHCH'OH

How to Get There

Náàts'ihch'oh is accessed by float-plane from the villages of Norman Wells, Tulita, and Fort Simpson, Northwest Territories, and Watson Lake in Yukon. The flight in over the mountainous landscape is spectacular. Flight-seeing tours can be arranged. Check the park's website for Parks Canada's Náàts'ihch'oh Trip planner *(www.pc.gc.ca/eng/ pn-np/nt/naatsihchoh/Visit.aspx)*, which lists the various air services.

The Little Nahanni River in the western part of the park can be accessed by a gravel road known as Highway 10—the Nahanni Range Road in the Yukon Territory. The road is not always maintained as it leads to the off-and-on-again Cantung mine in the Northwest Territories.

Just before the mine, the Howard's Pass Access road begins, providing access to Flat Lakes, the main starting point for Little Nahanni paddlers. The river flows from the lakes into Nahanni, then Náàts'ihch'oh. It may be possible to drive past Flat Lakes to access the Little Nahanni River below some of the more challenging rapids. Check with the park for information on conditions before starting the drive.

When to Go

June through early September sees the mildest weather and longest days, although temperatures can get below freezing (-5° C, 23°F) in June and September. It can be very hot in the summer (30°C, 86°F). Around the summer solstice, night is only a few hours long; in August, the sky is dark enough for northern lights viewing.

How to Visit

Náàts'ihch'oh is very remote. Visitors must bring everything they need, and they are unlikely to see many other people. There are no lodges and no trails. Travel is by maps, compass, and reading the landscape. Registration is required. Contact the park at (867) 588-4884 or naatsih choh.info@pc.gc.ca.

Visitors can also engage an experienced wilderness outfitting and guiding company to look after all arrangements for river trips in the park (see p. 339).

Parks Canada's Náàts'ihch'oh Trip planner gives an excellent overview of the park's recreational opportunities.

PADDLING THE SOUTH NAHANNI RIVER

517 km/321 mi; 18 to 23 days

The full trip down the **South Nahanni River** from the Moose Ponds at the western end of Náàts'ihch'oh to Nahanni Butte is one of the world's top paddling experiences.

The headwaters section of the South Nahanni River in Náàts'ihch'oh features the **Rock Gardens,** deemed by expert canoeists as very technical with lots of rocks along the way. It takes seven to nine days from the Moose Ponds at the foot of Náàts'ihch'oh through the Rock Gardens to **Gahnjhthah Mje (Rabbitkettle Lake)** in Nahanni, where air service is available. This stretch of the river is best run from mid-June through July, before water levels drop. Take along the *South Nahanni River Touring Guide* ($5.00) to navigate the river. Order via email, nahanni.info@pc.gc.ca, or phone (867) 695-7750.

Less experienced paddlers should begin trips downstream in Nahanni at either **Gahnjhthah**

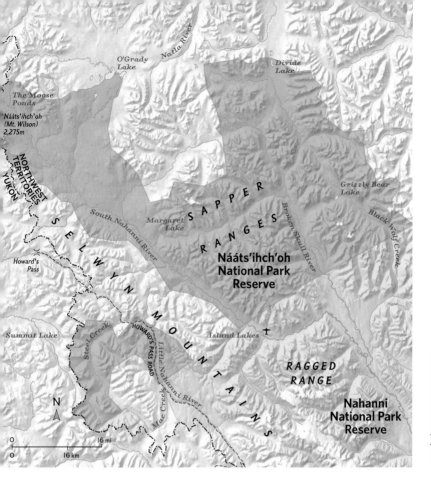

Mįe (Rabbitkettle Lake) or **Nájlįcho (Virginia Falls)**. Rafting is also available from these points.

PADDLING THE LITTLE NAHANNI RIVER

85 km/53 mi; 8 to 12 days

With intense Class II–V whitewater, the **Little Nahanni River** is a very technical paddle with lots of blind hairpin turns, where back-ferrying may be necessary to avoid being caught by sweepers.

  The best time to canoe from Flat Lakes to **Gahnįhthah Mįe (Rabbitkettle Lake)** is mid-June to mid-August. For more information check out the

Little Nahanni trip planner (*www .pc.gc.ca/eng/pn-np/nt/naatsihchoh /Activities/15act1/pad2.aspx*).

PADDLING THE BROKEN SKULL RIVER

150 km/93 mi; 6 to 8 days

With continuous Class I–II whitewater, the **Broken Skull** is a good option for experienced paddlers going on their first northern wilderness river trip. The run starts at **Divide Lake** and ends at **Gahnįhthah Mįe** (Rabbitkettle Lake) on the South Nahanni River, where there is air access. The best time to make this trip is mid-June to mid-August.

Beauty perfectly reflected

From the Broken Skull River you can access two undeveloped natural hot springs. **Broken Skull Hot Springs** (NTS map 105 I/16), which has a remarkable soaking pool, is a 2.5-km (1.5 mi) hike from the river. **Grizzly Bear Hot Springs** (NTS map 95 L/12) is a 10-km (6 mi) hike from the river up a creek bed that involves multiple creek crossings.

PADDLING THE NATLA-KEELE RIVER
480 km/298 mi; 18 to 21 days

O'Grady Lake, on the park's northwestern edge, is an access point for the Natla-Keele River system, which offers white-water paddling trips through vast wild valleys outside the park to Tulita.

HIKING

The high country along the northern boundary of Náàts'ihch'oh offers a true wilderness adventure in a little-known landscape. The park encourages exploration of this area and invites visitors to share their dis-coveries of interesting places to hike and camp. To locate hiking areas in Náàts'ihch'oh, Parks Canada uses map or GPS co-ordinates. National Topographic System Maps are available: *www.nrcan.gc.ca/earth-sciences /geography/topographic-information /maps/9771.*

Several floatplane-accessible hiking opportunities have already been identified. More will be added to the list over the next few years. The routes are concentrated in high areas because the park's river valleys are notoriously brushy and difficult to walk.

Grizzly Bear Lake (NTS map 95 L/12) offers open-tundra walking among beautiful alpine streams and the park's highest mountains. Longer backpacking options are available in the mountains to the northeast.

Divide Lake (NTS map 105 P/01) is another starting point for rewarding hiking options above the Broken Skull Valley. Hiking the high country can precede the descent of the river by canoe for a nicely varied wilderness trip.

NÁÁTS'IHCH'OH NATIONAL PARK RESERVE
(Parc national du Nááts'ihch'oh)

INFORMATION & ACTIVITIES

HEADQUARTERS
The park reserve office is in Tulita, on the banks of the Mackenzie River, and can only be accessed by air, water, or by ice road in the winter. www.pc.gc.ca/pn-np/nt/naatsihchoh/Visit.aspx.

SEASONS & ACCESSIBILITY
June to September, though winter access is permitted. Contact the park reserve office for a complete list of air charter companies.

VISITOR & INFORMATION CENTRES
Telephone information (867) 588-4884. The park reserve's website serves as a virtual information centre. A park visitor centre will be built in **Tulita.**

ENTRANCE FEE
No park fees at time of writing. It is necessary to register with Parks Canada. You can register and get a park orientation by phone (867) 588-4884 or in person at the Parks Canada offices in Tulita or Fort Simpson.

PETS
Dogs on a leash only.

FACILITIES FOR DISABLED
Some scenic flights may be able to accommodate people with disabilities.

THINGS TO DO
Paddling, hiking, scenic flights, and cultural tours. Visitors must register for South Nahanni River trips through Nahanni National Park Reserve of Canada, (867) 695-7750. nahanni.info@pc.gc.ca. Parks Canada online trip planner www.pc.gc.ca/pn-np/nt/naatsihchoh.

OUTFITTERS
Blackfeather, The Wilderness Adventure Company (888) 849-7668. Info@blackfeather.com; www.blackfeather.com.
Canoe North Adventures (519) 941-6654. info@canoenorthadventures.com; www.canoenorthadventures.com. **Nahanni**

River Adventures (800) 297-6927. Info@nahanni.com; www.nahanni.com.
Nahanni Wilderness Adventures (888) 897-5223. adventures@nahanniwild.com; www.nahanniwild.com.

SPECIAL ADVISORIES
• Bear safety precautions required.
• Fire in fireboxes preferred.
• No fishing allowed.

OVERNIGHT BACKPACKING
The higher areas of the park, including **Grizzly Bear Lake** and **Divide Lake**, lend themselves to backpacking. Route-finding experience necessary. Check the park's website for updates on new areas.

CAMPGROUNDS
Random camping.

HOTELS, MOTELS, & INNS
(unless otherwise noted, rates are for a 2-person double, high season, in Canadian dollars)

Outside the park:
Tulita, NT X0E 0K0:
Two Rivers Hotel 17 Mackenzie Dr. (867) 588-3320 tworivershotel@outlook.com. $420.
Riverview Bed & Breakfast 28 Mackenzie Dr. (867) 588-3511. ronwenddyoe@hotmail.com. $300, including hot breakfast.

Norman Wells, NT X0E 0V0:
Canoe North Adventures Lodge 9 Beaver Ln., Box 148. www.canoenorthadventures.com/lodge. $200.
Heritage Hotel 27 Mackenzie Dr., Box 279. (867) 587-5000. www.info@heritagehotelnwt.com. $300–$330.
Sahtu Dene Inn 191 Mackenzie Dr. (867) 587-2511. www.sahtudeneinn.com, info@sahtudeneinn.com. $235 and up.
Yamouri Inn 1 Town Sq. (867) 587-2744. yamouri.inn@gmail.com. $250.

Fort Simpson, NT X0E 0N0:
See p. 333.

NÁÁTS'IHCH'OH

▶ **PARKS IN DEVELOPMENT (PROPOSED)**

Thaidene Nëné National Park Reserve

Great Slave Lake is the 10th largest freshwater lake in the world. The proposed Thaidene Nëné National Park Reserve would protect 14,000 sq km (5,405 sq mi) of the magnificent East Arm region of the lake as well as a wildlife-rich area of low ridges of granite and gneiss traversed by tumbling rivers that feed into it. Christie Bay, the deepest freshwater body in North America, is home to huge lake trout. Bald eagles hunt from the cliffs above.

Lockhart River waterfall

Located on the Canadian Shield, the exposed portion of the continental crust underlying the centre of North America, the proposed Thaidene Nëné National Park Reserve would protect a landscape of profound contrast. Here, deep winters give way to glorious summers, soaring cliffs fall into the deepest freshwater in North America, and vast forests open to great barren lands.

Just as the innumerable lakes of the Canadian Shield are connected by a network of rivers throughout the watersheds of Thaidene Nëné, various peoples have long been connected to Thaidene Nëné. Thaidene

Nëné means "Land of the Ancestors" in the Chipewyan language. The Łutsël K'e Dene First Nation consider it to be the "heart of the homeland." The Northwest Territory Métis Nation also has significant ties to the hunting, trapping, and trading routes of the area.

Thaidene Nëné is a culturally rich area whose longstanding traditions of hunting, fishing, gathering, and spiritual practice continue today as various northern peoples make their lives here.

Ts'akui Theda (the Lady of the Falls) is a beautiful and spiritual place where the people of Łutsël K'e go for healing and to pray. This site and Desnethche (the Lockhart River, which drains into Great Slave Lake) were once described by Steven Nitah, the chief negotiator for the Łutsël K'e Dene First Nation, as "the fundamental core of Denesoline cultural identity, the spiritual apex of our people." The park would help ensure the cultural continuity of its various inhabitants.

Visitors to the new park would have an unusual opportunity to experience an ecological transition from forest to tundra. On the land at the western end of the proposed park is forest of spruce and jack pine, with an understory of feather moss, lichens, blueberries, and cranberries. To the east it grades to more stunted taiga forest, which in turn gives way to Arctic tundra. This transition is known as the "tree line."

The East Arm of Great Slave Lake is known for its world-class fishing of giant whitefish and lake trout. It also features spectacular rivers waiting to be navigated by canoe and kayak enthusiasts, secluded bays for boating and sailing, and jaw-dropping scenery that will long be remembered.

In 1833, as part of an effort to explore the northern reaches of the area, explorer George Back set up Fort Reliance. It is from this base that he found the river (now called the Back River) that he followed to the Arctic Coast. The remains of the fort, recognized as a national historic site, can be found near the mouth of the Lockhart River.

Perched on the shore of the East Arm of Great Slave Lake, Łutsël K'e will be the gateway to Thaidene Nëné National Park Reserve. A community of 350, it is the home of the Łutsël K'e Denesoline. It has a small airport and a summer wharf, making it accessible year-round. Here, park visitors will be able to view the northern lights and experience Denesoline culture.

It is the dynamic, living connection between land and people, between the water and the land, between the forest and the barrens, that makes Thaidene Nëné one of Canada's national treasures. In terms of wildlife, the park would protect portions of the annual ranges of all three barren-ground caribou herds that populate the region.

In July 2015 Parks Canada publically released a proposed 14,000-sq-km (3,459,475 acres)Thaidene Nëné National Park Reserve boundary for public consultation. The Government of Northwest Territories also released proposed boundaries for additional portions of Thaidene Nëné that could be protected by territorial land-use mechanisms.

Given the widespread support, it is hoped that the national park reserve will be created soon.

THAIDENE NËNÉ

Back's chimney, Fort Reliance

The mighty La Roncière Falls and the Hornaday River

▶ TUKTUT NOGAIT

NORTHWEST TERRITORIES
ESTABLISHED 1998
18,181 sq km/4,492,622 acres

In an expanse of tundra scattered with rolling hills, barren plateaus, and remote lakes, three wild rivers carve their way across a vast land-scape to the Arctic Ocean. Spring melt rushes through sheer vertical canyons over chiselled beds of limestone, shale, and sandstone; roars through rapids; and crashes over waterfalls. This exceptional canyon scenery is reminiscent of that found in the more populated American Southwest, but here, standing on the wide open tundra above the Arctic Circle, you are likely to enjoy it in nearly total seclusion.

Although the Hornaday River runs for 360 km (224 mi), it was the last Canadian river of its size to be discovered. In its upper reaches, it is shallow, wide, and meandering, but downstream it transforms into 45 km (28 mi) of wild, white water. Red canyon walls soar 120 m (394 ft) above it. At one dramatic spot, the river is funnelled through a canyon 3 m (10 ft) wide before it plunges over the magnificent La Roncière Falls.

The tundra itself has varied features and climates. Long, harsh winters give way to summers that bring the landscape to life. Cliffs formed by the canyon walls provide nesting sites for one of the greatest concentrations of peregrines and gyrfalcons in Canada. Ancient, well-worn migration trails wind along the canyon rims and across plateaus, marking the route of thousands of caribou from the Bluenose West herd as they travel to their traditional calving grounds in the Melville Hills. And tracks of wolves, grizzlies, and wolverines along the sandy edges of the upper Hornaday testify to the presence of these hard-to-glimpse species.

Evidence of early cultures, such as the Thule and Copper Inuit (A.D. 1200–1500), can still be seen. More than 400 archaeological sites, including remnants of campsites on top of hills, food caches, graves, and kayak rests—some more identifiable than others—suggest that this vast landscape has been in use by indigenous people for hundreds of years.

Today the Inuvialuit people from the nearby community of Paulatuk still rely on the lands encompassed by the park to support a traditional lifestyle. The park protects the calving grounds for the Bluenose caribou—meaning "young caribou" in Inuvialuktun. Tuktut Nogait provides a tundra home for the young caribou born in early summer.

How to Get There

Tuktut Nogait is a remote park located 40 km (25 mi) east of the community of Paulatuk and 460 km (286 mi) northeast of the town of Inuvik. To access the park for backpacking or paddling trips, visitors typically fly from either Inuvik or Norman Wells in the Northwest Territories. Only water-based landings are permissible. As charter flights are very expensive, investigate sharing or splitting the costs with another group—contact the Parks Canada office in Inuvik for a list of planned trips.

Alternatively, if you're backpacking (and thus don't need to transport a canoe or kayak), take a scheduled flight (available three days a week) with Aklak Air from Inuvik to Paulatuk. From Paulatuk you can access the park on foot, or you can save some time and get a little closer to the park boundary by using a locally hired boat or an ATV. These options will take you across privately owned Inuvialuit lands. You are asked to contact the Inuvialuit Land Administration prior to your trip. Be aware that all travel may be delayed due to unexpected weather and environmental complications such as fog, high river water, pack ice, strong winds, or snow.

When to Go

Go after the ice has melted on the lakes and before the snow begins to fall. In the Arctic, that's mid-June to mid-August. During the summer months, expect anything from blue skies and warm breezes to fog and freak snowstorms. In late June, the tundra explodes into a carpet of wildflowers, and caribou are out in numbers. In early July, the river water levels are ideal, and the diversity of birds rich. In August, the land is ablaze with fall colours, and you'll finally be able to pack away your bug spray.

How to Visit

Extended backpacking or paddling trips of 10 to 12 days are the preferred methods for taking in this remote Arctic wilderness park. All trips require extensive logistical preparation several months in advance, and it is mandatory to register and receive an orientation session at the start of your trip. Detailed backpacking and paddling guides for the Hornaday River are available, and additional but limited information on

TUKTUT NOGAIT

other areas is available upon request.

Given the park's remote location and the potential for weather-related complications in air travel, be aware that in the event of an emergency, assistance could be days away. Therefore, it is highly recommended that visitors have backcountry survival skills and extensive knowledge of wilderness first aid.

HORNADAY RIVER CANYONS
About 7 to 10 days

Paddling the 45-km (28 mi) stretch of white water through the **Hornaday River Canyons** is not an option for the amateur adventurer. However, trekking along the rim is a thrilling experience, and you'll spend days soaking in the dramatic scenes of frothing water and jagged rock. Hiking on either side is on mostly level terrain with a mix of tundra and tussocks. Both hikes allow you to view the impressive 20-m-high (66 ft) **La Roncière Falls** (in the third canyon).

To backpack the west rim, fly into Uyarsivik Lake and hike back out to Paulatuk. From Uyarsivik Lake, 2 km (1 mi) from the first of three Hornaday Canyon sections, hike for several days until you reach the delta, approximately 10 km (6 mi) from the coast, and continue overland to **Paulatuk.** Allow 10 days for this 107-km (66 mi) hike. Given that this route does not require crossing the Hornaday River, it's the one most frequently taken by visitors.

To backpack the east rim, fly in to a small lake 4 km (2.5 mi) southeast of Roncière Falls. This seven-day hike follows the east rim of the canyons and river edge to the delta. From here, you must either have arranged for a boat pickup at a predetermined time and location, or make a river cross-

An Inuvialuit cultural host shows visitors the Many Caches archaeological site.

ing on foot. The latter should only be attempted by experienced backpackers at low-water levels.

HORNADAY (UPPER SECTION) & LITTLE HORNADAY RIVERS
About 10 days

Upstream of the canyons is a vast river valley scored by meandering waterways and large sweeping sandbars. Experience this section of the river by backpacking or paddling.

To backpack, fly to **Erly Lake** near the south border of the park. Hike across the open tundra for a couple of kilometres (1 mile) to reach the river. For 105 km (65 mi), you will follow the west bank to **Uyarsivik Lake,** the aircraft pickup spot just before the canyons begin. Mats of pink moss campion and white mountain avens guide the way.

In early July, 145 km (90 mi) of the **upper Hornaday** is navigable by canoe. Off the river, there are side valleys that offer hiking excursions among small hills and lakes. It takes a minimum of 10 days to complete this route from **Canoe Lake** (south

TUKTUT NOGAIT

White water in a slot canyon

end of the park) to Uyarsivik Lake (upstream of the canyons). You'll need flights in and out, as well as a short portage to and from the lakes.

Upstream from its confluence with the Little Hornaday (its one major tributary, see opposite), the **Hornaday River** is shallow, and alternates between short, calm, slow sections and long, fast, rocky riffles and chutes, though none of the white water is designated as anything over Class II. Good campsites are plentiful in this area. Downstream of the confluence, the current slows and the channel widens.

Some stretches, which are up to 800 m (2,625 ft) wide, resemble a lake more than a river. Lined by vast sandbars and dunes, the river wanders through an old bedrock river valley modified by glacial erosion.

Suitable campsites are more difficult to find in this section.

You can access the Hornaday River via the **Little Hornaday River,** which forms the outflow from **Hornaday Lake.** Fly to the eastern park boundary where Hornaday Lake borders Nunavut. Hornaday Lake is the park's largest lake and is located in the **Melville Hills** 512 m (1,680 ft) above sea level. The Little Hornaday River drops 150 m (492 ft) between the lake and the Hornaday River 89 km (55 mi) downstream. Spirited and fast flowing, the Little Hornaday is ideal for experienced Class III white-water paddlers. The river is narrow and shallow with riffles, rock gardens, and rapids. A trip from Hornaday Lake to the Hornaday River and then to Uyarsivik Lake is 185 km (115 mi). Allow a minimum of 10 days.

TUKTUT NOGAIT NATIONAL PARK
(Parc national Tuktut Nogait)

INFORMATION & ACTIVITIES

HEADQUARTERS
www.parkscanada.gc.ca/tuktutnogait.
Western Arctic Field Unit, Box 1840,
Inuvik, NT X0E 0T0. Phone (867) 777-
8800. Inuvik.info@pc.gc.ca.

SEASONS & ACCESSIBILITY
Peak visitor season is late July–August,
with 24-hour daylight in June and July.
Recommended winter travel is between
March and May. Scheduled flights
between **Paulatuk** and **Inuvik** are with
Aklak Air. Charter aircraft services are
available from Inuvik and **Norman Wells.**
All groups required to attend an orientation and have a landing permit. There are
no wheeled landing strips. Cost-sharing
opportunities may be available—contact
the Parks Canada office. Overland hiking
access from Paulatuk (40 km/25 mi).
Guides can be secured through Paulatuk
Hunters and Trappers Committee: (867)
580-3004. Winter access is by aircraft
equipped with skis, snow machine up to
park boundary, or skiing from Paulatuk.

ENTRANCE FEES
For backcountry camping $25 per person
per day, $147 per person per year. Fishing
permits $10 per person per day, $34 per
person per year.

PETS
Pets permitted; must be on a leash or
under physical control at all times.

ACCESSIBLE SERVICES
None.

THINGS TO DO
Hiking, fishing, paddling for paddlers with
strong wilderness first aid and backcountry
skills. No established hiking trails. Access to
Hornaday River for paddling via the **Little
Hornaday River** (Class III rapids) starting
at **Hornaday Lake** (185 km/115 mi) or starting directly on main river (145 km/90 mi).
Total paddling time is 8 to 12 days. Copies
of "Hornaday River Guide" available at park
office in Inuvik. More than 350 archaeological sites dating back to A.D. 1200.

SPECIAL ADVISORIES
• No campfires. Camp stoves and cooking
  fuel can be bought in Inuvik or Paulatuk.
• Fishing permits, required for anyone 16
  and older, allow a limit of one game fish.
  Daily catch-and-possession limit is one of
  either arctic char, lake trout, or grayling in
  addition to one broad whitefish.
• No commercial or sport hunting.

CAMPGROUNDS
Camp at identified sites and do not move
rocks. Appropriate camping sites along the
Hornaday River recommended.

HOTELS, MOTELS, & INNS
*(unless otherwise noted, rates are for a
2-person double, high season, in Canadian
dollars)*

Paulatuk Visitors Centre Hotel P.O. Box 52,
Paulatuk, NT X0E 1N0. (867) 580-3051.
paulatuk_hotel@northwestel.net. $360.

TUKTUT NOGAIT

ROSCOE & BROCK RIVERS

The beautiful waterfalls and deep,
narrow canyons of **the Roscoe,** in the
northeast, and **the Brock,** in the mid-
north, are also worth exploring, though
few visitors do, given the increased
logistical challenges of accessing these
areas. Less information is available for these routes. Hiking here
is more challenging than on the
Hornaday because of creek crossings
and uneven ground. On both rivers,
expect Class II and III white water
upstream of unnavigable canyon sections. Note that weather conditions
can delay travel for several days.

Muskoxen sightings are frequent along the lower Thomsen.

▶AULAVIK

NORTHWEST TERRITORIES
ESTABLISHED 1992
12,200 sq km/3,014,686 acres

While the rest of the world marches forward to the drums of progress, Aulavik National Park's spectacular wildlife-rich lowland tundra seems content to remain a timeless Arctic treasure. In this remote park, one can hear the howl of wolves, the *kee-yee-yip* of arctic foxes, the grunt of the muskoxen, and the relentless rush of wind. The tundra of Aulavik is home to 150 species of flowering plants that explode in a kaleidoscope of colour, making it easy to feel as though you have landed in a world totally removed from the one we live in.

In addition to the park's rich biodiversity, the western Arctic lowlands of Aulavik are breathtakingly beautiful, and the park protects over 280 archaeological sites, some of which date back 3,500 years. A visitor with sharp eyes will spot metal knives, tools crafted from bone and antler, and stone points scattered amid the remains of ancient meat caches and tent rings.

The more recent historical drama of the European quest for the Northwest Passage is evoked by the shore cache of the obsessed Capt. Robert M'Clure, whose British naval ship H.M.S. *Investigator* was frozen fast in Mercy Bay in 1851. The desperate crew was finally rescued in 1853, and the icebound vessel became a source of rare wood and metal for the Copper Inuit.

The level of commitment and cost required to access Aulavik prevents much human traffic: The park sees an average of 15 visitors per year—over 80,000 Arctic hectares (197,680 acres) per visitor. Translated as "the place where people travel" in Inuvialuktun, the language of the Inuvialuit, Aulavik is a must for any serious Arctic wilderness lover, despite the challenges of getting there.

How to Get There

Aulavik is one of Canada's most remote parks, and visitors must plan their visit well ahead. Charter a Twin Otter from Inuvik for the four-hour, 750-km (466 mi) flight northeast to the park. There is one stop en route to Aulavik: a refueling at Sachs Harbour (Ikahuak), the

A black-bellied plover

only settlement on Banks Island (pop. approximately 65).

From Inuvik, the only way into Aulavik National Park is by charter aircraft. To get to Inuvik, drive north from Dawson City on the iconic Dempster Highway (670 km/420 miles). There are also daily flights from Edmonton, Alberta, and from the Yukon. There may be opportunities to cost-share air charters from Inuvik—contact the Parks Canada office in Inuvik. There also are licensed outfitters offering trips into Aulavik.

The park is rich in cultural sites and has a long history of people travelling across and through the land. Please keep in mind during your own travels that many of these sites are easy to miss—please camp in recommended areas and do not move rocks or other features at cultural sites/potential cultural sites.

When to Go

Aulavik is best enjoyed at the fleeting height of the high Arctic summer. Paddlers will want to arrive after the river breaks up, usually in mid- to late June, and before the snowmelt ends in mid-July. After this, water levels drop dramatically, leaving the upper Thomsen River a shallow, rocky riffle, and the silty lower reaches become a frustrating maze of shifting sand and mud bars. Visit from late June to mid-July to hit the best paddling, peak flowers, and good bird- and wildlife-watching.

How to Visit

A visit to Aulavik requires detailed advance planning. This is a very isolated high Arctic wilderness and visitors need to be self-sufficient and prepared to meet a large range of obstacles and

AULAVIK

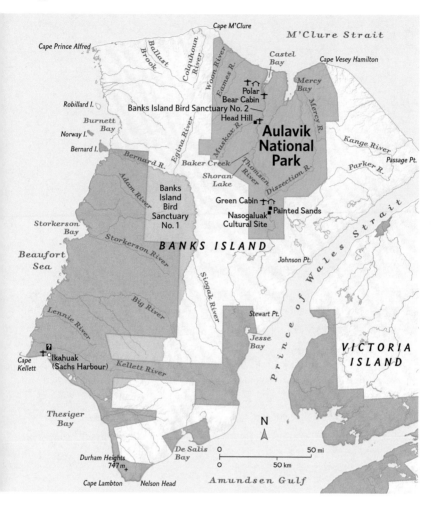

Cape M'Clure

M'CLURE STRAIT

Cape Prince Alfred

Ballast Brook

Colquhoun River

Woon River

Eames R.

Castel Bay

Cape Vesey Hamilton

Polar Bear Cabin

Mercy Bay

Mercy R.

Robillard I.

Banks Island Bird Sanctuary No. 2

Head Hill

Aulavik National Park

Burnett Bay

Norway I.

Egina River

Muskox R.

Kange River

Bernard I.

Bernard R.

Baker Creek

Thomsen River

Passage Pt.

Parker R.

Adam River

Banks Island Bird Sanctuary No. 1

Shoran Lake

Dissection R.

Green Cabin

Painted Sands

Storkerson Bay

Nasogaluak Cultural Site

Beaufort Sea

Storkerson River

BANKS ISLAND

Prince of Wales Strait

Johnson Pt.

Big River

Siogak River

Stewart Pt.

Jesse Bay

VICTORIA ISLAND

Lennie River

Cape Kellett

Ikahuak (Sachs Harbour)

Kellett River

Thesiger Bay

N

Durham Heights 747 m

De Salis Bay

0   50 mi

0   50 km

Cape Lambton   Nelson Head

Amundsen Gulf

complications, some more foreseeable than others.

All visits begin with a park orientation from Parks Canada staff in Inuvik. This one-hour presentation will acquaint you with the remote and sensitive nature of the unusual landscape on northern Banks Island. In a place where average July temperatures rarely exceed 10°C (50°F), you'll need to be prepared for cold weather conditions, and be aware of the risks of hypothermia. Although

temperatures on south-facing, sheltered slopes can reach 25°C (77°F), midsummer snow is still likely. Inland encounters with polar bears are less likely, but grizzly bear encounters are possible. With the changing conditions of glacial ice and the unpredictable bear behaviour observed in recent years, bear spray and approved protocols for travelling in bear country are necessary parts of safe travel in Aulavik. Contact the Parks Canada office in Inuvik for trip planning and logistics information and to learn more about using firearms in the park.

Local wildlife monitors may also be hired from the community of Sachs Harbour. While most visitors to Aulavik canoe or kayak the **Thomsen River,** billed as the world's most northerly navigable waterway, some prefer to ramble across the rolling tundra, an option that affords glimpses of Arctic wildlife from nearly every mountable ridge. Given the expense and travel time of an expedition to Aulavik, most parties wish to spend 10 days to two weeks exploring the park. This is sufficient time to canoe or kayak the entire length of the Thomsen River within the park and have plenty of time for hiking excursions along the way. This is also the minimum time needed to thoroughly explore part of the park on foot from a base camp, or to hike between two of the established airstrips. You need to factor in a couple of days for weather-related delays when you plan your trip.

FLOAT TRIP—THOMSEN RIVER

About 7 to 10 days

Although the park offers rewarding (if somewhat sodden) hiking, Aulavik is best experienced from a kayak or canoe. The entire 150 km (93 mi) from the south boundary to **Castel Bay** is an easy Class I float, with few hazards, save for some visible rocks and secondary channels. The valley is notorious for frigid headwinds howling inland off the ice-covered **M'Clure Strait,** sending whitecaps rolling upstream, so expect some lining and bumping. Many expedition groups prefer collapsible canoes and kayaks to cut down on the size and weight of their cargo, bearing in mind the Twin Otter payload restrictions.

There are four established tundra airstrips and one gravel strip inside the park. Paddlers often put in at **Thom Up** (Upper Thomsen) strip near the park's southern boundary. For shorter trips, or if low water

AULAVIK

A hiker looks over the lower falls of Mercy River.

Arctic wolf at the Thomsen River

An arctic tern nesting

Locoweed (*Oxytropis*)

levels preclude paddling the upper river, a good strip exists at **Green Cabin,** at the confluence of the Thomsen and **Painted Sands Creek.** The forest green plywood building is the only permanent structure near the Thomsen River, and is a popular put-in or pickup location for visiting groups. The ideal, two-week float takes parties from Thom Up or Green Cabin to established landing strips at the **Muskox River** or Castel Bay, where the Thomsen empties its snowmelt into the ice-choked M'Clure Strait. All charter aircraft companies must have a valid business licence to operate in the park.

Upstream of Green Cabin, crystal clear water hurries over a shallow, bouldery bed. A vibrant community of poppies, louseworts, and purple saxifrage dance in the wind on a gently rolling tundra. Plovers, sandpipers, snowy owls, jaegers, and sandhill cranes all nest here, and several active wolf dens have been established near the

AULAVIK NATIONAL PARK
(Parc national Aulavik)

INFORMATION & ACTIVITIES

SEASONS & ACCESSIBILITY
June until mid-August, accessible by airplane. Twenty-four-hour daylight between June and mid-August. Darkness throughout winter makes it difficult to land a plane. Charter air companies must have a valid business licence to operate in the park. Groups must obtain a landing permit and attend an orientation at the Parks Canada office.

HEADQUARTERS
Western Arctic Field Unit P.O. Box 1840, Inuvik, NT X0E 0T0. Phone (867) 777-8800. www.parks canada .gc.ca/aulavik.

ENTRANCE FEES
Backcountry camping fees $25 per person per day, $147 per person per year. Fishing permits $10 per person per day, $34 per person per year.

PETS
None permitted.

ACCESSIBLE SERVICES
None.

THINGS TO DO
Paddle down the **Thomsen River.** Hiking terrain throughout the park.

Visit pre-Dorset archaeological sites near **Shoran Lake.**

View Peary caribou, muskoxen, arctic foxes, arctic wolves, ermines, arctic hares, and both brown and collared lemmings. Marine mammals along the north coast include polar bears, ringed seals, bearded seals, beluga whales, and bowhead whales. Visit parkscanada.gc.ca/aulavik for information on licensed operators.

SPECIAL ADVISORIES
- Note daily fish catch-and-possession limit of one arctic char, one lake trout, and one grayling.
- Fires not permitted in the park.
- Be aware that many cultural sites do not always look like cultural sites.
- Camp at identified sites and do not move rocks.

CAMPGROUNDS
There are no designated campgrounds. Camping permitted everywhere in the park except in or around archaeological sites.

HOTELS, MOTELS, & INNS
A variety of accommodations is available in Inuvik; rates may vary according to season. For information about accommodations and things to do in Inuvik, go to www.destinationinuvik.com.

AULAVIK

riverbanks. Overlooking the river, *Xanthoria*-encrusted stone cairns mark archaeological sites, which attest to centuries of human activity in the region.

The **lower Thomsen** boasts rugged topography, with rocky outcrops and steep banks. Aulavik's unique microclimate produces some of the most diverse and dense Arctic flower growth imaginable. The river banks and slopes support nesting peregrines and rough-legged hawks, and are also home to fox dens. Explore the region around the Muskox and Thomsen Rivers, looking for rare Arctic plants like the giant mastodon flower while watching for the muskoxen to make their appearance. Although the lower river becomes muddier, the hiking becomes more interesting, and muskoxen sightings are virtually guaranteed. Aulavik boasts the highest density of these Ice Age mammals on the planet.

An elder shares stories at Ivvavik National Park.

Aerial view of the Firth River

▶IVVAVIK

YUKON
ESTABLISHED 1984
9,750 sq km/2,409,277 acres

High in the northwest corner of Yukon, stunted spruce trees pitch from the permafrost at wild angles. Arctic willow grows like a carpet low on the ground, where it's safe from the wind and close to sunlight-warmed soil. The Firth, Canada's oldest flowing river, cuts a turquoise trail through the rolling, unglaciated hills of the British Mountains.

A visit to Ivvavik National Park gives one a special sort of bragging right—this site sees an average of only 200 visitors yearly. Its Arctic location means it can be tough to access, but the pristine beauty of the place makes it well worth the challenge. Ivvavik (meaning "nursery" or "birthplace" in Inuvialuktun) was the first Canadian national park created as the result of an indigenous land claim settlement. One of the many provisions of the 1984

Inuvialuit Final Agreement (a constitutionally protected legal agreement that protects and preserves Inuvialuit culture in the North) established Ivvavik on the Yukon North Slope, which some of the Porcupine caribou herd use as calving grounds, while other parts of the herd continue each year to coastal calving grounds in Alaska.

Despite the rugged, isolated nature of the land here, human presence stretches back thousands of years. Radiocarbon-dated bison bones, found along the frigid Firth River, bear butchering marks that speak to hunting activity more than 10,000 years ago.

The remnants of tools—both primitive and advanced—are found in Ivvavik today. The park is more than a collection of ancient artifacts; it is a living cultural landscape on which Inuvialuit continue traditional practices, including subsistence harvesting, all of which are provided for in the land claim.

Throughout the park, you'll find evidence of stone and sod remains of Dorset, Thule, Eskimo, and Inuit habitation, tools used by Paleo-Arctic communities, and old fishing sites along the shores of the Firth.

Evidence of European occupation also exists in the form of fur-trading posts at Qikiqtaruk Herschel Island Territorial Park, artifacts from the mini gold rush at Sheep Creek in the 1970s, and traces of the Cold War— the remnants of one of America's Distant Early Warning Line stations at Komakuk Beach and Stokes Point.

How to Get There

From Inuvik, the only way into the park is by charter aircraft. To get to Inuvik, drive north from Dawson City on the iconic Dempster Highway (670 km/420 miles). There are also daily flights from Edmonton, Alberta, and from the Yukon.

When to Go

Winter conditions can occur from mid-September to mid-May. Summer is the best time to visit. Temperatures hover around 14°C (57°F) and the sun lasts 24 hours.

How to Visit

Enter Ivvavik and stay at the base camp at Imniarvik with Parks

Canada. If you have a couple of weeks, book a Firth River rafting trip with one of the licensed operators. The more adventurous can plan their own overnight adventures or take a day trip to Babbage Falls.

IMNIARVIK (SHEEP CREEK) BASE CAMP TRIP
17 km/11 mi; 5 days

Until 1986, a placer gold mine operated on **Sheep Creek.** Today, where this winding waterway drains into the **Firth River,** you'll find Imniarvik base camp. The only Parks Canada base camp facility in the park, the site boasts a shower and washroom. The facility is used for youth camps, research and monitoring, and for visitors on Parks Canada trips, such as this one. "Imniarvik" is the traditional Inuvialuktun name for the area, meaning "where the sheep are." Dall sheep are frequently seen on the slopes above the camp.

While there are no marked paths

IVVAVIK

King eider (*Somateria spectabilis*)

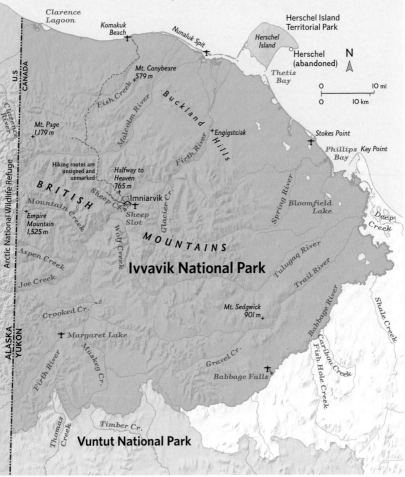

here, it is a hiker's paradise. Visitors on base camp trips can choose from an assortment of ridges and hikes to explore under the midnight sun. Routes with names like **Halfway to Heaven, Inspiration Point, Dragons Ridge,** and **Dragons Tor** give you a sense of the possibilities. If you're feeling less adventurous, take a stroll along the nearby Firth River and check out some of the Class V rapids at **Sheep Slot**—they contribute to the Firth River's reputation as a life list river for paddling fanatics. Keep an eye out for Dolly Varden char and arctic grayling in the crystal clear pool.

BABBAGE FALLS TRIP

5-km/3-mi hike; 6 hours

Bush planes, such as a Twin Otter on tundra tires, are best suited to landings at most of the wilderness airstrips in Ivvavik. Charter airline companies may have busy

Beluga whales in Ivvavik National Park

schedules, so contact them early in your planning. Your chosen company must have a business licence with Parks Canada, and your group will require a landing permit. All visitors must register with Parks Canada and attend an orientation before their trip.

Be sure to give yourself a two-day buffer when arranging transportation in and out of Inuvik. Weather in the Arctic can delay departures, particularly at **Babbage Falls,** where the site's proximity to the Beaufort Sea can make for foggy and windy conditions. Flying into the park, you'll pass over the **Mackenzie Delta,** one of the world's great river deltas, made up of a spectacular complex of lakes and streams that flow north into the Arctic Ocean. Watch for the transition from pancake-flat delta to the rounded, emerald peaks of the **British Mountains.** This range makes up two-thirds of the park's total area and is typical of Ivvavik's nonglaciated landscape. Thirty thousand years ago, a wide land bridge (called

Beringia) stretched west to Alaska and Siberia. The unique landscape visitors experience in Ivvavik is one of the oldest in the world, as it was unaffected by Ice Age glaciation.

The coast of the Beaufort, frozen eight months of the year, is fringed with ice. Babbage Falls is one of a number of places to spot *aufeis,* thick sheets of ice that form when underground springs freeze, often over existing river ice, and over such an expanse (several square kilometres) that these sheets frequently do not melt before winter weather begins freezing them again.

From the airstrip, the hike to Babbage Falls descends 420 m (1,380 ft) over about 5 km (3 mi) and generally takes two to three hours. The terrain here is dry tundra until you reach the base of the falls, where small peat hummocks crop up. Beside the slopes alongside the Babbage River, you can find the worn trail made by generations of grizzly bears. The short, sparse vegetation makes for easy trailblazing.

IVVAVIK

Top: A snowy owl Middle: Arctic willow Bottom: A walrus

FIRTH RIVER RAFTING TRIP

130 km/81 mi; 13 days

More than half of Ivvavik's visitors come to raft the **Firth River**—a stunning Class IV waterway with temperatures as low as minus 7°C (19°F). Because of this, private groups must be able to deal with emergencies and self-rescue in a remote Arctic setting. Those who are not so well equipped should look into booking a guided trip with a licensed outfitter.

The rafting season is late June to early August. Charters drop off at **Margaret Lake,** at the southwest corner of Ivvavik, close to the Alaska border, where rafters put in to begin the journey to **Nunaluk Spit** on the Arctic Ocean, a distance of 130 km (80 mi).

From here, north is the only direction you can go. The wide river valley at Margaret Lake narrows near **Joe Creek,** speeding up to Class II and III rapids as it moves toward the boulder gardens of **Sheep Slot.** Before **Engigstciak,** narrow canyons (10 m/ 33 ft across in some places) lead the way to Class IV rapids.

For those who still have energy (or adrenalin) at the end of the day, there are a number of hikes along the way. An 11-km (7 mi) loop at Margaret Lake summits a series of three peaks, offering views of the **Firth River Valley** and the **aufeis field** to the south and north. The hike at **Crooked Creek** is an easy 6-km (4 mi) trek to a scenic ridge overlooking the Firth River. Watch for hummocks and tussocks as you hike—it's easy to twist an ankle on their shaggy heads.

During the final leg of the trip, the river enters the coastal plain and mingles with sandbars to form a long delta. **Nunaluk Lagoon** is the take-out location for the trip. In the late summer months, it's one of many coastal lagoons that host moulting sea ducks like the white-winged scoter and common eider. A 100-m-wide (328 ft) band of warm water near the shore here also acts as a major migration corridor for the least and arctic cisco of the Mackenzie River. Newborn caribou and cows, seals, and, rarely, polar bears can be seen from the spit.

IVVAVIK NATIONAL PARK
(Parc national Ivvavik)

INFORMATION & ACTIVITIES

HEADQUARTERS
Western Arctic Field Unit P.O. Box 1840, Inuvik, NT X0E 0T0. Phone (867) 777-8800. Inuvik.info@pc.gc.ca; www.parkscanada.gc.ca/ivvavik.

SEASONS & ACCESSIBILITY
Charter aircraft services from Inuvik, 200 km (124 mi) east of the park, to **Margaret Lake, Sheep Creek, Stokes Point, Nunaluk Spit,** and **Komakuk Beach.** A commercial company must have a business licence to land in the park. All groups are required to have a landing permit and must attend an orientation before their trip. Landing strips are not maintained. Cost-sharing opportunities may be available—contact the Parks Canada office (see above). Winter travel recommended in March and April.

ENTRANCE FEES
Backcountry camping fees $25 per person per day, $147 per person per year. Fishing permits $10 per day, $34 per year.

PETS
Pets permitted; must be under physical control at all times.

ACCESSIBLE SERVICES
None.

THINGS TO DO
Rafting on the **Firth River** (Class IV wilderness). Limited rescue assistance. Hiking along the mountain ranges to coastal lowlands. Twenty-four-hour daylight in summer months.

Wildlife viewing of Porcupine caribou migration between June and early July from central Yukon to calving grounds along the coast. Fishing in early June to August for Dolly Varden char. Fishing catch-and-possession limits are one Dolly Varden char with an aggregate of three game fish total. Permit required.

Hiking: No marked hiking trails means the park is yours to explore. Hikers should have a topographic map or can join a Parks Canada base camp trip. Details at www.parkscanada.gc.ca/ivvavik. Air access points at Sheep Creek, Margaret Lake, Komakuk Beach, Babbage Falls, and Stokes Point.

Aircraft charter companies such as Aklak Air, (867) 777-3555, www.aklakair.ca, must have valid national parks business licence to operate in the park. Winter access via aircraft equipped with skis or by snow machine as far as park boundary. More information available at the Parks Canada office in Inuvik.

SPECIAL ADVISORIES
- No facilities, services, established trails, or campgrounds in the park. Visitors must be entirely self-sufficient.
- Flash flooding potential hazard.
- Ivvavik is home to grizzly bears and, on the coast, the occasional polar bear. All necessary precautions should be followed. Contact Parks Canada for more information on travelling in bear country.

CAMPGROUNDS
Camping permitted throughout the park except at archaeological sites. Recommended sites included in Firth River map and guide available at Parks Canada office. Wind-resistant tents recommended. Campfires forbidden. Camp stoves and bottled fuel must be used.

HOTELS, MOTELS, & INNS
(unless otherwise noted, rates are for a 2-person double, high season, in Canadian dollars)

Outside the park:
Inuvik, NT X0E 0T0:
Nova Inn Inuvik Box 3169, 300 Mackenzie Rd. (866) 374-6682. inuvik@novahotels.ca; www.novainninuvik.ca. $159–$179.

A variety of accommodations are available in Inuvik: Rates may vary according to season. Learn about where to stay and all the things to do in Inuvik at www.destinationinuvik.com.

IVVAVIK

View of ice floes in Discovery Harbour from Fort Conger

▶ QUTTINIRPAAQ ᖁᑦᑎᓂᕐᐹᖅ

NUNAVUT
ESTABLISHED 1988
37,775 sq km/9,334,406 acres

Quttinirpaaq National Park is a sprawling, expansive high Arctic park situated at the northern end of Ellesmere Island, the last piece of land before Canada gives way to the Arctic Ocean. Visitors to Quttinirpaaq will encounter wildlife that has almost certainly never laid eye on humans, including arctic wolves, Peary caribou, muskoxen, and arctic hares. In the brilliance of a 24-hour sunlit day, visitors can trek through a landscape sculpted by glaciers.

Quttinirpaaq (pronounced koo-tin-ear-paak) refers to a "place at the top of the world" in Inuktitut. Originally created as Ellesmere Island National Park Reserve in 1988, this expanse of land became Quttinirpaaq National Park in 2001 under the Nunavut Land Claim Agreement. It is the second largest national park in Canada, and is also the most northerly. It is only 800 km (497 mi) from the North

Pole and is the last stop on land for adventurers headed there.

Visitors to the North Pole begin their journey at Ward Hunt Island, which is also a part of this vast park. Before they step off this island and out of the park, adventurers must be utterly self-sufficient and skilled in wilderness travel and survival, because designated trails do not exist. Rescue capabilities are limited and may take several days. Pickup must be arranged in advance with the air company that visitors use to start their North Pole journey.

Visitors who come to Quttinirpaaq to hike, ski, mountain climb, or mount expeditions across the ice caps or glaciers in the park must have and be able to read topographical maps, as hiking in this backcountry does not involve groomed trails but, instead, suggested routes. Quttinirpaaq is a land of contrasts. It's home to the highest peak in eastern North America—Barbeau Peak. It has an ice cap a kilometre (0.6 mi) thick, but also shelters a very productive thermal Arctic oasis at Lake Hazen, which at 70 km long and 10 km wide (43 mi by 6 mi) is one of the largest and deepest lakes in the circumpolar world. Quttinirpaaq also contains some geological features that suggest that perhaps this part of the world was not always situated so far north.

Inside the park, visitors can hike various loops, or ski and hike between Lake Hazen and Tanquary Fjord. Accompanied by Parks Canada staff, visitors can explore the historic base camp at Fort Conger, site of American Robert Peary's North Pole expeditions. From Fort Conger on a clear day, you can see Greenland 20 km (12 mi) away.

In summer, temperatures can reach 23°C (73°F) at Lake Hazen, making it warmer than Nunavut's capital of Iqaluit 2,000 km (1,240 mi) to the south. However, weather is always unpredictable and any visit demands advance planning and preparation.

How to Get There

Get to Iqaluit daily by air from Ottawa or three times weekly from Montreal. There are also flights to Iqaluit from Yellowknife. The two airlines that fly to Iqaluit are First Air and Canadian North. Upon reaching Iqaluit, take a First Air flight to Resolute.

Quttinirpaaq is 800 km (497 mi) northeast from the community of Resolute, which is the last leg of the journey you can make via scheduled flights. Beyond Resolute, Kenn Borek's chartered aircraft is the only option available. These 10-seat charter Twin Otters are the workhorses of the high Arctic.

The easiest way to access the park is to purchase a seat on Parks Canada's charter flight. Alternatively, you can book a private charter. Charter costs vary from year to year, depending on the cost of fuel. In 2016, a return flight to Tanquary Fjord for 10 passengers and their gear cost $26,000 to charter. To stay any length of time, two return flights are needed. Contact park staff for assistance.

QUTTINIRPAAQ

Arctic hare

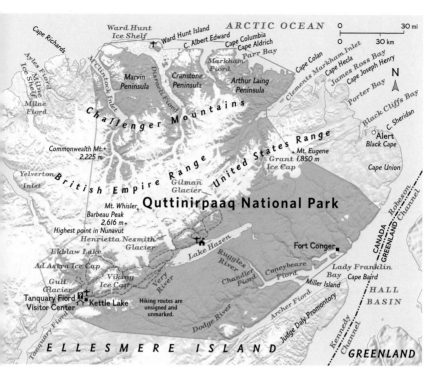

When to Go

Park staff spend the spring and summer in Quttinirpaaq, usually from mid-May until about mid-August. It is not recommended that visitors venture into the park when staff are not there, as this is an extremely isolated and remote location. May is still snowy and cold, although 24 hours of bright sun illuminates any adventure. With thousands of square kilometres of glaciers and skiable terrain, the opportunities for ski touring for the experienced visitor in Quttinirpaaq are almost endless.

Mid-June until mid-August is the best time for hiking in the park. Hikers can explore the park from drop-off points at Tanquary Fjord or Lake Hazen, but should be mindful that in such a remote high Arctic location, any sort of weather is possible, even in summer. From September to March even charter flights to the park are not possible, as pilots won't fly into the park during these cold, dark months.

How to Visit

Most visitors travel in guided groups (contact Parks Canada's partner Black Feather: The Wilderness Adventure Company), plan one- or two-week excursions, and take advantage of shared flights in and out of the park. Each year Parks Canada charters a Twin Otter from Resolute to Tanquary and sells individual seats ($8,000 in 2016).

Visitors alone or in guided groups must arrange mandatory registration and orientation in advance of their arrival in the park. This will ensure that Quttinirpaaq park staff are available at Tanquary as visitors arrive and will be there for their debrief at the end of their journey. Visitors must be self-sufficient, and bring their own gear, tents, clothing, stoves, fuel, and food. It's a good idea to pack more supplies than you think you'll need, in case weather-related delays extend your trip.

Between 1992 and 2010 expedition cruise ships visited the park almost every year for either day or multiday visits to Tanquary Fjord, and occasionally to Fort Conger. However, due to changes in marine shipping laws, icebreaker-class ships using heavy oil can no longer ply high Arctic or Antarctic waters, and as of this writing, it is unknown whether expedition cruises to Quttinirpaaq will resume. The result is that increasingly the park is accessible only to the hardiest of adventurers.

TANQUARY FJORD

At Tanquary Fjord, visitors can see a small **museum** with exhibits on the Cold War–era Defence Research Board's influence in the area, prior to the park's establishment. Military interest in the North was high during the height of the Cold War, and the displays illustrate Canada's response to the tensions. The park was also the site of committed academic research: In 1957–1958, which was an International Polar Year, McGill University students wintered here while they conducted extensive scientific research.

Travel in Quttinirpaaq will introduce you to the remains of an ancient culture predating the modern Inuit: The Paleo-Eskimo (Independence I and Independence II cultures) lived in what is now the national park 4,500 years ago. Evidence of their inhabitation can be found in various locations. Park staff can educate you further on the resilient and adaptive people who called this land home.

ARCTIC LIFE CYCLES

Because the park is in the extreme high Arctic, the landscape is unlike anything most visitors will ever have seen. Vegetation is sparse across most of the landscape, though it is lush in a few locations, such as

QUTTINIRPAAQ

Camping in one of the park valleys in Quttinirpaaq National Park

QUTTINIRPAAQ NATIONAL PARK
(Parc national Quttinirpaaq ᖁᑦᑎᓂᖅᐸᖅ ᒥᖕᒍᑎᕆᖅᓯᕝ ᓄᓇᑕᒥ)

INFORMATION & ACTIVITIES

VISITOR CENTRE
Contact the Parks Canada office for mandatory registration and orientation. Phone (867) 473-2500.

SEASONS & ACCESSIBILITY
Park open year-round; summer season lasts late May to late August. Notify Parks Canada about upcoming trip and upon arrival. Park accessible by charter aircraft from Resolute Bay or Grise Fjord. Kenn Borek Air provides Twin Otter aircraft. Call (867) 252-3845.

HEADQUARTERS
P.O. Box 278, Iqaluit, NU X0A 0H0. Phone (867) 975-4673 or (844) 524-5293 (toll free). www.parkscanada.gc.ca/quttinirpaaq.

ENTRANCE FEES
Day use: $12 per person per day for commercial groups. $25 per person per day or $147 per person per year for backcountry excursions and camping. Check parkscanada.gc.ca/quttinirpaaq for up-to-date fees.

PETS
None permitted.

ACCESSIBLE SERVICES
None.

THINGS TO DO
Hike in **Lake Hazen** and **Tanquary Fjord** in the summer. Take an expedition to the North Pole starting on **Ward Hunt Island** along the northern coast. Guided historic tour of **Fort Conger** by special permission. Ski-touring or ski-mountaineering on the ice cap and glaciers in the spring. If accessing the North Pole from parklands, inform park staff at Iqaluit headquarters.

SPECIAL ADVISORIES
• Contact Parks Canada in advance for pre-trip information, to register, and to book the mandatory orientation. During orientation, you must provide park staff with a detailed itinerary, including side trips.
• Weather may delay flights to the North.
• Allow for scheduling flexibility.
• Practise proper food management when camping to avoid problems with wildlife.
• Be able to recognize and prevent the onset of hypothermia.
• When crossing glaciers, travel with

Lake Hazen. The life cycle of organisms seems to operate in slow motion here: An array of wildflowers and other plants take years to produce seeds, though in the meantime they support a range of herbivores that roam the area. Insects like the woolly bear caterpillar also may take up to 14 years to mature from egg to butterfly.

Migrating birds from Africa, Europe, and the southern tip of South America come to the area to nest and raise their young. Muskoxen, the Peary caribou, arctic wolves, and arctic hares remain in Quttinirpaaq year-round and raise their young during the brief, bright summer months. The ice cap that covers much of the park results in the creation of many glaciers; the peaks seen barely poking through this ice are called *nunataks,* which is a Greenlandic word for a ridge or a peak surrounded by ice. **Barbeau Peak** is the highest of these. Guided or very experienced independent visitors can ski and climb Barbeau Peak.

At the north end of the park, near **Ward Hunt Island,** the last fragments of 300,000-year-old ice shelves remain. Until recently, the **Ward Hunt Ice Shelf** acted as a dam at the mouth of the **Disraeli Fjord,** containing a giant epishelf lake. A crack began to develop in the ice shelf, and in 2002 the lake drained into the Arctic Ocean.

ropes. Individuals should be experienced in crevasse rescue.

- When hiking, avoid rock walls and cliffs with bare, freshly broken rock. Be particularly careful when it is raining and during the spring and fall.
- Visitors should be experienced in recognizing avalanche hazards, have good route-finding skills, and be skilled in self-rescue techniques.
- Water should be fine-filtered and treated or boiled before drinking.
- Be cautious on riverbanks when crossing rivers and streams. Cross major waterways early in the day (2 a.m.–7 a.m. if possible, and if water levels are high, wait for them to drop).
- Emergency radios provided in the park buildings at Tanquary Fjord and Lake Hazen. In case of emergency call dispatch line (780) 852-3100.

CAMPGROUNDS

No designated campgrounds. Select campsites in durable locations where signs of your occupation will be minimized, such as areas with little or no vegetation. Avoid camping in steep terrain or near potential wildlife habitat, such as sedge meadows. Do not dig trenches around tents or build rock windbreaks.

HOTELS, MOTELS, & INNS

(unless otherwise noted, rates are for a 1-person, high season, in Canadian dollars; all hotels offer a shuttle to and from the airport.

Outside the park:
Grise Fjord, NU X0A 0J0:
Grise Fjord Lodge P.O. Box 11. (867) 980-9135. $210 per person.

There is no restaurant in Grise Fjord and lodge accommodations are rudimentary. It is suggested you bring a sleeping bag.

Resolute, NU X0A 0V0:
The Qausuittuq Inn P.O. Box 270. (867) 252-3900. www.resolutebay.com. Restaurant. $225.
South Camp Inn P.O. Box 300. (867) 252-3737. www.southcampinn.com. $275 per person.

OUTFITTERS

Contact Parks Canada at (867) 975-4675 or via email at nunavut.info@pc.gc.ca for an up-to-date list of licensed outfitters and guides.

Visit Nunavut Tourism at http://nunavut tourism.com for additional information.

QUTTINIRPAAQ

A polar bear and cub

Moonrise over snow-blanketed mountains

▶ SIRMILIK ᓯᕐᒥᓕᒃ

NUNAVUT
ESTABLISHED 1999
22,200 sq km/5,485,739 acres

Sirmilik National Park is home not only to breathtaking views of the sea, mountains, and broad valley vistas, but also to an amazing variety of marine and avian wildlife. One of Canada's most accessible high Arctic parks, Sirmilik is truly a jewel in Canada's celebrated national parks network. Bylot Island offers stunning sights: navy blue waters setting off glistening white glaciers and icebergs that rise out of them, tinged with turquoise. Visitors may catch sight of some of the hundreds of narwhals and seals that swim in the waters here.

For thousands of years, right up to the present, the rich diversity of Arctic wildlife in the park supported the nomadic Inuit people. For centuries, they centred their existence around the demands of the land and its weather: Their survival depended on it. When the wind blew and the temperature plummeted, they stopped and found shelter, and continued only when the weather eased. Their culture and history is still well documented today for visitors to Sirmilik National Park.

Sirmilik, pronounced siir-mi-lick, means "place of glaciers" in Inuktitut. The park covers much of the north tip of Baffin Island,

and is bordered by the communities of Arctic Bay and Pond Inlet. Established as a national park as the result of the Nunavut Land Claim Agreement in February 2001, Sirmilik is still a fairly unknown expanse of land. The park encompasses the Bylot Island Bird Sanctuary, jointly managed by Parks Canada and the Canadian Wildlife Service, where greater snow goose research has been conducted for more than three decades. Bylot Island is the nesting site for more than 40 species of migratory birds.

How to Get There

From Iqaluit, travel to Pond Inlet (one of the two gateway communities into Sirmilik National Park) is possible in six or seven days with either First Air or Canadian Northern airlines. First Air also offers flights that will take you to the other, smaller gateway community of Arctic Bay. Air travel between Arctic Bay and Pond Inlet is possible only via Iqaluit, although spring travel by snow machine and summer travel by boat can also get you from one to the other.

From Pond Inlet or Arctic Bay, hire a snow machine for transport, or engage an outfitter or guide to lead you into Sirmilik National Park, preferably in spring when the ice is still safe to traverse. You can also ski across the ice of Eclipse Sound—approximately 25 km (16 mi) from Pond Inlet—in spring to get to the park. Floe edge tours from the sea ice are also available in the spring.

If travelling with the comfort of modern conveniences appeals to you, you can visit the park in summer as a passenger on one of the many expedition cruise ships that spend up to two days sailing the sounds and inlets around Sirmilik. Depending on the itinerary of the cruises, passengers may be able to go ashore for some exploration within the park. In summer, you can also hire a kayak guide to lead you on a trip into the waters of the park.

When to Go

Sirmilik is in the high Arctic wilderness, so the best time to go is in spring or summer, which in this region means May through September when the sun is shining for the better part of 24 hours. July is ice-breakup month and the park is not accessible, as the ice will no longer support ski or snow-machine travel. Boats and ships can't travel the waters around this time either, because of the hazards posed by the breaking ice. August to mid-September is the best season for boating and hiking in the park. From late September to late March, Sirmilik's weather turns harsh and stormy. The dark season, during which the sun is hardly in evidence at all, lasts for two solid months around the time of the winter solstice.

How to Visit

Sirmilik offers a variety of activities for hardy travellers eager to learn about the park's geology and wildlife. If you're willing to put forth some effort, you can get a close-up look at glaciers, icebergs, and the marine life residing off the floe edge. The park's population of Arctic seabirds make it a wonderful destination for the avid bird-watcher. If you're feeling adventurous, you can dive under the sea ice for intimate encounters with the marine life living in the waters, including narwhals and beluga whales and walruses. Summer is the best time to meet Inuit residents and learn about their culture, ancient and modern. Watch craftsmen at work, and take in Inuit art and performances in either Pond Inlet or Arctic Bay.

SIRMILIK

To ensure your safety on kayak, boat, ski, or hiking expeditions, rely on the skills of outfitters and guides to arrange your visit into the park. As in all national parks in Nunavut, Sirmilik expeditions are backcountry adventures and are generally not suitable excursions for small children or elderly travellers. As this is still a relatively new park, it doesn't yet have established routes for you to follow through the park. However, by the same token, Sirmilik offers you the opportunity to blaze your own trails, depending on what you wish to see and how skilled a hiker you are. Make sure you bring a good camera with you: The beauty and awesome vastness of Sirmilik National Park afford visitors a wealth of photo opportunities.

HIKING & PADDLING

One of the most frequently hiked areas of the park is the **Mala River Valley** on the **Borden Peninsula.** Some camping and hiking around **Pond Inlet** is possible, though these excursions won't necessarily take you into the park. Exploring the area around Pond Inlet will give you the opportunity to examine the remnants of sod huts built in past centuries by the North Baffin Inuit, which are a testament to their resilient culture.

Outfitters will take you into Sirmilik to explore the cultural sites protected within the park's boundaries. A single row of 10 sod houses built at the foot of the mountains along the north coast of Borden Peninsula is one of the most important and evocative cultural

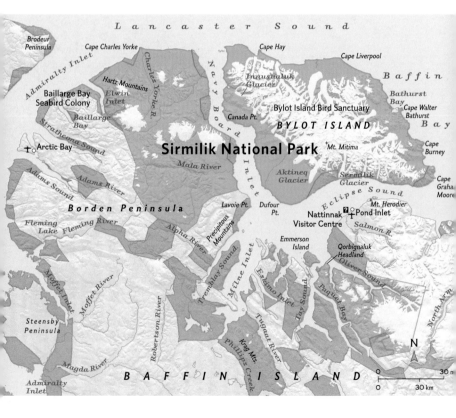

Black-legged kittiwake gull rookery on a cliff

sites along this coast. These durable Thule-era houses are constructed of stone, whalebone, and sod.

BYLOT ISLAND & BORDEN PENINSULA

Guided kayak trips of various lengths and to various parts of the park can be arranged. Floe-edge excursions near **Bylot Island** will give you close-up encounters with marine mammals and can be booked in the spring. You can also arrange to partake in diving expeditions, guided by outfitters and based out of **Arctic Bay.** Only the most experienced skiers and climbers should attempt spring glacier crossings on Bylot Island.

Many of Bylot Island's 16 alpine glaciers are visible from the waters of **Eclipse Sound** and from **Navy Board Inlet.** Oliver Sound's deep waters, glaciers, and sheer cliffs shelter a rich variety of sea life from the inclement weather of North Baffin Island. The sprawling Borden Peninsula is also within park boundaries. Partially covered with glaciers, its tortuous geo-

logical formations are composed of red sandstone that's layered, striped, and folded with shades of ochre and magenta. These cliffs are home to thousands of nesting seabirds. Colonies of murres, kittiwakes, and fulmars come here to prey on fish from Lancaster Sound to feed their nestlings. The **Baillarge Bay bird sanctuary,** a small crescent of cliffs that is habitat for seabirds, is also protected as part of the park.

Sirmilik National Park's high concentration of seabirds and other Arctic life like narwhals, seals, and polar bears is a result of the rich, highly productive waters of **Lancaster Sound,** just north of Bylot Island and the Borden Peninsula. The waters of the sound are capable of supporting a hugely diverse array of life, and Parks Canada is studying the feasibility of creating a national marine protected area in Lancaster Sound to extend the park's protection to this rare Arctic marine ecosystem.

There's a healthy polar bear population in this park, especially along the Lancaster Sound area, so if you're planning to traverse parts of the

SIRMILIK

SIRMILIK NATIONAL PARK
(Parc national Sirmilik ᓯᕐᒥᓕᒃ ᒥᕐᖑᐃᓯᕐᕕᒃ ᓄᓇᖓᑦ)

INFORMATION & ACTIVITIES

VISITOR CENTRE
Nattinnak Visitor Centre Phone (867) 899-8225. **Sirmilik Park Office** Phone (867) 899-8092

SEASONS & ACCESSIBILITY
Park office open year-round. The park is inaccessible during ice breakup in mid-June to late July and when the ice freezes in mid-October to early November. Travel to the park is not advisable November to February. Access is by boat from late July to September or by snow machine from late September to early July from **Pond Inlet** or **Arctic Bay.** Contact Nattinnak Visitor Centre to make arrangements with outfitters. Endless daylight May–August; no daylight in December and January. Late March–early June is the best time of year for winter activities.

HEADQUARTERS
P.O. Box 300, Pond Inlet, NU X0A 0S0. Phone (867) 899-8092. www.parks canada.gc.ca/sirmilik.

ENTRANCE FEES
The daily backcountry excursion fee per person is $25, or $147 for a season's pass. For large commercial groups the fee is $12 per person for short stays on shore (such as a cruise ship visit). Check www .parkscanada.gc.ca for up-to-date fees.

PETS
Pets are not recommended as they can attract polar bears. If a pet is taken into the park it must be leashed at all times.

ACCESSIBLE SERVICES
None.

THINGS TO DO
Skiing, mountaineering, and winter camping. Windslab is the common form of snow; deep powder rare. In late July to early September, sea kayaking and boating in **Oliver Sound** south of Pond Inlet; **Lancaster Sound** between Devon Island and Sirmilik; **Eclipse Sound** waterway to Bylot Island, **Navy Board Inlet,** and **Borden Peninsula.**

SPECIAL ADVISORIES
• Before visiting, contact the park to book an appointment for mandatory registration and pre-trip orientation, during which you will need to provide park staff with a detailed itinerary of your planned trip and arrange a post-trip deregistration.
• Weather may delay flights to the North.
• Allow for flexibility in scheduling.

Iceberg on Pond Inlet dwarfs human visitor.

landscape on foot, it is very advisable to travel with a qualified guide who knows the region and can provide you the necessary gear for a safe trek.

INUIT COMMUNITIES

Hotel accommodations are available in the local communities; you can also arrange a home stay with an Inuit family. If you'd rather brave the elements, Arctic camping is possible at **Salmon River** just outside Pond Inlet. If you do plan to camp

- Talk to park staff to identify areas with thinner ice. Sea ice close to river mouths is generally thin. Do not approach areas with deep snow and water on top, as this indicates open water beneath. Avoid travelling through bays and inlets with narrow channels, as they often have strong currents in spring.
- Boaters should be prepared for strong winds, floating ice, and strong tides.
- No campfires allowed. Campers are advised to bring white gas and portable stoves.
- Visitors must be prepared for white-outs, avalanches, and extreme weather. Travel in groups of at least four is advised. Individuals must have training in glacier travel and crevasse rescue.
- Avoid polar bears, which are most active along the coast of the Borden Peninsula and along the north, west, and east coasts of Bylot Island. Avoid females and cubs in March and April and from July to October.

CAMPGROUNDS

No designated campgrounds. Select campsites in durable locations where signs of your occupation will be minimized. Avoid camping in steep terrain or near potential wildlife habitat, such as sedge meadows. Do not dig trenches around tents or build rock windbreaks. Camping near floe edge can be dangerous.

OUTFITTERS

Contact Parks Canada, (867) 975-4675 or nunavut.info@pc.gc.ca for an up-to-date list of licensed outfitters and guides.

HOTELS, MOTELS, & INNS
(unless otherwise noted, rates are for a 2-person double, high season, in Canadian dollars)

Pond Inlet, NU X0A 0S0:
Sauniq Hotel P.O. Box 370. www.pond inlethotel.com. (867) 899-6500. $225 per person.

Arctic Bay, NU X0A 0A0:
Tangmaarvik Inn P.O. Box 130. (867) 439-8005. $250 per person. Restaurant. Breakfast, 6–9 a.m. $40. Lunch, 12–1 p.m. $50. Dinner, 6–7 p.m. $60. In nearby Pond Inlet there is one fast-food restaurant.

Visit Nunavut Tourism at nunavuttour ism.com for additional information on accommodations and activities.

SIRMILIK

in Sirmilik, be sure to confirm with an outfitter what equipment and supplies you should bring with you. If you're eager to immerse yourself in local culture, some outfitters can arrange a visit with the Inuit at their outpost camps. This may give you a chance for a taste of local cuisine, too. Recently harvested local food is sometimes offered as part of this experience. Near the communities of Arctic Bay and Pond Inlet, there are opportunities to fish for arctic char or to pick berries in the late summer.

Community visitor centres provide a rich offering of local art, including hand carvings, dolls (Pond Inlet is known for dolls that reflect the culture and customs), fabric painting, hats, jewellery, and items crafted from narwhal tusks. These unique pieces are also available for purchase at the local co-op store. This is a wonderful opportunity to come away from your trip with a locally made item that evokes the culture and traditions of the people of Sirmilik.

▶ NATIONAL MARINE CONSERVATION AREA (PROPOSED)

LANCASTER SOUND
NUNAVUT

The Northwest Passage may have been a starvation coast for dozens of 19th-century explorers, but its eastern entrance is a sea of plenty for seals, walruses, and whales such as narwhals, belugas, and bowheads. Christened Lancaster Sound by explorer William Baffin in 1616, it is also one of the great ornithological wonders of the world. More than 700,000 breeding pairs of seabirds lay their eggs in crevices and on the ledges of the cliffs that border the Sound. And every spring, a million dovekies stop here to fatten up on the way to their summer haunts in northwest Greenland.

Stopping for a close-up view

Lancaster Sound is poised to become part of the largest protected marine area in Canada. About twice the size of Lake Erie, it is 400 km (230 mi) long by as much as 200 km (120 mi) wide.

High tides and strong currents combine to make Lancaster Sound rich for birds and marine mammals. The current flows west near Devon Island and east off Bylot Island. This constant refreshing of nutrients provides a moveable feast for Arctic marine wildlife.

A glance at the numbers shows the almost supernatural abundance of this primeval waterway: It nourishes 70,000 narwhals, 7,300 bowhead whales, 2,500 polar bears (the largest subpopulation in Canada) and 20,000 beluga whales. Vast clouds of thick-billed murres, northern fulmars, and black-legged kittiwakes—one-third of all the colonial seabirds in eastern Canada—flutter about the cliffs, dropping into the water to feed on arctic cod and smaller marine creatures. Lancaster

Sound is also a stopping point for thousands of king and common eiders on their way north.

Six hundred meters (2,000 ft) down, at the bottom of Lancaster Sound, could be billions of barrels of oil. The conservation area would protect the wildlife over this resource.

First proposed in 1987, the protected area would include not just Lancaster Sound proper but all the waters around glaciated Bylot Island, which is itself the site of Sirmilik National Park. The proposed protected area is bordered to the north by Devon Island, the world's largest uninhabited island, and to the west by the murre colonies of Prince Leopold Island. Bylot and Devon Islands combine a forbidding shield of tidewater glaciers and cliffs with areas of verdant meadows good for hiking. Like most high Arctic waters, Lancaster Sound freezes for much of the year. Yet strong currents make for a patchwork of moving ice. The unstable surface, while traditionally perilous for Inuit hunters and their dog teams, is an ideal platform for polar bears wandering in search of ring, bearded, and harp seals.

Tough, well-adapted humans have lived in the Lancaster Sound region for thousands of years, drawn by the reliable food supply. The Thule (prehistoric Inuit) culture arrived sometime after A.D. 1000. Unlike earlier peoples, they brought with them dog teams and kayaks, along with bows and arrows and a three-pronged fish spear known as a *kakivak*.

Daily flights go from southern Canada to Iqaluit, the capital of Nunavut, on southern Baffin Island. From here, a small aircraft conveys passengers several times a week to the Inuit village of Pond Inlet, population 1,500, on the shores of the proposed protected area. Right before this book went to press, a local outfitter, Polar Sea Adventures, began bringing groups by snowmobile to the very edge of the open water, a fertile zone known as the floe edge. Camp is set up, and over several days, visitors have a chance to see and photograph polar bears, narwhals, seals, birds, and other Arctic animals feeding on the bounty of Lancaster Sound. Multiday kayaking options are also available.

Later in the summer, many visitors experience the region by cruise ship. Several cruises explore Lancaster Sound from departure points at Resolute Bay, southern Baffin Island, and Greenland. Passengers can day hike southern Devon Island and take excursions within view of the bird cliffs.

For more information, go to *www.polarseaadventures.com*, *www.adventurecanada.com*, or *www.quarkexpeditions.com*.

For details on the **Lancaster Sound National Marine Conservation Area,** go to *www.pc.gc.ca/eng/progs/amn cnmca/lancaster/index.aspx*.

LANCASTER SOUND

Lancaster Sound harbours vast numbers of seabirds.

Reversing Falls, at the mouth of Ford Lake, with 8-m (26 ft) tides surging in and out.

▶UKKUSIKSALIK ᐅᖃᓯᒃᓴᓕᒃ

NUNAVUT
ESTABLISHED 2003
20,880 sq km/5,159,560 acres

Ukkusiksalik National Park surrounds Wager Bay, which was often mistaken for the Northwest Passage during early European explorations. The park has extraordinarily rich concentrations of marine wildlife and was home to Inuit until the late 1960s. In the wake of centuries of human activity, Ukkusiksalik has become the site of more than 500 documented archaeological sites that date back more than a thousand years.

On August 23, 2003, an Inuit Impact and Benefit Agreement for Ukkusiksalik National Park was signed by the Government of Canada and the Kivaaliq Inuit Association. Since then, final park boundaries have been set, and the park was established and protected under the Canada National Parks Act in 2014.

Ukkusiksalik (pronounced oo-koo-sick-sa-lick) is the Inuktitut word meaning "place where there is stone to carve pots and oil lamps." Given the size of Wager Bay, and the fact that the park completely encompasses this large body of water, the best way to see it is by boat.

There's a great deal to see and

do in Ukkusiksalik. Venturing into Wager Bay places you in the territory of the explorers who once sought the Northwest Passage—the first "Qablunaat" (white man) sailed into Wager Bay in 1742 hoping it was the long-sought-after passage. Wager Bay has been called an inland sea, and visiting it by boat will help visitors understand how the early explorers might have mistaken it for a passage to the Pacific.

This history of exploration, the archaeological record of the Inuit on the land, and the more recent presence of the Hudson's Bay Company's trading post in Ukkusiksalik make this park an exciting destination for the history buff.

The historic Hudson's Bay Company buildings date from the 1920s and are where Iqungajuk, the only Inuk Hudson's Bay post manager, lived and worked. The site is located on Ford Lake and can be accessed through the reversing tidal falls.

There are numerous archaeological sites around Wager Bay. *Inuksuit* (plural of *inuksuk*), wayfinding stone markers used by Inuit, are plentiful across the park landscape. Often, trails used by caribou herds were marked with inuksuit, which could also serve as hunters' blinds for when the caribou passed by. A seemingly unusual rock pile may have been a cache once used to store meat and protect it from wolverines and foxes.

Ukkusiksalik is located on a continental flyway, and visitors will encounter a great number of migratory birds nesting in or passing through its sprawling landscape. These include species such as predator hawks and peregrine falcons. The peregrine falcon, while rare in other parts of the continent, is quite plentiful in the park.

The park is also well populated with polar bears. Any travel to Ukkusiksalik is best done in the company of guides and outfitters who are trained and equipped to deal with the hazards of polar bear country. But the beauty of this park, with its rolling ochre and grey hills, its waterfalls and rare tidal reversing falls, will make travel to Ukkusiksalik well worth your while.

How to Get There

Fly from Winnipeg, or Yellowknife via Edmonton, to Rankin Inlet, the hub of the Kivalliq Region (central Arctic). Charter flights into the park can be arranged most easily from Baker Lake or Rankin Inlet. Check with Ukkusiksalik park staff about the status of airstrip conditions prior to chartering an aircraft, because the runways are remote and often unmaintained. Access to Ukkusiksalik National Park can also be achieved by contracting a licensed outfitter and chartering a boat from Naujaat (the closest community to the park) or from Rankin Inlet and other communities in the Kivalliq Region.

Spring snow-machine access is also possible in April and May, with the help of licensed outfitters. Make sure you factor in the time needed to cover the distances to Ukkusiksalik by land or by water, and always allow an additional couple of days in case weather intervenes.

When to Go

July and August are the best months to see the park. While it may be possible to fly into the park by charter earlier or later in the spring and summer season, July is when the area is awash in wildflowers. You

UKKUSIKSALIK

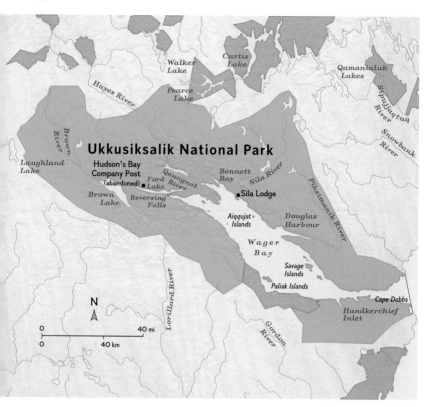

Ukkusiksalik National Park

can see the fall colours beginning to form on the tundra, along with ripening berries, in August. Travelling to the park in April by airplane or snow machine is also possible, since the sun will be high in the sky and you'll have 16 hours a day of bright sunlight glinting off the snow.

How to Visit

If **Sila Lodge** (Wager Bay) is operating, the staff there can arrange guided hikes and guided boat trips. If the lodge is not operating, visitors will need to seek tour operators and guides to facilitate onshore excursions or rely on a chartered boat to explore the park. For more information on Sila Lodge, contact the park office.

Intrepid visitors have explored small parts of the park via kayak. The presence of polar bears in the water and along the shores of Wager Bay makes kayaking inadvisable.

Park staff work year-round at the Parks Canada office in Naujaat. They are available in **Repulse Bay** to discuss your trip throughout the planning stages.

WILDLIFE

A trip to Ukkusiksalik centres upon life on **Wager Bay**. Boating from place to place around the shore offers visitors the quickest and best way to access the myriad smaller bays along the coast of Wager Bay. One of these excursions can expose

Top: A visitor at Thule site near Brown River. Middle left: Astarte fritillary. Middle right: Arctic ground squirrel. Bottom: Aurora borealis near Wager Bay.

UKKUSIKSALIK NATIONAL PARK

(Parc national Ukkusiksalik ᐅᒃᑯᓯᒃᓴᓕᒃ ᒥᕐᖑᐃᕐᓯᕐᕕᒃ ᓄᓇᑦᓯ)

INFORMATION & ACTIVITIES

HEADQUARTERS

P.O. Box 220, Naujaat, NU X0C 0H0.
Phone (867) 462-4500. ukkusiksalik
.info@ pc.gc.ca; www.parkscanada
.gc.ca/ukkusiksalik.
Field Unit Office Box 278, Iqaluit, NU,
X0A 0H0. Phone (867) 975-4673.

SEASONS & ACCESSIBILITY

Park open year-round; park office
open weekdays. Park accessible by
boat in July and August from **Rankin
Inlet,** Naujaat, **Chesterfield Inlet, Baker
Lake,** or **Coral Harbour,** or a charter
flight from Baker Lake or Rankin Inlet.
Travel restricted or impossible during
ice breakup in May and June. Travel to
the park not recommended in fall and
winter. Flights and charters to Naujaat,
Chesterfield Inlet, Baker Lake, and Coral
Harbour available from Winnipeg via
Rankin Inlet, from Ottawa via Iqaluit,
or Edmonton via Yellowknife. Charters
into the park must be by Single Otter if
the runway is suitable. Contact the park
office for information about air companies flying charters in the area.

ENTRANCE FEES

Daily backcountry excursion fee is
$24.50 per person; $147.20 per season.
For large commercial groups, such as
cruise passengers, the short-stay fee is
$12 per person. Check www.parkscanada
.ca/ukkusiksalik for the most up-to-date
fees.

PETS

All pets must be on a leash.

ACCESSIBLE SERVICES

None.

THINGS TO DO

Contact the Parks Canada office in Naujaat
to book your mandatory registration and
pre-trip orientation. At the orientation, visitors must provide park staff with a detailed
itinerary of the trip, including side trips.
The park is mostly navigable by water.
Boating and paddling in **Wager Bay,** hiking
with experienced guides and outfitters, and
wildlife viewing (polar bears, seals, beluga
whales, narwhals). Archaeological sites
can be seen throughout the park, including
an ancient gymnasium-like structure, food
caches, and tent circles. To find outfitters
contact Nunavut Tourism office in Kivalliq
(866-686-2888) or Parks Canada office in
Repulse Bay.

OUTFITTERS AND GUIDES

Contact Parks Canada in Naujaat for an up-
to-date list of licensed outfitters and guides.

SPECIAL ADVISORIES

• Exercise polar bear safety procedures.
• Twenty-four-hour daylight in summer.
• Tides and currents may affect boating.
  Boating only possible between July and

visitors to several of the park's most
exciting features, such as the archaeological sites, fabulous views, and hilltop and river valley hikes. Moreover,
from the boat you'll get a good look
at some of the marine life and wildlife that inhabit the park, too.

Ukkusiksalik National Park is first
and foremost about Arctic wildlife.
Visitors to the park may see caribou
wandering by, alone or in groups. In
the waters, whales and fish abound;
the sky is filled with a huge range
of bird species. Sik-siks (arctic
ground squirrels) will sit on their
haunches and chatter at you.

You may see a fox or a wolf, but
you're almost guaranteed to catch
sight of a polar bear and probably
more than once, sometimes at a
distance, but perhaps much closer.

You may see polar bears with
their cubs, harvesting seals,
scrounging along the coastline

September. Consult the Canadian Ice Service on the Environment Canada website for sea-ice conditions.

- If travelling in the spring, talk to park staff to identify areas with thinner ice. Do not approach areas with deep snow with water on top, as this indicates open water beneath. Avoid travelling through bays and inlets with narrow channels, as they often have strong currents in spring.
- Be able to recognize and prevent the onset of hypothermia.
- Water should be fine-filtered and treated or boiled before drinking.
- Be cautious crossing rivers and streams and do not cross during episodes of high water—wait for water levels to drop.
- Visitors should be experienced in recognizing avalanche hazards, route-finding skills, and self-rescue techniques.
- Visitors must be self-sufficient and able to handle medical or wildlife-related emergencies.
- In case of emergency call Jasper National Park Emergency Dispatch (780) 852-3100.

CAMPGROUNDS

No designated campgrounds. Visitors must stay in hard-sided accommodations or camp with bear fencing or overnight in closed boats. Campsites and food containers should be bearproof. Camping near floe edge can be dangerous.

HOTELS, MOTELS, & INNS
(unless otherwise noted, rates are for a 2-person double, high season, in Canadian dollars)

Outside the park:
Baker Lake, NU X0C 0A0:
The Iglu Hotel P.O. Box 179 (867) 793-2801. www.bakerlakehotel.com. $215 per person.
Baker Lake Lodge P.O. Box 239. (867) 793-2905. ookpikaviation.ca/bakerlake-lodge. $215
Nunamiut Lodge P.O. Box 369. (867) 793-2127. www.nunamiutlodgehotel.ca $235–$275.

Rankin Inlet, NU X0C 0G0:
Iglu Hotel (867) 793-2801. www.baker landhotel.com. $215 per person.
Katimavik Suites P.O. Box 73. (867) 645-2275. www.katimaviksuites.com. $239.
Nanuq Lodge P.O. Box 630. (867) 645-2650. www.nanuqlodge.com. $229.
Siniktarvik Hotel and Conference Centre P.O. Box 40. (867) 645-2807. www .rankininlethotel.com. $224.
Turaarvik Hotel P.O. Box 40. (867) 645-4955. $210–$250.

Chesterfield Inlet, NU X0C 0B0:
Tangmavik Hotel P.O. Box 43. (867) 898-9975. www.chesterfieldinlet.com. $250 per person.

UKKUSIKSALIK

looking for fish or a whale carcass, or feeding on seaweed. Because the polar bear population is so high, it is important for visitors to travel with licensed tour operators and guides who are familiar with polar bear behaviour and know how to keep bears at a safe distance from humans. Contact park staff for the latest information on the companies providing services to the park.

Barren-ground caribou at Ford Lake

Parks Canada's International Leadership Role on National Parks

National parks have been a defining aspect of Canada's self-image. The pride Canadians feel in their national parks has extended to the country's international identity. Images of the national parks of the Canadian Rockies can be found all over the world. Canada has become synonymous with wild mountain beauty—so much so that when heads of state visit they often ask to see Banff even though it is thousands of kilometres away from the nation's capital.

Kayaking the Rouge River, Rouge National Urban Park

Canada's early enthusiasm for national parks resulted in the creation of the world's third national park (Banff) and several others, which led to the need to manage them in a co-ordinated manner. In 1911 J. B. Harkin was called on to organize what would become the world's first national park service and to develop ideas about a national park system. In 1914 he wrote a framework for thinking about park management. Poetically entitled "Just a Sprig of Mountain Heather," it classified parks whose emphasis was enjoyment of wild scenery and those whose emphasis was wildlife protection and gave guidance to what activities did and did not belong in parks. Harkin was in close contact with U.S. park administrators who subsequently organized the U.S. Park Service.

The world's first Peace Park was established in 1932 when the Parliament of Canada and the U.S. Congress together created Waterton-Glacier International Peace Park along the Alberta–Montana border. The Peace Park idea has since spread around the globe.

The World Heritage Convention was adopted in 1972. Nahanni National Park Reserve was among the first five natural sites recognized under the Convention as being of outstanding universal value to humanity. Since then, national parks across Canada from Gros Morne in Newfoundland to Kluane in Yukon Territory have been declared World Heritage Sites.

In 1976, Parks Canada adopted the national park reserve concept as a means to establish national parks in areas where there were unsettled land claims. Parks Canada has become adept at working with indigenous people to create national parks and to co-operatively manage them. This innovative approach has resulted in the creation or expansion of a number of parks and has been studied by other countries.

Parks Canada was a pioneer in endangered species conservation and has played notably important roles in preserving plains bison and whooping cranes from extinction. Parks Canada moved beyond simple species protection to focusing on ecosystem function. In a globally significant development for national parks management, the year 2000 saw maintenance or restoration of ecological integrity through protection of natural resources and natural processes legally established as the first priority in all aspects of management of Canada's national parks.

Large landscape conservation that involves interconnected series of protected areas also has origins in Canada's national parks. The binational Yellowstone to Yukon Conservation Initiative started in 1993 intends to link up the national parks of the Rocky Mountains of Canada and the U.S. with corridors so species can move around the landscape in search of mates and breed securely. It has become the global icon of a field that is becoming known as connectivity conservation. Banff National Park's highway crossing structures for wildlife are the most comprehensive in the world.

Canada has been very active in the development of global expertise in park management. The CEO of Parks Canada has twice chaired the World Protected Areas Leadership Forum. Canadian park experts have also held many leadership positions with the World Commission on Protected Areas of the International Union for Conservation of Nature (IUCN), which sets global standards. Parks Canada has a Memorandum of Understanding with China's State Forest Administration to collaborate on managing national parks and has provided financial support for Kenya's national parks to enhance resilience to climate change and for the restoration of forest and savannah habitats. It also has agreements with Mexico, Chile, and Colombia to collaborate on building resilience to climate change in national parks. Many delegations from other countries have come to Canadian national parks to learn about park management.

More recently, Parks Canada is achieving new highs in providing exceptional visitor experiences through new and innovative programs. In an increasingly urbanized world, these programs are creatively meeting the evolving needs of visitors and are beginning to inspire similar approaches in other parks systems.

Canada is a signatory to the Framework Convention on Climate Change and the Convention on Biological Diversity. Climate change and the biodiversity extinction crisis increase the need for large parks, connectivity conservation, and international cooperation. Given the challenges, in the 21st century national parks will play an even bigger role in the country's life and in the role Canada plays on the global stage.

— HARVEY LOCKE, *Member of the IUCN's World Commission on Protected Areas*

INTERNATIONAL LEADERSHIP ROLE

A climber on Mount Thor

▶AUYUITTUQ ⊲▷⊰∆ᶜ⊃ˤᵇ

NUNAVUT
ESTABLISHED 1972
19,089 sq km/4,716,995 acres

Auyuittuq (pronounced ow-you-wee-took) is the most geologically dynamic of the national parks in Nunavut. It is a relatively young landscape, with new mountains thrusting sharp granite peaks skyward. Sculpted by glaciers, this park is 85 percent rock and ice. It encompasses the Penny Ice Cap, which is bisected by Akshayuk Pass, the main travel route through the park. Countless glaciers have flowed off the ice cap and into the pass.

Auyuittuq has the highest peaks in the Canadian Shield, and the internationally famed Thor Peak and Mount Asgard are dream destinations for rock climbers all over the world. Marine life, like the narwhal and ringed seal, thrive in the coastal fjords of Auyuittuq. You'll find evidence of the changing geology of the park and of the erosive effects of ice, wind, and water everywhere as you explore the park's challenging terrain.

Auyuittuq means "land that never melts" in Inuktitut, the language of the region's Inuit citizens. Auyuittuq was the first national park established in what is now Nunavut. It was signed into existence as a national park reserve in 1976 and became Auyuittuq National Park with the signing of the Nunavut Land Claim Agreement and the creation of Nunavut in 1999.

Climbers and those who simply appreciate stunning scenery are drawn to Auyuittuq, Nunavut's most visited national park. Akshayuk Pass offers a natural route through the heart of the park while providing access to the park's interior peaks and its glacier-fed rivers and lakes. The park's late June and July explosion of wildflowers, the potential for encounters with foxes, weasels, or hares, and the diversity of marine life make a visit to Auyuittuq an incredibly rewarding backcountry experience.

Auyuittuq's world-famous sheer cliff faces and tumbling scree slopes, glaciers and mountain peaks, and crystal clear air will make your visit unforgettable. Adventurers can test themselves in a rugged, wild landscape that is still only a day's travel from Nunavut's capital, Iqaluit. This proximity to Iqaluit makes Auyuittuq the most accessible and affordable of Nunavut's national parks.

Its terrain is great for multiday backpacking trips and mountain climbing in summer. Glacier expeditions and ski trips in spring are more easily organized in Auyuittuq than in any of the other national parks in Nunavut. A day trip to the Arctic Circle marker is possible from Pangnirtung. It's even possible to enjoy a boat ride to the park, take a short hike, and still manage to spend the night in a local hotel. With planning, you can also enjoy an Inuit homestay in the local community. Additionally, each year a select few cruise companies access the park.

How to Get There

There are twice-daily flights to Iqaluit from Ottawa with First Air and Canadian North. Flights to Iqaluit from Edmonton via Yellowknife by First Air and Canadian North are scheduled three times a week. Iqaluit serves as a hub for all air travel in the eastern Arctic.

Scheduled flights leave from Iqaluit to Pangnirtung and Qikiqtarjuaq six days a week; both communities act as gateways to the park. For a through-hike or ski trip, start in Qikiqtarjuaq, make your way to Pangnirtung, and fly out from there. If you plan a mountain-climbing expedition, a trip across the Penny Ice Cap, or a hiking or ski loop trip of the pass to the Arctic Circle, Windy Lake, Glacier Lake, Thor, or Summit Lake, you may choose to start and end your trip in Pangnirtung. Another option is a boat trip into the park's beautiful fjords from Qikiqtarjuaq.

To access the park via Qikiqtarjuaq you will need either a boat or snow-machine outfitter to bring you to the northern end of the Akshayuk Pass at the inner tip of the North Pangnirtung Fjord, an 85-km (53 mi) ride. From Pangnirtung, your boat or snow-machine outfitter will take you to the southern end of the Akshayuk Pass at Overlord, some 32 km (20 mi) from the community. To access this point, it must be high tide in Pangnirtung Fjord. It is also possible to hire a local outfitter during the spring season to take you by snow machine or dog team through the entire pass, or as far as the Arctic Circle marker.

When to Go

Auyuittuq's spring season for ski and glacier expeditions and ice-cap travel is from mid-March to late April. For much of May and most of June, the park is not accessible because the ice is soft and dangerous to traverse

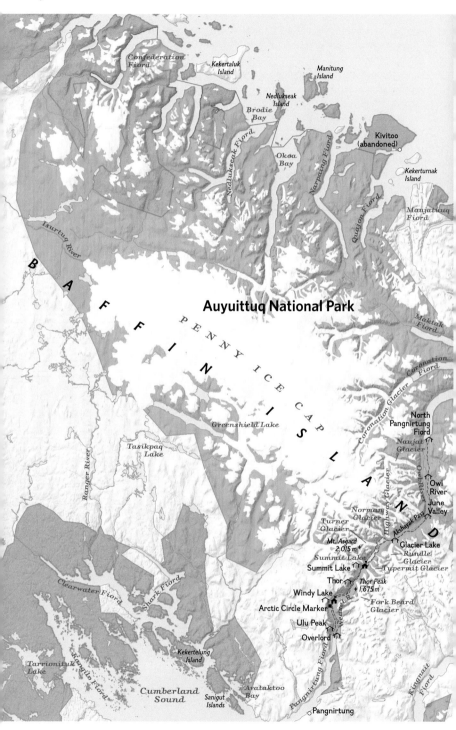

Confederation Fiord

Kekertaluk Island

Manitung Island

Nedluhseak Island

Brodie Bay

Okoa Bay

Narpaing Fiord

Kivitoo (abandoned)

Kekerturnak Island

Nedluhseak Fiord

Manjatuuq Fiord

Qudjon Fiord

Isurtuq River

B A F F I N

Auyuittuq National Park

P E N N Y I C E C A P

Maktak Fiord

Coronation Fiord

Greenshield Lake

Coronation Glacier

North Pangnirtung Fiord

Tasikpaq Lake

Naujat Glacier

Ranger River

Highway Glacier

Owl River

Owl River

June Valley

Norman Glacier

Akshayuk Pass

I S L A N D

Turner Glacier

Mt. Asgard 2,015 m

Summit Lake

Summit Lake

Thor

Thor Peak 1,675 m

Glacier Lake

Rundle Glacier

Typermit Glacier

Clearwater Fiord

Shark Fiord

Windy Lake

Arctic Circle Marker

Fork Beard Glacier

Ulu Peak

Weasel R.

Overlord

Pangnirtung Fiord

Kekertelung Island

Kingnait Fiord

Tarrionituk Lake

Kargilo Fiord

Cumberland Sound

Sanigut Islands

Avataktoo Bay

Pangnirtung

by snow machine yet still too dense for boat travel. Day trips, backpacking, hiking, and expedition climbing start the last week of June from Pangnirtung. Hiking through the entire pass starts in late July from the Qikiqtarjuaq side, and activities continue until early September. Expedition cruise visits occur in either August or September. After that, conditions in the park deteriorate: Waning hours of daylight, high winds, and extreme cold blowing off the Penny Ice Cap make the park an uncomfortable and dangerous place to be.

How to Visit

Auyuittuq, like all the national parks in Nunavut, is a wilderness backcountry experience. All visitors must register, pay the park visitor fee, and take the mandatory orientation at the park office/visitor centre in either Pangnirtung or Qikiqtarjuaq before entering the park. Book your appointment in advance with park staff. Auyuittuq National Park also has a free Visitor Information Package, which is available by email (Nunavut .info@pc.gc.ca). It also can be mailed to you in advance of your trip. Park staff are happy to answer your questions by phone (867-473-2500) or email as you plan your itinerary. After your trip, you will be required to meet with park staff again to deregister and provide a post-trip debrief.

Very few visitors bring young children into the park, unless it is for a day trip within a kilometre or two of Overlord. Skiers, hikers, backpackers, and expedition climbers are expected to be experienced. Otherwise, visitors should consider hiring a qualified and licensed outfitter or guide. Park staff recommend visitors travel in groups of at least six people.

AUYUITTUQ

Harp seal

HIKING

Within Auyuittuq you will find routes rather than trails. The park is a spectacular destination because of its active, changing landscape, but be aware that the weather is variable too: Prepare for fierce winds, storms, and periods of low visibility due to fog and snow. Also be prepared to deal with rushing cataracts of glacier meltwater following a few warm days or a rainstorm. Include enough extra time in your itinerary that you won't be rushed if weather conditions slow you down.

Within the park, visitors need to be self-sufficient, and bring with them tents, enough food for their trip, stoves, first aid kits, and all the gear necessary (including spares) for their planned activities. Consider hiring a licensed outfitter and guide to help ensure a safer journey and to provide the gear you need. There are no lodges or stores in the park, though emergency shelters and outhouses are stationed about 15 to 29 km (9–18 mi) apart.

Most visitors experience Auyuittuq National Park by going into the park via **Akshayuk Pass,** but for seasoned hikers, there are other ways to see the park. From the pass, it's possible to take side trips up the valleys that radiate off the pass. You can also gain access to the park through other fjords with the help of local boat outfitters, depending on the season. It also is possible to spend most of your trip on the **Penny Ice Cap,** which covers an area the size of Prince Edward Island. This is recommended only for veteran explorers, as it's difficult to access and requires a high level of glacier travel skills.

If your trip takes you through the community of **Pangnirtung,** which has a population of approximately 1,300 people, be sure to include enough time in your itinerary to take in the **Uqqurmiut Centre of the Arts** and spend some time looking around the tapestry and printmaking studios. You can also take a side trip to hike **Mount Duval** or visit the site of the former whaling station at the **Kekerten National Historic Site.**

AUYUITTUQ NATIONAL PARK
(Parc national Auyuittuq ⊲⊳⊰⊲⊃ᵇ ΓˢᵠJ∆ρˢᐱᵇ ᑲᐊᑕΓ)

INFORMATION & ACTIVITIES

VISITOR CENTRES
Pangnirtung: Auyuittuq Visitor Centre, exhibits and office (867) 473-2500. nunavut.info@pc.gc.ca. Angmarlik Interpretive Centre (867) 473-8737. **Qikiqtarjuag:** Piqalujaujaq (867) 927-8161

SEASONS & ACCESSIBILITY
Visitors can access the park either using licensed outfitters or independently. If you are using a snow machine, motorboat, or dog team, you must hire a licensed outfitter. Visitors can ski, hike, and mountain climb independently. Travel is discouraged between October and February. Contact park for ice conditions.

HEADQUARTERS
Pangnirtung Office Phone (867) 473-2500; **Qikiqtarjuaq Office** Phone (867) 927-8834. www.parkscanada.gc.ca/auyuittuq.

ENTRANCE FEES
Park backcountry user fees are $25 per day per person or $147 for a season pass. For large commercial groups such as cruise ships the fee is $3 per person in an educational group, or $12 per person for a small group for backcountry excursions.

PETS
Pets not recommended, but if brought to the park, must be leashed at all times.

ACCESSIBLE SERVICES
None.

THINGS TO DO
Snow-based activities early March to late April when fjords are frozen, or by boat after ice breakup from Pangnirtung Fjord (late June–Sept.) or Broughton Island (late July–Sept.). Skiing and hiking in **Akshayuk Pass** (97 km/60 mi) between North Pangnirtung Fjord and Overlord. No designated ski or hiking trails.

Boat tours from Qikiqtarjuaq. Dogsledding and snow-machine rides with outfitters, ski-touring on the ice fields, and mountain climbing.

SPECIAL ADVISORIES
• Contact Pangnirtung or Qikiqtarjuaq offices to register, participate in orientation, provide skiing or hiking itineraries, and deregister.
• Travel not advisable between October and February.
• Emergency shelters with two-way radios found at Overlord, Windy Lake, Thor, Summit Lake, Glacier Lake, June Valley, Owl River, and North Pangnirtung.
• No cooking or sleeping in emergency shelters. Use only in an emergency.
• Carry satellite phones.
• To prevent encounters with wildlife, avoid camping near wildlife habitats or leaving food around campsites.

CAMPGROUNDS
In **Akshayuk Pass,** warden cabins and emergency shelters with radio and outhouse on trail one-day hike apart. Visitors can camp wherever they like, but near emergency shelters recommended. In Pangnirtung there is the **Pisuktinu Tungavik Territorial Campground** (minimal services) or homestays; contact Angmarlik Interpretive Centre.

OUTFITTERS & GUIDES
Contact Parks Canada in Pangnirtung for an up-to-date list of licensed outfitters and guides.

HOTELS, MOTELS, & INNS
(unless otherwise noted, rates are for a 2-person double, high season, in Canadian dollars)

Outside the park:
Pangnirtung, NU X0A 0R0:
Auyuittuq Lodge (867) 473-8955. www.pangnirtunghotel.com. Restaurant. $225 per person. Includes airport pick-up.

Qikiqtarjuag, NU X0A 0B0:
The Tulugak Hotel (867) 927-8874. www.qikiqtarjuaq.com. Restaurant (the only one in Qikiqtarjuaq). $250.

AUYUITTUQ

▶ NATIONAL HISTORIC SITES OF CANADA

57-63 St. Louis Street N.H.S. Part of an historic significant streetscape. Québec, QC

Abbot Pass Refuge Cabin N.H.S. Early stone alpine cabin used by climbers, 1922. Banff NP, AB

Alexander Graham Bell N.H.S. Commemorates famous inventor. Baddeck, NS

Ardgowan N.H.S. Residence of Father of Confederation William Henry Pope, circa 1850. Charlottetown, PE

Athabasca Pass N.H.S. Major fur trade transportation route. Jasper NP, AB

Banff Park Museum N.H.S. Early natural history museum in Rustic style, 1902-03. Banff NP, AB

Bar U Ranch N.H.S. Historic ranch in AB foothills, 1883. Longview, AB

Batoche N.H.S. Métis village; site of 1885 Battle of Batoche; Northwest Rebellion. Batoche, SK

Battle Hill N.H.S. Site of Battle of the Longwoods, 1814; War of 1812. Wardsville, ON

Battle of Cook's Mills N.H.S. Site of British victory; War of 1812. Cook's Mills, ON

Battle of the Châteauguay N.H.S. Site of 1813 battle in defence of Lower Canada; War of 1812. Allans Corners, QC

Battle of the Restigouche N.H.S. Site of last naval battle in Seven Years' War. Pointe-à-la-Croix, QC

Battle of the Windmill N.H.S. American invasion mission foiled, 1838. Prescott, ON

Battle of Tourond's Coulee/Fish Creek N.H.S. Site of battle between Métis and Canadian forces, Northwest Rebellion 1885. Fish Creek, SK

Battlefield of Fort George N.H.S. War of 1812, capture of Fort George by Americans, 1813. Niagara-on-the-Lake, ON

Beaubassin N.H.S. Major Acadian settlement; pivotal place in the 17th- and 18th-century North American geopolitical struggle between the British and French empires. Fort Lawrence, NS

Beaubears Island Shipbuilding N.H.S. Archaeological site associated with 19th-century shipbuilding in NB. Beaubears Island, NB

Bellevue House N.H.S. Important Italianate villa 1840s; home of Sir John A. Macdonald, Prime Minister (1867-73, 1878-91). Kingston, ON

Bethune Memorial House N.H.S. Birthplace of Dr. Norman Bethune, a national hero to the Chinese and possibly Canada's most prominent international humanitarian. Gravenhurst, ON

Bloody Creek N.H.S. Site of two French-English combats, 1711 and 1757. Bridgetown, NS

Bois Blanc Island Lighthouse and Blockhouse N.H.S. Wooden blockhouse part of the defences of Fort Malden, 1839; point of attack by Canadian rebels and their American sympathizers; January 1838. Bois Blanc Island, ON

Boishébert N.H.S. Acadian refugee settlement, 1756-59. Beaubears Island, NB

Butler's Barracks N.H.S. Complex represents 150 years of military history. Niagara-on-the-Lake, ON

Canso Islands N.H.S. Site of fishing centre, 16th- to 19th-century. Canso, NS

Cape Spear Lighthouse N.H.S. Oldest surviving lighthouse in Newfoundland, 1836. Cape Spear, NL

Carillon Barracks N.H.S. Early 19th-century stone military building. Carillon, QC

Carillon Canal N.H.S. Operational canal; site of two earlier canals, 1826-33. Carillon, QC

Carleton Martello Tower N.H.S. Fortification built to defend Saint John during War of 1812. Saint John, NB

Carrying Place of the Bay of Quinte N.H.S. Site of 1787 treaty between British and Mississauga. Carrying Place, ON

Cartier-Brébeuf N.H.S. Wintering place of Jacques Cartier, 1535-36. Québec, QC

Castle Hill N.H.S. 17th- and 18th-century French and British fortifications. Placentia, NL

Cave and Basin N.H.S. Hot springs, birthplace of national parks. Banff NP, AB

Chambly Canal N.H.S. Operational canal; nine locks, swing bridges. Chambly, QC

Charles Fort N.H.S. Charles Fort (formerly known as Scots Fort) was built in 1629 by the son of Sir William Alexander. Annapolis Royal, NS

Chilkoot Trail N.H.S. Transportation route to Klondike gold fields. Chilkoot, BC

Coteau-du-Lac N.H.S. 18th-century transportation and defence structures. Coteau-du-Lac, QC

Cypress Hills Massacre N.H.S. 1873 attack on Assiniboines by wolf hunters, North West Mounted Police restored order. Fort Walsh, SK

Dalvay-by-the-Sea N.H.S. Queen Anne Revival summer home, 1896-99. Prince Edward Island NP, PE

D'Anville's Encampment N.H.S. Encampment of failed French expedition to recover Acadia, 1746. Halifax, NS

Dawson Historical Complex N.H.S. Important collection

of buildings from the Klondike Gold Rush. Dawson, YT

Dredge No. 4 N.H.S. Symbolizes importance of dredging operations (1899-1966) with the evolution of gold mining in the Klondike. Bonanza Creek, YT

First Oil Well in Western Canada N.H.S. First commercially productive oil well in the West. Waterton Lakes NP, AB

Fisgard Lighthouse N.H.S. First permanent lighthouse on Canada's West Coast, 1859-60. Colwood, BC

Forges du Saint-Maurice N.H.S. Remains of Canada's first industrial village. Trois-Rivières, QC

Former Territorial Court House N.H.S. Substantial frame judicial building, 1900-01. Dawson, YT

Fort Anne N.H.S. 1695-1708 fortifications. Annapolis Royal, NS

Fort Battleford N.H.S. North West Mounted Police headquarters, 1876. Battleford, SK

Fort Beauséjour – Fort Cumberland N.H.S. Remnants of 1750-51 French fort; captured by British and New England troops in 1755. Aulac, NB

Fort Chambly N.H.S. Restored and stabilized 1709 stone fort. Chambly, QC

Fort Edward N.H.S. Played a role in the struggle for predominance in North America, 1750-1812; oldest blockhouse in Canada, 1750. Windsor, NS

Fort Espérance N.H.S. Remains of two North West Company fur-trade posts. Rocanville, SK

Fort Gaspareaux N.H.S. Military ruins and cemetery of 1751 French fort. Port Elgin, NB

Fort George N.H.S. Reconstructed British fort from War of 1812. Niagara-on-the-Lake, ON

Fort Henry N.H.S. British fort completed 1836 to defend Rideau Canal. Kingston, ON

Fort Langley N.H.S. Early 19th-century Hudson's Bay Company post. Langley, BC

Fort Lawrence N.H.S. English fort, 1750-55. Fort Lawrence, NS

Fort Lennox N.H.S. Outstanding example of early 19th-century fortifications. Saint-Paul-de-l'Île-aux-Noix, QC

Fort Livingstone N.H.S. Original headquarters of North West Mounted Police. Pelly, SK

Fort Malden N.H.S. 19th-century border fortification; Fort Amherstburg; War of 1812. Amherstburg, ON

Fort McNab N.H.S. Fort built in 1889 to defend Halifax Harbour. Halifax, NS

Fort Mississauga N.H.S. 19th-century brick tower within star-shaped earthworks; War of 1812. Niagara-on-the-Lake, ON

Fort Pelly N.H.S. Remains of Hudson's Bay Company fur trade post. Pelly, SK

Fort Rodd Hill N.H.S. Late 19th-century fort to defend Victoria-Esquimalt fortifications. Colwood, BC

Fort Sainte Marie de Grace N.H.S. First permanent French settlement in Acadia, 1632. LaHave, NS

Fort St. James N.H.S. Fur trade post founded by Simon Fraser, 1806; Hudson's Bay Company. Fort St. James, BC

Fort St. Joseph N.H.S. British military outpost on western frontier, 1796-1812; War of 1812. St. Joseph Island, ON

Fort Ste. Thérèse N.H.S. Site of French fort for defence against Iroquois, 1665. Chambly, QC

Fort Témiscamingue N.H.S. Remains of French fur trading post. Ville-Marie, QC

Fort Walsh N.H.S. Early North West Mounted Police post. Merryflat, SK

Fort Wellington N.H.S. Military remains of 1813-38 fortifications; War of 1812. Prescott, ON

Fortifications of Québec N.H.S. 4.6-km (2.9 mi) network of walls, gates, and squares. Québec, QC

Fortress of Louisbourg N.H.S. Reconstruction of 18th-century French fortress. Louisbourg, NS

Forts Rouge, Garry and Gibraltar N.H.S. Fort Rouge, - La Vérendrye, 1728; Fort Gibraltar, - North West Company, 1810; Fort Garry – Hudson's Bay Company, 1822. Winnipeg, MB

Frenchman Butte N.H.S. Site of 1885 battle, Cree and Canadian troops; Northwest Rebellion. Frenchman Butte, SK

Frog Lake N.H.S. Site of Cree uprising, Northwest Rebellion 1885. Frog Lake, AB

Georges Island N.H.S. Harbour fortification; contains Fort Charlotte. Halifax, NS

Gitwangak Battle Hill N.H.S. 18th-century Gitwangak hilltop fortification surrounding five longhouses, Tawdzep. Gitwangak, BC

Glengarry Cairn N.H.S. Conical stone monument, with stairway, to the Glengarry and Argyle Regiment, erected in 1840. Cairn Island, ON

Grand-Pré N.H.S. Commemorates Acadian settlement and expulsion. Grand Pré, NS

Grassy Island Fort N.H.S. Centre of English fishery in 18th century. Canso, NS

Grosse Île and the Irish Memorial N.H.S. Quarantine station for immigrants from 1832-1937. Grosse-Île, QC

Gulf of Georgia Cannery N.H.S. Outstanding West Coast fish processing complex, 1894. Richmond, BC

Halifax Citadel N.H.S. Restored British masonry fort, 1828-56. Halifax, NS

Hawthorne Cottage N.H.S. Picturesque cottage, home of Captain Bob Bartlett from 1875-1946. Brigus, NL

HMCS Haida N.H.S. Last of World War II tribal class destroyers. Hamilton, ON

Hopedale Mission N.H.S. Symbol of interaction between Labrador Inuit and Moravian Missionaries; representative of Moravian Mission architecture in Labrador. Hopedale, NL

Howse Pass N.H.S. First crossed by David Thompson in 1807. Banff NP, AB

Inverarden House N.H.S. Important 1816 Regency cottage with fur-trade associations. Cornwall, ON

Jasper House N.H.S. Archaeological remains of 1829 fur trade post, Hudson's Bay Company. Jasper NP, AB

Jasper Park Information Centre N.H.S. Picturesque fieldstone park building of Rustic design, 1913-14. Jasper NP, AB

Kejimkujik N.H.S. Important Mi'kmaq cultural landscape. Kejimkujik NP, NS

Kicking Horse Pass N.H.S. Traversed by Palliser expedition, 1857-60; adopted by Canadian Pacific Railway as their new route through the Rockies, 1881. Yoho NP, BC

Kingston Fortifications N.H.S. Protection for the Royal Naval Dockyard and the entrance to the Rideau Canal; War of 1812. Kingston, ON

Kootenae House N.H.S. Site of North West Company post, 1807-12. Invermere, BC

L.M. Montgomery's Cavendish N.H.S. Intimately associated with Lucy Maud Montgomery's formative years and early productive career. Cavendish, PE

La Coupe Dry Dock N.H.S. Site may represent 18th-century Acadian construction. Aulac, NB

Lachine Canal N.H.S. Operational canal; five locks, railway/road bridges. Montréal, QC

L'Anse aux Meadows N.H.S. Only authenticated Viking settlement in North America. St. Anthony, NL

Laurier House N.H.S. Second Empire home, built in 1878, of two prime ministers, Sir Wilfrid Laurier and William Lyon Mackenzie King. Ottawa, ON

Lévis Forts N.H.S. Part of Québec fortification system. Lévis, QC

Linear Mounds N.H.S. Aboriginal burial mounds from A.D. 1000-1200. Melita, MB

Louis S. St. Laurent N.H.S. Childhood home of Louis S. St. Laurent, Prime Minister, 1948-57. Compton, QC

Louis-Joseph Papineau N.H.S. Stone house built in 1785, associated with Louis-Joseph Papineau. Montréal, QC

Lower Fort Garry N.H.S. Major centre in 19th-century fur trade, Hudson's Bay Company. Selkirk, MB

Maillou House N.H.S. Fine example of 18th-century QC town architecture, 1736. Québec, QC

Manoir Papineau N.H.S. 19th-century manor, home of Patriot leader, Louis-Joseph Papineau. Montebello, QC

Marconi N.H.S. Site of first wireless station in Canada. Table Head, NS

Melanson Settlement N.H.S. Pre-expulsion Acadian farm community, 1664-1755. Lower Granville, NS

Merrickville Blockhouse N.H.S. Part of lock system of Rideau Canal, 1832-33. Merrickville, ON

Mississauga Point Lighthouse N.H.S. Site of first lighthouse on great lakes, 1804. Niagara-on-the-Lake, ON

Mnjikaning Fish Weirs N.H.S. Largest and best preserved wooden fish weirs known in eastern North America, in use from about 3300 B.C. Atherley, ON

Montmorency Park N.H.S. Site of bishop's palace; Parliament 1851-55. Québec, QC

Monument-Lefebvre N.H.S. Multi-function building, symbol of Acadian cultural revival. Memramcook, NB

Motherwell Homestead N.H.S. Farm of William Richard Motherwell built in 1882, noted politician and scientific farmer. Abernethy, SK

Murney Tower N.H.S. Mid 19th-century British imperial masonry fortification. Kingston, ON

Nan Sdins N.H.S. Remains of Haïda longhouses and totem poles. Gwaii Haanas National Park Reserve, BC

Navy Island N.H.S. Archaeological remains related to ship building. Niagara Falls, ON

Peterborough Lift Lock N.H.S. World's highest hydraulic lift lock, 1896-1904. Peterborough, ON

Point Clark Lighthouse N.H.S. Imperial tower and lightkeeper's house, 1859. Amberly, Point Clark, ON

Pointe-au-Père Lighthouse N.H.S. Early reinforced concrete lighttower at strategic location. Pointe-au-Père, QC

Port au Choix N.H.S. Pre-contact burial and habitation sites. Port au Choix, NL

Port-la-Joye—Fort Amherst N.H.S. Remains of British and French forts. Rocky Point, PE

Port-Royal N.H.S. Reconstruction of 1605 French settlement. Port Royal, NS

Prince of Wales Fort N.H.S. 18th-century stone fur trade fort; Hudson Bay Company. Churchill, MB

Prince of Wales Tower N.H.S. Late 18th-century stone defence tower, 1796-99. Halifax, NS

Province House N.H.S. Neoclassical birthplace of Confederation. Charlottetown, PE

Québec Garrison Club N.H.S. Only private military club in Canada perpetuating the British colonial tradition of assembling military officers in a social environment, 1879. Québec, QC

Queenston Heights N.H.S. Site of 1812

Battle of Queenston Heights; includes Brock Monument; War of 1812. Queenston, ON

Red Bay N.H.S. 16th-century Basque whaling industry complex. Red Bay, NL

Rideau Canal N.H.S. Operational canal; 202-km route, forty-seven locks. Ottawa/Kingston, ON

Ridgeway Battlefield N.H.S. Site of battle against Fenian raiders, 1866. Ridgeway, ON

Riding Mountain Park East Gate Registration Complex N.H.S. Three rustic buildings built under depression relief programs. Riding Mountain NP, MB

Riel House N.H.S. Family home of Métis leader Louis Riel. Winnipeg, MB

Rocky Mountain House N.H.S. Rival Hudson's Bay Company and North West Company posts. Rocky Mountain House, AB

Rogers Pass N.H.S. Canadian Pacific Railway route through Selkirk Mountains. Glacier NP, BC

Royal Battery N.H.S. Role in the 1745 and 1758 sieges of Louisbourg. Louisbourg, NS

Ryan Premises N.H.S. East Coast fishing industry complex. Bonavista, NL

S.S. Keno N.H.S. Wooden steamboat built 1922, 140 feet x 30 feet, three decks. Dawson, YT

S.S. Klondike N.H.S. Largest and last YT commercial steamboat. Whitehorse, YT

Saoyú-Ehdacho N.H.S. Expression of cultural values through the interrelationship between landscape, oral histories, graves and cultural resources. NT

Sainte-Anne-de-Bellevue Canal N.H.S. Operational canal; site of earlier 1843 canal. Sainte-Anne-de-Bellevue, QC

Saint-Louis Forts and Châteaux N.H.S. Integral part of Québec's defence system; the seat of colonial executive authority for over 200 years. Québec, QC

Saint-Louis Mission N.H.S. Site of Huron village destroyed by Iroquois in 1649. Victoria Harbour, ON

Saint-Ours Canal N.H.S. Operational canal; 1933 (and remains of 1849) lock. Saint-Ours, QC

Sault Ste. Marie Canal N.H.S. First electrically-powered lock, 1888-94. Sault Ste. Marie, ON

Shoal Tower N.H.S. Mid 19th-century British imperial masonry fortifications. Kingston, ON

Signal Hill N.H.S. Commemorates defence of St. John's; includes the Cabot Tower. St. John's, NL

Sir George-Étienne Cartier N.H.S. Double house of prominent 19th-century politician, 1830s. Montréal, QC

Sir John Johnson House N.H.S. House of famous Loyalist, 1780s. Williamstown, ON

Sir Wilfrid Laurier N.H.S. House interprets life of Sir Wilfrid Laurier, Prime Minister (1896-1911). Laurentides, QC

Skoki Ski Lodge N.H.S. Ski lodge in rustic vernacular, 1930-31. Banff NP, AB

Southwold Earthworks N.H.S. Rare and well-preserved example of an Aboriginal fortified village completely surrounded by earthworks; Attiwandaronk Indian village, circa A.D. 1500. Iona, ON

St. Andrews Blockhouse N.H.S. Restored wooden blockhouse from War of 1812. Saint Andrews, NB

St. Andrew's Rectory N.H.S. Example of mid 19th-century Red River architecture, 1852-1854. St. Andrews, MB

St. Peters N.H.S. French trading post and fort, 1650-1758. St. Peter's, NS

St. Peters Canal N.H.S. Operational canal; structures dating from 19th century. St. Peter's, NS

Stanley Park N.H.S. Outstanding large urban park, 1890s. Vancouver, BC

Sulphur Mountain Cosmic Ray Station N.H.S. Remains of high altitude geophysical laboratory. Banff NP, AB

The Forks N.H.S. Historic meeting place, junction of the Red and Assiniboine rivers. Winnipeg, MB

The Fur Trade at Lachine N.H.S. Stone warehouse used as depot, 1803; North

West Company and Hudson's Bay Company. Lachine, QC

Trent–Severn Waterway N.H.S. Operational canal; 386 km route, forty-four locks. Trenton/Port Severn, ON

Twin Falls Tea House N.H.S. Early rustic tea house in Yoho National Park, 1923-24. Yoho NP, BC

Wolfe's Landing N.H.S. Successful landing led to capture of Louisbourg, 1758. Kennington Cove, NS

Woodside N.H.S. Boyhood home of William Lyon Mackenzie King, Prime Minister (1921-26, 1926-30, 1936-48). Kitchener, ON

Wrecks of HMS Erebus and HMS Terror N.H.S. Shipwrecks associated with Sir John Franklin's 1845 expedition in search of a Northwest Passage. Queen Maud Gulf, King William Island, Nunavut

Yellowhead Pass N.H.S. Transportation route through Rocky Mountains. Jasper NP, AB

York Factory N.H.S. Hudson's Bay Company's principal fur trade depot from 1684-1870s. York Factory, MB

York Redoubt N.H.S. Major seaward defences of Halifax Harbour from the American Revolutionary War until World War II. Halifax, NS

National Historic Sites information from the Parks Canada website: www.pc.gc.ca/progs/lhn-nhs/index_e.asp

MAP LEGEND

AREAS

- Featured national park
- National park marine areas
- Other national park
- Other parkland
- Canadian aboriginal land

LINES

- Freeway
- Main highway
- 831 Other road
- Unpaved road
- Winter road
- Ferry
- Trail or suggested hiking route
- Railroad

POINT SYMBOLS

- ○ Town
- ■ Point of interest
- ? Visitor or information centre
- ▲ Campground
- ⚠ Backcountry campground
- ⊼ Picnic area or shelter
- ⚥ Overlook, viewpoint
- ⌂ Ranger station, warden cabin, operation station
- ⌂ Emergency cabin
- ⊺ Lighthouse

- ✝ Airport, landing strip
- ⚐ Golf course
- ⚬ Swimming, beach
- ⚑ Downhill skiing
- + Peak
- ⚣ Pass
-) (Tunnel
- — Dam
- ‖ Waterfall
- ℘ Spring

NOTE: Parks Canada excludes all representations, warranties, obligations and disclaims all liabilities in relation to the use of the maps included in this book.

ACKNOWLEDGEMENTS

National Geographic would like to thank all who generously gave time and talent to the creation of this book especially John Thomson, Lori Bayne, Barbara Brownell Grogan, Bill O'Donnell, Susan Straight, Sheila Buckmaster, Kay Hankins, Susan Blair, Marlena Serviss, Kevin McNamee, David Murray, Francine Mercier, Julie Hahn, Lee Montgomery, Per Nilsen, Dena Rozon, Laani Uunila, Geoffrey Hancock, Joanne Huppe, Brock Fraser, Geordon Harvey, Steve Duquette and the many supporting Parks Canada team members from coast to coast.

ILLUSTRATIONS CREDITS

The following images were provided by and are © Parks Canada:

4: W. Lynch; 6-7: E. Le Bel; 8: Dale Wilson; 12 (LO): Dale Wilson; 14-15: Dale Wilson; 17: Rod Cox; 18: W. Lynch; 20: Nick Langor; 25: Dale Wilson; 26: Dale Wilson; 27: André Cornellier; 28: Heiko Wittenborn; 31 (UP): Geoff Goodyear; 31 (LO): Heiko Wittenborn; 32 (LE): Heiko Wittenborn; 32 (RIGHT): Heiko Wittenborn; 34: Sheldon Stone; 35: Scott Taylor; 36: Scott Taylor; 38: Sheldon Stone; 40-41: Parks Canada; 42: Parks Canada; 47: Parks Canada; 48: Dale Wilson; 49: Ron Garnett; 50: Parks Canada; 53: Parks Canada; 54: S. Coffen-Smout; 56: Dale Wilson; 61 (UP): Chris Reardon; 61 (CT): Dale Wilson; 61 (LO): A. Fennel; 66: John Sylvester; 68: Wayne Barrett; 70 (UP): Wayne Barrett & Anne MacKay; 70 (CT): John Sylvester; 70 (LO): Wayne Barrett & Anne MacKay; 71 (UP): John Sylvester; 71 (LO): John Sylvester; 74: Wayne Barrett & Anne MacKay; 75: Chris Reardon; 77: Wayne Barrett & Anne MacKay; 79: Chris Reardon; 80: Brian Townsend; 84 (LO): Chris Reardon; 87: Brian Townsend; 88 (UP): Mark Mills; 88 (CT): Jacques Pleau; 88 (LO): Willy Waterton; 89: Brian Morin; 94: Éric Le Bel; 95: Éric Le Bel; 99: Éric Le Bel; 102 (LO RT): Jean-François Bergeron; 105: Marc Loiselle; 106: Marc Loiselle; 107 (UP): Louis Falardeau; 107 (LO): Nelson Boisvert; 108: Jacques Pleau; 111: Michel Houde; 112 (UP): Jacques Pleau; 112 (LO LE): Jacques Pleau; 112 (LO RT): Michel Houde; 113: Jacques Pleau; 115: Jacques Pleau; 118: Brian Morin; 121: André Guindon; 122 (UP): Parks Canada; 122 (LO): André Guindon; 124 (UP): Parks Canada; 124 (CT): John Butterill; 124 (LO): Parks Canada; 125 (CT): John Butterill; 125 (LO): André Guindon; 126: Parks Canada; 128: Parks Canada; 130: Scott Munn; 132: Willy Waterton; 135: Ethan Meleg; 136 (UP): Ethan Meleg; 136 (LO): Ethan Meleg; 138 (UP): Madeleine Lahaie; 139: John Butterill; 140: Don Wilkes; 144 (UP): Robin Andrew; 146: Don Wilkes; 150: S. Kenney; 153: André Guindon; 155: Parks Canada; 164 (UP): Wayne Lynch; 164 (LO): Kevin Hogarth; 174: Parks Canada; 176: Sandy Black; 178 (UP): Parks Canada; 178 (LO RT): Wayne Lynch; 181: Parks Canada; 182: Parks Canada/Prince Albert National Park; 186 (UP): Brad Muir; 186 (LO): Kevin Hogarth; 188: Glen & Rebecca Grambo; 189: Wayne Lynch; 190: Robert Postma; 193: Wayne Lynch; 194 (UP): Greg Huszar; 196: Parks Canada; 200 (UP): D. Tuplin; 202: Wayne Lynch; 206 (LO): Jean-François Bergeron; 212: Chris Siddall; 217: Parks Canada; 226 (CT): Amak Athwal; 226 (LO): John Evely; 227 (UP): Rafa Irusta; 227 (CT): Parks Canada; 227 (LO): Patricia Kell; 229: Parks Canada; 235 (LE): Ryan Bray; 235 (UP RT): Ryan Bray; 237 (UP): Rogier Gruys; 237 (LO): Ted Grant; 238-9: Nick Alexander; 245: Parks Canada; 246: Parks Canada; 247: Jacques Pleau; 252 (UP): Chris Siddall; 252 (LO LE): Chris Siddall; 252 (LO RT): Wayne Lynch; 255 (UP): Parks Canada; 255 (LO): Parks Canada; 256: Jacques Pleau; 258: John Woods; 264: R.D. Muir; 267: Jacolyn Daniluck; 268: (UP LE): Wayne Lynch; 268 (LO): John Woods; 270 (UP): Josh McCulloch; 270 (LO): John Butterill; 271: Fritz Mueller Photography; 272-3: Josh McCulloch; 274: Miles Ritter; 277: Chris Cheadle; 279 (UP): Emily Gonzales; 279 (LO): Christian J. Stewart; 281 (UP): Ken Mayer Studios; 281 (CT): Chris Cheadle; 281 (LO): John Butterill; 282: Tom Tomascik; 284: Scott Munn; 291: Wayne Lynch; 297 (UP): Daniel McNeill; 297 (LO): Debbie Gardner; 299: Mark Hiebert; 301: Chris Cheadle; 302: Wayne Lynch; 306 (UP): Jean-François Bergeron; 306 (CT LE): Fritz Mueller; 309 (UP): Wayne Lynch; 309 (LO): Fritz Mueller; 310 (UP): Lee Narraway; 312-313: Wayne Lynch; 315: Wayne Lynch; 317 (UP): Wayne Lynch; 317 (LO): Wayne Lynch; 318 (UP): Wayne Lynch; 318 (LO): Wayne Lynch; 319: Wayne Lynch; 320: Parks Canada; 322: Parks Canada; 324: Parks Canada; 326: Wayne Lynch; 328: Fritz Mueller; 331: Fritz Mueller; 334: Fritz Mueller; 338: Fritz Mueller; 340: Parks Canada; 341: Parks Canada; 342: Charla Jones; 345: Charla Jones; 346: Rob Buchanan; 348: Wayne Lynch; 349: Wayne Lynch; 351: Wayne Lynch; 352 (UP): Parks Canada; 352 (LO LE): Wayne Lynch; 352 (LO RT): Wayne Lynch; 354-5: Fritz Mueller; 357: Wayne Lynch; 359: Wayne Lynch; 360 (UP): Wayne Lynch; 360 (CT): Wayne Lynch; 360 (LO): Parks Canada; 362: Wayne Lynch; 363: Wayne Lynch; 365: David Andrews; 367: Wayne Lynch; 372: Lee Narraway; 374: Diane Blanchard; 375: Francine Mercier; 376: Lee Narraway; 379 (UP): Lee Narraway; 379 (CT LE): Lee Narraway; 379 (CT RT): Lee Narraway; 379 (LO): Lee Narraway; 381: Lee Narraway; 382: Scott Munn; 388: Parks Canada.

Additional images were provided by the following:

Cover: Jason Kasumovic/Shutterstock; 2-3: Carr Clifton; 12 (UP): Raymond Gehman/NG Creative; 12 (CT): Chris Alcock/Shutterstock; 13: Raymond Gehman/NG Creative; 16: Michael S. Lewis/NG Creative; 22: Duncan de Young/Shutterstock; 62: V. J. Matthew/Shutterstock; 67: Taylor S. Kennedy/NG Creative; 72: Steve Irvine/National Geographic My Shot; 84 (UP): Melissa King/Shutterstock; 90-91: Richard Olsenius/NG Creative; 92: Pierdelune/Shutterstock; 96: Michael Melford/NG Creative; 98: Jean-Francois Rivard/Shutterstock; 101: Jean-Francois Rivard/Shutterstock; 102 (UP): Daniel Zuckerkandel/Shutterstock; 102 (LO LE): iStock.com/Jean-Paul Lejeune; 116: © Whyte Museum of the Canadian Rockies/V263/NA-3436/ Byron Harmon; 125 (UP): iStock.com/Eric Ferguson; 138 (LO): Wayne Adam; 142: Kateryna Dyellalova/Shutterstock; 144 (LO): Scott Currie; 148: Michael S. Lewis/NG Creative; 156: Carr Clifton; 160: Rob Huntley/Shutterstock; 162: © GaryandJoanieMcGuffin.com; 163: © Garyand JoanieMcGuffin.com; 164 (CT): Raymond Gehman/NG Creative; 165: Linda Drake/National Geographic My Shot; 166-7: Norbert Rosing/NG Creative; 168: David Schultz/ National Geographic My Shot; 171: Norbert Rosing/NG Creative; 172: Keith Levit/Shutterstock; 178 (LO LE): Raymond Gehman/NG Creative; 185: Raymond Gehman/NG Creative; 194 (LO LE): Raymond Gehman/NG Creative; 194 (LO RT): Raymond Gehman/NG Creative; 200 (LO): Raymond Gehman/NG Creative; 206 (UP): Klaus Nigge/ NG Creative; 208 (UP): Michael Melford/NG Creative; 208 (CT): Raymond Gehman/NG Creative; 208 (LO): James P. Blair/NG Creative; 209: Tim Fitzharris/Minden Pictures/NG Creative; 210-211: Maria Stenzel/NG Creative; 215: Raymond Gehman/NG Creative; 218: Caleb Foster/ Shutterstock; 222: Adrian Baras/Shutterstock; 223 (UP): IPK Photography/Shutterstock; 223 (LO LE): Artifan/ Shutterstock; 223 (LO RT): iStock.com/morganry; 226 (UP): Raymond Gehman/NG Creative; 228: Marmaduke Matthews, Bow River (with Bourgeau Range in background), 1887, oil on canvas, Collection of Whyte Museum of the Rockies; 230: Raymond Gehman/NG Creative; 235 (LO RT): Raymond Gehman/NG Creative; 240: Lowell Georgia/NG Creative; 244: Michael Melford/NG Creative; 248: Michael Melford/NG Creative; 268 (UP RT): 2009fotofriends/Shutterstock; 270 (CT): Paul Nicklen/ NG Creative; 275: naturediver/Shutterstock; 288: Rich Reid/NG Creative; 290: Raymond Gehman/NG Creative; 292: Pete Ryan/NG Creative; 296: Raymond Gehman/ NG Creative; 305: George F. Mobley/NG Creative; 306 (CT RT): Murray Lundberg/Shutterstock. 306 (LO): Michael S. Quinton/NG Creative; 310 (CT): Michael Melford/NG Creative; 310 (LO): Paul Nicklen/NG Creative; 311: Gordon Wiltsie/NG Creative; 314: Peter Essick; 356: James P. Blair/NG Creative; 368: Paul Nicklen/NG Creative; 371: Gordon Wiltsie/NG Creative; 384: Michael Nichols/NG Creative.

INDEX

NATIONAL GEOGRAPHIC
GUIDE TO THE

National Parks
of Canada

Since 1888, the National Geographic Society has funded more than 12,000 research, exploration, and preservation projects around the world. National Geographic Partners distributes a portion of the funds it receives from your purchase to National Geographic Society to support programs including the conservation of animals and their habitats.

National Geographic Partners
1145 17th Street NW
Washington, DC 20036-4688 USA

Become a member of National Geographic and activate your benefits today at natgeo.com/jointoday.

For information about special discounts for bulk purchases, please contact National Geographic Books Special Sales: specialsales@natgeo.com

For rights or permissions inquiries, please contact National Geographic Books Subsidiary Rights: bookrights@natgeo.com

ISBN: 978-1-4262-1756-2

Printed in Canada

16/FC/1

All maps have been produced by National Geographic Partners based on data provided by the Parks Canada Agency or made available through Natural Earth. The incorporation of data sourced from the Parks Canada Agency or made available through Natural Earth within this book shall not be construed as constituting an endorsement by them of this book.

Parks Canada excludes all representations, warranties, obligations and disclaims all liabilities in relation to the use of the maps included in this book.

The information in this book has been carefully checked and to the best of our knowledge is accurate. However, details are subject to change, and the publisher cannot be responsible for such changes, or for errors or omissions. Assessments of sites, hotels, and restaurants are based on the author's subjective opinions, which do not necessarily reflect the publisher's opinion.